Material Worlds

Simon J. Bronner, Series Editor

CULINARY

TOURISM

EDITED BY LUCY M. LONG

THE UNIVERSITY PRESS OF KENTUCKY

Publication of this volume was made possible in part
by a grant from the National Endowment for the Humanities.

Scholarly publisher for the Commonwealth,
serving Bellarmine University, Berea College, Centre
College of Kentucky, Eastern Kentucky University,
The Filson Historical Society, Georgetown College,
Kentucky Historical Society, Kentucky State University,
Morehead State University, Murray State University,
Northern Kentucky University, Transylvania University,
University of Kentucky, University of Louisville,
and Western Kentucky University.
All rights reserved.

Editorial and Sales Offices: The University Press of Kentucky
663 South Limestone Street, Lexington, Kentucky 40508-4008
http://www.kentuckypress.com

08 07 06 05 04   5 4 3 2 1

Library of Congress Cataloging-in-Publication Data

Culinary tourism / edited Lucy M. Long.
    p.   cm. — (Material worlds)
ISBN 0-8131-2292-9 (Hardcover : alk. paper)
1. Food. 2. Tourism. I. Long, Lucy M., 1956– II. Series.
TX357.C83   2003
641.3—dc21   2003008804

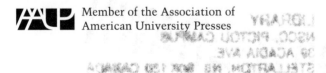

This book is dedicated to someone
who approaches food and all of life
as a big adventure—
my mother, Peggy Bradford Long.

Contents

Acknowledgments

In many ways, this book reflects my own travels in life and the people that I have met along the way. My early years were spent between cultures: southern cities and small towns, American suburbia, rural North Carolina, the southern Appalachian mountains, military bases and missionary compounds in Korea, Taiwan, Thailand, and Vietnam. Along with introducing me to the vast array of ways of living that are possible, this between-ness frequently gave me a sense of being a tourist, even in places that were familiar. While this perpetual state of tourism was disconcerting at times, I want to credit my parents, Rufus Long and Peggy Bradford Long, with making it an adventure. New places, new people, and new foods were considered opportunities for discovery. And discovery was fun!

My parents encouraged me to follow educational and professional paths that allowed me to continue to explore. I am indebted to professors at Davidson College, the University of Maryland, and the University of Pennsylvania who provided direction, support, and the occasional nudge. Among others, Kenny Goldstein kept after me to get my work done; Don Yoder introduced me to the concept of foodways, while Margaret Mills introduced me to the fluidity of ethnicity and identity; and Dan Ben-Amos liked some of my ideas. Colleagues in foodways have also been supportive. Yvonne Lockwood, particularly, has encouraged me and brought me into the American Folklore Society's Foodways Section early on. Conversations with her and others—Kathy Newstadt, Marlyn Motz, Amy Bentley,

Barbara Kirshenblatt-Gimblett, Jack Santino, Chris Geist—have stimulated my thinking.

The editors at The University Press of Kentucky have done a superb job of encouraging, guiding, and cajoling me, as well as the individual authors in this collection, throughout this endeavor. Zig Zeigler and Allison Webster first realized the potential of the topic and encouraged me to submit a proposal for a book. Jennifer Peckinpaugh saw me through the ins and outs of pulling together a cohesive collection of essays and refining the subject matter and concepts. Her editing helped me immensely in improving my own writing and thinking. Nichole Lainhart has done a wonderful job of tying up loose ends and completing the final details of editing. All of them have been extremely patient and helpful, and I am greatly indebted to them.

The biggest adventure of all has been my own family. My children, Ian, Will, and Hannah, have been served culinary theories along with their veggie burgers and frozen pizza and have courageously tried interesting new foods and eating situations. They gamely picked through the Galician octopus boil for the potatoes; they willingly (usually) ordered unusual dishes in restaurants around the world; and they cheerfully ate cold cereal when various food experiments failed. Throughout all the trials and tribulations that go into producing a book, my husband, Jack Santino, has been there with encouragement, a willingness to listen to the latest version of an idea, and the ability to operate the microwave oven when I am too busy writing about food to prepare it or consume it. He deserves a home-cooked meal as well as my gratitude.

Foreword

Barbara Kirshenblatt-Gimblett

Culinary tourism, an exploratory relationship with the edible world, is the subject of this beautifully conceived book. Whether you go to food or food comes to you, the nature of the encounter is what defines a food experience as culinary tourism.

Where food is the focus of travel, as in gastronomic tourism, itineraries are organized around cooking schools, wineries, restaurants, and food festivals—in the case of Sardinia, this includes festivals celebrating the sea urchin, mullet, wild boar, chestnuts, or torrone, among others. Food magazines and epicurean guidebooks, which have long celebrated the gastronomic opportunities afforded the mobile eater, orient the reader to particular foods, dishes, and cuisines, their pleasures, their histories, and their locales. Often, these publications include recipes; and, whether read like a musical score or actually performed in the kitchen, such recipes prompt the culinary tourist to relive vividly remembered but ephemeral travel experiences in rich sensory detail, while still offering vicarious travel for the armchair tourist.

Even when food is not the main focus of travel, one must eat, regardless of whether or not a memorable experience is the goal. Making experiences memorable is a way the travel industry adds value—and profit—to an essential service such as food. Indeed, the tourism and hospitality industries design experiences, including culinary ones, within the constraints of the tourist's time, space, and means. They do this by making the world an exhibit of itself. A collaboration between highly self-conscious producers and consumers, culinary tourism is a space of contact and encounter, negotiation and transaction, whether at home or abroad.

While the question of authenticity does not generally arise in the course of ordinary life, it is a hallmark of touristic experiences, culinary included. Why, if we do not debate the authenticity of the toast and coffee of our daily breakfast, do we become anxious about the authenticity of an ethnic restaurant or gastronomic travel experience? Restaurants, as several essays in this volume show, are prime sites of designed experiences, collaboratively produced. As businesses, not museums (though often similar), restaurants adapt themselves to their market, including both their customers and their competition. Our preoccupation with their authenticity goes to the heart of the concept of culinary tourism that informs this volume: namely, how self-consciousness arises from encounters with the unfamiliar and challenges what we know—or think we know—about what is before us. What provokes anxiety or delight is our ability to recognize ourselves in what is presented and our uncertainty about the rest— that is, the visibility of the seam between the familiar and the unfamiliar, our heightened sense of the distinct components in the mix, and our inability to experience the coalescence as such. While we tend to speak not only of the authenticity of a dish or a restaurant, but also of an authentic experience, without clearly distinguishing them, *authentic experience* makes the question of authenticity—and debating that question—constitutive of such experience.

Not authenticity, but the *question* of authenticity, is essential to culinary tourism, for this question organizes conversation, reflection, and comparison and arises as much from doubt as from confidence. The ensuing conversation tests and extends one's knowledge and discernment. Whether culinary tourism is inspiring, boring, or frustrating depends on the balance between challenge and mastery, a balance that is recalibrated with the accumulation of experience.[1] This way of thinking about authenticity is in keeping with the focus of *Culinary Tourism* on the culinary tourist as an active agent.

Culinary tourism creates opportunities to find, test, and push thresholds of the unfamiliar. Newness arises from unpredictability, and culinary tourism, to the degree that it constitutes a break with one's daily routine and even with the predictability of the tourism industry, affords innumerable occasions for new experiences. New experiences expand the ways we create and know ourselves because they dehabituate and estrange much that we take for granted: they unsettle habitus, those embodied dispositions and tacit understandings that require little shocks to come into consciousness. Culinary tourism is shock treatment. It brings "life" into view through the surprises afforded by the unexpected and the un-planned—"Life is what happens to you while you're busy making other plans," as John Lennon is to have said. As the essays in this volume so vividly demonstrate, culinary tourism familiarizes the new and estranges the familiar, redrawing their relationship with each new experience.

While openness to variety makes the species adaptable, wariness of the unknown puts new and potentially dangerous foods to the test before they pass the threshold of the mouth. This is why, as several essays in this volume show, challenging foods are highly charged, whether they are be-loved, detested, stigmatized, or reclaimed. As Jill Rudy's essay shows, such foods may form the centerpiece of an initiation rite among Mormon mis-sionaries newly arrived in Guatemala, for whom the challenge is to man-age disgust—or, rather, to subject oneself to the possibility of a culinary conversion experience. Such foods may be the subject of deep play, as in the Hawaiian festival discussed in Kristin McAndrews's essay, where *poke*, a stigmatized dish, is reclaimed, with humor, and subjected to playful differentiation, elaboration, and mobility within the shifting hierarchies of the cultural field. Relentless focus on a single food or dish, like the gauntlet thrown down to Iron Chefs, encourages ingenuity, while mix-tures (*poke*, chili, bouillabaisse, chowder), because they combine differ-ent elements in different proportions, are subject to almost infinite, if minute, variation, before mutating into something else. Culinary compe-titions based on mixture dramatize what it takes to make a coalescence hold still as an identifiable dish. They mark—and contest—the point where a dish becomes something else. Synthetic and indeterminate, such mix-tures calibrate distance, placement, and relations between generations, communities, locations, and times. They make the map edible. They tell you, by their variation, where you are—in whose home or in what town.

What is it about food that distinguishes culinary tourism from tour-ism in general? Not only do food experiences organize and integrate a particularly complex set of sensory and social experiences in distinctive ways, but also they form edible chronotopes (sensory space-time convergences). The capacity of food to hold time, place, and memory is valued all the more in an era of hypermobility, when it can seem as if everything is available everywhere, all the time. Shopping, cooking, and eating become more like accessing an edible database of infinite permuta-tion than stepping into a culinary world that is defined by slower moving coalescences of geology, climate, history, and culture captured by the idea of *terroir* and protected by appellation. Though wine is bottled and even air is canned (a humorous souvenir that suggests the impossibility of trans-porting the effable quality of being there), it is the relative immobility of a coalescence—the specificity of experiencing it on the spot, in relation to season, ripeness, freshness, perishability, and total world of which it is a part—that requires that you go there. Indeed, this is the raison d'étre of tourism proper. Going there, however, is a matter also of invention, in the case of "Jewish" restaurants in what was once the Jewish quarter of Kazimierz, a suburb of Cracow, where such restaurants mark an absent presence, as Eve Jochnowitz's essay demonstrates. Not only invention, but also intensification, can be seen in celebrations of soul food or down-home cooking in the Catskills or heritage cuisines in the Midwest, as discussed in Rachelle Saltzman's essay.

Even as the edible database and its permutations expand exponen-tially—and perhaps as a result of this expansion—so too do allergies, food restrictions, and special diets. À la carte becomes the norm, even during the domestic family dinner, to the degree that the family dinner survives at all. Meanwhile, culinary tourism on the road adapts to the constraints of kashruth or vegetarianism, even as foods associated with such diets go mainstream, as evidenced by the burgeoning kosher food industry and growing market for soy products. Such diets, whether medically, religiously, or otherwise mandated, make many attributes of culinary tourism a regu-lar part of everyday life—as much through saying no to what is not al-lowed as saying yes to what is.

As the study of tourism attends more closely to lived experiences and the study of food continues to explore its transactional character, these fields will find in *Culinary Tourism* a powerful conceptual framework and rich case studies. From kosher Oreos to the gentrification of Mexican cuisine, from the charismatic cooking of Basque communities in Spain and the United States to the mainstreaming of Southwestern foodways, *Culinary Tourism* maps a lively cultural and intellectual terrain for fu-ture research.

Barbara Kirshenblatt-Gimblett
New York University

Note

1. See Mihaly Csikszentmihalyi, *Beyond Boredom and Anxiety* (San Fran-cisco: Jossey-Bass Publishers, 1975).

Introduction

Lucy M. Long

One of my favorite activities when I travel is eating. I am not alone. The tourism industry thrives on providing food experiences—of new and exotic foods, of foods authentic to a particular culture, of foods familiar and safe to a traveler. Food is central to traveling, and it is a vivid entryway into another culture, but we do not have to literally leave home to "travel." Movies, books, postcards, memories all take us, emotionally if not physically, to other places. Food as well can carry us into other realms of experience, allowing us to be tourists while staying at home. Restaurants, cookbooks, televised cooking shows, food magazines, and the recipe sections of local and national newspapers enable us to experience vicariously the cuisines and foodways of others.

Culinary tourism is more than trying new and exotic foods. The basis of tourism is a perception of otherness, of something being different from the usual. Such perception can differ from individual to individual and from culture to culture, and it can include other times, belief systems, lifestyles, and ways of being, not only other places. Furthermore, food itself can be a destination for tourism, not only a vehicle. We can enjoy trying new foods simply for the experience of those foods, not for where the foods might lead us.

Much of my thinking on culinary tourism and on foodways in general comes from my own background. Because my father worked with the U.S. State Department, I grew up in Asian countries (Korea, Taiwan, Thailand, Vietnam) and the Southeastern United States (North Carolina mountains and Piedmont region). My childhood was filled with contrasting food experiences: Asian versus American foods, Korean versus Japanese, mountains versus flatland, wealthy versus poverty level, urban versus rural, "hillbilly" versus mainstream, Northern versus Southern. Food experiences that were commonplace to me often seemed novel, even strange, to my peers in other cultural settings. Grits or hominy for breakfast was normal in the South; rice and seaweed were normal in Korea; grilled octopus was normal in Thailand. While for me these were familiar, even nostalgic foods, individuals outside of those cultures found them to be exotic, a touristic entry into another culture. At the same time, standard American foods—steak and baked potatoes, fast-food hamburgers—were an exotic treat for me, offering me an experience of what was to most Americans the culinary mainstream. These early experiences made me very aware of the dynamic and fluid quality of tourism, of how the familiar can be exotic, and the exotic familiar. This sense of wonder at the potentially multiple and emotionally powerful meanings of food was carried into my work on culinary tourism. It also made me aware that the motivations for eating particular foods are complex and varied. The political intertwines with the personal, the individual with the communal, and the aesthetic with the functional. Critiques of cultural behaviors must allow for that complexity.

This volume explores food as both a destination and a vehicle for tourism. Consuming, or at least tasting, exotic foods can be the goal of a touristic experience, but food can also be a means by which a tourist experiences another culture, an entree, so to speak, into an unfamiliar way of life. These essays address different aspects of the intersection of food and tourism, ultimately adding to our understanding of both realms of phenomena.

The Literature

Scholarship relevant to culinary tourism comes primarily from three fields: anthropology of tourism, folklore, and food studies. The literature in these fields often overlaps, and their interdisciplinarity, particularly of the latter two fields, tends to not only cross the boundaries between the humanities, arts, and social sciences, but also bridges the academic and public or applied domains. Theories are put into action and translated into festival presentations, public displays, nutritional guidelines, and restaurant development as well as marketing and education. This makes a survey of the literature quite unwieldy, but it also highlights the potential role of food in exploring issues of authenticity and the cultural politics of representation.

Surprisingly, none of these fields have focused on food specifically as a subject and medium of tourism. Food is included with other aspects of culture on display for tourists. Eating, particularly at festivals and restaurants, is mentioned along with other tourist activities; however, no study has been published that looks at how food and the activities surrounding it might shape the touristic experience or vice versa, how tourism may be shaping the foodways of a culture, community, or individual. Works by folklorists come the closest to addressing the construction of foodways and the role of tourism as potentially one of the forces in that construction.

The anthropology of tourism emerged as a distinct field in the mid-1970s. Valene L. Smith marks its inauguration as 1974, when a conference on the subject was held. Publications soon followed.[1] Since then, anthropological tourism research has followed two primary directions, as characterized by James Lett: "[M]ost anthropologists have either described the ways in which tourism is used as a symbolic means of expressing and maintaining human identity, or they have described the social, political, economic, and environmental effects that result from using touristic modes of production to maintain human life" (1989:277).

Within the first approach, a primary endeavor has been a refining of the concepts of tourism and the tourist, which initially involved developing typologies of tourists, tourist destinations, and tourist activities. Dean MacCannell, for example, draws from semiotics and Marxism to analyze the tourist experience, stating, "touristic consciousness is motivated by its desire for authentic experience" (1989:1). He proposed a number of key concepts that have contributed significantly to tourism scholarship, among these the notion of "site sacralization"; that is, the five-stage process by which something becomes a tourist attraction. He also suggests the notion of "staged authenticity" to describe the ways in which the presentation of cultural forms can create an illusion of familiarity with that culture.[2]

Valene Smith continued in a similar vein as MacCannell, offering further thoughts on definitions and typologies. He defined a tourist as "a temporarily leisured person who voluntarily visits a place away from home for the purpose of experiencing a change" (1989:1). He posits that three key elements—leisure time, discretionary income, and positive local sanctions—make tourism possible and help determine the type of tourism selected by an individual (1989:1). He then delineated seven types of tourists based on their goals, their mode of travel, and their adaptability, and constructed a typology of five forms of tourism based on the destination and purpose of the tour.[3]

This work on typologies and classification helped to establish the anthropology of tourism as a legitimate field of study, and scholars have continued to refine both definitions and typologies. The paradigm shift from text to context and from product to process that begin occurring in the humanities in the 1970s is evident in a number of the reworkings of definitions. For example, Nelson Graburn shifted the definitional focus from tourism to the touristic experience, describing it as a journey from the profane (everyday life) to the sacred (vacation, new experiences, new cultures) in that it is a way that people "embellish and add meaning to their lives" (1989:22). Graburn sets contemporary tourism in a historical context in which the increasing secularization of Western society has pushed individuals to seek renewal from outside their everyday sphere of life.

One of the most influential scholars to explore tourism as a way of experience is John Urry, who proposed the notion of the "tourist gaze," arguing that tourism is essentially different from "everyday looking" (1990). It attends to difference, seeking objects that contrast with familiar experience: "A crucial feature of tourism . . . [is that the] potential objects of the tourist gaze must be different in some way or other. They must be out of the ordinary. People must experience particularly distinct pleasures which involve different senses or are on a different scale from those typically encountered in everyday life" (1995:45). Urry further qualifies the tourist gaze by dividing it into two broad types: the "romantic," which is a "personal, semi-spiritual relationship with the object of gaze," and the "collective," which involves a group and communal sense of carnival; that is, a festive turning upside down of the routine and ordinary (1995:45–46).

Most contemporary scholars of tourism seem to accept it as a complex and multifaceted activity, and their definitions reflect that complexity, focusing on a quality of experience rather than types of behaviors (Baranowski and Furlough, 2001). For example, Pierre Van den Berghe, in his study of ethnic tourism in Mexico, states: "the boundaries of tourism are not as self-evident as they might first, appear" (1994:4). He continues with an attempt at definition: "It is not objective behavior by itself that defines tourist status . . . what transforms a person into a tourist is taking a leap out of ordinary life" (1994:5). The departure from the everyday is a recurring theme in other conceptions of tourism as well and is treated as a defining characteristic in determining whether or not an activity constitutes tourism.

Another theme in the contemporary research on tourism is the recognition of the institutions of tourism as social and cultural constructions. As such, they reflect specific historical circumstances and specific cultural worldviews for framing difference and the everyday. In some cases this stance leads to a critique of tourism as peculiar to modern life and tied directly to contemporary economies and power structures. "Tourism heralds postmodernity; it is a product of the rise of consumer culture, leisure and technological innovation" (Caplan 1996, quoted in Bell and Lyall 2002:3).

Some scholars have addressed this notion of tourism as construction by deconstructing the elements making up the experience itself. One element that has been singled out is that of authenticity and its role in making a touristic experience satisfying to the viewer. The literature at this point crosses disciplines to include folklore. Significant work has been done by folklorist Barbara Kirshenblatt-Gimblett, who critiqued MacCannell's work, questioning his reliance on authenticity as a criterion for tourism since, she points out, "authenticity is not a given in the event but is a social construction" and "the preoccupation with the authentic is a culturally and historically specific phenomenon" (1998:303). Her later work on museums further challenges the notion of authenticity as a useful concept in understanding tourism and explores the ways in which it has made both scholarship and the tourist experience problematic (1998).

A further direction of scholarship in the anthropology of tourism—and one very relevant to this volume—is an attention to different types of tourism as producing qualitatively different kinds of experience. The destination and types of activities form the basis of defining these types, so that there is ecotourism, ethnic tourism, cultural tourism, adventure tourism, and others. For example, Jane Desmond, in her study of Hawaiian hula dancing and Sea World, explores how the focus on bodies shapes the tourist industry and the experience itself: "The public display of bodies and their materiality (how bodies look, what they do, where they do it, who watches, and under what conditions) are profoundly important in structuring identity categories and notions of subjectivity. And that, when commodified, these displays form the basis of hugely profitable tourism industries" (1999:xiii). Desmond's work sheds light on the peculiarities of culinary tourism, in which the materiality of food helps to ground the experience for many tourists, helping them relate it to their everyday lives.

Surprisingly, none of this theorizing involves the role of food in tourism. This volume, while indebted to the theoretical frameworks in this literature, attempts to remedy that. It continues the quest for definitions by exploring the nature of tourism as related to food and eating. Because food is a physiological necessity as well as a social and cultural construct and expressive medium, it highlights the complexity of touristic involvement in eating. An individual may be a tourist in an objective sense, but at a particular time and place may eat out of hunger rather than curiosity. Similarly, an individual may sit down to a meal with trepidation because of the otherness of the food, but may continue consuming the meal after the first bite because it is aesthetically satisfying and pleasing to taste. A variety of motivations, even contradictory ones, can occur simultaneously, and ways of experiencing food sometimes occur unbidden. This nature of food contributes to exploring tourism as a stance, a process, and a way of approaching an object or activity, rather than a category of behavior. This allows us to see tourism as occurring in a multitude of activities, not necessarily traveling to "foreign" lands. It means that not only can one stay home and still experience the "exotic," but one may also stay home and view the familiar and mundane as exotic.

The second approach in the anthropological literature addresses the impact of tourism on the host culture, with the nature of that impact being given a moral evaluation based more on the scholar's ethos than on the responses of the culture being impacted. A critique of tourism as exploitation is a frequently stated theme, as represented early in the literature by Dennison Nash, who concluded that tourist/host relationships were marked by an inequality of power and represented a form of imperialism (1989). Tourism as a potentially positive force, however, has also been explored and promoted. Valene Smith claimed that tourism is not necessarily damaging to a culture and should be seen in a larger context as one of a variety of forms of modernization (1989). Furthermore, different types of tourism pose different potentials for impact, and some features of a host culture are more susceptible to impact than others. Davydd Greenwood explored the nature of the impact of tourism as having to do with meaning of activities, not merely the activities themselves (1989). He concludes that while an activity may be rendered meaningless through the commodification and adaptation that occurs with tourism, that same tourism "can engender processes of reflection that lead to cultural elaboration" (1989:185). Renewed interest in local culture, appreciation for local traditions, and an improved sense of cultural worth can result. More recent scholarship, some of which overlaps with folklore, utilizes a notion of culture as dynamic process rather than static artifact. Benetta Jules-Rosette found that African tourist arts represent the interplay of tradition with the particular social contexts posed by tourism. Similarly, folklorist Regina Bendix, in her study of an Alpine festival, concluded, "tourism is merely one component contributing to the types of actions and choices made by locals." (1989:144) Meaning is not necessarily negated by tourism; tourism calls for the construction and negotiation of new meanings.

Tourism, according to these and other scholars, is not an inherently negative force for cultural stability and continuity. The concept of dynamic tourism, developed by Priscilla Boniface, promotes relationships between "host societies, target sites, their visitors, and the tourism industry itself" that work toward making tourism beneficial for all (2001:ix). She writes: "[T]ourism can have harmful, cultural, and environmental effects. On the other hand, as a tool for change, tourism is widely seen as a chance for social, cultural and economic benefits. Tourism can solve problems, offering new development in some places, regeneration in others" (2001:ix).

While the industries associated with tourism—travel agents and packaged tours, hotels and restaurants catering to tourists, displays and presentations specifically for tourists—have been made possible by the availability of leisure time and expendable cash, the phenomenon of individuals exploring other cultures out of curiosity is neither postmodern nor peculiarly Western. I see tourism as a universal human impulse—curiosity and an adventurous spirit are facets of personality that are shaped in their expression by the ethos and institutions of specific cultures, but the impulse itself is not dependent upon particular historical circumstances. Food is an arena in which that impulse can be exercised regardless of the institutionalized practices of tourism.

The disciplines of food studies and folklore have also addressed data and issues related to culinary tourism. Although food studies emerged as an academic field as recently as the 1980s, it has long been, and still is in many cases, embedded in other disciplines—American studies, folklore, anthropology, history, sociology, and psychology. It crosses the boundaries between the arts, humanities, and sciences, blending nutrition and health professions with the culinary arts and hospitality management. A number of scholarly and professional organizations, notably the Association for the Study of Food and Society, have helped to bring together individuals representing this array of backgrounds, providing a wealth of perspectives on food. The field is currently developing cohesive theories and models for understanding food and food-related behaviors, and culinary tourism is one area in which food scholars are theorizing about food as a cultural, social, and communicative phenomena. An indication of that interest appeared in a 1996 conference sponsored by the International Commission for Ethnological Food research.[4] These papers raised questions of identity politics, construction of nationalism, the processes of adaptation to tourist venues, and the meaning of commodification of food traditions. Such questions are recurring themes in much of the work done on food and tourism.

Folklore as an academic discipline has a long history of including food as a subject for study and theorizing. Along with providing studies of individual food items and food traditions in specific folk groups, folklore scholarship has addressed the aesthetic and sensory nature of food, the use of food in expressing and constructing cultural identities and social relationships, as well as the emergence and imposition of meaning in relation to food.

The European ethnographic method of identification and description of the details of peasant life included food and was adapted by American folklorists first to cultural groups outside the European-Protestant-based mainstream and later to include any community constituting a folk group. Publications on various "folk foods" appeared as early as 1895, and this approach has continued into the present.[5] Such scholarship is represented by the work of Don Yoder, who used the methods of ethnographic research to demonstrate the concept of foodways.[6] Foodways refers to the network of behaviors, traditions, and beliefs concerning food, and involves all the activities surrounding a food item and its consumption, including the procurement, preservation, preparation, presentation, and performance of that food (Yoder 1972). As a conceptual model, foodways systematizes the exploration of how food is woven into everyday life and personal history. It is this intertwining of everyday life that frequently gives a particular food item emotional meaning: a bagel purchased from the local neighborhood deli run by old family friends carries very different associations from one purchased from the freezer section of a supermarket chain.

Consistent with the formulation of folklore as "artistic communication in small groups,"[7] folklorists also explored food as an aesthetic and sensory domain. Michael Owen Jones emphasized the importance of recognizing eating as an artistic activity that satisfies aesthetic needs as well as nutritional, social, and cultural ones.[8] This approach has tended to distinguish folklore scholarship from anthropological and sociological studies, as has an attention to the individual and to specific communities of individuals as opposed to cultures as a whole (Georges and Jones, 1995; Toelken, 1996). Underlying this work and central to folklore studies are questions of meaning: What does food mean to people? How is that meaning constructed? How is food experienced in a meaningful way?

A base from which to begin exploring culinary tourism is offered by folklorists, cultural geographers, culinary historians, and social scientists who have mapped distribution of food items, described consumption and production trends, and identified specific food communities and regions. Although tourism was usually not the focus of earlier work, it was often included in the analysis of the maintenance and construction of food traditions.[9] Research also demonstrated that food is a resource for enacting and constructing group identity as well as for symbolic communication, and that tourism has shaped the ways in which that resource is used.[10] The significance of tourism in identifying and defining regional foods has also been studied.[11] The lobster, for example, became iconic of Maine because of tourism on the coastal part of the state, overshadowing the inland culture that did not emphasize seafood (Lewis 1998:65–84). Similarly, pasties, a savory turnover traditional to Michigan's Upper Peninsula, became a symbol of both region and ethnicity partially through tourism and marketing (Lockwood and Lockwood 1998:21–37). In Louisiana, festivals, songs, stories, and souvenirs created for tourists have celebrated the crawfish, changing the social status of the creature and turning it into a positive and highly lucrative symbol of Cajun ethnicity (Guitierrez 1998:139–44).

Public displays and festivals are frequent venues for culinary tourism and contribute significantly to the meanings of food traditions. These events allow for food to be treated simultaneously as commodity and symbol. As such, the emotional attachment to that food item or process can be ambiguous; its value is now shaped by an audience's response to it rather than by the memories it holds. Sabina Magliocco explored this ambiguity in her analysis of an Italian-American festival designed by non-Italians specifically to attract tourists to a town. Food in this event is skillfully manipulated by the Italian-American community to both present a positive image to the tourists and retain the private symbolic meanings held within the community (1998:145–62). She concludes that this instance of tourism utilizing food has created a safe context in which meaning is suspended: "For non-Italians and tourists, the foods and activities at the festival can offer a taste of Italianness without any of the shock or inconvenience of total immersion in a foreign culture" (1998:158).

The issues of meaning that Magliocco raises are central to my conception of culinary tourism and to this volume as a whole. How has tourism shaped the accepted meanings of particular foods; but also, how has it shaped foodways as a meaningful domain of experience? As foods become a commodity within the tourist marketplace, what happens to the functions and roles they may have had for their original users?

A number of "food biographies," historical and ethnographic studies of single food items, demonstrate that tourism has often invented meanings for foods as well as intensified the meanings that are in use.[12] Oranges, cranberries, apples, peppers, and many other foods have become advertising icons for attracting tourists to particular states and regions.[13]

At the same time, according to historian Donna Gabaccia, tourism has helped Americans cross "the boundaries of taste" with which they were familiar in their various ethnic communities. In her study of American food, *We Are What We Eat: Ethnic Food and the Making of Americans*, she argues that as food items were introduced to new consumers and became "American," they sometimes lost their original meaning as markers of ethnicity. However, those foods that maintained a tourist status also maintained their ethnic symbolism (1998). Similarly, tourism can also help to maintain the continuity of a culinary tradition, particularly if that tradition historically included room for outsiders to participate. For example, clambakes, a New England festive event in which clams, fish, corn, potatoes, and other food items are cooked in a pit dug into the sand of a beach, have continued as a meaningful tradition because they represent continuity with community identity, and that identity includes hospitality (Neustadt 1992).

Kathy Neustadt's study on clambakes represents scholarship in folklore that addresses an experiential approach to understanding meaning. Echoing Jones's call for attention to foodways as a sensory domain, she emphasizes the material quality of food and the need to actually touch, taste, and swallow it in order to understand how other people experience it (1992). I discuss this kind of understanding as "meaningfulness"; that is, the "felt" meanings of a food—the ways in which it functions emotionally, psychologically, and socially for individuals within a group, and the ways those individuals experience that food. My conceptualization of culinary tourism attempts to understand the role of tourism in the meaningfulness of food experiences. How does tourism shape the ways in which food connects us to our past, our place, and to other people, not only on a cognitive and intellectual level but also on an emotional one?

Culinary Tourism as Conceptual Framework

This volume examines examples of the intersection of food and tourism, offering a conceptual framework for approaching culinary tourism.[14] It begins with an essay on culinary tourism as a theoretical and methodological concept and includes a case study of strategies used in the manipulation of culinary tourism. The remaining essays are organized into three sections according to the context in which the tourist activity occurs: public and commercial contexts, private and domestic contexts, and constructed and emergent contexts.

Following the anthropological literature on typologies, the volume offers several of its own: types of otherness, foodways, venues for tourism, and strategies of negotiating otherness in culinary tourism. Otherness in relation to food tends to be thought of as cuisines representing ethnicity or exotic cultures vastly different from one's own. Food, however, can represent many types of other: time-related, religious/ethical, regional, gendered, age-related, and socioeconomic as well as the more common cultural or ethnic. While most of the essays focus on the cultural other, Lucy Long's essay gives examples of each of them. The essay by Miryam Rotkovitz on Kosher food explores the religious other, and Liz Wilson, in her essay on Asian foods, analyzes the intersection of ethical and socioeconomic other. Eve Jochnowitz's study of Jewish restaurants in Poland touches upon the past as other. Further elaboration of tourism utilizing the varieties of others would be a contribution to the field.

A second typology as well as a key idea in the culinary tourism model is the incorporation of the concept of foodways to allow for more activities than consumption to be considered as potential tourist experiences. While eating "foreign" or "ethnic" foods is the most obvious activity of tourism, procurement and preparation are frequently used vehicles for exploration as well. Visiting an ethnic market to obtain ingredients can be a touristic act, as is thumbing through cookbooks of "foreign" cuisines. Most public venues for tourism highlight consumption, while private and domestic contexts usually allow for a broader spectrum of foodways to be explored. The essays by Jill Rudy on Mormon missionaries in Guatemala, Miryam Rotkovitz on American Jews, and Jacqueline Thursby on Basques and Basque Americans describe how preparation as tourism enables the tourist to experience more fully the cultures represented by the cuisines being prepared. Barbara Shortridge and Liz Wilson mention procurement as tourism in their studies of ethnic heritage food in the American Midwest.

A third typology identifies venues in which food is presented as tourist attraction. This includes business ventures, such as restaurants, groceries, advertising, and marketing, as well as educational and celebratory venues, such as schools, museums, and festivals. The venues can also be public or private, communal or individual. This typology challenges the perception of travel as necessary to tourism. Individuals need not leave familiar territory in order to experience otherness. The tourist gaze can be turned inward to look at the familiar and everyday, recognizing them as potentially offering a different kind of experience. This frequently involves seeing from another's perspective, for example, viewing a standard menu as if one came from another place or time. Foods we take for granted suddenly become strange. Similarly, the tourist gaze can illuminate the meanings of a familiar food, attending to the ways in which it embodies a personal and cultural past and expresses perceptions of identity.[15]

A fourth typology outlines some of the strategies used by individuals and groups to present their foods in tourist venues. Central to these strategies is the idea of tourism as a negotiation of experiential realms of exoticness and familiarity, edibility and palatability. Tourism is a process by which meanings are assigned to activities and objects and by which activities and objects are interpreted. It is a perspective; a way of viewing and experiencing that attends to contrast with the familiar. As such, it is also a resource for expressing identity, satisfying aesthetic needs, and enacting social roles and relationships. This theme of tourism as process runs throughout the essays and is analyzed as rhetorical strategies in the first chapter. It is particularly emphasized by Amy Bentley in her discussion of Southwestern cuisine and by Jeffrey Pilcher is his analysis of Mexican culinary tourism. Rachelle Saltzman explores tourism as intensification of identity in her essay on restaurants in the Catskill Mountains of New York State, while Kristin McAndrews demonstrates that ethnic identity as represented by food can be fluid and negotiable in touristic events.

Underlying all the essays in the book is the use of ethnography as both a research tool and conceptual model. Tourists and hosts have been observed in action; tourist sites have been visited; individuals interviewed; and food eaten in order to identify the perceptions of the participants of tourism. As ethnographers, we are concerned with the meanings assigned by those individuals and institutions. Those are the meanings that are being acted upon, that are understood by the people using them. Ethnography tells us what choices were available to individuals and why they made the selections they did, giving us insights into how people experience culinary tourism.

Ethnography rests on context, on observing the immediate setting and surroundings of an event as well as the historical, social, cultural, and personal background of the event and the participants. People react to all these forces, so that context shapes their actions. Exploring tourism according to context, then, enables us to understand the particulars of individual instances of tourism as well as the broader patterns of culinary tourism in general.

The cultural context of much of the research in this volume is American. While the volume does not claim to define the American experience of culinary tourism, it does raise questions concerning culinary tourism in the United States. Is the experience of tourism by Americans within their own country distinctively different from tourism elsewhere or by non-Americans? How do our varied backgrounds and histories influence what we eat, when we eat, and how we eat? How do they influence our approach to trying new things, whether at home or abroad? Is there a peculiarly American form of culinary tourism? Such questions turn us to issues of national identity and cultural politics. Who, after all, decides what is American food and who is American? Who defines what it means to eat in the United States?

The mobility, individualism, affluence, and consumerism that characterize American culture have also shaped American foodways. Individuals commonly move away from family and neighborhood to pursue educational and professional opportunities. Foods and foodways are carried along and introduced and established in new places. Historical ties with place, then, are becoming less and less a physical reality. However, there may be a corresponding increase in nostalgia for place as well as in awareness of distinctions between the various regions and types of place in the United States. Individuals moving outside their home regions discover that their foodways, even though heavily shaped by mass-produced foods, carry distinctive aspects that seem strange or uncommon in other regions—hot dogs have different toppings in Chicago, New York, or Detroit; carbonated drinks go by different names according to region—pop, tonic, soft drinks, soda.

A characteristic of contemporary American eating—and perhaps a result of the general affluence of American society—is the treatment of food as entertainment. Dining out, preparing new recipes, attending cooking classes, and purchasing cookbooks and cooking magazines are not necessarily required for nutritional purposes but provide hobbies and entertainment for many Americans. This can also be seen as culinary tourism and as ways for Americans to explore not only "foreign" and exotic foods but foods closer to home. Foods thought to be familiar are turned into subjects for the tourist gaze when they are recognized as carrying identity.

American foodways draw from the wealth of immigrant and native foodways available throughout the history of the country. Although a homogenization of this variety seems to occur on a national level, regional and ethnic foodways have not only retained their distinctive identity but tend to traditionalize the commercial and mass-produced foods that usually define our national cuisine. According to historian Donna Gabaccia in her study of ethnic food in America, Americans were and are no more conservative in their culinary preferences than any other culture. In fact, they have displayed a flexible and open approach to trying new foods and incorporating them into their foodways as well as adapting their own food traditions to new circumstances and resources. She interprets this treatment of food as representing an open approach to the variety of cultures making up the nation. She states: "The foods we eat commemorate a long history of peaceful cultural interaction; our multi-ethnic eating daily proclaims our satisfied sense of affiliation with one another" (1998:231).

Culinary tourism, then, does not challenge one's identity as an American. This perhaps explains the history of adoption of foods introduced by cultural groups holding low social status. Dishes from Chinese (particularly Cantonese), Mexican, and even African-American cuisines originally entered mainstream foodways from the ground up, so to speak, from the working classes who ate what was affordable and filling. Contemporary American food habits now include a wide array of items that started their culinary life carrying specific ethnic associations with little status.

The essays in this volume explore culinary tourism in the United States from a number of perspectives. My essay identifies strategies used in restaurants and festivals to market foods to tourists. Amy Bentley analyzes tourism within the economic structures of American culture, exploring the meanings and uses of the cuisine of the southwestern United States. She examines the appropriation of this cuisine by food industries, and the political implications of the large-scale acceptance of this hybrid cuisine by mainstream America. Rachelle Saltzman's essay describes food in the Catskills resorts, exploring the culinary other not as the unfamiliar but as the ideal. Her work demonstrates the complexity of tourism and the ways in which it can turn inward as well as lead outward. Liz Wilson writes about the adaptation of Asian foodways by the '60s generation—"again baby boomers"—tying this movement to specific historical and cultural trends. She explores not only the changing status of a set of foods from exotic to familiar, but also the incorporation of culinary tourism into an everyday norm for eating. In the final chapter, Barbara Shortridge examines a number of venues for ethnic food tourism in the midwestern

United States. Restaurants, souvenir shops, and festivals all frame particular foods as representing ethnicity and heritage and therefore available for tourism. The idea of culinary tourism, however, is not unique to American culture. It occurs in every culture and every level of society, and the observations made in these essays are relevant to culinary tourism in other contexts.

Concluding Invitation

This book offers theory and data with which to think about food and tourism, hopefully challenging and expanding our understanding of both. Food is more than simply the dishes we consume; tourism is more than traveling to a culture different from one's own. A basic question underlying any research in culinary tourism is that of why food is so often central to the touristic experience. I know from my own experiences that food seems to provide us with a sense of the "realness" of things. Because of food's commonality to all cultures, it allows us to experience the diversity within that commonality, providing us with groundedness from which we can embark on adventures into otherness. This book is meant to provide a taste of such adventures.

Notes

1. Influential publications were Dean MacCannell's *The Tourist: A New Theory of the Leisure Class*, published in 1976 (reprinted in 1989), and Valene L. Smith's *Hosts and Guests: The Anthropology of Tourism*, published in 1977 (with an updated edition in 1989).

2. MacCannell draws from Erving Goffman's work on social space and his divisions of social establishments into front and back regions. MacCannell delineates six settings in which different degrees of intimacy are allowed between the host culture and the tourist, creating perceptions of authentic engagement with the culture by the audience (1989:101–4).

3. Smith's typology of tourists includes: "explorer, elite, offbeat, unusual, incipient mass, mass, charter" (1989:11–14). His typology of tourism forms includes: ethnic tourism, cultural tourism, historical tourism, environmental tourism, and recreational tourism (1989:4–6).

4. The proceedings from this conference were published as *Food and the Traveller: Migration, Immigration, Tourism and Ethnic Food*, edited by Patricia Lysaght (Nicosia, Cyprus: Intercollege Press, 1998).

5. John Gregory Bourke, 1895, "The Folk-foods of the Rio Grande Valley and of Northern Mexico," *Journal of American Folklore* 8: 41–47.

6. Yoder worked primarily with the traditional culture of Pennsylvania, fo-

cusing on the German ethnic groups in that area. Examples of his work include Don Yoder, 1961, "Sauerkraut in the Pennsylvania Folk-Culture," *Pennsylvania Folklife* 12 (summer): 56–69, and Yoder, 1961, "Schnitz in the Pennsylvania Folk-Culture," *Pennsylvania Folklife* 12 (fall): 44–53.

7. This definition of folklore is one of the most frequently cited. It was formulated by Dan Ben-Amos in his 1972 article, "Toward a Definition of Folklore in Context," in *Toward New Perspectives in Folklore*, ed. Americo Paredes and Richard Bauman, 3–15. Austin: University of Texas Press.

8. See the "Prologue" and "Part I: The Sensory Domain" in Michael Owen Jones, Bruce Giuliano, and Roberta Krell, eds. 1983 *Foodways and Eating Habits: Directions for Research*, Los Angeles: The California Folklore Society.

9. Several essays in a seminal volume, *Ethnic and Regional Foodways in the United States: The Performance of Group Identity*, addressed the role of tourism in the maintenance and construction of food traditions (Brown and Mussell 1984). Kalcik's analysis of food traditions as the performance of identity provides concepts for exploring food in tourism (1984:37–65).

10. These include essays on the foodways of the New Jersey Pine Barrens (Gillespie 1984:145–68), crawfish in Louisiana (Gutierrez 1998:169–82), and Italian American food in Utah (Raspa 1984:185–94).

11. A collection of essays published in 1998 and edited by geographers Barbara Shortridge and James Shortridge, *The Taste of American Place*, represents a number of disciplines and includes tourism as one of the forces shaping the foodways of different regions within the United States.

12. Andrew Smith has written a number of food biographies—tomatoes, popcorn, catsup—and an edited volume, *Rooted in America: Foodlore of Popular Fruits and Vegetables* (Wilson and Gillespie 1999) follows this vein. These essays focus on a single food, often examining the influence of tourism on invented meanings for foods.

13. Oranges, for example, were advertising icons for Florida and also served to attract tourism to the state (Mechling 1999:120–41). Displays and festive events use cranberries, peppers, and watermelons to attract tourists (Gillespie 1999, Wilson 1999, Turner 1999:211). Apples and apple butter are frequently the focus of festivals in the Midwest.

14. This book grew out of a panel presented in 1996 at the annual meeting of the American Folklore Society. The panel included Yvonne Lockwood, Susan Kalcik, Rachelle Saltzman, and me. Approaching food as an arena for tourism was an obvious subject for folklorists and one that emerged in discussions concerning a number of topics, particularly issues surrounding food in commercial, public contexts and in the appropriation of traditional foodways. Questions of cultural intervention arose in these discussions, as did explorations of the manipulation of food as symbol of identity by ethnic and regional groups. It seemed apparent that we needed a framework for tying together these seemingly disparate food phenomena and the issues emerging from them.

I had recently completed my dissertation examining the impact of folksong collectors and tourists on the dulcimer tradition in a North Carolina mountain community. In my readings of the anthropology of tourism, I was struck by how relevant much of this scholarship was to understanding contemporary foodways. As a folklorist, I was also struck by the potential contributions of our discipline to the models presented in this literature. Because of our recognition of the artistic impulse in everyday interactions, folklorists attend to the aesthetic dimensions of foodways, allowing foodways to be approached through its own universe of logic. Simultaneously, our perspective on foodways as a weave of activities, beliefs, and cultural systems enables us to integrate food with history and economics as well as with the personal and the aesthetic. With these perspectives in mind, I explored tourism theories in light of foodways. My paper at the 1996 meeting provided a framework for studying the intersection of food and tourism, and the essays in this volume have built upon that framework.

15. This idea builds upon Urry's concept of the personal in contrast to the collective experience of tourism. One of the contributions of the field of folklore is its attention to the individual as an agent in the enactment of culture and in the enactment of tourism. This is not to ignore the institutionalization of tourism and the political implications of these institutions. However, we ask how individuals' cultural backgrounds, personal histories, and immediate circumstances intersect in their construction and interpretation of tourism.

Works Cited

Baranowski, Shelley and Ellen Furlough, eds. 2001 *Being Elsewhere: Tourism, Consumer Culture, and Identity in Modern Europe and North America.* Ann Arbor: University of Michigan Press.

Bell, Claudia and John Lyall. 2002. The Accelerated Sublime: Landscape, Tourism, and Identity. Westport, Connecticut and London: Praeger.

Ben-Amos, Dan. 1972. "Toward a Definition of Folklore in Context." In *Toward New Perspectives in Folklore,* ed. Americo Paredes and Richard Bauman, 3–15. Austin: University of Texas Press.

Bendix, Regina. 1989. "Tourism and Cultural Displays: Inventing Traditions for Whom?" *Journal of the American Folklore Society* 102:131–46.

Boniface, Priscilla. 2001. *Dynamic Tourism: Journeying With Change.* Buffalo: Channel View Publications [published in Clevedon, England].

Brown, Linda Keller and Kay Mussell, eds. 1984. *Ethnic and Regional Foodways in the United States.* Knoxville: University of Tennessee Press.

Desmond, Jane C. 1999. *Staging Tourism: Bodies on Display from Waikiki to Sea World.* Chicago: University of Chicago Press.

Gabaccia, Donna Ro. 1998. *We Are What We Eat: Ethnic Food and the Making of Americans.* Cambridge, Mass.: Harvard University Press.

Georges, Robert, and Michael Owen Jones. 1995. *Folkloristics: An Introduction.* Bloomington: Indiana University Press.

Gillespie, Angus K. 1984. "A Wilderness in the Megalopolis: Foodways in the

Pine Barrens of New Jersey." In *Ethnic and Regional Foodways in the United States: There Performance of Group Identity*. Eds. Linda Keller Brown and Kay Mussell, 145–68. Knoxville: The University of Tennessee Press.

Goffman, Erving. 1963. *Behavior in Public Places: Notes on the Social Organization of Gatherings*. New York: Free Press of Glencoe.

Graburn, Nelson H. H. 1989. "Tourism: The Sacred Journey." In *Hosts and Guests: The Anthropology of Tourism, 2nd ed.* Ed. Valene L. Smith, 21–36. Philadelphia: University of Pennsylvania Press.

Greenwood, David. 1989. "Culture by the Pound: An Anthropological Perspective on Tourism as Culture Commoditization." In *Hosts and Guests: The Anthropology of Tourism, 2nd ed.* Ed. Valene L. Smith, 171–85. Philadelphia: University of Pennsylvania Press.

Gutierrez, C. Paige. 1998. "Cajuns and Crawfish." In *The Taste of American Place: A Reader on Regional and Ethnic Foods*, eds. Barbara G. Shortridge and James R. Shortridge, 139–44. New York: Rowman and Littlefield Publishers.

Jones, Michael Owen, Bruce Giuliano, and Roberta Kress, eds. 1983. *Foodways and Eating Habits: Directions for Research*. Los Angeles: The California Folklore Society.

Jules-Rosette, Benetta. 1984. *The Messages of Touristic Art: An African Semiotic System in Comparative Perspective*. New York: Plenum Press.

Kalcik, Susan. 1984. "Ethnic Foodways in America: Symbol and the Performance of Identity." In *Ethnic and Regional Foodways in the United States: The Performance of Group Identity*. Eds. Linda Keller Brown and Kay Mussell, 37–65. Knoxville: The University of Tennessee Press.

Kirshenblatt-Gimblett, Barbara. 1998. *Destination Culture: Tourism, Museums, and Heritage*. Berkeley: University of California Press.

Lett, James. 1989. "Epilogue to Touristic Studies in Anthropological Perspective." In *Hosts and Guests: The Anthropology of Tourism, 2nd ed.* Ed. Valene L. Smith, 265–79. Philadelphia: University of Pennsylvania Press.

Lewis, George H. 1998. "The Maine Lobster as Regional Icon: Competing Images Over Time and Social Class." In *The Taste of American Place: A Reader on Regional and Ethnic Foods*, eds. Barbara G. Shortridge and James R. Shortridge, 65–83. New York: Rowman and Littlefield Publishers.

Lockwood, Yvonne R. and William G. Lockwood. 1998. "Pasties in Michigan's Upper Peninsula: Foodways, Interethnic Relations, and Regionalism." In *The Taste of American Place: A Reader on Regional and Ethnic Foods*, eds. Barbara G. Shortridge and James R. Shortridge, 21–36. New York: Rowman and Littlefield Publishers.

Long, Lucy. 2001. *Stirring Up the Past: The Grand Rapids Apple Butter Fest*. Documentary video. Bowling Green, Ohio: WBGU-TV.

MacCannell, Dean. 1989 [1976]. *The Tourist: A New Theory of the Leisure Class*, 2nd ed. New York: Schocken Books.

Magliocco, Sabina. 1998. "Playing With Food: The Negotiation of Identity in the Ethnic Display Event by Italian Americans in Clinton, Indiana." In *The Taste of American Place: A Reader on Regional and Ethnic Foods*, eds. Barbara G.

Shortridge and James R. Shortridge, 145–61. New York: Rowman and Littlefield Publishers.

Mechling, Jay. 1999. "Oranges." In *Rooted in American: Foodlore of Popular Fruits and Vegetables.* Eds. David Scofield Wilson and Angus Kress Gillespie, 120–41. Knoxville: The University of Tennessee Press.

Nash, Dennison. 1989. "Tourism as a Form of Imperialism." In *Hosts and Guests: The Anthropology of Tourism, 2nd ed.* Ed. Valene L. Smith, 37–52. Philadelphia: University of Pennsylvania Press.

Neustadt, Kathy. 1992. *Clambake A History and Celebration of an American Tradition.* Amherst: University of Massachusetts Press.

Raspa, Richard. 1984. "Exotic Foods Among Italian-Americans in Mormon Utah: Food as Nostalgic Enactment of Identity." In *Ethnic and Regional Foodways in the United States: The Performance Group Identity.* Eds. Linda Keller Brown and Kay Mussell, 185–94. Knoxville: The University of Tennessee Press.

Shortridge, Barbara G. and James R. Shortridge. 1998. *The Taste of American Place: A Reader on Regional and Ethnic Foods.* New York: Rowman and Littlefield Publishers.

Smith, Valene L., ed. 1989 [1977]. *Hosts and Guests: The Anthropology of Tourism, 2nd ed.* Philadelphia: University of Pennsylvania Press.

Smith, Valene L., and William R. Eadington, eds. 1992. *Tourism Alternatives: Potentials and Problems in the Development of Tourism.* Philadelphia: University of Pennsylvania Press.

Toelken, Barre. 1996. *The Dynamics of Folklore.* Logan: Utah State University Press.

Turner, Patricia A. 1999. "Watermelons." In *Rooted in American: Foodlore of Popular Fruits and Vegetables.* Eds. David Scofield Wilson and Angus Kress Gillespie, 211–23. Knoxville: The University of Tennessee Press.

Turner, Victor, and Edward Bruner. 1984. *The Anthropology of Experience.* Chicago: University of Illinois Press.

Urry, John. 1990. *The Tourist Gaze: Leisure and Travel in Contemporary Societies.* London: Sage.

———. 1995. *Consuming Places.* London: Routledge.

Van den Berghe, Pierre L. 1994. *The Quest for Other: Ethnic Tourism in San Cristobal, Mexico.* Seattle: University of Washington Press.

Wilson, David Scofield. 1999. "Hot Peppers." In *Rooted in American: Foodlore of Popular Fruits and Vegetables.* Eds. David Scofield Wilson and Angus Kress Gillespie, 89–119. Knoxville: The University of Tennessee Press.

Wilson, David Scofield, and Angus Kress Gillespie, eds. 1999. *Rooted in American: Foodlore of Popular Fruits and Vegetables.* Knoxville: The University of Tennessee Press.

Yoder, Don. 1972. "Folk Cookery." In *Folklore and Folklife: An Introduction.* Ed. Richard M. Dorson, 325. Chicago: University of Chicago Press.

CHAPTER 1

Culinary Tourism

A Folkloristic Perspective
on Eating and Otherness

Lucy M. Long

Culinary tourism is about food as a subject and medium, destination and vehicle, for tourism. It is about individuals exploring foods new to them as well as using food to explore new cultures and ways of being. It is about groups using food to "sell" their histories and to construct marketable and publicly attractive identities, and it is about individuals satisfying curiosity. Finally, it is about the experiencing of food in a mode that is out of the ordinary, that steps outside the normal routine to notice difference and the power of food to represent and negotiate that difference.

Definitions

Folklorists, food scholars, and food aficionados have long been fascinated by occasions of exploratory eating—instances of eating the new, the unfamiliar, the alien—and by the institutions and artifacts that enable those occasions, such as "ethnic" restaurants, international cookbooks, and folklife festivals.[1] These occasions and institutions include a wide variety of food-related behaviors and reflect complex networks of cultural, social, economic, and aesthetic systems as well as individual preferences. The definition of what constitutes adventurous eating is a contextual one that depends on the perspective and motivations of the eater. In this essay I propose the concept of "culinary tourism" as a framework for tying together the notion of perspective and the variety of instances in which a foodways is considered representative of the other.[2] I define culinary tourism as the intentional, exploratory participation in the foodways of an other—participation including the consumption, preparation, and presentation of a food item, cuisine, meal system, or eating style considered to belong to a culinary system not one's own.[3] This definition emphasizes the individual as active agent in constructing meanings within a tourist experience, and it allows for an aesthetic response to food as part of that experience.[4]

Exploration and intentionality define these instances as tourism. Participation occurs specifically because of the perceived otherness of the foodways, and that otherness elicits curiosity. Although scholarship concerning the anthropology of tourism primarily addresses exploration of new spaces, it has generated concepts applicable to the exploration of new culinary domains as well. Valene Smith defined a tourist as "a temporarily leisured person who voluntarily visits a place away from home for the purpose of experiencing a change" (1989:1). The culinary tourist anticipates a change in the foodways experience for the sake of experiencing that change, not merely to satisfy hunger. Nelson Graburn proposed that the tourist experience is a journey from the profane to the sacred as a way to embellish and add meaning to one's life (1989:22). The tourist experience offers not only new cultures and new sights, but also new ways of perceiving those sights, and these new ways of perceiving ultimately enhance the individual. John Urry developed this notion of tourism as a qualitative category of experience, defining it as a kind of viewing he refers to as "the tourist gaze" (1990). This gaze is distinctive from "everyday looking" in that it attends to difference (1990, 1995). It notices contrast and distinctiveness; it shifts objects and actions out of the common and mundane world, enabling or encouraging viewers to recognize their power as symbols, entertainment, and art. In this sense, foodways may be one of the fullest ways of perceiving otherness. Sightseeing is only a partial engagement with otherness, whereas culinary tourism, utilizing the senses of taste, smell, touch, and vision, offers a deeper, more integrated level of experience. It engages one's physical being, not simply as an observer, but as a participant as well.[5]

A key concept in these definitions is the idea of tourism being voluntary; becoming a tourist is a choice, and with that choice there is an implied openness to the new. New experiences may be tried, however, for a variety of reasons, not all of which we would consider touristic. For example, individuals may participate in an exotic foodways out of consideration for one's host, in response to a challenge, as a statement of rebellion against the status quo, to conform to social obligations or norms, and so on. Tourism, on the other hand, involves new experiences for the sake of the experience itself. Through tourism, we satisfy our curiosity about otherness; we confront the impulse to explore the unknown, to climb the mountain because it is there. And we expect to find pleasure in seeking the unknown, perhaps not in the unknown itself, but in the conducting of that search; we may not like the food after all, but we can have fun trying it. Furthermore, the pleasure we find in food and eating can be of an aesthetic nature, satisfying our sensibilities of taste, proportion, and appearance, so that the pleasure stems from the food itself and not from what it represents.

Intentionality also assumes the perception, or categorization, of a food complex as other, and it is this perception that shapes our approach to the food. We must think of a food as being somehow different, new, or exotic in order to think of exploring it. This perception can shift with experience, and the shift can move us toward tourism or away from it. What may begin as touristic eating may change with familiarity. We may try a new food with trepidation, but once we discover the taste is pleasing, we may then eat that food for aesthetic enjoyment. An example of such a shift occurred personally during a meal at a Taiwanese restaurant in the United States in which I came across a chunk of unknown substance in a seafood stew. Because the other ingredients were sea creatures and the chunk resembled marbled fat, my dinner companions and I tried to identify what animal it may have belonged to. After a tentative taste, we realized it was plant—more specifically, taro—and we ate it with hunger rather than curiosity.

Similarly, we have probably all had the experience of unknowingly eating something that we otherwise would have considered inedible or unappealing and would have approached with curiosity, with the sense of trying something different. An example that plays upon ethnic stereotypes occurred while I was traveling in Burma and was served dog-fried rice at a small lunchroom. Not knowing the ingredients but recognizing the general category of the dish and being hungry, my Western traveling companions and I ate enthusiastically. During the meal, however, the cook responded to our questioning gestures about the meat in the dish with an "arf, arf." We immediately lost our appetites. Those of us who continued to eat did so out of curiosity rather than hunger, and with a definite sense of eating something outside our usual boundaries of what was edible. Our initial consumption of this food was not a voluntary participation in an other, but a misperception of the familiar. We moved from eating to satisfy physical hunger to eating as outsiders.

Foodways

"Participation in foodways" implies the full spectrum of activities surrounding food. The term "foodways" suggests that food is a network of activities and systems—physical, social (communicative), cultural, economic, spiritual, and aesthetic. Folklorist Don Yoder borrowed the term from anthropologist John J. Honigman to refer to "the total cookery complex, including attitudes, taboos, and meal systems—the whole range of cookery and food habits in a society."[6] As such, food touches every aspect of our lives. Participation in this multifaceted universe involves the procurement and/or the production of raw materials; the preparation of those materials into food; the preservation of foods; the planning of menus and meal systems; the presentation of dishes; the performance of eating styles or techniques; the system of food habits, food ethos, and aesthetics; as well as the actual consumption of food. It also includes a wide range of behaviors connected to thinking and talking about food—the metaculinary universe; for example, collecting recipes and cookbooks; producing and viewing televised cooking shows; participating in cooking classes or instances of teaching and learning techniques of food preparation, presentation, and consumption. Participation, then, includes the whole range of activities surrounding food.

The concept of foodways opens up the range of activities available for tourism. Since food is more than the dishes we eat, we can be tourists by exploring these other aspects of the food systems. It means that we can mix the new with the old, the exotic with the familiar. For example, we can procure familiar ingredients from a new market, try new preparation methods for an old favorite, or substitute known spices for novel ones in a new dish. It also means that we can be culinary tourists without actually eating, or without leaving home. Perusing cookbooks and cooking magazines and watching cooking shows or films with food scenes offer mental and emotional journeys to other food worlds. Similarly, foodways can help to ground tourism in the everyday. By turning normally routine activities, such as shopping, cleaning up, and storing foods, into tourist sites, we can more easily contrast and negotiate the sense of difference with the familiar.

Otherness

"Other" in this definition refers to the anthropological notion of humans defining the world according to their own socially constructed perceptions of reality, perceptions that divide the world into the known and familiar as opposed to the unknown or other.[7] Otherness is a construction by the individual as well as by the culture within which that individual moves. Foods are not inherently strange or exotic; the experiences of an individual are what determine the status of a food. In this sense, tourism depends on a perception of otherness rather than an objective reality of an item's relationship to that individual.

The other can be distinguished from the familiar along a variety of dimensions. In the context of foodways, I suggest five major categories: culture, region, time, ethos/religion, and socioeconomic class. Gender and age can also be types of other, but do not seem to be used frequently. In reality, all of these categories frequently overlap.

Culture, which includes ethnicity and national identity, is one of the most obvious ways of distinguishing food systems as other. It is also the most frequent category in which culinary tourism is enacted, giving us international dinners, cookbooks, and restaurants specializing in the cuisine of particular cultures, and classes and televised cooking shows demonstrating cooking techniques from a variety of cultures. This category is based partly on spatial distance and physical boundaries between groups of people. A food system physically removed from the familiar can automatically, though not necessarily, represent the unknown and therefore be potentially strange. This spatial distance also refers to the juxtaposition of foodways of varying cultures that have historically had physical distance, usually with the locating of one identity within the context of another, turning the former identity ethnic.[8] Ethnicity, like otherness, is a dynamic cultural construct and is more usefully thought of as a process of contextualization rather than an actual objective state. Ethnic identity is based on perceptions of shared heritage and of living within a dominant host culture (Oring 1986:24). In a way, within tourism, all cultures are ethnic, since it is the contrast with the individual's familiar cultural identity that makes the contrasting one appropriate for the tourist gaze.

Region as other also refers to spatial distance, but it is distance occurring within national boundaries. Regions are cultural landscapes shaped by and resulting from specific natural environments and the particular cultures utilizing them. As a basic necessity of survival and therefore a central aspect of everyday life, food plays a prominent role in the manipulation of the natural environment and serves as a window into the histories, ethos, and identities of the specific cultures tied to that environment.[9]

Region exists within cultures and often offers a localization of a broadly cultural foodways as well as a foodways unique to and distinctive of that geographic area. For example, in the American Southwest, salsa frequently

1-1. Packages from the same company but three products. One emphasizes ethnic other—"traditional Middle Eastern." The second package highlights an ethical other—vegetarianism—as does the bottle drink advertising "Soy to the World," since soy is associated with organic and vegetarian diets. *Photo by David Hampshire.*

1-2. These two food items play upon the cultural or ethnic other. The first specifies the cultural identity—"Thai Kitchen," "Thai Ginger and Vegetable." It then includes an explanation, "Instant Rice Noodles" and a photo of the product. Smaller letters at the top of the package proclaim "Authentic Thai Cuisine," just in case there was any doubt. The second product makes no claims to a specific ethnicity, but the brand name "Maruchan Ramen" identifies it as ethnic American. Originating in Korea and Japan, these instant noodles are usually packaged with "Oriental" seasonings; however, this flavor—tomato—has adapted to American tastes, incorporating Italian American cooking. *Photo by David Hampshire.*

1-3. Regional others are highlighted by these items, as is spelled out by the potato chip package that proclaims "Tastes of America." Stereotypes of Southern California are used—palm trees, skateboard, cool kid in sunglasses. The cookies imply the coastal aspect of Boston, perhaps harking back to the Boston Tea Party and the essential American-ness of the city. The package also uses the ethical other—vegan—"Egg and Dairy Free" and the socioeconomic other "Premium Gourmet." The postcard defines Louisiana in terms of its food, showing its distinctiveness from other regions and implying its ethnic otherness by presenting Cajun seafood and sausages. *Photo by David Hampshire.*

tops hamburgers in place of ketchup, representing a local food item added to a national one. There is simultaneously a distinctive Southwestern cuisine blending the Anglo, Hispanic, and Native American foodways of that region. Regional awareness is becoming more widespread in the United States as Americans attempt to define themselves as a nation but still recognize individual histories. Numerous festivals, restaurants, and cookbooks celebrate region, and place is currently used as a potent marketing tool for tourism as well as for entertainment and patriotism.

Separation by time refers to foodways of eras other than the present. The past is a rich source of culinary otherness; for example, historical reenactment feasts, samples of food served in living history demonstrations, or cookbooks offering re-creations of past recipes. Such foods frequently represent a highly selective past, and sometimes an invented one.

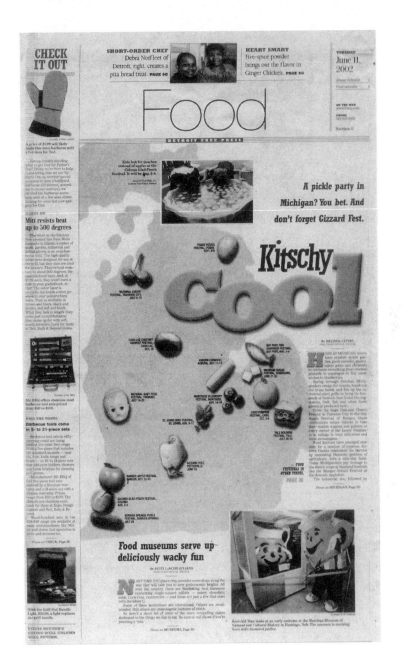

1-4. Region is again presented as other. The map of Michigan as well as the headline presents a region normally thought of as mainstream American, as having distinctive traditions, even if they are "Kitschy." The article also tends to make exotic the familiar by looking at common foods—cherries, pickles, Kool-Aid—as a source of "wacky fun." *Photo by David Hampshire.*

Heritage is a construction of the past based on contemporary identity and represents the interpretive stance and purposes of whoever is doing the interpreting (Lowenthall 1985; Handler and Gable 1997). It is a common destination for tourism, and food frequently plays a role in "making history come alive," as living history museums commonly express it, allowing viewers to glimpse the routines of everyday life in a past era. The full range of foodways is frequently included at these museums—from growing crops and raising livestock to harvesting and even butchering, to cooking and eating.[10]

Time as other can also refer to futuristic foods; for example, dried "astronaut" ice cream, the pelletlike "ice cream of the future" sold in amusement parks, or preparation techniques imagined for the future. Some items categorized as health foods, such as soy products, quinoa and other high protein grains, and organically grown produce, are marketed as foods that a civilized, environmentally aware nation will move toward adopting as a standard part of its cuisine in the future, while simultaneously identifying the foods with a preindustrialized, romanticized tribal past. As with foods representing the past, futuristic foods reflect a selective view of what we hope will come to pass, a time when technology will provide for all the world's population without depleting natural resources or destroying the environment—or in such a way that environmental concerns are no longer relevant.

Time as other can also include special foodways set aside for holiday celebrations or rituals. These events can be considered "time out of time" and are frequently embedded in religions and cultural others as well. Holiday traditions commonly, if not universally, involve some aspect of foodways, from foods specially designated for that holiday (candy canes for Christmas, cakes with candles for birthdays, turkey and dressing for Thanksgiving) to preparation methods (cookie exchanges for winter holidays, tamale making among Mexican-American women at Christmastime, outdoor grilling for America's Independence Day) to designated styles of consumption (family-style serving for Thanksgiving, picnic and informal eating for the Fourth of July) (Santino 1994). Candy packaged with the colors and motifs of a particular holiday signal an opportunity to get in the spirit of that holiday by purchasing and consuming that candy. Cereal, cake mixes, snack crackers, and other foods are now marketed in this way (Santino 1996). Religious rituals frequently involve food in overtly symbolic ways: Christian communion includes bread and wine as symbols of the body and blood of Jesus; Jewish Passover utilizes matzo (unleavened bread) as a reminder of Moses leading the Israelites out of Egypt.

1-5. National identity is evident in the packaging for these foods. By using motifs from the American flag ("Stars & Stripes"; red, white, and blue colors; and the character on the cake mix waving a flag) a patriotic other is emphasized. These products were all sold around the fourth of July, the date of American Independence Day, so that not only do they evoke images of the nation, but also images of that holiday—picnics and barbecues, fun with family and friends, fireworks, a day off from work. *Photo by David Hampshire.*

Ethos and religion also define the other. While both refer to worldview and systems of evaluating human actions and products, religion, as used here, implies formal, institutionalized rules for behavior based on an interpretation of the spiritual and the sacred. The religious culinary other would include food taboos and meals or food preparation methods following religious dietary requirements, such as those proscribed by Judaism, Islam, Seventh Day Adventists, and other religions. Also used for tourist purposes, as mentioned above, are dishes corresponding to calendrical cycles or ritual observances. Three kings cake for Epiphany,[11] Polish jelly doughnuts for Lent, and rice cakes for Chinese New Year are commonly sold in supermarkets where I live and are advertised as a way to experience those holidays. Church festivals, in-school demonstrations, and folklife festivals frequently offer foods representing this type of other as a way to educate outsiders about a specific religion or religious group. The foods selected for such presentations are frequently ones that are felt to be "safe," as they do not challenge the normative perceptions of what defines food and appealing tastes.

1-6. Time as other is evident in this newspaper special of recipes for this season. Although hot dogs and oranges are eaten throughout the year, they are associated here with summertime activities and vacations. *Photo by David Hampshire.*

Ethos may also be formally organized but less associated with the spiritual world. Vegetarians and vegans, for example, represent a growing population in the Western world and constitute a significant enough number to be recognized in the American marketplace. Vegetarian meals, meat substitutes, restaurants offering vegetarian menus, and cookbooks and food magazines designed specifically for non–meat eaters, offer venues by which tourists can experience this ethos. Similarly, organic produce offers an entrée into a philosophical stance on the relationship of humans to nature. Breastfeeding can, though not necessarily, also represent an ethos of the nature of the mother-child relationship. Diet foods and dieting schedules reflect a concern with body image that represents a contemporary ethos related particularly to the female body. Any of these foods can be offered as a way of trying out those belief systems.

Socioeconomic class as culinary other divides foodways according to recognized social levels within a society. In the United States, we find genres such as white trash cookbooks, down-home diners, upscale "fancy" dining in expensive hotels or four-star restaurants, and gourmet cooking classes. Some of these foods, particularly lower-class cuisine, are presented in a humorous, satirical manner that mocks not only the cuisine, but also the cultural group producing it. For example, the cookbooks featuring Southern working-class and mountain foods tend to use stereotypes and negative imagery of these populations, presenting their food as consisting of "trash animals," such as opossums, groundhogs, throw-away parts of animals (squirrel brains), unusual grains and fruits (hominy, persimmons), and using unhealthy cooking techniques (everything fried in lard). At the same time, these books do address a somewhat morbid curiosity about groups considered outside the mainstream, and there is the potential that they can be read and their recipes tried as culinary tourism. Similarly, as commercial, mass-produced foods disseminated through grocery store chains and fast-food restaurants have become more popular and are perceived as taking over American foodways, the home cooking and plain foods of the middle classes and middle America are being presented as an other cuisine not only ripe for touristic exploration, but also rich in political implications.

Gender and age are two more categories of otherness, but neither seems to play a significant role in either marketing or intentional tourism. An example of gendered foodways would be a woman carving the Thanksgiving turkey or overseeing the barbecue grill, not out of necessity or skill, but out of curiosity to experience what are usually considered male activities. Similarly, the 1970s phrase "real men don't each quiche" can be turned into a tourist call for men to taste quiche in order to experience femininity (or possibly homosexuality). Age as the basis for an other foodways would include items such as commercial baby food, infant formula, or breast milk. There may even be certain foods that we associate with our childhood and youth; tasting them may flood us with memories of another age, allowing us to revisit experiences tied to age. For example,

I occasionally consume grape Popsicles or soda pop to see if I can recapture the intensity of flavor they seemed to hold for me as a child.

All of these others can be enacted in a variety of arenas, commercial and domestic, public and private, festive and ordinary. Restaurants, festivals, cookbooks, grocery stores, private festive food events, cooking classes, televised cooking shows, advertising, and tourism brochures are some specific sites for culinary tourism. These arenas serve as interfaces between individuals and cultures, reflecting the expectations and contexts bearing upon each exchange. Interactions with foodways are seen through the lenses of our own experiences and cultural history; our perceptions of an other are uniquely our own. Simultaneously, our expectations will shape the interchange. Using the term "interface" highlights the self-reflexive potential of such sites and the possibility for dynamic, negotiated interactions within them. The term also reminds us that encounters with the other frequently teach us more about ourselves than about the other.

Each enactment of such tourism involves at least two actors, real or imagined, the host and the guest, the producer and the consumer—each having their own perspectives on what defines otherness. Consumers select those foodways contrasting with their own culinary system; while producers, individuals, or institutions attempting to present potentially other foodways must take into account the foodways systems of their audience. An individual shapes the presentation of his or her ethnicity according to the cognitive model held of the audience's culture (Coggeshall 1986). Producers of instances and artifacts of culinary tourism will likewise adapt their presentations to their understanding of their audience's culinary aesthetics and experiences. Studies of culinary tourism, then, need to address instances of such tourism as interactive, communicative events within a larger conceptual symbolic system.[12]

Realms of Culinary Experience

In the context of foodways, the crux of otherness involves three realms of experience—what I call the realms of the exotic, the edible, and the palatable. The *exotic* is a continuum from the familiar to the strange that defines the similarity of things to our known socially constructed universe. It is based on our individual histories and personal tastes as well as on the collective cultural experience and the generally accepted culinary aesthetic.

The realm of the *edible* consists of cultural categories of what can and cannot be eaten, in the sense that one's humanity is tied to observing such categories. While this realm has similarities with Claude Lèvi-

Strauss's categories of raw and cooked (Lèvi-Strauss 1966; 1978), I do not treat it as expressive of universal cognitive structures. Edibility is culturally specific, and as Mary Douglas has demonstrated in her work on taboos and food patterns, it can be a reflection of a culture's social structure. The question of edibility automatically occurs at the extreme end of the exotic continuum since the unknown raises questions not only about whether a food can be eaten, but also whether it should be eaten (Douglas 1966).

The realm of the *palatable* is an aesthetic rather than cognitive one, dealing with what is considered pleasing within a culinary system. Foods may be considered edible, but their selection for consumption will depend on whether or not they are considered savory, appetizing, or appropriate for particular contexts. Palatability can be seen as a "shadow" realm of edibility, since the two tend to be collapsed by many eaters. Certain food items or aspects of a food system may be considered culturally edible but unpalatable to a particular eater or group of eaters, and therefore would appear inedible. Vegetarians, for example, may find meat not only unpalatable, but also inedible. The children's categories of "yuk" and "yum" also blur the distinction between these realms, translating them into a culinary philosophy shaping everyday consumption, much to the dismay of nutrition-minded parents.

The difference between the realms of edible and palatable is perhaps most clearly seen in how we use them to evaluate other eaters. The eater of the "not edible" is perceived as strange, perhaps dangerous, definitely not one of us, whereas the eater of the unpalatable is seen as having different tastes. Both realms refer to the potential consumption of a particular food or aspect of foodways, but edibility refers to the categorical possibility; palatability to the aesthetic. The first is what we can eat; the second is what we want to eat.

By treating these categories as dynamic cultural resources available for individual manipulation and responsive to change, I hope to leave the model open to the historical, the situated, the contingent, and the diversity within cultures. In keeping with this approach, it is perhaps more accurate to portray these realms as axes that cross each other, forming four quadrants. These quadrants allow for overlapping, so there can be foods that are exotic but edible and foods that are familiar but inedible.

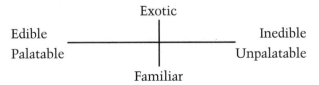

Since the boundaries of these realms depend on the past experiences, personal tastes, and personalities of the potential eaters and producers, as well as on the cultural categories and aesthetics of those actors, these realms are flexible and dynamic. Food items can shift in their location within these realms, because individuals' and society's perceptions of edibility and exoticness can shift. This shifting can occur in any direction along these axes: from the exotic to the familiar or the familiar to the exotic, and from the edible to the inedible or the inedible to the edible. It can occur on an individual basis or on a larger scale as a regional or national trend, either informal or institutionalized. It can also occur with any aspect of foodways—a specific ingredient, a particular dish, eating style, or preparation method—as well as entire cuisines.

Shifts in Perspective and the Multivocality of Food

The shifting from the exotic to the familiar and the inedible to the edible occurs constantly in the marketing of new foods to the American public. A good example is kiwi fruit, ten years ago a rarity in grocery stores in my part of the Midwest, but now commonplace enough to be included in school lunches. Pizza provides another example, beginning as an ethnic food with some question as to its palatability. With acceptance it has become a common meal for many Americans and has lost much of its otherness, to the extent that it is now considered a genre of food with certain structural features: dessert pizzas consist of a sweet dough or cookie base covered with whipped cream or sweetened cream cheese and topped with fruit or candies; ice-cream pizzas are similar but with an ice cream base. Ironically, some producers are shifting pizza back to the exotic end of the continuum by the addition of trendy, expensive, or unusual items—whole-wheat crusts, sun-dried tomatoes, shiitake mushrooms, goat cheese, grilled shrimp, and lobster. A pizza carryout restaurant in Philadelphia owned by a Korean couple deftly mixed the familiar and the exotic by offering a dish called "Korean Pizza," a standard pizza crust with Korean grilled beef and vegetables. Similarly, tostados and tacos have moved from the realm of questionable edibility to such familiarity that they are being served in school cafeterias. Chopsticks, rice steamers, shish kebab, barbecue, hot pepper sauces, and salsa dips are other common examples of this type of shift.

While American foodways appear to be expanding, the opposite directional shift occurs also, particularly in the definitions based on ethos. Some foodways that were once mainstream, even normative, have been moved to the inedible by some segments of the population because of nutritional or health concerns. Cooking green beans (and other vegetables) for hours with lard or bacon, as is common in traditional Southern cooking, is no longer in favor in health-conscious restaurants in the South. Butters and creams are suspect, as are traditional sauces and gravies that call for these ingredients. Rich desserts full of fats and sugar are deemed taboo for those who are health-conscious, and women's magazines frequently give alternative recipes and cooking methods for popular but cholesterol-laden foods like fried chicken, grilled cheese sandwiches, and ice cream. Similarly, vegetarians have placed animal products in the realm of the inedible, sometimes replacing them with foods formerly treated as exotic (bean curd, mashed bean pastes, and bean and grain patties) or even inedible (soybeans, seaweed, fermented dairy products). In these cases, the foodways that have shifted to inedible remain familiar to the larger population.

These shifts occur on a personal level as well, reflecting an individual's history, personality, experiences, and circumstances. Food, like any cultural product, is multivocal and polysemic, and new meanings can be recognized in new contexts. This frequently occurs when one's perceptions of foods are challenged in some way. An example of such a shift in perspective is an incident in which a friend requested suggestions of an exotic food that his young daughter could make for a school project. When I suggested that he look to his own background, he stated that he remembered only "normal foods" like bubble and squeak, toad-in-the-hole, tudgies (mashed turnips), Yorkshire pudding, and odds and sods. Although he had grown up in the urban Midwest, he lived with his Irish immigrant grandparents and was raised with their foodways, assuming that that was standard to the area. When he realized that these foods represented his Irish heritage, he looked at them differently, recognizing that they could be exotic to the Midwest. He then helped his daughter select a recipe for potato pancakes from an Irish cookbook. (The project was very successful; her classmates found the pancakes both foreign and tasty.)

A similar shift in perspective can occur when an individual physically changes location and finds him or herself living within a new foodways system. The contrast between what is accepted as normal in the new location and what is familiar from past experience can lead to foods not normally perceived as different being held up as subject for "the tourist gaze." I offer an experience of my own as an example. Twelve years ago I moved from the urban East Coast to a small town in the Midwest. In restaurants and homes, I was introduced to some regional specialties—canned sauerkraut juice, fried sauerkraut balls; Cincinnati chili (cinnamon-flavored meat sauce served over spaghetti, with a choice of beans, onions, and cheese on top);[13] mashed potatoes mixed with gravy and noodles; sweetened tomato pudding; gelatin-and-mayonnaise layered salads; thick, syrupy, bitter homemade apple butter; the word "pop" for soft drinks, while the word "soda," which I was used to, referred to an ice cream mixture. I was now in the heart of America—meat-and-potato country—with a cuisine featuring an abundance of starch and protein with few seasonings other than salt.

At the same time, I was dismayed at the paucity of ethnic, vegetarian, and "health" foods available. Whereas I had been used to small ethnic grocery stores, market stalls, and street vendors as well as inexpensive, family-run ethnic restaurants, foods that had been a part of my everyday diet—tofu, numerous fresh vegetables and fruits, items from Vietnamese, Ethiopian, Korean, Chinese, and Afghan cuisines—were not immediately available and were largely unfamiliar to my neighbors. It was with much interest, then, that I read an edition of the local university student newspaper that was titled "International Foods in Local Restaurants." The paper listed Mexican food available at Taco Bell and at Kaufman's Family Restaurant for their weekly Tuesday night special; Italian food at the numerous pizza parlors catering to the student population and on Italian night at Kaufman's; German and Polish sausages at Kaufman's; and Chinese food at two Cantonese lunchrooms specializing in chop suey and chow mein. For real novelty, but somewhat risky, one could order Peking and Szechwan dishes at another Chinese restaurant. To an outsider from the urban East Coast, the selection was not only dismally small, but also was inaccurate in its designation of items as ethnic foods. Of course, none of the local foods I found rather exotic were listed in this article, while those foods considered exotic by the local aesthetic to me were familiar and even mundane. As an outsider, I was discovering the exotic in what was familiar to natives of the area.

Tourism as Negotiation

As this anecdote illustrates, exoticness, edibility, and palatability, like any cultural categories, are contextual, social and personal constructs that can undergo redefinition by specific cultures as well as by individuals. Likewise, they are a resource to be potentially manipulated for creative, expressive, economic, even political ends. The maneuvering between the realms of the exotic and the edible is a dynamic, creative process that is perhaps best thought of as a negotiation of the realms with the needs, interests, and aesthetics of all the actors involved. This negotiation should be examined, then, from the point of view of both the producer and the consumer, and in terms of individual choices as well as group inclinations. There will always be some individuals who are more conservative in their tastes than others, just as there are individuals who will "push the palate," so to speak. Likewise, some populations, for whatever reason, will be more open to new culinary experiences than others. One of my children's preschool teachers actively taught the children to be good taste-testers, willing to take at least one bite of everything. Her concern was primarily a nutritional one, but she was teaching an exploratory approach to food that contrasted dramatically with the "better safe than sorry" approach pushed by some parents who cautioned children against trying new foods.

While exploratory eating can be a matter of personal preference and accessibility, it can also be promoted for commercial or ideological reasons. Individuals may want to introduce new foodways as a matter of ethnic or regional pride, as a statement of identity, as a demand for public recognition, or as social or cultural capital. They may also be a way to consolidate group belonging, define difference, and demonstrate distinctiveness. New foods may also be presented as a commodity, either as an innovation based on a tradition or as a tradition viable for new groups or uses. In such cases, producers explicitly manipulate the realms of the exotic, the edible, and the palatable to attract consumers.

Strategies of Negotiation

In examining attempts to present and explore new foods, I found five basic strategies for negotiating these realms: *framing, naming* or *translation, explication, menu selection,* and *recipe adaptation.* In the following discussion of these strategies, I focus on the producers/presenters of food, and I draw data primarily from two kinds of arenas: ethnic restaurants, specifically Korean restaurants in Philadelphia in the mid-1980s, and community-based seasonal festivals in the Midwest.[14] Ethnic restaurants are a particularly valuable arena for observation, because the need to be commercially viable forces restaurant owners to be aware of their potential customers' tastes, pocketbooks, and prior exposure to different foodways systems. The anticipated clientele, then, is a major factor in the negotiation of edibility and exoticness, and ethnic restaurants must frequently emphasize the edibility of the exotic in order to attract non-native customers.

Community-based festivals, on the other hand, tend to exoticize the familiar; they present the mundane as celebratory and the ordinary as extraordinary. In the Midwest, many of these festivals highlight the region's agricultural roots by using as a theme a particular food item or crop associated with the locale—northwest Ohio, for example, boasts apple butter, cherry, radish, tomato, and pumpkin festivals as well as an "Eggstravaganza" featuring eggs.

Framing, the first strategy of negotiation, involves designing a context surrounding a food item that then defines that food's edibility and exoticness. I draw here on ideas from Richard Bauman (1977) and Erving Goffman (1963) to emphasize the need to situate performances in particular physical contexts. The languages used on menus and signs, the decor, the spatial arrangement of tables, and the location of public and private areas are means by which actors can emphasize the exotic or the familiar. The Korean restaurants in Philadelphia signaled their anticipated clientele through such framing. Those catering to primarily Korean customers frequently displayed signs and menus only in Korean, had Korean paintings or objects, but had none of the stereotypical Asian decor. Those anticipating both Korean and non-Korean customers had menus and signs in Korean and English and more of the Asian decor. They also had designated back rooms for in-group customers. These usually were rooms upstairs set aside for large group dinners and parties where the eaters would sit on cushions on the floor at low tables. One establishment even had a disco and bar that was not publicly advertised to non-Koreans. The restaurants expecting a non-Korean clientele tended to use the more stereotypical Asian decor, such as beaded curtains, dragon motifs, and red napkins, with a familiar large dining room seating arrangement.

Similarly, placing an otherwise familiar food in an unusual context can signal a potentially new interpretation of that food. The community-based festivals in Ohio juxtaposed local history with particular foods, assigning those foods associated (both imagined and actual) with cultural heritage and identity. Such framing essentially signifies the need to recognize familiar foods as potentially other, to see them as outsiders would.

The second strategy of negotiation, naming or translation, involves the identification of items. This may be a literal translation of the name of a dish or food item or the invention of a new name. For example, the Korean dish *bulgogi* is translated literally as "fire meat" but is frequently identified as "grilled beef strips." Such names frequently draw from the familiar end of the continuum in order to demonstrate their similarities to the larger foodways system. In doing so, the naming places the food analogously within a framework accessible to Americans. For example,

1-7. A menu from a restaurant plays upon regional as well as cultural and ethical other. Indiana can represent the American Midwest (an exotic region for many Americans) and therefore represent the wholesome values of rural America. The restaurant offers Amish cooking, a culture that is felt to value purity, quality, and tradition in its food as well as in its lifestyle. *Photo by David Hampshire.*

the Korean dish *kimchi* is frequently identified as a pickle, although it is not made with vinegar. It could more accurately by identified as "cabbage and turnip fermented with salt, garlic, hot pepper, and rotted shrimp," but such a description would push it toward the inedible—or at least the unpalatable—for many American consumers.

Festivals also used this strategy to draw attention to the exotic quality of otherwise familiar foods. Prefixes such as "old-tyme" or "old-fashioned" emphasize the foods' representativeness of the past. Similarly, local regional or geographic ties may be made explicit by adding place names to the identification of a food item—Grand Rapids apple butter, Cincinnati chili, Ohio buckeyes (for a chocolate and peanut-butter confection made to resemble horse chestnuts). Religious identities associated with an area were also highlighted—Amish chickens and eggs, Mennonite whole-grain breads—as were characteristics felt to be representative of the region's ethos—homegrown, family-farmed, handpicked.

A third strategy is that of explication: description and explanation of the ingredients, manner of cooking, context for eating, or history and symbolism of the item. In this strategy, the consumer is drawn into the foodways system of the item and given a "native" perspective on it. In an

1-8. More food products that are packaged emphasizing regional others. The scone mix blends a variety of others: "Southern Delicious Contagious" is blended with an ingredient, cranberries, associated with New England and Thanksgiving and a food item, scones, associated with British cuisine. It also implies an ethnical other in its use of "folk art," which, according to the blurb on the package symbolizes this company's food because it "is the very definition of homemade; it's simple, pure and from the heart." Black-eyed peas are associated with Southern and African-American cooking, and in case a consumer is unaware of that, the package states, "Popular in Southern Culture." A drawing of a farm tells us that this food represents a down-home, rural other as well. The jar contains candy in the shape of pebbles and is identified with a city in North Carolina. *Photo by David Hampshire.*

1-9. Jars of apple butter with the packaging highlighting the rural and wholesome associations with this food. *Photo by David Hampshire.*

intentionally humorous use of this strategy, a Thai restaurant in Milwaukee, The King and I, identified the spiciness of the dishes on their menu
according to a scale that began with one star for "coward," two stars for
"careful," three stars for "adventurous," and four stars for "Native Thai."
Similarly, waiters and waitresses in most Korean restaurants were prepared to give a complete description of the ingredients and preparation
methods of the dishes being offered. Likewise, they would demonstrate
techniques for holding chopsticks, for cooking one's meal with the tableside
grill—the *sinsullo*, and for serving oneself from the communal dishes. I
played a similar role at the Festival of American Folklife at the Smithsonian
Institution in Washington, D.C., in the early 1980s when I was a pre-
senter for a Korean foodways section. While two older Korean women,
neither of whom spoke a great deal of English, demonstrated preparation
techniques for a number of dishes, I fielded questions, most of which were
about the edibility of those dishes, particularly *kimchi*. This dish is known
among Americans for its extreme spiciness and powerful odor, features
that have been played upon in American images of Koreans. In my explanations of the diversity of recipes for the dish and of its central role in
Korean foodways, I attempted to make the audience familiar enough with
kimchi to see it as at least edible. They may not personally like the item,
but they gained an appreciation for why some people do.

Many cookbook authors attempt a similar negotiation of the exotic
by including introductions to the food system being presented or by including narratives and anecdotes about the recipes. For example, a Korean
cookbook written in English specifically for Americans provides descriptions of the basics of Korean cuisine and of Korean table settings and has
photographs of ingredients potentially unfamiliar to that audience. Another cookbook compiled of recipes used at various Smithsonian folklife
festivals includes descriptions of the significance of a recipe in a community or family tradition along with quotations from the original cooks.
Such a strategy personalizes, and therefore humanizes, otherwise exotic,
potentially inedible foods. A recipe for octopus, for example, is accompanied by the cook's memories of her family's procuring and eating of the
creature (Kirlin and Kirlin 1991:95).

The local festivals in Ohio, on the other hand, frame the commonplace as worthy of attention through descriptions of the history and social
uses of the item and through explanations of the otherness of familiar
foods. Frequently, the food items are familiar, but the cooking methods
are not, being "old-fashioned" ones used historically in that region. The
Grand Rapids Apple Butter Festival, for example, offers apple butter pre-

pared in large iron pots over outdoor fires, a method that used to be common in the region. While apple butter itself is still a familiar item in the region's foodways, that preparation method is not. During the festival, volunteers demonstrate the cooking method and discuss it with the audience. Similarly, some dishes are not recognized as being representative of the region until their distinctiveness—and their potential exoticness to an outsider—is pointed out. Items such as potpie (a thick chicken or turkey stew with large flat noodles) or Cincinnati chili, apple butter, and tomato ketchup are now being included as part of presentations of regional identity. Other food items may be presented as representative because of their commonness and therefore interrelatedness to other aspects of the regional culture. Recognizing a food item does not shift it toward the realm of the exotic so much as it clarifies the symbolic weight of that food.

Menu selection, the fourth and perhaps the most common strategy, is the selecting of particular dishes thought to best appeal to the consumer. This strategy involves the producer's cognitive model of the tastes of the potential eater as well as the producer's notions of which dishes best represent the cuisine. In Korean restaurants, waitresses frequently suggest the blander dishes to American customers, assuming that too much garlic and hot pepper is offensive to most Americans. Several dishes in particular are thought to be unpalatable to anyone except Koreans—*kimchi chigye* or stew, and *naengmyun*, a cold buckwheat noodle soup served with a thick, black, fermented soybean paste and a raw egg. Several restaurants have actually refused my order of these dishes.

Menu selection clearly reflects the intentions of the producer and the anticipated consumer. Korean restaurants catering to a primarily Korean clientele featured specifically Korean dishes prepared in an "authentic" manner, that is, using more spices. Those anticipating a mixed clientele frequently highlighted on the menu those dishes thought to appeal to non-Koreans. Restaurants targeting mostly non-Koreans selected those dishes using ingredients and quantities of spices known to be acceptable and liked by most American customers. A common strategy among these last establishments was to offer Korean food alongside other Asian cuisines, such as Japanese or Chinese, already established in the United States. By juxtaposing the relatively unfamiliar Korean cuisine with the others—still exotic but more familiar—Korean food was brought into the realm of the edible.

Similarly, a Cantonese restaurant owner in Memphis described to me how he "educated" American children to eat Chinese food by offering them Chinese dishes such as egg rolls and chop suey that he felt would not be too strange to them. Once they were familiar with these foods, he gradually offered them a larger selection until they had acquired a taste for Chinese cuisine. Ironically, his teaching was too effective, and the children, when they became adults, went on to acquire tastes for the Peking and Szechwan styles offered by other restaurants. He concluded that his Cantonese-style cooking was too bland for them, too familiar, and no longer offered the excitement of the exotic.[15]

Using the same strategy, the community-based festivals selected dishes thought to be familiar to the crowds but also fitting of a particular public identity, one that was usually based on an imagined past. Apple butter or popcorn was standard demonstration fare at these festivals; neither needed explanation to regional audiences. By grounding foodways in the familiar, these festivals emphasized the similarities, the unity of the area, thereby helping it qualify as a cultural region, one of the underlying themes of many of these festivals.

The final strategy, recipe adaptation, involves the manipulation of the ingredients and preparation methods of particular dishes in order to adapt to the foodways system of the anticipated consumers. Potentially offensive ingredients, or those not easily obtained, may be omitted or replaced with more familiar ones. Again, *kimchi* provides an excellent example. The dish comes in numerous variations of ingredients depending on the season, the locale, the occasion, and the social status of the eaters. The most typical kind, a winter *kimchi*, is made of, among other things, Chinese cabbage, turnips, green onions, garlic, red pepper, ginger, shrimp and oysters, water, and salt. The mixture is left in a cool place to marinate for at least four to five days, preferably several months. As mentioned above, the result is very hot and pungent. When preparing *kimchi* for American customers, most of the Korean restaurants in Philadelphia made a less spicy version. One cook described how she left out the shrimp and decreased the amount of pepper and garlic for her "American *kimchi*." She also told of another restaurant that substituted paprika for the red pepper normally used, keeping the red color of the *kimchi* but reducing its spiciness.

In a reverse process, festivals frequently adapted recipes to produce foods that would seem familiar yet still out of the ordinary and with an aura of exoticness. These adaptations often emphasized the rural background and "hands on" attitude of the region. Instead of store-bought, canned, or frozen foods, festivals used homegrown, freshly picked ingredients prepared home style in a family setting, such as freshly picked cherries, homegrown pumpkins, farm fresh eggs, or apple butter prepared over outdoor fires instead of in crock pots.

This look at some of the strategies used in negotiating the realms of

1-10. This T-shirt displays the basic idea of culinary tourism—shopping at this store is more than simply stocking your pantry; it enables one to "taste" the whole world. *Photo by David Hampshire.*

exoticness and edibility confirms the need to locate culinary tourism in the perspectives of the individuals involved; that is, tourism is in the eye of the beholder—or on the tongue of the taster. What to one individual is a culinary adventure may be mundane and familiar to another and vice versa. As with any cultural tradition, there can be a discrepancy between the meanings assigned to food by the producers and those assigned by the consumers. Furthermore, foodways serve a multitude of functions in our culture; culinary tourism is but one.

Concluding Thoughts

Locating culinary tourism in the perspectives of individual consumers and producers addresses the question of why it occurs. Some scholars have interpreted the impulse to eat the other as a colonialist, hegemonic act, a taking over of another group by appropriating its cultural traditions, or as representing the capitalist inclinations to display superiority by mastery over ever-expanding arenas, including new cuisines (Goody 1982; Mintz 1985; Montano 1997; Heldke 2001). Culinary tourism can also be seen as a sign of prosperity, allowing producers and consumers to elevate food from being mere sustenance to the realms of art and recreation, and therefore tools for the expression and manipulation of social power (Appadurai 1981, 1986; Bourdieu 1984). A more optimistic interpretation sees culinary tourism as the willingness of humans to experience the cultural worlds of other people, as the result of curiosity about other experiences and other ways of life. This is not to deny the political implications of tourism or the ethical responsibilities attached to it. Nor does it ignore the fact that tourism turns culinary traditions into commodities to be bought and sold. Beginning at the level of individual involvement in tourism, however, illuminates the complexity of cultural productions and allows us to see the workings of personal meaning within larger institutional meanings.

In my research, I found the motivations for culinary tourism to be complex and to reflect what appears to be a basic and universal impulse. People intentionally consume an other because they are curious, and that curiosity stems from any number of reasons: because they are bored with the familiar, they do not want to be rude to a host, they want to balance their nutritional intake, they want to belong to a specific community of eaters, they feel pride in the heritage represented by a foodways, or they want to authenticate an experience by relishing it, so to speak. As both social system and aesthetic system, food is a powerful medium through which to enter another culture. Through food we can communicate identity, relationships, ideologies, and emotions, as well as fulfill basic physical needs. Food offers us an aesthetic experience, and like other aesthetic realms—music, dance, art—it draws us into its own universe of meaning. The materiality of food allows an individual to experience an other on a sensory level, not just an intellectual one. By consuming the foods of a group distinct from us, we may be acting out larger cultural impulses, but the aesthetic and material nature of food, I think, explains the pervasiveness of food in tourist sites. The act of eating offers a way to share our basic humanity, while also acknowledging and negotiating our differential identities.

The model of culinary tourism suggested here provides a framework for seeing the varieties of interfaces in which adventurous eating occurs as instances of negotiating individual and social perceptions of the exotic. As such, they represent a movement toward expanding the definitions of edibility and palatability and the horizons of the familiar. These instances are connected to a multitude of culinary experiences occurring throughout our culture, all characterized by the dynamic exploration and redefining of our culinary universes. As destination and vehicle for tourism, food expands our understanding of both food and tourism.

Notes

1. For contemporary folkloristic approaches to the study of food and foodways see Jones, Giuliano, and Krell 1983; Brown and Mussell 1984; Neustadt 1992; Gutierrez 1992; and Lockwood and Lockwood 1991. For examples of a folkloristic approach to recipe collections see Kirlin and Kirlin 1991, and Kaplan, Hoover, and Moore 1986.

2. I borrow here from folklorist Barbara Kirshenblatt-Gimblett's use of the phrase "gastronomic tourism" (personal communication, February 1996). Kirshenblatt-Gimblett is well known for "pushing" the boundaries of folklore and for her insightful critiques of the discipline (see, for example, Kirshenblatt-Gimblett 1988). She has also been a major influence in the folkloristic study of foodways.

3. I draw here from the extensive body of literature on the anthropology of tourism and on the critique of touristic productions. Three classics in the field are Smith 1989; MacCannell 1976; and Jules-Rosette 1984. For more experiential and ethnographic-based approaches, see Urry 1990, 1995; Smith and Eadington, 1992; Baranowski and Furlough 2001; and Desmond 2001. The journal *Annals of Tourism Research* specializes in tourism. Tourism has also been of particular interest to folklorists, partly because it raises questions over such issues as the nature of authenticity, the relationship between producer and consumer, and the aesthetic and political quality of cultural representations.

4. This conception of culinary tourism draws heavily from contemporary folklore theory, hence the title, "a folkloristic perspective." Some scholars use the term "folkloristic" to distinguish the field of folklore studies from its subject matter (Georges and Jones 1995). The definition of folklore offered by Dan Ben-Amos in 1972—"artistic communication in small groups"—is still useful today, succinctly characterizing folklore. Folklore is generally thought of as those products and patterns of behavior expressing a communal ethos and aesthetic and being transmitted over time and place in a way that allows for individuals and

groups to create variations, enacting their particular histories, identities, and circumstances in each performance. I draw from a number of scholars in my own formulation of folklore as the processes and products by which individuals construct, negotiate, and maintain meaningful connections with past, place, and people (see Toelken 1996).

5. Jane Desmond's work on public displays of bodies as sites for tourism demonstrates the power of the materiality of things to ground experience. She states that Western thought reflects a philosophy "dependent on the body to anchor systems of knowledge that articulate social difference" (2001:xiv). Furthermore, she points out that "live performers not only authenticate these packages' differences: they also offer the possibility of contact with them" (2001:xv). Food similarly grounds the tourist experience in our own bodies and physicality.

6. The quote is taken from Yoder 1972:325. Yoder's source is Honigman 1961.

7. The notion of other has informed the field of folklore studies since the 1970s and has drawn from both anthropological models and literary theory as well as from philosophical inquiries into the nature of knowledge. See, for example, Turner and Bruner 1984.

8. For more discussion on ethnic identity as a contextualization process, see Royce 1982.

9. For folkloristic approaches to region and regional foodways, see Jones 1976; part 3 of Brown and Mussell 1984; and Allen and Schlereth 1990.

10. Personal communications with historian and folklorist, Dr. Chris Geist, who has worked at Colonial Williamsburg, have made me aware of the extent to which food is used in heritage tourism.

11. Three kings cake is baked with several "fortune-telling" items inside—a thimble for spinsterhood, a ring for marriage, a coin for wealth. Although usually associated with Catholic communities, it is spreading in popularity. A Protestant church in Findlay, Ohio, holds an "Epiphany Party" every year and serves a three kings cake. A small figure is wrapped in foil and, along with other items similarly wrapped, is baked inside the cake. Whoever gets the figure has to make the cake the following year.

12. This approach draws from performance theory (see Bauman 1977) to attend to actual incidents of consuming an other with awareness of the varying levels of context present. It also reframes Dell Hymes's ethnography of speaking model as "ethnography of eating" (see Hymes 1962 and 1974).

13. For a full discussion of this dish, see Lloyd 1981.

14. In the fall of 1983, for a course in folklife taught by Don Yoder, I began an ethnography of Korean foodways in the Philadelphia area, looking specifically at the varieties, uses, and symbolic meanings of the dish *kimchi*. This work resulted in a term paper, a paper on *kimchi* read at the 1986 American Folklore Society meeting, and an unpublished paper on varieties of restaurant experiences. My work on festivals in the Midwest began in 1986 and has continued to the present. In 2002, I produced a documentary video on a local apple butter festival titled *Stirring Up the Past: The Grand Rapids Apple Butter Fest.*

15. This interview was a part of a larger survey on Asian communities in Memphis that I conducted for the Center for Southern Folklore in Memphis, Tennessee, from January through June of 1980.

Works Cited

Allen, Barbara, and Thomas J. Schlereth, eds. 1990. *Sense of Place: American Regional Cultures*. Lexington: University Press of Kentucky.

Appadurai, Arjun. 1981. "Gastropolitics in Hindu South Asia." *American Ethnologist* 8: 494–511.

———. 1986. "Introduction: Commodities and the Politics of Value." In *The Social Life of Things: Commodities in Cultural Perspective*. Ed. Arjun Appadurai, 3–63. Cambridge, U.K.: Cambridge University Press.

Baranowski, Shelley, and Ellen Furlough, eds. 2001. *Being Elsewhere: Tourism, Consumer Culture, and Identity in Modern Europe and North America*. Ann Arbor: University of Michigan Press.

Bauman, Richard. 1977. *Verbal Art as Performance*. Rowley, Mass.: Newbury House.

Bourdieu, Pierre. 1984. *Distinction: A Social Critique of the Judgement of Taste*. Cambridge, Mass.: Harvard University Press.

Brown, Linda Keller, and Kay Mussell, eds. 1984. *Ethnic and Regional Foodways in the United States: The Performance of Group Identity*. Knoxville: University of Tennessee Press.

Coggeshall, John M. 1986. "One of Those Intangibles: The Manifestation of Ethnic Identity in Southwestern Illinois." *Journal of American Folklore* 99: 273–90.

Desmond, Jane C. 2001. *Staging Tourism: Bodies on Display from Waikiki to Sea World*. Chicago: University of Chicago Press.

Douglas, Mary. 1966. *Purity and Danger: An Analysis of Concepts of Pollution and Taboo*. New York: Praeger.

Gabaccia, Donna R. 1998. *We Are What We Eat: Ethnic Food and the Making of Americans*. Cambridge, Mass.: Harvard University Press.

Georges, Frank and Michael Owen Jones. 1995. *Folkloristics: An Introduction*. Bloomington: Indiana University Press.

Goffman, Erving. 1963. *Behavior in Public Places: Notes on the Social Organizations of Gatherings*. New York: Free Press of Glencoe.

Goody, Jack. 1982. *Cooking, Cuisine and Class: A Study in Comparative Sociology*. Cambridge, U.K.: Cambridge University Press.

Graburn, Nelson H.H. 1989. "Tourism: The Sacred Journey." In *Hosts and Guests: The Anthropology of Tourism, 2nd ed.* Ed. Valene L. Smith, 21–36. Philadelphia: University of Pennsylvania Press.

Gutierrez, C. Paige. 1992. *Cajun Foodways*. Jackson: University Press of Mississippi.

Handler, Richard, and Eric Gable. 1997. *The New History in an Old Museum: Creating the Past at Colonial Williamsburg*. Durham, N.C.: Duke University Press.

Heldke, Lisa. 2001. "Let's Cook Thai: Recipes for Colonialism." In *Pilaf, Pozole, and Pad Thai: American Women and Ethnic Food.* Ed. Sherrie A. Inness, 175–98. Amherst: University of Massachusetts Press.

Honigman, John J. 1961. *Foodways in a Muskeg Community: An Anthropological Report on the Attawapiskat Indians.* Ottawa: Northern Coordination and Research Center.

Hymes, Dell. 1962. "The Ethnography of Speaking." In *Anthropology and Human Behavior.* Eds. T. Gladwin and William.C. Sturtevant. Washington, D.C.: Anthropological Society of Washington.

———. 1974. "Ways of Speaking." In *Explorations in the Ethnography of Speaking.* Eds. Richard Bauman and Joel Sherzer, 433–52. New York: Cambridge University Press.

Inness, Sherrie A., 2001. *Pilaf, Pozole, and Pad Thai: American Women and Ethnic Food.* Amherst: University of Massachusetts Press.

Jones, Michael Owen, Bruce Giuliano, and Roberta Krell, eds. 1983. *Foodways and Eating Habits: Directions for Research.* Los Angeles: California Folklore Society.

Jones, Suzi. 1976. "Regionalization: A Rhetorical Strategy." *Journal of the Folklore Institute* 13: 105–18.

Jules-Rosette, Benetta. 1984. *The Messages of Tourist Art: An African Semiotic System in Comparative Perspective.* New York: Plenum Press.

Kaplan, Anne R., Marjorie A. Hoover, and Willard B. Moore, eds. 1986. *The Minnesota Ethnic Food Book.* St. Paul: Minnesota Historical Society Press.

Kirlin, Katherine S., and Thomas M. Kirlin, eds. 1991. *Smithsonian Folklife Cookbook.* Washington, D.C.: Smithsonian Institution Press.

Kirshenblatt-Gimblett, Barbara. 1988. "Mistaken Dichotomies." *Journal of American Folklore* 101: 140–55.

———. 1998. *Destination Culture: Tourism, Museums, and Heritage.* Berkeley: University of California Press.

Lèvi-Strauss, Claude. 1966. "The Culinary Triangle." *Partisan Review* 33: 586–95.

———. 1978. *The Origin of Table Manners.* Trans. John and Doreen Weightman. New York: Harper and Row.

Lloyd, Tim. 1981. "The Cincinnati Chili Culinary Complex." *Western Folklore* 40: 28–40.

Lockwood, Yvonne R., and William G. Lockwood. 1991. "Pasties in Michigan's Upper Peninsula: Foodways, Interethnic Relations, and Regionalism." In *Creative Ethnicity: Symbols and Strategies of Contemporary Ethnic Life.* Eds. Stephen Stern and John Allan Cicala, 3–20. Logan: Utah State University Press.

Lowenthal, David. 1985. *The Past Is a Foreign Country.* Cambridge, U.K.: Cambridge University Press.

MacCannell, Dean. 1976. *The Tourist: A New Theory of the Leisure Class.* New York: Schocken Books.

Mintz, Sidney W. 1985. *Sweetness and Power: The Place of Sugar in Modern History.* New York: Penguin.

————. 1996. *Tasting Food, Tasting Freedom: Excursions into Eating, Culture, and the Past.* Boston: Beacon Press.

Montaño, Mario. 1997. "Appropriation and Counterhegemony in South Texas: Food Slurs, Offal Meats, and Blood." In *Usable Pasts: Traditions and Group Expressions in North America.* Ed. Tad Tuleja, 50–67. Logan: Utah State University Press.

Neustadt, Kathy. 1992. *Clambake A History and Celebration of an American Tradition.* Amherst: University of Massachusetts Press.

Oring, Elliott. 1986. "Ethnic Groups and Ethnic Folklore." In *Folk Groups and Folklore Genres: An Introduction.* Ed. Elliott Oring, 23–44. Logan: Utah State University Press.

Royce, Anya Peterson. 1982. *Ethnic Identity: Strategies of Diversity.* Bloomington: Indiana University Press.

Santino, Jack. 1994. *All Around the Year: Holidays and Celebrations in American Life.* Urbana: University of Illinois Press.

————. 1996. *New Old-Fashioned Ways: Holidays and Popular Culture.* Knoxville: University of Tennessee Press.

Stern, Stephen, and John Allan Cicala. 1991. *Creative Ethnicity: Symbols and Strategies of Contemporary Ethnic Life.* Logan: Utah State University Press.

Smith, Valene L., ed. 1989. "Introduction." In *Hosts and Guests: The Anthropology of Tourism, 2nd ed.* Ed. Valene L. Smith, 1–17. Philadelphia: University of Pennsylvania Press.

Smith, Valene L. and William R. Eadington, eds. 1992. *Tourism Alternatives: Potentials and Problems in the Development of Tourism.* Philadelphia: University of Pennsylvania Press.

Toelken, Barre. 1996. *The Dynamics of Folklore.* Logan: Utah State University Press.

Turgeon, Laurier, and Madeleine Pastinelli. 2002. "'Eat the World': Postcolonial Encounters in Quebec City's Ethnic Restaurants." *Journal of American Folklore* 115/456: 247–68.

Turner, Victor W., and Edward M. Bruner. 1984. *The Anthropology of Experience.* Urbana: University of Illinois Press.

Urry, John. 1990. *The Tourist Gaze: Leisure and Travel in Contemporary Societies.* London: Sage.

————. 1995. *Consuming Places.* London: Routledge.

Yoder, Don. 1972. "Folk Cookery." In *Folklore and Folklife: An Introduction.* Ed. Richard M. Dorson, 325. Chicago: University of Chicago Press.

Culinary Tourism in Public
and Commercial Contexts

Part 1 addresses culinary tourism in public contexts. These venues are usually commercial, where food is being not only presented but also sold to outsiders. Such contexts shape the relationship of the producer to the food—food is literally a commodity and, as such, complicates and frequently distances the emotional content of the food for those offering it and receiving it. The public commercial context also shapes the relationship between the producer and the consumer, mediating it as a monetary interaction in place of, or perhaps as well as, a social one. Public settings often include festive or ritual activities. Special foods are frequently used to mark an event or setting as festive, but the reverse is true as well. A festive setting may frame a particular food as special and imbue it with new meanings specific to that context.

Jennie Germann Molz's essay begins this section by examining the concept of authenticity—a quality often held as the ideal in tourism. Using Thai restaurants in Texas as a case study, Molz explores the ways in which authenticity is central to the touristic experience and yet is constructed out of the experiences of the consumers. Jeffrey Pilcher then discusses the development of a tourism industry that surrounds Mexican food. By offering Mexican culture as a touristic subject, producers and promoters have had to negotiate the stereotypes held by Anglo-Americans. Utilizing a different context, Kristin McAndrews focuses on a food festival in Hawaii, exploring how it frames a particular foodways as both exotic and festive. The festival offers tourists a safe arena for trying new foods and also serves as a means through which they can feel they are experiencing the local culture by eating the local foods.

Eve Jochnowitz also addresses culinary tourism in restaurant settings but demonstrates the multivalent nature of food and commercial transactions. She examines Jewish food in contemporary Poland, observing that the commercial foods offered on a main street in Cracow function as a Jewish "theme park." Jochnowitz concludes that the presentation of Jewish food in Poland reflects the position of Jews in Polish folklore, and culinary tourism allows the Polish people to "taste" the experiences of Jews in their culture.

CHAPTER 2

Tasting an Imagined Thailand

Authenticity and Culinary Tourism in Thai Restaurants

Jennie Germann Molz

Food and tourism have long been linked in the popular mindset. Lifestyle magazines such as *Gourmet* and *Travel & Leisure,* for example, reveal the connection between food and tourism. The former rarely excludes a travel section, while the latter is never without its food reviews. At the other end of the budget, backpacker guides like *Lonely Planet* always include sections on local foods and where to eat while traveling. As these magazines and travel guides demonstrate, eating and tourism go hand in hand. But when eating *is* tourism, a whole new theoretical framework arises. Culinary tourism, the exploration of foreign foodways as representative of an other (Long 1998), provides a framework for interrogating the various intersections between tourism and foodways. This essay will investigate one such intersection, the concept of authenticity, in an effort to outline the usefulness of this concept in examining instances and arenas of culinary tourism. The term "authenticity" has been widely, and somewhat contentiously, applied to the study of both foodways and tourism. I will explore how the concept of authenticity can be applied within the framework of culinary tourism to better understand the social dynamics, particularly the processes of identity construction and validation, that accompany adventures in eating.

One site of culinary tourism in which the concepts of authenticity and identity making are particularly evident is the ethnic restaurant. Unlike tourists in the traditional sense, culinary tourists can explore the exotic without leaving their own neighborhood. Ethnic restaurants are one of an increasing number of arenas in which people can engage in touristic practices within their own culture and as part of their everyday life. When John Urry, in his study of tourism, comments that "people are much of the time tourists" (1990:82) he is referring to the process by which everyday local sights and experiences come under the tourist gaze. Ethnic restaurants are an example of how dining establishments have come under the tourist gaze and how dining out has become a touristic practice. Eating out has been described as a form of identity work (Lu and Fine 1995), where the restaurant is "a theater for thinking and fashioning a self" (Shelton 1990:507). The ethnic restaurant, then, is a symbolic stage upon which the exploration of the exotic, facilitated through the concept of authenticity, becomes an expression of identity. While these social dynamics play out in a variety of ethnic restaurants, this essay focuses on Thai restaurants in the United States, with their connotation of exoticness, as particularly valuable venues in which to examine culinary tourism and authenticity.

Authenticity

Authenticity has been categorized as one of those plastic words that "have come to mean so much that they really mean very little while nonetheless signaling importance and power" (Bendix 1992:104). In a brief essay on culinary authenticity, Arjun Appadurai expresses how the term "authenticity," in spite of its relatively simple definition, can be so difficult to grasp:

> Authenticity measures the degree to which something is more or less what it *ought* to be. It is thus a norm of some sort. But is it an immanent norm, emerging somehow from the cuisine itself? Or is it an external norm, reflecting some imposed gastronomic standard? If it is an immanent norm, who is its authoritative voice: The professional cook? The average consumer? The gourmand? The housewife? If it is an imposed norm, who is its privileged voice: the connoisseur of exotic food? The tourist? The ordinary participants in a neighboring cuisine? The cultivated eater from a distant one? (1986:25).

Appadurai's questions outline the basic debate over authenticity: where is it located and by what authority is it judged? Appadurai believes the term should not be applied to culinary systems at all, because it cannot account for the inevitable evolution that occurs in cultures and their cuisines. He claims, "the idea of authenticity seems to imply a timeless perspective on profoundly historical processes. Thus, the transhistorical ring of authority with which the word authenticity is sometimes used in the evaluation of foreign cuisines is spurious" (1986:25). Appadurai's rejection of the term "authenticity" lies in his perception that it connotes an *objective* reality. In contrast, many scholars believe that authenticity is a subjective or emergent quality that is constructed and negotiated within a social context (Moscardo and Pearce 1986; Evans-Pritchard 1987; Cohen 1988; Lu and Fine 1995; Edensor 1998). The debate Appadurai brings up here in terms of ethnic foodways is also evident in tourism studies.

The notion of authenticity as a motivation for tourism first appears in Dean MacCannell's work *The Tourist: A New Theory of the Leisure Class.* In this early study of tourists, MacCannell suggests that modern society has become inauthentic and that the modern tourist is on a quest to recover this lost authenticity. According to MacCannell, "Modern Man is losing his attachments to the work bench, the neighborhood, the town, the family, which he once called 'his own' but, at the same time, he is developing an interest in the 'real life' of others" (1973:91). MacCannell's tourist locates authenticity in some premodern realm—in people, places, and times that have not yet been dispossessed of their authenticity by the processes of modernity. However, MacCannell's tourist can never find or experience true authenticity, for the tourist world is constructed in such a way as to thwart the tourist's quest. "Touristic consciousness," he explains, "is motivated by its desire for authentic experience, and the tourist may believe that he is moving in this direction, but it is very difficult to know for sure if the experience is in fact authentic" (1973:101). MacCannell says that tourists are almost always caught in a paradoxical situation where what they think is an authentic experience is really an experience of staged authenticity.

He derives the concept of "staged authenticity" from Erving Goffman's (1959) study of social performance, in which Goffman divides the social world into back regions and front regions. Back regions, which are off-limits to outsiders or audience members, are areas where social actors prepare their performances and store props, and relax between performances. Front regions are areas where social actors actually perform in front of an audience. MacCannell says that the true back region is not available to tourists, but that the travel industry, understanding the modern tourist's desire for authenticity, has created a middle ground: staged authenticity. In between the inauthentic front region and the authentic back region, he argues, is a continuum of representations that are more or less authentic, depending on how close they are to the back or front region, respectively. This explains the tourist's confusion over whether an experience is authentic or not, because a front region may be presented *as if* it were a back region. It appears to be a behind-the-scenes peek at another culture, when in fact it is as carefully orchestrated as any other presentation for the tourists.

The Thai restaurant, a representative enclave of Thai culture within the United States, is a good example of staged authenticity. A Thai restaurant is a behind-the-scenes peek, if you will, at Thai-ness. Thai restaurants use several strategies to imbue their food and the overall dining experience with a sense of authenticity. But as MacCannell asserts, these representations ultimately fail to be truly authentic, because they are arranged to fool the tourists into believing they are having an authentic experience. The Thai restaurant tends to reflect the American perception of what constitutes an authentic Thai experience, even when this perception veers from the reality of Thai culture. According to MacCannell's framework, Thai restaurants are, at best, examples of staged authenticity.

The Thai Restaurant as "Staged Authenticity"

Participant observation in several Thai restaurants, most located in the Dallas metropolitan area, initially substantiates MacCannell's theory.[1] Restaurant owners and designers obviously realize and attempt to cater to their customers' desire for an authentic experience. The menu and ingredients, as well as the décor, appear to be created to engender a sense of authenticity, even when other factors expose the fact that these representations are not necessarily authentic.

The Menu

The most straightforward marker of authenticity in a Thai restaurant is usually found on the menu, where the restaurant often states that its food is authentic or original, or that its ingredients and cooking techniques adhere to traditional Thai recipes. Some restaurants, like Tuppee Thai, create this sense of authenticity by identifying the region in Thailand from which their food comes: "Original Thai country cuisine from the south of Thailand." The menu at Chiang Mai Thai restaurant asserts that its dishes "are prepared based on traditional methods." In addition to establishing the authenticity of the food and its preparation, the Chiang Mai menu tells diners how to have an authentic dining experience: "Thai food has always been *meant* to be shared with friends and family amid lively discussions and much laughter. This interaction is *what eating Thai style is all about*"(emphasis mine).[2]

Restaurants also imply culinary authenticity through the selection of dishes on the menus. The menus include those dishes commonly found in Thailand: rice and noodle dishes, soups, cold salads, stir-fry dishes, and beverages such as Thai iced tea. Occasionally, a parenthetical note, such as "(A favorite Thai Noodle Dish)," will assure the authenticity of the dish by implying that Thai people themselves eat this dish. By making these claims of authenticity on their menus, Thai restaurants appeal to what they perceive as their customers' desire for an authentic culinary experience.

While most Thai menus include typical dishes, such as Tom Yum soup and Pad Thai noodles, other equally authentic dishes and preparation techniques may be omitted with the customers' preferences in mind. For example, although in Thailand it is common to put a fried egg on top of a dish of fried rice, most Thai restaurants will only do this as a special request and usually charge extra for this authentic addition. Serving fried rice *kai dao* (with a fried egg) does not appeal to most Western diners, and therefore Thai chefs omit the egg. The Thai restaurant's menu, then, is self-contradictory, claiming authenticity on one hand, but adapting to the Western parameters of culinary acceptability on the other.

The Ingredients

Thai restaurants also attempt to provide an authentic experience by using typical Thai ingredients. More than any other ingredient, the chili pepper has come to stand for Thai-ness. Thai restaurants understand this equation, and spiciness is indicated in every menu. The Thai restaurants in this study use the chili and spiciness as measures of authenticity. Chiang Mai Thai explains in its menu that "Thai food is famous for being spicy." This menu uses small red fireballs next to spicy dishes to indicate how hot the dish is. The menu at Bangkok City offers the following scale for indicating how spicy diners want their food: "When ordering 'Please' Specify Degree of Spice Desired. *Coward, **Careful, ***Adventurous, ****Native Thai." This scale implies that the hotter the dish, the more authentic, or native, the food will be. These menus indicate that the kitchen is capable of making each dish as hot as it would be made in Thailand ("If you want, you can have *all* the chilies in the kitchen"), but every restaurant caters to diners' requests for milder food ("All meals are individually prepared and suited to your palate"). Again, the need to cater to the customer requires Thai restaurants to adapt their representation of authentically seasoned dishes to their customers' palates.

In addition to diners' delicate taste buds, local availability of ingredients can also thwart attempts at authenticity. Even when restaurants claim to use traditional ingredients, they often must substitute ingredients that are more easily available in the United States. Bangkok City, for example, uses prepackaged frozen mixed vegetables in its stir-fries. Other restaurants use button mushrooms in place of oyster mushrooms in the Tom Yum, or American broccoli instead of Asian broccoli in the stir-fries. These allowances to local palates and conditions undermine the authenticity that the restaurants try to uphold.

Again, allowances to authenticity are made as much by what is served as by what is *not* served. Since most Americans are averse to eating certain animal parts, Thai restaurants in the United States avoid the authentic practice of serving chicken entrails or fish heads with particular dishes. In these cases, the restaurants' need to attract local patrons undermines their ability to present a truly authentic experience to their diners. The Thai restaurant is not the only ethnic restaurant where authenticity is bowed for commercial reasons. Jeremy MacClancy (1992) explains that "if immigrant restaurateurs want to draw Westerners in to their establishments, they are often forced to adapt their recipes. It is hard to imagine a Chinese eatery that served items like 'chicken's blood porridge' and 'soyed pig's bowel' pulling in the crowds"(205).

The Décor

Thai restaurants often attempt to create a sense of authenticity beyond the food. They use native artwork, decorations, and music to suggest that the restaurant really is an enclave of Thai culture. Common in these Thai restaurants are photographs of King Bhumipol, the current king of Thailand, or of King Rama V, the revered nineteenth-century king who modernized Thailand. Several of the restaurants also have spirit houses, small altars with offerings of oranges, water, jasmine, and incense. Since the photographs of the monarchs and the spirit houses are usually placed near the kitchen or cashier's area, they seem to be more for the staff than for the patrons. On his continuum between front and back, MacCannell would probably consider these items as closer, both literally and metaphorically, to the authentic back region since they are not necessarily displayed for the benefit of the diners.

But other decorations are certainly exhibited to create a Thai atmo-

2-1. Traditional appliqué wall hanging on display in a Thai restaurant. *Photo by Joe Ownbey.*

sphere for the diners. Paintings of temples and posters from the Tourist Authority of Thailand direct the tourist gaze to those sights that ought to be seen while visiting Thailand. The posters at Krua Thai Kitchen depict various scenes such as the floating market in Bangkok, silversmiths in northern Thailand, or Thai dancers in full regalia. Two large oil paintings at Thai Soon show Wat Phrakao and Wat Arun, famous temples in Bangkok. These particular sights would almost certainly be on any tourist's itinerary in Thailand.

Native artwork tends to adorn most Thai restaurants as well. Sequined appliqué wall hangings of elephants or Thai soldiers, wood carvings painted in gold, large fans painted with bucolic scenes of rice paddies and fishing villages, five-color porcelain dishes, wooden lotus flowers, and wooden statuettes of Thai women, hands pressed together in a welcoming *wai* pose, all serve to create an atmosphere of Thai-ness. The fact that all of these typically Thai items can be bought in the souvenir shops in Bangkok contributes to the feeling that the restaurant is a stage for Thai-ness.[3] A tape of traditional Thai classical or folk music usually plays in the background, enhancing these visual and culinary markers of Thai culture.[4]

2-2. The counter near the entrance at Tuppee Thai restaurant displays several Thai statues, including wooden statues of Thai women in the welcoming *wai* pose. *Photo by Joe Ownbey.*

This music, and all of the props typically found decorating a Thai restaurant, set the stage upon which Thai-ness, in the form of a dining experience, is performed for the culinary tourist. In spite of these efforts to present traditional food in a genuine setting, Thai restaurants conjure a contested version of an authentic experience for their diners. Because the Thai restaurant is constrained by social and economic factors, such as obtaining traditional ingredients or catering to customers' palates, its attempt at presenting an authentic culinary and cultural picture of Thai-ness is merely staged authenticity. Rather than displaying true Thai culture, the Thai restaurant plays out the American perceptions of Thai culture. But even in light of the constraints placed on Thai restaurants' efforts toward creating a space of genuine Thai-ness, is a staged experience, by definition, inauthentic?

Although MacCannell's notion of staged authenticity is useful in examining the way Thai restaurants represent otherness, his theory has limited application to understanding authenticity in a culinary tourism context. To begin with, several scholars have questioned MacCannell's assertion that all tourists are on a quest for authenticity. Erik Cohen (1979), among others (Pearce 1985; Feifer 1985; Smith 1989; Urry 1990), says that there are several motivations for travel, just as there are many types of tourists. Later I will discuss these tourist typologies, along with the suggestion that some tourists travel specifically to engage in *in*authentic experiences.

Second, MacCannell bases his notion of staged authenticity on Goffman's framework of front and back regions even though Goffman does not necessarily equate back regions with authenticity.[5] To Goffman, the back region and the front region are two sides of the same coin of self-presentation. By assigning the term staged authenticity to representations constructed for tourist consumption, MacCannell paints all host/guest interactions with the brush of inauthenticity, when in fact there may be aspects of this interaction that *are* authentic. Gianna Moscardo and Philip Pearce argue, "tourists can achieve an authentic experience or insight into the lives of others through relationships with people within tourist settings" (1986:470). Representations of authenticity are informed by tourists' expectations, which are, of course, culturally defined.[6] Therefore, the interface between the tourist and the host culture reflects a wider cultural code that, even as an example of staged authenticity, is a valuable source of insight into the cultural mindset.

Finally, MacCannell dismisses what may be authentic about these interactions because he perceives authenticity as an objective quality that exists in a fixed place or time. Like his questing tourist, MacCannell can never find authenticity, because he is looking for it in the wrong place. He is looking for authenticity only in the secret back regions of the foreign other, when in fact authenticity also, and primarily, exists in the modern mindset of the Western tourist. MacCannell defines modernization as the loss of authenticity, but it is principally in modern Western culture that the notion of authenticity exists at all. MacCannell places the burden of authentic representation on the travel industry or on the other, but not on the tourists themselves. For the purposes of understanding culinary tourism, a more fruitful way of considering authenticity is as a mutually negotiated concept where the diners' perceptions are as responsible for the construction of authenticity as is the representation produced by the Thai restaurant.

Negotiating Authenticity in Thai Restaurants

In contrast to MacCannell's claim that authenticity is an objective quality, many scholars suggest that authenticity is negotiable, emergent, and socially constructed. Tourists bring their own symbolic systems and cultural experiences to bear on this negotiation of authenticity. As Cohen explains, "the question here is *not* whether the individual does or does not 'really' have an authentic experience in MacCannell's sense, but rather what endows his experience with authenticity in his *own* view" (1988:377–78). In other words, authenticity is created as much through the tourist's own perceptions as it is by the host's performance of otherness.

Therefore, in addition to looking at how Thai restaurants construct authenticity through the menu, ingredients, and décor, it is necessary to consider how diners determine authenticity in such an environment. As demonstrated above, Thai restaurants bend their own representation of authenticity to meet the expectations of their diners and remain commercially viable. In this sense, the restaurant owners and designers are constructing a new definition of authenticity, one that is based on an American perception of Thai culture rather than on a purely Thai point of view. At the same time, the diners themselves also construct a definition of authenticity, albeit a definition that continues to be constrained by Western stereotypes of Thai-ness and otherness, as well as by personal taste preferences. By looking at these constraints we can understand the cultural code with which diners are "reading" or understanding the authenticity of their culinary experience. What this code reveals is not necessarily a depiction of Thai culture and cuisine, but rather a Western picture of what Thai-ness is or should be.

Culinary tourists in Thai restaurants are like the respondents in Shun Lu and Gary Fine's study of Chinese restaurants who "define authenticity in association with their own social experience" (1995:543). They construct a set of criteria by which they judge authenticity. This set of criteria is based primarily on comparisons to their social experiences of Thailand or Thai culture, including media images of Thailand, their own travel experiences, and experiences in other Thai restaurants or other Asian restaurants. In addition to setting the criteria for determining authenticity, these diners also decide when to apply this measuring stick, and they judge their own level of expertise in deciding whether or not their experience is authentic.[7]

Respondents who have traveled to Thailand before use their travel experiences to set criteria for authenticity. One respondent considers the food at the Thai restaurant she eats at in the United States authentic "because it seems most like the food I ate in Thailand." Another decides that a restaurant's menu is authentic if it includes dishes she ate while traveling in Thailand, such as green mango salad, and she describes what she expects an authentic Thai restaurant to look like: "Thai umbrellas hanging everywhere, wooden Thai carvings on the wall and in restrooms, celadon dishes, perhaps, plus a picture of the king hanging on the wall. Because that would be . . . the way you would see it in Thailand, or the items described would lend themselves to a Thai environment, as one would find these kinds of things in Thailand."

Even respondents who have never been to Thailand, though, have some sort of expectation of what authentic Thai food and décor should be. Of the décor, they expect bamboo and greenery, red and gold decorations, gold and wood statues, and Asian-influenced or Buddhist art. Several respondents acknowledge that they judge a Thai restaurant's authenticity, in part, based on media images they have seen of Thailand. Their expectations of gold décor, wooden statues, and colorful textiles come from images they have seen in movies.

Regarding the food, the main criterion for authenticity is the degree of spiciness. In addition, diners look for typical Thai ingredients, such as coconut milk, lemon grass, and basil. Most of the diners who had not been to Thailand still had opinions about what constituted authentic Thai food and a genuine Thai atmosphere. Frequently, these criteria are based on comparisons to other Thai restaurants. For example, to one respondent, Star of Siam is more authentic than Thai Soon because Star of Siam puts bowls of chili sauce, shrimp paste, and sugar on the table. She bases her judgment not on experiences in Thailand, but rather on an experience in another Thai restaurant. To a certain extent, Thai restaurants are formulaic, both responding to and creating their diners' expectations of authenticity. The formula, then, becomes another point of comparison in judging authenticity.

Another criterion that most respondents use to determine the authenticity of a restaurant is the perceived ethnicity of the staff and other diners in the restaurants. Roger Abrahams notes that American diners "look for public places where the cuisine is served with such authenticity that the 'ethnics' themselves eat there" (1984:23). The respondents in this study seemed embarrassed to admit that they look to the ethnicity of the chef, the servers, the other diners, and even the delivery person who brings their take-out orders, to determine if the restaurant is authentically Thai. Some even admit that it doesn't matter if the staff and other diners are Thai, as long as they appear to be Asian. Thus, this particular criterion is important, but not strictly applied.

In addition to establishing the criteria by which they judge a restaurant's authenticity, these diners also ascertain their own or others' authority for making this determination. Some respondents were open to giving their opinions, whether or not they had been to Thailand. As one respondent qualified her response: "In the perspective of someone who has never visited Thailand, Krung Thai is the most authentic [restaurant] because most of their entrées are spicy (even if you ask for mild)." But several others acknowledge that they are not qualified to judge the authenticity of Thai restaurants, because they have never been to Thailand. One respondent explained, for example, that he is "a little scared of Thai food, so I'm not a good judge of authenticity." Another refused to answer any questions regarding authenticity, because "I am not Thai and I have never been to Thailand." And one respondent admitted that even though he has "a sneaking suspicion that all [of the Thai restaurants] pacify their dishes to cater to the delicate American palate which can't tolerate the spice that a Thai can," he cannot prove his suspicion, because "I haven't been to Thailand; I also haven't been told by anyone who knows whether the places I eat at are authentic or not."

In addition to establishing the various criteria for judging authenticity, these respondents also determine that the authority to measure authenticity lies in one's ethnicity (being Thai) or must be learned or acquired through travel. Not all of the respondents felt comfortable assessing authenticity, but every one of them felt qualified to make judgments regarding taste. Respondents were asked to rate the importance of authenticity against the importance of palatability in their decision to patronize a Thai restaurant. While all of the respondents claimed that they want to have an authentic experience at a Thai restaurant, they overwhelmingly admitted that they would not go to an "authentic" restaurant if the food did not taste good to them. So, regardless of the criteria they establish to judge the authenticity of the restaurant and the food, diners do not consider authenticity as the only—or even the most important—factor in deciding where to eat. All of the respondents claimed to want an exotic, authentic experience, but not at the expense of palatability and familiarity.

Thus, in constructing their notion of authenticity, these diners express and validate their individual and social identities. The concept of authenticity is a useful theoretical tool for exploring the discourse concerning identity construction and validation as it occurs in culinary tourism. The way the culinary tourist defines and uses the notion of authenticity to negotiate his or her experience of the other is clearly more indicative of the diner's identity and mindset than it is of the other. Although the Thai restaurant purports to express authentic Thai-ness, these restaurants serve as the backdrop of otherness and difference against which the culinary tourist's Western identity is defined. The negotiation of authenticity brings to light the processes of identity making that occur in arenas of culinary tourism.

Culinary Tourism as Identity Work

Foodways and tourism converge within the wider social discourse concerning identity making. Both include processes of identity construction that occur along a perceived cultural divide between that which is familiar and that which is different, between the edible and the exotic, the self and the other. Culinary tourists contest and explore this dividing line by using food as a means of interacting with and experiencing the other while expressing and validating their own social identities.

As many food scholars point out, food is a means of expressing and reinforcing identity (Douglas 1971, 1982; Brown and Mussell 1984; Abrahams 1984). Individual preferences and tastes are a clear indication of a person's identity, as the cliché phrases "You are what you eat" and "One man's meat is another man's poison" imply. Food and identity are intimately connected, not only at the individual level, but in terms of group identity as well. According to Mary Douglas, food is a form of social communication that speaks of a group's identity through "different degrees of hierarchy, inclusion and exclusion, boundaries and transactions across boundaries" (1971:61).[8] Food systems "bind individuals together, define the limits of the group's outreach and identity, [and] distinguish ingroup from out-group" (Brown and Mussell 1984:5). By participating in certain food behaviors, therefore, individuals can clearly express their particular group affiliations. The in-group/out-group or familiar/exotic identifications expressed through food behaviors imply more than just culinary preferences. They indicate wider cultural differences between groups. As Allison James explains: "[T]he very concept of 'foreign' food . . . derives from the marking out of difference: 'foreign' food is food from abroad consumed at home, food of the 'other,' strange and unfamiliar. Shared patterns of consumption thus mark our difference from others and mapping, as they often do, on to other signs of difference—from the organization of domestic space through to the division of labor and concepts of sexual intimacy—food consumption practices provide confirmation of wider differences between cultural orders" (1996:78–79).

Culinary difference can also express cultural difference. If the cultural identity of the other can be expressed via food, then it is through food that the culinary tourist can interact with the other. Unlike the foreign language or other cultural processes or rituals, food is accessible to outsiders and therefore makes cultural difference accessible to tourists. Culinary tourism is predicated on this notion that foodways can be a stage upon which a group's identity is performed.

Many studies of tourism are similarly focused on the issues of identity expression (Lanfant, Allcock, and Bruner 1995; Rojek 1993, 1997). In his study of tourists at the Taj Mahal, Tim Edensor (1998) approaches his topic from Mark Neumann's (1988) view that: "Tourism is a metaphor for our struggle to make sense of our self and world within a highly differentiated culture . . . it directs us to sites where people are at work making meaning, situating themselves in relation to public spectacle and making a biography that provides some coherency between self and world" (cited in Edensor, 22). It is worth noting that the meaning making that occurs in a tourist site has more to do with the self than the other. The tourist's project is to understand and locate the self, and this project often takes place in relation to the other.

The idea that an interaction with the other reveals more about the self is a common theme in tourism studies. Daniel Boorstin quips, as tourists "we look into a mirror instead of out a window and we see only ourselves" (1961:117). Any touristic interaction is filtered by the tourist's own cultural mindset. Not only can the notion of exotic be defined only against what the tourist understands as everyday, but any experience of the other is necessarily viewed through the tourist's own historically and culturally located lens. Sometimes an encounter with the other is needed to bring the tourist's own cultural identity into better focus. This is what occurs in Thai restaurants, where diners, while experiencing a taste of Thai culture, are really validating their own individual identity and affiliating themselves with a particularly American identity.

In instances of culinary tourism, then, food is doubly expressive. By participating in a food system, the culinary tourist is expressing and reinforcing his or her own identity while exploring the identity of the other that is represented by that food system. Consider MacClancy's description of eating in ethnic restaurants: "Just like those cannibals who gobbled up others to strengthen their own identity as a group, Westerners who today dine on ethnic or regional meals are indirectly reminding themselves of what is their own 'national cuisine.' By eating the Other, they redefine the Self" (1992:204). As Lucy Long suggests, while culinary tourism is "the intentional, exploratory participation in the foodways of an Other" (1998:181), it often results in "teach[ing] us more about ourselves than about the Other" (1998:185).

This identity expression is negotiated through the concept of authenticity, and, as I will discuss later, through the concept of inauthenticity. Though Thai restaurants attempt to create a sense of authenticity, the result is generally a formulaic representation that mirrors American expectations of Thai-ness rather than reflecting the reality of Thai culture. At the same time, American diners in Thai restaurants use the concept of authenticity to contextualize their experience of the exotic other within their own field of apprehension. In the end, this interface reveals more about the Western mindset and culture in which the Thai restaurant operates than it reveals about the other that the restaurant purports to represent.

Authenticity and Identity

Authenticity has been both an implicit and explicit inspiration for classifying tourists and tourist behaviors. Valene Smith's (1989) typology classifies tourists and tourism into five categories: ethnic tourism, cultural tourism, historical tourism, environmental tourism, and recreational tourism. Though Smith does not overtly identify her tourist types with the concept of authenticity, an implicit connection exists. Whereas recreational tourism focuses on rest and relaxation, ethnic, cultural, and environmental tourism—and to an extent, historical tourism—are motivated by a desire to "get off the beaten path" of mass tourism, to engage personally with the other, and to glimpse vanishing cultural practices. This latter motivation resonates with MacCannell's theory of tourist motivation. Even if they are not explicitly on a quest for authentic experience of the other, these tourists are certainly motivated by a desire to get closer to the other than mass tourism structures allow.

On the other hand, Erik Cohen (1979, 1988) does overtly use the concept of authenticity to create a typology of tourists and touristic experiences that provides a useful framework for understanding how authenticity facilitates identity construction and validation in Thai restaurants. Cohen bases his typology on the tourist's use of the concept of authenticity in negotiating their experience of the other. Those tourists who are motivated by a desire to have a deeply meaningful encounter with the other will require a more authentic experience than those tourists who are motivated by fun and recreation. Thus Cohen establishes a scale of touristic experience with existential tourists at one end and diversionary tourists at the other. The existential tourist is intensely interested in the authenticity of his or her experience and maintains a very rigid and objective set of criteria for judging that authenticity. A little further down the scale is the experimental tourist, who continues to hold in mind strict criteria for authenticity. Even further down the scale is the experiential tourist, whose criteria for authenticity is not as strict as the first two, but who nevertheless seeks "to participate vicariously in the authentic life of others" (1988:377). Holding even looser criteria for authenticity is the recreational tourist, who is more interested in having fun than in having an authentic experience. Finally, the diversionary tourists do not consider authenticity an important quality and "remain totally . . . unconcerned with the problem of authenticity of their experiences."

Culinary tourists can also be classified within this typology depending on how they engage with the concept of authenticity in their ethnic eating experiences. I propose that the level of importance tourists attach to authenticity is indicative not only of the depth of experience they desire, but also of the identity characteristics they are likely to express or try to validate in their interactions with a culinary other. The existential, experimental, and experiential tourists, who prioritize authenticity in their touristic experiences, will tend to associate their culinary explorations as signs of their own sophistication and competence. Forays into foreign foodways are opportunities for these tourists to display their access of the other by their ability to go native even when this directly challenges their definition of edibility. These are tourists who will insist on eating with chopsticks to demonstrate their competence of the other's food behaviors. They will ask for their fried rice *kai dao*. I observed a woman in one Thai restaurant encouraging her dinner companions to order black rice pudding, a Thai dessert, because it would give them a taste of an authentic Thai dish. When the dessert arrived, the others at the table were put off by the appearance of the gelatinous pudding. She displayed a sense of competence by knowing what to order, as she had presumably had this dish before. So the sense of daring with which she took the first bite of the black rice pudding was more an assertion of competence than adventurousness. By authorizing herself as the arbiter of authenticity, this woman expressed her own competence and sophistication in this encounter. These culinary adventurers are similar to ego-tourists. Like tourists who travel to remote, unspoiled areas, these types of culinary tourists pride themselves on insisting on authentic experiences.

Recreational tourists, in contrast, temper their insistence on authenticity by prioritizing their own enjoyment of the experience. As one respondent in this study says: "I enjoy educating myself on the cuisine of other cultures because I love food in general and want to try it all, but I won't eat somewhere where I don't like the food just to be able to men-

2-3. On Lower Greeville Avenue in Dallas, Thai Soon is surrounded by other ethnic restaurants, including Teppo, a Japanese restaurant, next door. *Photo by Joe Ownbey.*

tion it at a cocktail party to appear 'cultured.'" The recreational tourist engages with authenticity differently than the existential, experimental, or experiential tourist, and therefore expresses and validates different identity characteristics. Among these characteristics are a sense of playfulness, flexibility, and democratic tolerance. According to Cohen, recreational tourists "seek in the Other mainly enjoyable restoration and recuperation, and hence tend to approach the cultural products encountered on their trip with a playful attitude of make-believe, [and therefore] will entertain much broader criteria of authenticity" (1988:377). Tourists at the existential end of the typology scale are exclusive, while recreational tourists are inclusive. Recreational tourists are democratic in their culinary exploration and fit Abrahams's description of American diners: "[W]e seem to want to be able to say of ourselves as eaters that we will try anything once. We become equal-opportunity eaters, especially in situations where we can sample unaccustomed foods" (1984:23). For American diners in ethnic restaurants, exploring cultural and culinary diversity is a reflection of democratic openness. They also reflect the shifting culinary identity of American cuisine.

The American cuisine contains cultural difference by embracing the proliferation of ethnic restaurants and culinary styles. Eating in Thai restaurants is only a small part of the overall ethnic eating experience of most Americans. A survey of the locations of the Thai restaurants in this study reveals that these restaurants are part of a smorgasbord of ethnic and regional restaurants. In Dallas, for example, Thai restaurants are found literally next door to Italian, Mexican, Cajun, Middle Eastern, and Japanese restaurants.

This variety of ethnic food may be the best way to define the American identity and cuisine at all. Sidney Mintz recounts the reaction he received from a class of students when he casually mentioned that America did not have a cuisine. After several students responded that America *did* have a cuisine, "another student took a different tack. He talked happily about 'eating Thai' one night, and 'eating Chinese' the next, and asked rather plaintively whether *that* couldn't be 'our cuisine.' He plainly felt that having access to a lot of different 'cuisines' was a wonderful idea—and certainly better than meat loaf" (1996:107). To Mintz, the American identity is expressed by our tendency "to try new foods, seeking novelty in eating, as we do in so many aspects of life" (1996:116). This sense of novelty and playfulness directs us to another way of considering authenticity and identity in culinary tourism.

The Culinary "Post-Tourist"

Cohen's recreational tourist is synonymous with what other scholars refer to as the "post-tourist" (Feifer 1985; Urry 1990). Cohen's recreational tourist is "prepared playfully to accept a cultural product as authentic, for the sake of the experience, even though 'deep down' they are not convinced of its authenticity" (1988:377). Unlike MacCannell's tourist, who is motivated by a quest for authenticity, post-tourists "delight in the *inauthenticity* of the normal tourist experience" (Urry 1990:11)(emphasis mine). Post-tourists are primarily characterized, as Cohen and Urry describe, by their playfulness and disregard for authenticity. Urry describes the "post-tourist," a term introduced by Feifer, as someone who "delights in the multitude of choice, . . . [who] knows that they are a tourist and that tourism is a game, or rather a whole series of games with multiple texts and no single, authentic tourist experience" (1985:100). The term, deriving from Feifer's self-proclaimed "postmodernist" excursions through Paris, connotes a contemporary tourist who negotiates the visually and sensually prolific culture of postmodernity with savvy. For the post-tourist, the novelty and variety of experience is paramount to concerns over authenticity. In fact, the post-tourist enjoys experiences often *because* they are inauthentic.

This tourist revels in the culinary and cultural pastiche that marks contemporary America. In his own exposition on postmodern culture, David Harvey describes the compression of the world's cuisines into the supermarket: "Kenyan haricot beans, Californian celery and avocados, North African potatoes, Canadian apples, and Chilean grapes all sit side by side"; and into the restaurant culture: "Chinese take-aways, Italian pizza parlours (run by a U.S. chain), Middle Eastern felafel stalls, Japanese sushi bars . . . the list is now endless in the Western world" (1990:300). Harvey criticizes this concentration of culinary styles as evidence that the modern Western individual engages only in vicarious, inauthentic experiences of simulacre. Taking a different view, MacClancy claims, "some people thrive on this cultural jumbling" (1992:208). He recounts an advertisement from a restaurant in suburban Cincinnati that read: "'The Italian restaurant with the Spanish name hosted by the Jewish couple with the Greek partner featuring American steaks, French onion soup, Ecuadorian ceviche and Swiss fondue.' Dare you ask for couscous?"(1992:208). Harvey, like MacCannell, seems to mourn the disappearance of authenticity in the culinary realm, but others, like MacClancy and the post-tourist, find inauthenticity a small price to pay for culinary variety and the spice it adds to everyday life.

Take, for example, the respondents quoted earlier. All of the respondents had eaten at Thai restaurants, but within a context of many other types of restaurants. They said that, besides Thai, they eat out at Chinese, Japanese, Indian, Malaysian, Vietnamese, Korean, Middle Eastern, French, Italian, Mexican, Spanish, Mediterranean, German, Cuban, and Caribbean restaurants. Their ethnic dining experiences are defined by variety rather than by authentic difference. As they admitted, authenticity is important but not paramount in their experience at an ethnic restaurant. To them, enjoyment of the experience is more important than the authenticity of the experience. According to one respondent who loves Thai peanut sauce: "If 'authentic' peanut sauce had shells in it—plah! [*sic*] I would not order it. If someone told me that the sauce I love was really a Mexican recipe, [I] wouldn't care. Olé, I'd say!" By qualifying authenticity this way, the culinary post-tourist self-consciously plays with the symbols that encode the ethnic restaurant. The post-tourist is aware of the social and commercial constraints to authenticity and decides to overlook them. In this way, the post-tourist copes with the proliferation of culinary signs and styles that would overwhelm the seeker of authenticity. The post-tourist's more liberal engagement with authenticity allows for the culinary boundaries to be constantly redrawn and expanded, accommodating new culinary behaviors.

Conclusion

This paper has attempted to outline some of the ways in which the concept of authenticity can be used in exploring the social dynamics that occur in instances of culinary authenticity. Authenticity, considered in the context of the touristic interaction, is one means of understanding the processes of identity construction and validation that take place in arenas of culinary tourism. As a tool for classifying tourist motivation and interaction with the other, authenticity reveals various identity characteristics that culinary tourists express and validate while eating out. The typologies outlined by Cohen (1979) and Smith (1989) are initially quite valuable in providing a theoretical approach to classifying culinary tourists and identifying general behaviors and motivations shared by tourists and culinary tourists. But as Edensor admonishes, "there is a danger that such categorisations become reified as immutable. . . . While there are certain regularities, dominant tourist conventions are open to challenge and are contingent upon historical and geographical contexts" (1998:61). Indeed, typographies established to classify culinary tourists are only as useful as they are flexible and accommodating to cultural exigencies and, as Edensor points out, historical and geographical contexts.

This study focuses on the Thai restaurant, but the concept of authenticity can be applied to other locales of culinary tourism, such as cookbooks, food festivals, or cooking classes. Folklorists and ethnographers must be careful, though, to understand that the concept of authenticity is an invention of Western modernity. As such, the concept is limited in what it can reveal about touristic interactions. Other theoretical approaches must be used in conjunction with authenticity to illustrate and examine the social dynamics that occur at all sites of culinary tourism. For example, authenticity is a valuable tool for investigating the tourist's identity construction, but perhaps other approaches will be more fruitful in examining culinary tourism from the host's point of view. Other typologies of tourist motivation and behavior may also be valuable constructs for assessing culinary tourists. The concept of authenticity may be slippery and problematic, but it continues to have currency in teasing out the complex interactions that take place between the self and the other in instances of culinary tourism.

Notes

1. This information is derived from participant observation at ten Thai restaurants. I visited each restaurant at least once to eat, observe, take notes and photographs, and to talk informally with the waitstaff and/or owners. Most of these restaurants are located in the Dallas metropolitan area, with one located in Minneapolis. While Minneapolis has recently become a magnet for Asian immigrants, Texas already has the fourth largest Asian/Pacific Islander populations in the United States after California, New York, and Hawaii. According to U.S. Census Bureau estimates for 1999, the Dallas metropolitan population is around 4.9 million, with an Asian/Pacific Islander population of roughly 562,000. Dallas continues to attract Asian immigrants and has increased its Asian population by over half during the 1990s. Unfortunately, statistics specific to the Thai population are not available from the U.S. Census Bureau or from the Asian American Chamber of Commerce in Dallas.

Thai restaurants tend to be spread throughout the Dallas metropolitan area rather than concentrated in one specific area or neighborhood. Some of the restaurants I observed were near downtown (in the Lower Greenville restaurant area), while others were located in suburban areas such as Plano and Richardson. They were all mid- to upper-range restaurants catering mostly for dinner but also offering a sit-down or buffet lunch. Many of these restaurants also offer take-out or delivery service.

2. Another interesting example of establishing authenticity in the menu comes from a Thai restaurant in England where the menu invited diners to: "Please relax and savor the flavor of the East. Why not try a Thai beer to help you experience a true taste of Thailand. We cook from fresh ingredients. So be patient. Some of the fish is still in the sea in Thailand and it's a long way to go on a busy night."

3. For further discussion regarding souvenirs and tourist art, see Graburn (1976) and Evans-Pritchard (1987).

4. Classical Thai music is distinctive in its flowing rhythms. It is meant to resemble the sounds of a stream. For a description of traditional classical and folk music, refer to <http://www.seasite.niu.edu/Thai/music/classical/default.htm>, which also includes audio clips.

5. James Chriss (1999) provides a useful discussion on how Goffman's theories have been interpreted to support notions of authenticity and inauthenticity.

6. For examples of how culturally constructed stereotypes and expectations affect the authenticity of touristic products, see Deirdre Evans-Pritchard's (1987) discussion of how tourists' stereotypical definitions of Native American authenticity influence the art that Indians sell in Santa Fe and Stanton's (1989) study of Polynesian tourism.

7. I interviewed twelve people for this part of the paper. Respondents range in age from twenty-three to forty-seven and live in different areas of the United States, including Dallas, Philadelphia, San Francisco, Minneapolis, and New York. They are all employed or are students and could be classified as middle to upper-middle class. Three of the respondents are Asian-American. Five of the respondents had traveled to Thailand before. An additional four respondents had traveled to Asia, though not to Thailand. Respondents eat out an average of 2.8 times per week and eat at Thai restaurants once or twice a month on average. In general, I would characterize the respondents as experienced and frequent customers of ethnic restaurants. Interviews were conducted in person and through e-mail with telephone and e-mail follow-up. Many thanks go to those who participated.

8. For further discussion, see the chapter "Food as a System of Communication," in Mary Douglas's *In the Active Voice* (1982).

Works Cited

Abrahams, Roger. 1984. "Equal-Opportunity Eating: A Structural Excursus on Things of the Mouth." In *Ethnic and Regional Foodways in the United States.* Eds. Linda K. Brown and Kay Mussell. Knoxville: University of Tennessee Press.

Appadurai, Arjun. 1986. "On Culinary Authenticity." *Anthropology Today* 2: 25.

Bendix, Regina. 1992. "Diverging Paths in the Scientific Search for Authenticity." *Journal of Folklore Research* 29(2): 103–32.

Boorstin, Daniel J. 1961. *The Image, or, What Happened to the American Dream.* London: Weidenfeld and Nicolson.

Brown, Linda K., and Kay Mussell, eds. 1984. *Ethnic and Regional Foodways in the United States.* Knoxville: University of Tennessee Press.

Chriss, James J. 1999. "Role Distance and the Negational Self." In *Goffman and Social Organization: Studies in a Sociological Legacy.* Ed. Greg Smith. London: Routledge.

Cohen, Erik. 1979. "A Phenomenology of Tourist Experiences." *Sociology* 13: 179–201.

———. 1988. "Authenticity and Commoditization in Tourism." *Annals of Tourism Research* 15: 371–86.

Douglas, Mary. 1971. "Deciphering a Meal." In *Myth, Symbol, and Culture.* Ed. Clifford Geertz. New York: Norton.

———. 1982. *In the Active Voice.* London: Routledge & Kegan Paul.

Edensor, Tim. 1998. *Tourists at the Taj: Performance and Meaning at a Symbolic Site.* London: Routledge.

Evans-Pritchard, Deirdre. 1987. "The Portal Case: Authenticity, Tourism, Traditions, and the Law." *Journal of American Folklore* 100(397): 287–96.

Feifer, Maxine. 1985. *Going Places.* London: Macmillan.

Goffman, Erving. 1959. *The Presentation of Self in Everyday Life.* Garden City, N.Y.: Doubleday.

Graburn, Nelson H.H., ed. 1976. *Ethnic and Tourist Arts: Cultural Expressions from the Fourth World.* Berkeley: University of California Press.

Harvey, David. 1990[1989?]. *The Condition of Postmodernity: An Enquiry into the Origins of Cultural Change.* Cambridge, Mass.: Blackwell.

James, Allison. 1996. "Cooking the Books: Global or Local Identities in Contemporary British Food Cultures?" In *Cross-cultural Consumption: Global Markets, Local Realities.* Ed. David Howes. London: Routledge.

Lanfant, Marie-Françoise, J.B. Allcock, and Edward M. Bruner, eds. 1995. *International Tourism: Identity and Change.* London: Sage.

Long, Lucy M. 1998. "Culinary Tourism: A Folkloristic Perspective on Eating and Otherness." *Southern Folklore* 55(3): 181–204.

Lu, Shun, and Gary A. Fine. 1995. "The Presentation of Ethnic Authenticity: Chinese Food as Social Accomplishment." *The Sociological Quarterly* 36(3): 535–53.

MacCannell, Dean. 1973 [1976?]. *The Tourist: A New Theory of the Leisure Class.* Berkeley: University of California Press.

MacClancy, Jeremy. 1992 [1993?]. *Consuming Culture: Why You Eat What You Eat.* New York: Henry Holt.

Mintz, Sidney W. 1996. *Tasting Food, Tasting Freedom: Excursions into Eating, Culture, and the Past.* Boston: Beacon Press.

Moscardo, Gianna M., and Philip L. Pearce. 1986. "Historic Theme Parks: An Australian Experience in Authenticity." *Annals of Tourism Research* 13: 467–79.

Neumann, Mark. 1988. "Wandering through the Museum: Experience and Identity in a Spectator Culture." *Border/Lines* (summer): 19–27. Quoted in Tim Edensor, *Tourists at the Taj: Performance and Meaning at a Symbolic Site* (London: Routledge, 1998), 6.

Pearce, Philip L. 1985. "A Systematic Comparison of Travel-Related Roles." *Human Relations* 38(11): 1001–11.

Rojek, Chris. 1993. *Ways of Escape: Modern Transformations in Leisure and Travel.* London: Macmillan.

———. 1997. "Indexing, Dragging, and the Social Construction of Tourist Sites." In *Touring Cultures: Transformations of Travel and Theory.* Eds. Chris Rojek and John Urry. London: Routledge.

Shelton, Allen. 1990. "A Theater for Eating, Looking, and Thinking: The Restaurant as Symbolic Space." *Sociological Spectrum* 10: 507–26.

Smith, Valene L., ed. 1989. *Hosts and Guests: The Anthropology of Tourism, 2nd ed.* Philadelphia: University of Pennsylvania Press.

Stanton, Max E. 1989. "The Polynesian Cultural Center: A Multi-ethnic Model of Seven Pacific Cultures." In *Hosts and Guests, 2nd ed.* Ed. Valene L. Smith. Philadelphia: University of Pennsylvania Press.

Urry, John. 1990. *The Tourist Gaze: Leisure and Travel in Contemporary Societies.* London: Sage.

CHAPTER 3

From "Montezuma's Revenge" to "Mexican Truffles"

Culinary Tourism across the Rio Grande

Jeffrey M. Pilcher

President Jimmy Carter arrived in Mexico City for a state visit on February 14, 1979, and proceeded to recall for his hosts a previous encounter with Mexican culture, decades earlier as a naval officer, in which he had contracted what he described as "Montezuma's revenge." This indelicate reference to tourist's diarrhea became something of an international incident; Mexican President José López Portillo insisted that his country be treated with respect, while the local press denounced the remark as a "typical Yankee slur."[1] Culinary tourism thus transcended a private experience to become an important facet of inter-American relations. By inspiring such visceral reactions, encounters with exotic foods have long helped to construct national identities. Justifiably proud of their sophisticated regional cuisines, Mexicans resented being stereotyped as underdeveloped by the people who had created such gastronomic marvels as the microwave oven and the drive-through window. For their part, many in the United States considered wholesome, industrial processed foods to be one of the great advances of capitalism and civilization. Nevertheless, such views were far from homogeneous in either country. Visitors from the United States have often embraced the exoticism of supposedly primitive Mexico as a release from an overly materialist society. The practice of culinary tourism has meanwhile helped to construct social identities within Mexico, as Hispanic elites went in search of previously disdained indigenous foods. This essay examines the historical evolution and contemporary expression of these encounters, with particular emphasis on the Native American subjects of the tourists' gaze. Native efforts to mediate the contradictory demands of culinary tourism have been a vital part of their survival strategies, as individuals and communities, when confronted with the present-day globalization of commodities and identities.

Any discussion of tourism, whether culinary or otherwise, must always consider the multiple perspectives on the site of tourism. That Mexican self-images and views north across the Rio Grande have influenced the attitudes and stereotypes held by U.S. tourists becomes clear in the history of the so-called "Mexican truffle." Unlike the prized European mushroom, which grows unobtrusively in forests, the Native American fungus (*Ustilago maydis*) infects ears of corn, making it the bane of midwestern farmers, who burn whole fields to prevent the spore from spreading. By contrast, the pre-Hispanic inhabitants of Mexico, having no domesticated animals except for turkeys and small dogs, valued it as a source of protein, along with a variety of insects, small animals, and lake algae. As corn worshippers, they referred to the black fungus with the Nahuatl word *cuitlacoche*, meaning roughly "excrement of the gods." The Spanish conquistadors found the indigenous appetite for spores and *animalitos* to be proof of the superiority of European civilization. Affluent Mexicans still considered eating *cuitlacoche* to be a disgusting Indian habit until the 1940s, when gourmet Jaime Saldívar first devised an acceptable way of presenting the fungus in crêpes with béchamel sauce. French haute cuisine thus cleansed it of the lower-class stigma, and by the 1990s it became all the rage as part of the *nueva cocina mexicana*. European-trained chefs in Mexico City created endless variations of *cuitlacoche* mousse, and farmers in the United States purposely injected their corn with spores to supply upscale Mexican restaurants in New York, Chicago, and Los Angeles. A Mexican elite eager to claim a distinctive place on the buffet table of international cuisine had rehabilitated the formerly disdained smut as a New World truffle. U.S. tourists who overcame their fear of "Montezuma's revenge" to savor the "excrement of the gods" thus followed a path already marked by their Mexican counterparts.[2]

The social controversy surrounding corn smut can be clarified analytically using Lucy Long's distinction between the cognitive category of edibility and aesthetic quality of palatability.[3] For lower-class Mexicans, including mixed-race mestizos, who were often erroneously assumed to be Native Americans, *cuitlacoche* was a palatable food—delicious when used as a filling for the corn pastries known as *quesadillas*. Even before the *nueva cocina* became fashionable, the Mexican elite recognized the edibility of *cuitlacoche*—one might even buy a quesadilla from a street vendor as a form of slumming—but moral restrictions prohibited serving such an Indian food to family or guests. In the United States, by contrast, the fungus lay beyond the boundaries of edibility, so that any corn infected with it was immediately destroyed. Only contemporary culinary tourists have discovered the palatability of indigenous foods, and many adventurous gastronomes now seek out corn fungus, cactus worms, and ant eggs with the same fervor they lavish on truffles, escargots, and caviar.

The modern transgression of these boundaries of palatability and edibility by wealthy Mexican and U.S. culinary tourists alike derives largely from a quest for authenticity. Indeed, sociologist Dean MacCannell maintains that the entire tourist industry depends on the need to escape temporarily from the wired network of Western society into a more primitive form of human existence.[4] Exotic dishes such as *cuitlacoche* appeal to many U.S. tourists as a natural alternative to processed and packaged industrial foods. The Mexican elite has meanwhile embraced these lower-class foods because of their pre-Hispanic lineage, which, like the pyramids, help legitimate their claim to an ancient and sophisticated civilization. Nevertheless, John Urry has complicated this view of tourism by pointing out that pristine environments, whether untouched wilderness or primitive societies, constitute only one subject of the tourist gaze, and many vacationers prefer the crowds and commercialism of Cancún or Disneyland.[5] Moreover, as Pierre van den Berghe observed, ethnic tourism to indigenous locations contains a conscious element of commercialism. Purchasing native handicrafts provides an important part of this particular tourist experience, and yet the image of authenticity loses value when the supposedly primitive villagers are themselves talking on cellular phones.[6] And the tourists' dilemma is minor compared with the difficulties experienced by natives attempting to negotiate favorable terms for their labor in the global marketplace at the same time that they reconcile capitalism with communal traditions and identities.

The Origins of Culinary Tourism in Mexico

The diverse regional cuisines of Mexico have long offered a rich source for culinary tourism, yet its development has been impeded until the twentieth century by distinctions of race and class. Although the magnificent banquets of Montezuma astounded the conquistadors, their desire for familiar foods led them to transplant European livestock and plants in an attempt to transform the colony, literally, into a New Spain. Elite disdain for the indigenous culture persisted through the nineteenth century and prompted an enduring preference for continental cuisine over local dishes. U.S. travelers, when they began arriving in large numbers at the start of the twentieth century, were likewise wary of culinary experimentation, but for different reasons. Spicy chile peppers would have come as a shock to people accustomed to the bland northern European diets at any time, but the late-nineteenth-century rise of the food processing industry made Americans particularly suspicious of unknown foods. Eventually restaurants appeared in Mexico and the southwestern United States that alleviated this fear by offering a toned-down and reassuring version of Mexican dishes for foreign tourists.

Mexican cuisine exhibits a distinct regionalism that dates back to pre-Hispanic times and continued through the colonial period. Food vendors in the great market of Tlatelolco sold the many different *moles* (chile pepper stews) and *tamales* (corn dumplings) characteristic of the ethnic groups within the Aztec Empire. When the Spaniards arrived, they tended to settle in the central highlands around Mexico City and to the north, which had been home only to fierce nomadic peoples until the Spaniards discovered silver mines. Farther south, by contrast, the large populations of Zapotecs and Mixtecs in Oaxaca and the Maya of the Yucatán retained their village lands and indigenous culture. The most pronounced ethnic differences appeared in the staple grains, for the Spaniards preferred wheat bread, while the Native Americans retained corn tortillas. Culinary blending occurred as New World beans and chile peppers gained acceptance on European tables and while meat from Old World livestock was incorporated into indigenous dishes, thereby forming the basis for a *mestizo* (mixed) cuisine. Nevertheless, the culinary literature produced after independence in 1821 revealed the elite preference for European culture in the multiple recipes for Spanish *pucheros* (stews) and desserts as well as in the neglect for regional dishes of Native American origin. Nineteenth-century cookbook authors questioned the morals of any housewife who served such street foods as tamales, which were considered appropriate only for "the lower orders."[7]

Rather than explore the variety of foods within their own republic, wealthy residents of Mexico City generally chose to tour the cuisines of Europe. Salvador Novo has chronicled Mexico's fin-de-siècle infatuation with French cooking, exemplified in the kitchen of the renowned Parisian chef Sylvain Daumont, who opened his eponymous restaurant in 1892.[8] Less well remembered, but equally attractive at the time were restaurants established by Italian immigrants such as Signores Fulcheri and Gambrinus. The popularity of pasta and Chianti should come as no surprise, given the fashion among Mexico's elite for pilgrimages to see the Pope in Rome. Meanwhile, boisterous German beer gardens and pseudo-Chinese chop suey joints attracted more adventurous diners in Mexico City. Several Mexico City hotels offered American-style dining where visitors could taste familiar foods, but *Campbell's Guide* warned, "with few exceptions, the restaurant advertised as English or American is to be avoided."[9]

Tour guides at the turn of the century referred to "French style" foods, but they used the term advisedly, for discerning palates recognized the tendency for chefs to "Mexicanize" their dishes, transforming them completely from the Parisian originals. A writer for the *Mexican Herald* explained that Italian restaurants also "are becoming, in a way, Mexican, in their desire to obtain Mexican patronage." Moreover, the author revealed the nostalgic historical memory involved in the restaurant trade: "The history of Mexico's excellent cooking dates back to the period of the second empire" and the court of the ill-fated Austrian Archduke Maximilian (1864–67). That glorious era did not meet its final end, the journalist maintained, until 1905, when the Concordia restaurant closed, taking with it the "memories of Austrian and French officers stalking down through its mirrored rooms."[10]

Notwithstanding this nostalgia for a defunct European empire, turn-of-the-century Mexicans did begin to revive a form of internal culinary tourism. Perhaps the foremost proponent of this exploration was cookbook author Vicenta Torres, who began publishing *Cocina michoacana* in 1896 as a serialized guide to the foods of Michoacán. Sold by subscription, it included recipes submitted by readers from all over the state and eventually the country. What started as an exaltation of the *patria chica* (local fatherland) therefore became one of the first media for imagining a national cuisine in Mexico. Late-nineteenth-century railroad construction offered another way for Mexicans to experience regional cuisines by purchasing foods in train stations en route. In 1910, an Englishwoman wrote: "To my horror I saw these educated people lapping up dreadful little mixtures offered them on leaves, made with Heaven knows what ingredients."[11] Thirty years later, an American traveler concluded, "everybody in Mexico, when viewed from a train, is selling something, especially food and lottery tickets. . . . I cannot say exactly what sort of an agreement the villagers have among themselves, but it did appear as if the survival of each town depended on what could be sold to the train."[12]

Travelers from the United States often carried with them cultural baggage that impeded their exploration of culinary differences. The military defeat of Mexico in 1847 and the subsequent seizure of half its national territory confirmed to their minds the superiority of American civilization. William H. Prescott's popular *History of the Conquest of Mexico* (1843), with its lurid tales of Aztec cannibalism, led them to suspect that every dish contained, if not human flesh, then at least something unmentionable. Encounters with the so-called Chili Queens—one of the leading tourists attractions in San Antonio, Texas, since the 1880s—seemingly validated their fears of culinary (and sexual) danger from dark-skinned women serving "various savory compounds, swimming in fiery pepper, which biteth like a serpent."[13] In 1896, a German immigrant, William Gebhardt, developed a way of mass-producing chili powder, which was marketed under the Eagle brand name, and which introduced Americans to a pale industrial copy of *moles*. Even such a knowledgeable guide as Reau Campbell referred to the Mexican dishes generically as chili con carne.[14]

The industrialization of food production in the United States during the second half of the nineteenth century reinforced long-standing suspicions about unknown dishes. Americans came to expect their foods to come out of factory-sealed containers: crackers individually wrapped in plastic by Nabisco rather than the stale contents of a general store cracker barrel; meats canned under government supervision by Armour, not wrapped in paper by a blood-stained butcher. The prospect of Mexican food must have seemed terrifying indeed for people accustomed to eating cold cereal for breakfast and bland white sauce for dinner. In the 1930s, a visitor from California, Bess Adams Garner wrote: "I believe that a few precautions about food and drinking-water are reasonable and necessary in any strange country. I don't believe that it is necessary to rouse heaven and earth telling about the fact that you are taking them." As an example of tourist behavior in restaurants, Garner described two women who "asked for an order of canned salmon and to see the can the salmon came out of." The Swedish cook, a Mrs. Thimgren, "came out of the kitchen with a can of Del Monte salmon in one hand and one of Iris in the other. I wish you could have seen her face—and the faces of—*los turistas*."[15]

Of course, not all early tourists were so closed-minded. As Fredrick Pike observed, each generation has spawned its own counterculture, suspicious of Anglo-Saxon civilization and eager to embrace a seemingly more natural way of life.[16] Such Bohemians depended on the assistance of local intermediaries, for as the *Mexican Herald* food critic observed: "Of the myriad Mexican restaurants, many could be recommended, but they are useless, unless one is accompanied by some one who knows all the luscious joys of Mexican cooking, and can order those dishes for which the country is famous."[17] Travelers without such a local expert were directed to the German restaurant Bach's for their Saturday evening special of turkey *mole*. Historian Helen Delpar described the vogue among American leftist intellectuals in the 1920s for Mexican culture following the Revolution of 1910. One of these cultural pilgrims, Anita Brenner, editor of the journal *Mexican Folklore*, ran articles on Mexico's regional cuisines, including native dishes. She later collected this material for her popular travel guide, which offered such suggestions as: "*Gusanos de maguey*, literally maguey worms, don't shudder, look like nothing you ever saw before. A highland delicacy."[18]

Nevertheless, for the majority of American tourists, Mexican food meant Sanborns. Housed in the historic Casa de Azulejos (House of Tiles), former residence of the elite Jockey Club, this restaurant and soda fountain was opened to the public in 1910 by pharmacists Walter and Frank Sanborn. The building soon acquired another layer of tourist interest, when, in 1915, Agustín Casasola photographed an incongruous pair of rustic revolutionaries, followers of Emilian Zapata, wearing cartridge belts and broad sombreros, drinking coffee in the ornate interior. By the 1940s, *Terry's Guide to Mexico* recommended it as "the premier restaurante in the Mexican Republic," emphasizing that "one can drink the certified pure water with safety," while "the milk is from certified Jersey cows kept on the Sanborn Farm under scrupulously clean conditions."[19] The chefs at Sanborns, such as the formidable Mrs. Thimgren of the canned salmon fame, greeted American travelers with familiar hotcakes and ice cream sodas in addition to a nonthreatening selection of Mexican cuisine, including their signature dish, *enchiladas suizas* (Swiss enchiladas) topped with cream and cheese.

Counterparts to Sanborns also began arising in the United States in an attempt to gain a mainstream clientele for Mexican cuisine. In 1930, for example, the Café La Golondrina opened in Los Angeles as the centerpiece for a Hispanic Old Town, which was renovated at the initiative of an Anglo woman, Christine Sterling. This tourist location, and similar ones throughout the Southwest, appeared at the same time that San Antonio authorities were closing down the "Chili Queens" as a supposed menace to public health.[20] The first stage of commercializing Mexican cuisine for foreigners was thus to compress its regional variety to a few typical dishes, to give the tourists an entrée without overwhelming them with exoticism. At the same time, the restaurateurs did everything possible to alleviate fears of contamination. To this day, many tourists, perhaps a majority, never transcend this introductory level. Nevertheless,

Mexicans naturally wished to encourage visitors to begin exploring the riches of their regional cooking.

Marketing Mexican Cuisine

The U.S. rise to global domination from about 1940 to 1970, or roughly from World War II to Vietnam, was also a time of rapid economic growth in Mexico. Although based on agricultural modernization and urban industrialization, this so-called Economic Miracle also emphasized tourism as a vital source of foreign exchange and internal employment. The gap between rich and poor remained broad, however, and an authoritarian political system assured that popular unrest did not disturb capitalist investment. The ruling party legitimized its monopoly on power through a program of assimilating Native Americans into the national community that was referred to somewhat misleadingly as *indigenismo*. Popularized in the murals of Diego Rivera, this goal was enunciated earlier by anthropologist Manuel Gamio in a book entitled *Forjando patria* (Forging the Fatherland, 1916). Mexico was therefore attempting to eliminate the folkloric indigenous communities that ironically became a major tourist attraction for young people who established the counterculture as a rebellion against a conformist corporate lifestyle that was emerging in both countries.

Mexican officials, aware of the tourist dollars lost due to unsanitary conditions, made concerted efforts to transform the country's image. A national commission for tourism was founded as early as 1929 to coordinate public and private sector efforts, and the Department of Health established a program for certifying the hygienic standards of tourist restaurants. Historian Alex Saragoza has identified two, at times conflicting, ideals guiding the federal tourism campaign. At first the government sought to portray an authentic Mexico fitting the propaganda of revolutionary nationalism and featuring pre-Hispanic monuments, ballets, *folklóricos,* and indigenous handicrafts. By the 1940s, politicians had realized the benefits of a more "modern" commercial tourism emphasizing sea, sand, and sun, and centered on the port city of Acapulco.[21]

Middle-class Mexicans responded enthusiastically to the call of the vacation, driving across newly built highways to visit ancient pyramids, colonial cathedrals, and modern resorts. En route they sampled the countless variations of regional cooking from the *moles* of indigenous Oaxaca to the *ceviches* (fresh seafoods "cooked" in lime juice) of Acapulco. They continued to desire those delicious foods upon returning home, thereby creating opportunities for regional restaurants in the nation's capital and other big cities during the 1940s and 1950s. Perhaps the most successful of the new restaurateurs was José Inés Loredo, from the Gulf port of Tampico, who built a chain of gourmet establishments around his signature dish, *carne asada a la tampiqueña* (butterflied steak served with green enchiladas, roasted chile strips, and grilled cheese). Cookbook author Josefina Velázquez de León meanwhile fueled the curiosity of Mexican women about their national cuisine by publishing more than 150 books, including the influential *Platillos regionales de la República mexicana* (Regional Dishes of the Mexican Republic, 1946).

This nostalgia for folkloric cuisine did not impede the desire of middle-class Mexicans for the benefits of industrialization. Urban housewives purchased modern ranges and refrigerators as soon as their budgets allowed, and blenders sold briskly even in impoverished rural communities as soon as electrification arrived so that women could replace the *metate* (grinding stone) for making chile sauces. American-style hotcakes were essential on modern breakfast tables, and when an Aunt Jemima restaurant opened in the Zona Rosa (Pink Zone) tourist district of Mexico City, it quickly became the hangout of the fashionable elite. When traveling, Mexicans demanded the highest standards of luxury they could afford and welcomed new hotels, restaurants, and other tourist accommodations as signs of national development.[22]

Just as Mexico acquired a mature tourist industry capable of providing modern amenities to American tourists, a new breed of traveler arrived in search of more authentic and natural experiences than those offered at commercial resorts such as Acapulco. The hippie counterculture emerged on college campuses in the 1960s and questioned the superiority of an American civilization that entailed corporate bureaucracy, conformist suburban lifestyles, and chemical pollution of the environment. In the hippie approach to eating, as historian Warren Belasco has noted, "two guidelines proved handy: Don't eat anything you can't pronounce (i.e., no propylene glycol alginate, a stabilizer used in bottled salad dressing) and if worms, yeast, and bacteria grew on it, then it must be natural, for no self-respecting bug would eat plastic. Inverting established notions of spoilage, the countercuisine equated preservatives with contamination and microbes with health."[23] Under the circumstances, a simple case of diarrhea in Mexico seemed preferable to dying of cancer from eating food contaminated by DDT or other carcinogens served up by the U.S. food processing industry. Dropping out to Mexico offered a particularly attractive alternative, both to get closer to nature and to avoid the Vietnam War draft. Yet the majority of these hippies were not genuine culinary tourists; the appeal of Oaxaca lay more in the hallucinogenic mushrooms of Huautla de Jiménez than in the fabled *moles* of Teotitlán del Valle. Local businesses disdained them as *turismo pobre* (poor tourism), spending little at hotels and restaurants, while the Mazatec folk healers were annoyed by their lack of respect for the rituals associated with the mushrooms.[24] The hippies made their greatest impact not in their youthful days, but rather as they matured, entered the workplace, and brought their social and environmental awareness into the corporate world as the "bourgeois Bohemians."[25]

The counterculture provided only one version of authenticity, for when America took notice of Mexico food, it did so in a variety of ways, once again confusing the expectations of culinary tourists. One source of this awareness of Mexican food came from established communities of Mexican Americans, who ate a basically *norteño* cuisine distinguished by tortillas made of wheat flour instead of corn and by large quantities of meat, especially beef. Their ethnic restaurants, predominantly Tex-Mex but also occasionally Santa Fe and Sonoran, began to spread beyond the Southwest in the 1970s, usually by toning down the heat of the chiles in order to appeal to mainstream consumers. Corporate purveyors of fast food meanwhile appropriated "Mexican" as a new category, likewise transforming the food in a search for product differentiation. Taco Bell initiated this rationalization process by creating the pre-formed taco shell, thereby dispensing entirely with the need for fresh tortillas, formerly the cornerstone of Mexican cooking. Mario Montaño has described the manner in which restaurateurs introduced fancy iron plates to serve the rustic grilled skirt steak known as *arrachera* or *fajita*, and then mutated the dish beyond all recognition to create the oxymoron "chicken fajitas."[26]

From under an avalanche of chips and salsa, Diana Kennedy called out for authentic regional foods with the publication of *The Cuisines of Mexico* (1972). This landmark cookbook introduced American readers to such classic recipes as *mole poblano*, snapper Veracruz, tamales from Michoacán, and Yucatecan pit-roasted pig. Even then, the collection had only scratched the surface, for as Kennedy later admitted, the village cooking of Mexico "was all too strange to publish in those days."[27] Nevertheless, Kennedy gathered a following, producing a second volume, *Recipes from the Regional Cooks of Mexico* (1978), and within a few decades authentic Mexican reached a critical mass in the United States.

One contribution to this trend came from upscale Southwestern restaurants pioneered, in 1980, by John Rivera Sedlar's approach to serving Mexican street foods, tamales and chiles, as haute cuisine. Although Sedlar and his contemporaries Robert Del Grande, Stephan Pyles, and Mark Miller freely adapted those foods using European cooking techniques, they continually returned to Mexico for inspiration and spread that influence among cooks in the United States. This "Latin turn" in fine dining also included more authentic restaurants, some of the first of which were the Frontera Grill in Chicago and Rosa Mexicano in New York. In 1989, Diana Kennedy produced her masterpiece, *The Art of Mexican Cooking*, including three recipes for *cuitlacoche*, although cooks still had little hope of finding the fungus in U.S. grocery stores. Together with Patricia Quintana's *The Taste of Mexico* (1986) and Rick Bayless's *Authentic Mexican* (1987), this volume inspired a flood of Mexican cookbooks in the 1990s. Moreover, starting in 1988, Kennedy's fans could experience the ultimate form of gastronomic tourism to Mexico by taking cooking classes with her through Culinary Adventures, a company organized by Marilyn Tausend.

The Contemporary Search for *México Profundo*

The Mexican elite's grudging acceptance of its multiethnic society and the slow abandoning of the myth of the cosmic race has facilitated the flowering of culinary tourism, both internal and external, in the 1990s. A herald of this change came with the extremely influential indigenous manifesto, *México profundo* (Deep Mexico, 1987), by the late Guillermo Bonfil Batalla. The most prominent Mexican anthropologist of the second half of the twentieth century, Bonfil Batalla reversed the goal of nationalist assimilation set out by Manuel Gamio and called instead for the recognition of indigenous rights. This movement gained both political urgency and international recognition when the Zapatista uprising began in Chiapas on January 1, 1994, purposely timed to coincide with the implementation of the North American Free Trade Agreement. Although widespread poverty in indigenous communities of southern Mexico forced large numbers of people to migrate to the United States in search of work, some have been able to parlay their ethnic identity into a marketable commodity. Abigail Mendoza, a resident of the Oaxacan weaving village of Teotitlán del Valle, exemplifies this native entrepreneurial ability through her talent as an interpreter of Zapotec cuisine. Together with elite cookbook authors, both Mexican and foreign, she has attempted to present her foods to a broad audience, yet contradictions inherent in culinary and ethnic tourism limit the success of their project.

Mexico's postwar consensus was shaken in 1968 with the political crisis of the Tlatelolco massacre, when the army killed hundreds of peacefully demonstrating students. The petroleum shock and stagflation of the early 1970s promptly derailed the economic "miracle" and caused a collapse of the peso. There followed a new search for national identity that rejected the folkloric symbols claimed by the ruling party and sought new ones based on the indigenous past. Following the international student movement, many young people began calling themselves *xipitecas* (pronounced "hippy tecas," like the Aztecas). Some formed groups to perform supposedly pre-Hispanic dances while dressed in plumed costumes. Meanwhile, anthropologists went back to the countryside, doing fieldwork among indigenous communities and contributing to what Claudio Lomnitz Adler described as a gentrification of rural food and drink.[28]

Despite the countercultural elements of this movement, Mexicans proved quite savvy about commercializing this newly authentic past. The tequila industry in Jalisco, led by Francisco Javier Sauza, acquired distilling technology as sophisticated as that of any single-malt Scotch or French brandy producer in order to make top shelf *añejo* tequila. The city of Puebla refurbished as a tourist attraction the convent kitchen where, according to legend, *mole poblano* was invented. Restaurants opened in Mexico City such as Fonda Don Chon, specializing in supposedly pre-Hispanic foods, while others began serving the *nueva cocina mexicana* of *cuitlacoche* crêpes, mousse, and ravioli. Virtually every one of these establishments has concocted some version of the "traditional" rose-petal *mole* featured in Laura Esquivel's novel, *Like Water for Chocolate*. That she invented this recipe, like all the others in the book, and that diners who had never heard of it before began demanding it in fancy restaurants, demonstrates still another modern construction of authenticity.

Oaxaca offered the natural focus for culinary tourism based on this pre-Hispanic past, and the state provided an important, although not exclusive, destination for Tausend's Culinary Adventures.[29] The participants numbered about twenty, several from the restaurant business but most simply adventuresome cooks and eaters from all over the country. They traveled first to Mexico City and began their experience with a visit to the world-renowned museum of anthropology, focusing not on the main pre-Hispanic displays, but on the less frequently visited second-floor ethnographic exhibits. Having marked the objects of tourist interest, primarily cooking utensils and ethnic textiles, the group proceeded by plane to the city of Oaxaca, where they met with Diana Kennedy. The elegant Englishwoman ruled her classes with the air of royalty, pronouncing edicts on environmentally sound cooking practices, banishing miscreants who disobeyed the rule against wearing the faintest trace of perfume, but mostly sharing her encyclopedic knowledge of Mexican cuisine gained through more than thirty years of research.

Culinary adventurers also experienced the uneasy tension, common to the tourist industry, of commercialized authenticity. When not in class, they toured the monumental ruins of Monte Alban and went shopping in Oaxaca's numerous folk art galleries. The highlight of the trip for many was a visit to a private home in the Zapotec village of Teotitlán del Valle, known for its elaborate weavings. The local merchant family of Abigail Mendoza demonstrated the preparation of traditional wedding festival foods of hot chocolate; *totopos*, large crisp tortillas; and *higadito*, a stew cooked with beaten eggs, reminiscent of Chinese soups and loaded with fertility symbols. Afterward she accompanied the group to a rustic distillery of *mescal*, a local counterpart of tequila, and then did a roaring business selling textiles to the tourists. A cooking class and dinner at the trendy restaurant Del Vitral left Kennedy fidgeting uneasily as the chef explained his *nueva cocina* creations. As a final examination, the students were turned loose on the Saturday market in Oaxaca City to purchase dried chiles and herbs, with the proviso that they had to pass through U.S. agricultural inspection before reproducing at home the dishes they had just learned. Diana Kennedy inspected the purchases, nodding sagely at the selection, and a friendly competition developed among the students as they attempted to carry back fragile earthenware pots and griddles—rarely with much success. Only airline luggage limits precluded the most ambitious of the group from returning with the Holy Grail of authentic Mexican, a stone *metate.*

Tausend's success prompted a number of other culinary tour groups to form. Nancy Zaslavsky began offering trips, which formed the basis for her cookbook, *A Cook's Tour of Mexico* (1995), as did an instructor at the Santa Fe Cooking School, Daniel Hoyer. Oaxacan residents, both native-born and American expatriates, also entered the fray. Susanna Trilling, a former New York chef and caterer who had traded the Big Apple for a little rancho outside Oaxaca City, opened the Seasons of My Heart Cooking School, which inspired a cookbook of the same name. Meanwhile, one of the bright young stars of Mexican cuisine, Iliana de la Vega Arnaud, began offering cooking classes in her stylish Oaxacan restaurant, El Naranjo. Nor were the opportunities limited to the local elite. A couple of recent college graduates signed up for a private cooking class in Oaxaca and found themselves in a rather proletarian home, preparing a large pot of turkey *mole* under the direction of a Mexican woman while her family hovered outside the kitchen, waiting to eat their leftovers. The sharp *señora* thus briefly reversed the international division of labor, turning hapless gringo tourists into migrant workers, and even getting them to buy the groceries.[30]

Cookbooks provide another important media of culinary tourism, both substituting for actual experience and encouraging it. Cooking authors serve as intermediaries between travelers and their subjects by pointing out authentic foods for tourists whether on vacation to Mexico, visiting Mexican restaurants, or traveling vicariously through books. Two of the foremost interpreters of the culinary México profundo, Diana Kennedy and Zarela Martínez, were outsiders who converted into prophets of Oaxacan cuisine. Martínez, a native of northern Mexico and successful New York City restaurateur, wrote her first cookbook, *Food from My Heart* (1992), as a personal memoir with an eclectic mix of regional dishes. Her volume *The Food and Life of Oaxaca* (1997), however, renounced the nouvelle tendencies of the previous work to portray the traditional cuisine of the southernmost Mexican state. Kennedy, meanwhile, has written her own culinary memoir, *My Mexico* (1998), which narrates her travels through the countryside and also propounds various ecological projects, such as replacing chemical fertilizer with compost from the waste of Mexico City markets.

Both volumes blend the genres of cookbook with travel writing, waxing poetic about the valley landscapes of Oaxaca. In addition, Martínez provides a number of glossy, black-and-white photos of cooks, food vendors, and people celebrating local festivals in distinctive indigenous costumes. The authors also clearly mark the authenticity of their recipes; for example, assuring readers that, "For local residents of Puerto Vallarta there is no *pozole* to compare with that of Señora Rafaela Villaseñor."[31] Such claims have become essential in the increasingly crowded Mexican cookbook market, as ever more exotic recipes offer a form of product differentiation. Although Kennedy had achieved novelty in the 1970s with a recipe for *mole poblano,* two decades later Martínez found it necessary to enumerate thirteen separate Oaxacan *moles,* specifically including those of Teotitlán del Valle and the Isthmus of Tehuantepec.

Culinary tourism has also provided business opportunities for ethnic intermediaries such as the Zapotec chef Abigail Mendoza. The primary intersection between village life and tourism has been the *guelaguetza,* originally a festival celebrating weddings or saints' days, and promoted by the federal government since the 1960s as a major tourist attraction culminating in a statewide pageant of folk dance. The term *guelaguetza* also referred to the system of loans needed to pay for these tremendously expensive festivals, which required feeding upward of five hundred people for days on end, all within a subsistence peasant economy. For merchant families such as the Mendozas, the international market for ethnic weaving has provided great opportunities, and Abigail's late father, Emiliano, served two separate terms as *mayordomo* (mayor), responsible for supporting the entire town's ritual life, without impoverishing himself.

Of course, much of the burden of these festivals fell on female members of the family, who did all of the cooking, but Mendoza parlayed this difficult work into an independent business opportunity in an otherwise patriarchal village society. One of the most difficult preparations, and one by which Zapotecs judge a festival meal, was the ceremonial chocolate used to greet wedding guests, especially the frothy texture of the foam on top. Local connoisseurs insist that this *espuma*, like fine champagne, must contain multitudes of tiny bubbles rather than a few large, flabby air pockets. For a party of five hundred, eight women are needed to grind the chocolate on the *metate* and eight more—the ones considered to be the cleanest, both morally and hygienically—to beat the *espuma*. Mendoza, always a talented cook, used the opportunity of the *mayordomías* to perfect the traditional village recipes and even to create some new ones of her own, which she served in a restaurant, Tlamanalli, to tourists visiting the village, and within the community through her business of catering weddings and other festivals. Mendoza's cooking soon found an appreciative audience far beyond the pueblo of Teotitlán del Valle; Diana Kennedy acknowledged her as "*the* star of the Zapotec kitchen," both *Gourmet* and *Saveur* magazines ran feature articles on her, and the *New York Times* declared Tlamanalli to be one of the ten best restaurants in the entire world. Her fame reached a pinnacle in 1999 with an invitation from the Culinary Institute of America in Napa Valley to give a demonstration of Zapotec cooking at a conference on Mexican cuisine.[32]

Yet these intermediaries faced dilemmas in their projects of allowing tourists to experience authentic foods in Mexico and to re-create them at home. Zarela Martínez observed: "In many of these villages, the everyday cooking is extremely simple, demanding absolutely fresh, flavorful ingredients. This aspect of the cooking is nearly impossible to capture in a cookbook. Giving 'recipes' for something like a very minimalistic vegetable stew using average U.S. commercial produce will only make it seem dull and tasteless."[33] She therefore filled the book with festival dishes like the *moles*, which were more easily explained through recipes but also enormously time-consuming and thus difficult for cooks to reproduce in the United States, even with access to the rare chiles and herbs. Diana

Kennedy faced similar problems in realizing her ecological goals of preserving traditional cuisines unspoiled by modernization, including the spread of tourism. As a result, she spoke candidly about the difficulty of culinary research: "I came across a street vendor selling shrimp *tamales*, which I had heard about for years and never had a chance to try. . . . The dough was roughly textured and heavy with lard. It was filled with a whole shrimp: the head with feelers, legs, shell, and tail, which made for a rather abrasive mouthful. . . . On such occasions I keep telling myself that, gastronomically speaking, it is always hit or miss when charting new territory."[34]

In adopting these narrative strategies, both Martínez and Kennedy had made their subjects exotic by emphasizing their otherness. This tendency to distance the cookbook buyer from the people who created the recipes is particularly unfortunate, given the global patterns of capital investment and labor migration. The sons and daughters of Teotitlán del Valle and other Oaxacan villages now work in large numbers as underpaid restaurant cooks and hotel maids throughout the United States. Unfortunately, the folkloric goodwill they gain from appreciative descriptions in cookbooks and from glossy photos wearing native costume is lost when they are taken out of the indigenous context and placed in the humble clothes and inherently disadvantageous situations of the service industry.

The contradictions between village life and international capitalism encountered by transnational cookbook authors are far worse in the case of ethnic intermediaries such as Abigail Mendoza. For traditional dishes to retain their cache, whether in Native American communities or in modern Mexican kitchens, they must remain carefully guarded secrets, and indeed many cooks still perform the crucial steps of a recipe alone. Mendoza insists that while the cooking secrets have leaked out at other pueblos, Teotitlán del Valle retains the most ancient and traditional preparations. In the case of chocolate, the secret lies in the preparation of white cacao (a six-month procedure involving multiple washings followed by extended periods buried underground beneath a *metate*). Yet unlike such fabled secret formulas of the corporate world as Kentucky Fried Chicken's eleven herbs and spices or Coca Cola's syrup, it would be impossible to mass-produce foamy chocolate using Mendoza's recipe. The Zapotec cook has also turned away visiting cookbook authors and even declined suggestions to write a book of her own.

The "Zapotec culinary secrets" heralded by the *Saveur* article served as simple advertising copy on mass-market publications, yet they constitute her very livelihood and status in the community. Whatever small compensation she might receive would be nothing compared to the profits accruing to multinational publishers if they could gain access to her secrets. An intelligent woman, Mendoza may also realize that her secrets do not lend themselves to written formulas, involving instead a nose for selecting the perfect ingredients from Oaxaca's rich local gardens and markets as well as the taste for combining them in a dish, skills that could never be captured in a cookbook. One even wonders about the long-term viability of the ethnic restaurant she operates as migration patterns and the inroads of capitalism increasingly distance village life from its former traditions—especially if rivals begin to import Italian cappuccino machines to mass-produce foamy chocolate.

Conclusion

Culinary tourism runs both ways across the Rio Grande as Mexican and American cultures blend in the modern world. Mexican food has become one of the top three most popular ethnic foods throughout the United States, along with Italian and Chinese, even though none of these truly represent the cuisines of the old countries. At the same time, American variants have become ever more present in Mexico itself, as tourists demand to eat their familiar fajitas, margaritas, chips, and salsa while on vacation, although the local consumers of these foods are primarily Americanized juniors. Virtually all purveyors of Mexican food assert at least a nominal claim to authenticity, and as a result the meanings of that term vary according to the context. An analysis of culinary tourism to Mexico or similar societies must therefore consider at least three situations: restaurants that attempt to reproduce the foods of distant regions, tourists who travel either physically or vicariously through cookbooks to those regions, and finally the indigenous subjects who perform for the tourists while at the same time attempting to preserve their own societies. All of these culinary performances, moreover, differ according to whether the audience comprises foreign visitors or members of the national elite.

Hackneyed reproductions of ethnic foods by restaurants outside of Mexico have prompted concerns that superficial culinary tourism will reduce authentic indigenous cuisines to the lowest common denominator of global fast-food chains.[35] For corporations such as Taco Bell, Mexico is little more than a low-cost product development laboratory, providing concepts such as *gorditas* and *chalupas* for food formulators and advertising executives to work over and then reexport around the world. Mexican culture thus becomes simply a raw material in the global marketplace, comparable to migrant workers, whose ubiquitous presence reinforces belief in the superiority of American civilization, especially since the U.S. media ignores their return migrations. Nevertheless, as the Pollo Loco chain has demonstrated, even fast food can attain a measure of authenticity. Corporate food processors do not necessarily herald the apocalypse of culinary homogenization and annihilation; rather, they can offer a rough introduction that leads people to seek out more authentic versions. Such dishes are available in large part because of migrant workers who carry their foods with them, making even exotic ingredients such as *cuitlacoche* available in some U.S. markets. The increasing presence and variety of regional Mexican restaurants demonstrates that culinary tourism is an ongoing process in which American consumers have grown more knowledgeable and demanding of genuine ethnic food.[36]

For members of the Mexican elite as well as foreign visitors, the search for authenticity through culinary tourism is more than just a gastronomic experience. The indigenous cuisine of Oaxaca provides the former with pre-Hispanic legitimacy for their nationalist claims, while the latter find temporary refuge from homogenized mass culture in slowly cooked *moles* and Native American textiles. An example of this exchange can be seen in the markets and restaurants of Oaxaca every time an American bites into a taco of *chapulines* (grasshoppers). Mexicans find these tiny insects quite palatable, tasting rather like coarsely ground chipotle peppers, and yet the tourist crossing the boundaries of edibility experiences an undeniable squeamishness that is almost a surrogate experience of "Montezuma's revenge." The discomfort lasts only a moment, and it provides a source of nationalist pride for Mexicans, who thereby conquer their foreign neighbors. The Bohemian aesthetic can be carried to extremes, as author Tony Cohan illustrates in describing his and his artist wife's search for inner peace in a provincial Mexican town. "We eat everything we see on the street," he writes. "Every few days one of us is ill with the *turistas*; even this seems to be part of the catharsis. Lomotil, Imodium, and Pepto-Bismol crowd the toothbrush and comb on the cloudy glass counter above the sink." They host an uptight friend from New York, who begins his visit in mortal fear of contagion and departs with a similar release: "'Montezuma's revenge!' Richard exclaims, hugging us each good-bye. 'Worth every miserable, dribbling bit of it!'"[37]

In Teotitlán del Valle, the authenticity of being an ethnic minority has provided Abigail Mendoza with a lucrative restaurant business opportunity and helped her become one of the leading citizens of the community in spite of patriarchal social restrictions. Nevertheless, the culinary tourism that has made her success possible depends on the continued marginality of her people, which forces them to spend much of their lives as migrant laborers to make enough money to support their families in Oaxaca. For the inhabitants of *México profundo*, as opposed to the culinary tourists, there are no medical cures for the predicament of globalization.

Notes

1. *New York Times*, February 15, 1979, 3.

2. Pilcher, Jeffrey M. 1998. ¡Que vivan los tamales! *Food and the Making of Mexican Identity*. Albuquerque: University of New Mexico Press, 131.

3. Long, Lucy M. 1998. "Culinary Tourism: A Folkloristic Perspective on Eating and Otherness." *Southern Folklore* 55, no. 3: 185–87.

4. McCannell, Dean. 1976. *The Tourist: A New Theory of the Leisure Class*. New York: Schocken Books, chapter 5.

5. Urry, John. 1990. *The Tourist Gaze: Leisure and Travel in Contemporary Societies*. London: Sage.

6. Van den Berghe, Pierre L. 1994. *The Quest for the Other: Ethnic Tourism in San Cristóbal, Mexico*. Seattle: University of Washington Press.

7. Pilcher, *¡Que vivan los tamales!*, 1–70, quote from 46.

8. Nove, Salvador 1993. *Cocina mexicana; o, Historia gastronómica de la Ciudad de México*. Mexico City: Editorial Porrúa, 125–35. See also René Rabell Jara. 1996. *La bella época*, vol. 6 of *La cocina mexicana a través de los siglos*. Mexico City: Editorial Clio.

9. Campbell, Reau. 1907. *Campbell's New Revised Complete Guide and Descriptive Book of Mexico*. Chicago: Rogers & Smith, 48; *Mexican Herald*, January 19, 1908.

10. *Mexican Herald*, January 19, 1908. See also Antonio García Cubas. 1946. *El libro de mis recuerdos: prólogo y selección de Manuel Carrera Stampa*. Mexico City: Secretaría de Educación Pública, 52–53.

11. Barton, Mary. 1911. *Impressions of Mexico with Brush and Pen*. London: Methuen, 16.

12. Miller, Max. 1937. *Mexico Around Me*. New York: Reynal & Hitchcock, 38–39.

13. Edward King quoted in Donna R. Gabaccia. 1998. *We Are What We Eat: Ethnic Food and the Making of Americans*. Cambridge, Mass.: Harvard University Press, 108.

14. Ibid, 108–09; Campbell, *Campbell's New Revised Guide*, 48.

15. Garner, Bess Adams. 1937. *Mexico: Notes in the Margin*. Boston: Houghton Mifflin, 24–25. See also, Harvey A. Levenstein. 1988. *Revolution at the Table: The Transformation of the American Diet*. New York: Oxford University Press, chapter 3.

16. Pike, Fredrick B. 1992. *The United States and Latin America: Myths and Stereotypes of Civilization and Nature*. Austin: University of Texas Press.

17. *Mexican Herald*, April 26, 1908.

18. Brenner, Anita. 1941. *Your Mexican Holiday: A Modern Guide*. New York: G. P. Putnam's Sons, 281; Helen Delpar. 1992. *The Enormous Vogue of Things Mexican: Cultural Relations between the United States and Mexico, 1920–1935*. Tuscaloosa: University of Alabama Press. Other early works include Natalie V. Scott. 1935. *Your Mexican Kitchen: A Compilation of Mexican Recipes Practicable in the United States*. New York: G. P. Putnam's Sons; Blanche and Edna V. McNeil. 1936. *First Foods of America*. Los Angeles: Suttonhouse Ltd.; Doris Aller. 1940. *The Epicure in Mexico: A Compilation by Doris Aller of Famous and Fine Mexican Dishes*. San Francisco: Colt Press.

19. Terry, T. Philip. 1944. *Terry's Guide to Mexico: The New Standard Guidebook to the Mexican Republic*. Boston: Rapid Service Press, 243.

20. Herrick, Elisabeth Webb. 1935. *Curious California Customs* (Los Angeles: Pacific Carbon & Printing, , 108–9; *La Opinión* (Los Angeles), April 22, 1930, 4; Mary Ann Noonan Guerra. 1988. *The History of San Antonio's Market Square*. San Antonio: Alamo Press, 14, 48.

21. Sargoza, Alex M. 2001. "Tourism and the Construction of *Lo Mexicano*, 1934–1952." In *Fragments of a Golden Age: The Politics of Culture in Postrevolutionary Mexico Since 1940*. Eds. Gilbert M. Joseph, Anne Rubenstein, and Eric Zolov. Durham, N.C.: Duke University Press.

22. Van den Berghe, *Quest for the Other*, 84–85.

23. Belasco, Warren J. 1993. *Appetite for Change: How the Counterculture Took on the Food Industry*. Ithaca, N.Y.: Cornell University Press, 40.

24. Zolov, Eric. 1999. *Refried Elvis: The Rise of the Mexican Counterculture*. Berkeley: University of California Press, 107–8; Van den Berghe, *Quest for the Other*, 47.

25. The phrase is from David Brooks. 2000. *Bobos in Paradise: The New Upper Class and How They Got There*. New York: Simon and Schuster.

26. Montaño, Mario. 1997. "Appropriation and Counterhegemony in South Texas: Food Slurs, Offal Meats, and Blood." In *Usable Pasts: Traditions and Group Expressions in North America*. Ed. Tad Tuleja. Logan: Utah State University Press, 50–67; Warren J. Belasco. 1987. "Ethnic Fast Foods: The Corporate Melting Pot." *Food and Foodways* 2: 1–30; Jeffrey M. Pilcher. 2001. "Tex-Mex, Cal-Mex, New Mex, or Whose Mex? Notes on the Historical Geography of Southwestern Cuisine." *Journal of the Southwest* 43, no. 4 (winter): 659–79.

27. Kennedy, Diana. 1998. *My Mexico: A Culinary Odyssey with More Than 500 Recipes*. New York: Clarkson Potter, 317.

28. Lomnitz-Adler, Claudio. 1992. *Exits from the Labyrinth: Culture and Ideology in the Mexican National Space*. Berkeley: University of California Press, 255–56.

29. The following account is based on the author's experience of a Culinary Adventures tour to Oaxaca, January 4–13, 1992.

30. Interview with Chris Magnuson, Williamstown, Massachusetts, September 29, 2001.

31. Kennedy, *My Mexico*, quote from 56; see also 282.

32. Ibid, 390. *Gourmet*, February 1991; *Saveur*, summer 1994; *New York Times*,

January 17, 1993. Background for this discussion comes from the excellent anthropological study by Lynn Stephen. 1991. *Zapotec Women.* Austin: University of Texas Press, 32–34, 178–207.

33. Martinez, Zarela. 1997. *The Food and Life of Oaxaca: Traditional Recipes from Mexico's Heart.* New York: Macmillan, 17.

34. Kennedy, *My Mexico,* 69–70.

35. This point is argued most persuasively by George Ritzer. 1998. *The McDonaldization Thesis: Explorations and Extensions.* London: Sage, 71–94.

36. Asimov, Eric. 2000. "Beyond Tacos: Mexican Food Gets Real.""*New York Times,* January 26, B14.

37. Cohan, Tony. 2000. *On Mexican Time: A New Life in San Miguel.* New York: Broadway Books, 16, 77.

CHAPTER 4

Flavors of Memory

Jewish Food as Culinary Tourism in Poland

Eve Jochnowitz

Every year since achieving independence, Poland has hosted greater and greater numbers of tourists from abroad, and in so doing has taken on the negotiation of the numerous issues in Poland's construction of its own heritage and the conflicting ideas about Polish history that visitors bring along. For non-Jewish Poles, Jewish tourists are both welcome signs of prosperity and unwelcome reminders of the past. For Jewish visitors, Poland is at once a site of abjection, both degraded and degrading, and a surrogate Holy Land.

Jewish settlement in Poland dates from the tenth century (Roth 1989:265); by the thirteenth century, Poland had become the haven of Ashkenazic Jews fleeing persecution and expulsion from France and Germanic lands. Poland's Jewish population was exceptionally fruitful, and on the eve of the Second World War, more than three million Polish Jews made up 10 percent of Poland's population and the largest Jewish population in Europe. Poland's history as a Jewish center ended horribly with the German occupation and the murder of 90 percent of Poland's Jews. Many of those who survived the war fled Poland in 1968 in response to the "anti-Zionist" purges. Depending on whom you ask, Poland's current Jewish population is somewhere between three thousand and twenty thousand.

Culinary tourism figures significantly in the encounter of Jews with contemporary Poland. For the purposes of this essay, I will examine both the culinary tourist productions intended for foreign visitors and the domestic culinary tourism of Poles living in Poland. The production of Jew-

A Jewish magazine examines Poland's interest in kosher food.

ish food and cooking in Poland sheds special light on the paradoxical role of Jews in Polish history and memory and the unique position of Poland in the Jewish collective imagination. It is useful to begin with a case study of Cracow's Szeroka Street.

"The Broadway of Jewish Cracow" was Roman Vishniac's name for Szeroka Street, the center market square of the Kazimierz neighborhood, which for six centuries was Cracow's Jewish section. Kazimierz is named for King Casimir the Great, king of Poland from 1333 to 1370, who in 1354 extended economic and political protection to the Jews of Poland. According to Jewish and Polish popular history, Casimir's kindness to the Jews was because of his love for his beautiful Jewish concubine, Ester. Before the war, Szeroka Street was the site of three synagogues, two cemeteries, and a *mikve* or ritual bath; it was the cultural and ceremonial center of Jewish life in Cracow. Szeroka Street today is the site of five Jewish restaurants, two Jewish coffee shops, a Jewish museum, and one functioning synagogue. It is no longer a ceremonial center, but in a way, the culinary has been rendered ceremonial. All five restaurants produce food primarily for the tourist market, and interestingly, all claim to offer their guests much more than food. Food functions as the medium of cultural transmission, real and imagined, for tourists, many of whom are Jewish, who visit Szeroka Street to taste Poland's Jewish past. In effect, Cracow's politicians and entrepreneurs have produced Szeroka Street as a Jewish theme park in a country where few Jews survive.

Szeroka Street is short but very wide (the word "*szeroka*" means wide in Polish) so that the street itself forms a small square. The center of the wide street, which once accommodated market carts, is now used as a car park, except during the annual festival of Jewish art and culture in Cracow, when Szeroka Street is the site of open-air concerts and performances for ten days. Many Jewish tourists come to Cracow for the festival each year, but the crowd of thousands that packs Szeroka Street is overwhelmingly Polish. Here is the paradox of the site of Szeroka Street: in the years since the advent of democracy, Cracow has been gentrifying at a rate that surpasses Warsaw, Lódz, and Gdansk. Coffee shops and retail establishments have thrived where they have appeared. At first, however, the Kazimierz, which is a poorer area, lagged behind the rest of Cracow. Topography was destiny for Kazimierz; the narrow and poorly paved streets and the tenement buildings that fronted on them were the legacy of the neighborhood's Jewish past and made the area unsuitable for a construction boom. The boomlet that has begun in Kazimierz has been driven almost entirely by domestic and foreign fascination with Jewish history in Poland. The gentrification of Szeroka Street has been the re-Judaization of Szeroka Street.

Of the buildings fronting on Szeroka Street, about one-quarter remain unrenovated dwellings; one-half are fully renovated buildings, all of which house Jewish sites; and the remaining quarter are under construction. It is by far the densest site of construction activity in Kazimierz.

If you stand in the center of Szeroka Street and face north, you will be looking directly at a little green park with two park benches and a small monument in front. The benches and the monument have the words "Fundacja Nissenbaumowa" (Nissenbaum Foundation) written on them. Beyond the park, looking straight ahead is the Jordan bookstore and coffee shop. If you turn clockwise, the Austeria restaurant in the building that housed the old *mikve* is at one o'clock, and the Galleria Judaica is at two o'clock. The east side of Szeroka Street has undergone massive renovation in the last few years and is now lined with handsome restaurant and retail fronts. In the middle of the east side of the street there is a synagogue cemetery. Continuing to turn clockwise, you will come to Ariel II, a brown building, then Ariel I, a much wider white building, and finally, the Hotel Ester, named for King Casimir's lovely mistress. The south end of the street is dominated by the courtyard and front of the *Stara Synagoga*, or Old Synagogue, which holds a museum and coffee shop. On the west side of Szeroka Street, there is a police station and several old, unrenovated apartment houses. At ten o'clock, there is the very imposing facade of the *Restauracja na Kazimierzu*, and finally, at eleven o'clock, is the Remuh Synagogue, Cracow's only regularly functioning synagogue. The Hebrew name of one of the oldest synagogues in Poland is *Beth ha kneseth ha khadasha de Remuh* or "The New Remuh Synagogue."

Tourists drawn to Szeroka Street frequent the local Jewish restaurants for nourishment and edification. For most Jewish visitors to Cracow, Jewish food means Ariel. The restaurants I referred to as Ariel I and Ariel II are both called, simply, Ariel. The proprietors of the two restaurants are currently in a legal battle over the right to use the name. The restaurant I referred to as Ariel I is the southernmost Ariel. This was actually the first Jewish restaurant on Szeroka Street and the first to be called Ariel. As soon as it opened, Ariel became the center of all nonceremonial Jewish activity in Cracow. Ariel also became the unofficial headquarters of Steven Spielberg's team during the filming of *Schindler's List*. Ariel I may have been the first Ariel restaurant on Szeroka Street, but it quickly fell to secondary status when the managers, Margot and Wojtek Ornat, opened their own restaurant next door. The Ornats' restaurant, Ariel II, has eclipsed Ariel I in terms of social importance. It is the official restaurant of Cracow's annual festival of Jewish arts and culture, and visitors and natives in Cracow will be only too pleased to tell you that Ariel II is the "real" Ariel. If you buy the postcard set of "Views of Jewish Kazimierz," you will get nine cards with images of synagogues and cemeteries and a shot of Ariel II. Inclusion in a set of postcards as one of the views of Jewish Kazimierz was a great public relations coup, but one that backfired since the view in the postcard is of the white building that is now the site of Ariel I.

The young waiters at both restaurants wear black vests and white tieless shirts. Ariel II has mismatched antique furniture, and Ariel I had large matched tables arranged in uncomfortable rows, but they have recently furnished their extra room with antique tables just like those at Ariel II. The menus at both Ariels are in English and Polish, and Ariel II has a Yiddish and Polish menu posted in the sidewalk cafe area. The menu at Ariel II is a small and elegant-looking burgundy-red booklet with gold parchment pages. The dishes that appear on the menu have widely differing Jewish pedigrees. Traditional Jewish dishes such as gefilte fish, matzoh pancakes, *czolent,* and stuffed goose neck appear side by side with fanciful dishes like "Purim chicken," which is chicken wrapped in a pastry crust and topped with a fried egg, and "Jankiel, the Innkeeper of Berdyczow's soup," which refers not to a soup in the Jewish repertoire, but to the most famous Jewish character in Polish letters, Jankiel the innkeeper. In *Pan Tadeusz,* the romantic epic by Adam Mickiewicz, the sympathetic Jankiel plays Polish patriotic music on his hammered dulcimer, an instrument particularly associated with Jewish music (Steinlauf 1997:10). Margot Ornat sees Jewish cuisine as being exotic, sweet, and spicy. Entrées like duck with apples, turkey with almonds, and goose liver with raisins and almonds reflect this sensibility. Ornat invented some of these dishes herself, and for the actual Jewish dishes, the restaurant uses the recipes provided by Roza Jakobowicz, the matriarch of Jewish Cracow.

Customers come to Ariel II less to eat than to see and be seen, to meet the younger members of Cracow's Jewish community who frequent Ariel II, and to hear the live music that owners feel is their main drawing card. Nevertheless, some of the food at Ariel II is quite good. The *borscht* is clear and flavorful, and the always-changing vegetarian salad is usually fresh and tasty. The menu at Ariel I is a black booklet with photocopied white pages inside. The Ariel I menu offers the same combination of real and fantasy Jewish food: Berdytchov soup, gefilte fish, Becalel's soup, and chicken livers à la Hertzel Street. The menu is also in Polish and English, but some of the Polish is not translated, and much of the English is incorrect. While the clientele at Ariel II is overwhelmingly foreign during the tourist season, the clientele at Ariel I is mixed tourist and native, and the tourists who frequent Ariel I are more likely to be German than American and Israeli. *Kroke,* Cracow's homegrown klezmer band, plays exclusively at Ariel I.

The coffee shop at the Jordan bookstore is also visited by many tourists seeking Jewish sites in Cracow. Numerous tours of Cracow, including the famous *"Schindler's List* Tour," originate at the Jordan. The bookstore has an eclectic collection of popular and scholarly books on Jewish subjects, many of them in English and at bargain prices, as well as postcards and pictures of Jewish interest. The coffee shop has posters on the walls of the Festival of Jewish Culture, *Fiddler on the Roof,* and some photographs of rabbis. A small bagel garland hangs over the bar, but bagels are not offered on the menu. There is, in fact, nothing Jewish about the menu in this coffee shop, and while none of the restaurants on Szeroka Street except for the *Restauracja na Kazimierzu* are kosher, Jordan is the only one that serves ham and kielbasa.

Two other Jewish venues on Szeroka Street serve no Jewish food. The Galleria Judaica is a small shop that offers many of the books and prints available at Jordan, as well as Jewish-themed toys and decorative pieces. Galleria Judaica does not serve any food. While there is no coffee shop here yet, an employee will switch on a tape of *Fiddler on the Roof* if a customer walks into the store.

The museum coffee shop at the Stara Synagoga is the most modest coffee shop on Szeroka Street and also the comfiest. Low black square stools and tables nestle in a corner of the museum bookstore, which sells handmade cards with Hebrew calligraphy and pressed flowers as well as the same selection of books and art found at the bookstores at Jordan, Galeria Judaica, and Ariel I.

Restauracja na Kazimierzu first opened in June 1995. It is the only kosher restaurant in a square with five Jewish eating establishments. A kosher oasis in a *treyf* (nonkosher) desert, the long-awaited restaurant was welcomed by hundreds of guests invited to the two opening celebrations on Friday evening and Saturday afternoon June 30 and July 1, 1995. To celebrate the opening of the restaurant, the owner, Zygmunt Nissenbaum, invited everyone who attended services at the Remuh *shul* to a lavish feast accompanied by free-flowing premium vodka. In traditional Jewish practice, every meal that includes bread begins with a ritual hand washing. At the opening of his restaurant, Mr. Nissenbaum personally washed the hands of every guest, a gesture of hospitality indigenous to the region.

Zygmunt Nissenbaum, a native of Warsaw, is head of the *Fundacja Nissenbaumowa,* the Nissenbaum Foundation, which works on restoring Jewish sites, mostly cemeteries and synagogues, in Poland (Nissenbaum Foundation 1988). Nissenbaum opened *Restauracja na Kazimierzu* partly in response to the requests of Jewish visitors who came to visit sacred sites in Poland and had no place kosher to eat. The restaurant could not be more different in style than the two Ariels. The four dining spaces—two informal dining rooms, one formal dining room and one outdoor cafe— are roomy and well lighted, where the Ariels are dim and snug. The enormous menu, available in English, Polish, German, and French, comes in a pale blue three-ring binder. The waitresses wear long pale blue aprons. Each piece of crockery is inscribed with the *Fundacja Nissenbaumowa* logo: a blue banner, a blue menorah, and three yellow leaves or candle flames. There is no live music, but Yiddish and Hebrew records play at a low volume.

The food at *Restauracja na Kazimierzu* is itself an intriguing combination of flavors and techniques unlikely to be found outside the Old World, or anywhere at all, really. The dishes offered on the sixteen-page menu are recognizable as classics of east European and Galician Jewish cooking. Fish, including gefilte fish and seven varieties of herring, dominate the selection of appetizers. Fish also dominate the main courses, but here the subtext begins to show through. In addition to steamed carp with vegetables and potatoes or grilled pike with potato pancakes, one may order *truite au bleu*. When the main course arrives, whether it is stuffed carp or blue trout, it is prettily garnished with julienne of red and yellow peppers and feathery *lolla rossa* lettuce. This bouquet garni owes nothing to traditional Polish Jewish cooking, and everything to the catering tradition of Europe's grand hotels and ocean liners, the training ground of the colorful Eugeniusz Wirkowski, the manager and executive chef of *Restauracja na Kazimierzu* and the *Arche Noah* kosher restaurants in Vienna and Berlin.

Eugeniusz Wirkowski's peculiar history as a chef, philosopher, and businessman suit him uniquely for this project and his partnership with Zygmunt Nissenbaum. Wirkowski escaped to Russia and served in the Soviet army during World War II. When he was discharged from the army with an officer's rank, he was eligible to enroll in culinary school. He and his son, Henryk, have been in the kosher restaurant business since 1983, when they temporarily ran a kosher catering establishment in Warsaw at the time of the fortieth anniversary of the Warsaw Ghetto uprising.

The senior Mr. Wirkowski belongs to a school of chefs trained for competitions such as the Culinary Olympics that emphasize elaborate decorations. Wirkowski once won a silver medal in the Culinary Olympics for his Jewish cooking. Olympic-style cooking is more often found in hotels than in restaurants and is almost never seen in Jewish restaurants, but for Wirkowski, the cuisine he loves and the style he has learned are not mutually exclusive, and this is why piped rosettes of liver on endive leaves appear at the lunch buffet.

The most important site in Jewish Cracow is the city's only functioning synagogue. Services are held every Friday night and Saturday morning for a small number of regulars and a much larger floating base of visitors. The character of the services can vary depending on what tour groups are in town, but it is always an Orthodox Ashkenazic rite. In the last ten years, a wedding and a bar mitzvah, both for outsiders, were celebrated at the Remuh *shul* (Kaufman 1985), but no Cracovian has had a Jewish wedding in more than twenty years. Many visiting orthodox groups use the back room at the Remuh *shul* as a lunchroom after services. They bring nonperishable food to *shul* on Friday and eat lunch on Saturday morning, because they may not carry, buy, or cook food on the Sabbath.

To function properly as a tourist attraction, food needs to fall sufficiently outside of the familiar, but sufficiently inside the circle of what is palatable. Paul Fussell attacks as a "tourist of the grossest kind" a traveler who wrote a letter to the editor of the *New York Times* travel section asking for advice on how to avoid Chinese food while visiting Hong Kong (1988:31). Eastern European food is less familiar than visitors might expect. The onions and garlic are missing from the Polish analogues of many familiar Jewish dishes, but all the same, the pedigree of the cuisine shows. The dill and parsley, the sour soups and pickles, the techniques of shaping the dumplings and pancakes all bear witness that the histories and memories of Jews and Poles are so closely intertwined as to be inseparable. All Jewish cooking resembles the cooking of adjacent cultures more than that of distant Jewish communities, but the connections between the Jewish and non-Jewish cuisines of Poland are not only regional.

Jewish visitors are not the only people in Poland interested in seeking out Jewish food. A domestic form of culinary tourism in Poland provides a market for many Jewish or putatively Jewish dishes, the appeal of which draws heavily on the role of Jews in Polish folklore. Of all the foods eaten by Jews or identified as Jewish, matzoh is the only food Jews are actually commanded to eat in the *Tanakh* (Hebrew Bible). In this sense, matzoh could be said to be the only truly Jewish food there is. Matzoh is baked and eaten in every Jewish community. Until the last century, matzoh was so prohibitively expensive that it was consumed only by Jews and only on Passover. Once

Label from Mis matzo
package.

machine manufacture of matzoh became fea-
sible, manufacturers promoted it for year-round
use. Matzoh—flat, hard, unsalted, unleavened
bread made only of wheat flour and water—is
very markedly a Jewish food. Nevertheless, in
Poland every large market carries at least one
brand of matzoh and many carry two. The packages of Poland's two brands of matzoh are amazing texts on the place of the Jews in the Polish
imagination.

Wit-Pol *maca*, the more common brand,
come the size of index cards. The little Wit-Pol
matzohs are appealing, but they are a bit too pale,
thick, and underbaked. The label copy reads:
"*Maca*—healthy, no fat, no yeast, no preservatives. Excellent for the diets of people with stomach ulcers and other ailments." In other words,
matzoh is a health food. This fits in perfectly with
the widely held Polish view that specifically Jewish products are somehow purer, safer, and better than their non-Jewish analogues.

Mis *maca*, also easy to find but not quite
as widely available as Wit-Pol, uses an entirely
different marketing ploy. There is no label copy
on the Mis brand *maca* package—just the
words "Mis Maca" and an illustration of a gorgeous Jewess made to look oriental (Figure 4-
1). With one hand she holds together her scanty
frock, and with the other she holds aloft a
square of matzoh. The Mis *maca* maiden also
fits in with a different set of Polish perceptions
of Jews—that they are a mysterious oriental
other—a sprinkle of spice in the country's otherwise bland broth. Mis matzohs are about half
again larger than Wit-Pol matzohs. They are
also thinner and more thoroughly baked.

Pushcarts on all the busiest streets in Warsaw and Cracow sell *obwarzanki* to busy pass-
ersby. These ring-shaped parboiled rolls are
clearly cousins of the bagel. *Obwarzanki* are

Obwarzanki for sale on a Cracow street.

available plain or topped with poppy seeds, sesame seeds, or coarse salt. The customer points at the desired piece, and the *obwarzanki*-monger fishes it out with a hooked metal rod. *Obwarzanki* are thinner and drier than bagels, and they have bigger holes. In flavor and texture, they are about halfway between bagels and the pretzels available in New York. Edouard de Pomiane, writing in 1929, called bagels, "A kind of zwieback, similar to German pretzels," and old photos of Jewish scenes in Poland show bagels as having very large holes. *Obwarzanki* and bagels are descendants of a common ancestor, but in a country that attaches Jewishness to some unlikely products, there seems to be no consciousness that *obwarzanki* are a Jewish food. Challah, the festive, egg-enriched braided Sabbath bread of Ashkenazic Jews is also sold in all of Cracow's bakeries, especially on Fridays. It is indistinguishable from challah anywhere else.

Kosher vodkas, beers, and water are a source of amazement, hilarity, delight, confusion, and offense to Jewish visitors in Poland. It is surprising to find matzoh and gefilte fish in Polish cuisine, but they are, after all, analogues of real dishes in Galician Jewish cuisine—foods that are actu-

Challah for sale in a Cracow bakery.

ally eaten. Beer, vodka, and water sold in Poland as kosher have no parallel in Jewish Europe, North America, or Israel. Kosher certification is put
on certain prepared foods to indicate that they were supervised at all stages
of manufacture. Foods that are likely to come into contact with nonkosher substances, such as baked goods, require kosher certification (it should
be noted that neither brand of Polish matzoh is kosher), but certain products—and vodka, beer, and water are among these—do not need to be
certified kosher even for the very strictest consumer. Why then the kosher alcohol?

A combination of factors are at work here. The virtues of the two
kosher matzohs, purity and orientalism, both apply. There is a complex of
popular beliefs afloat in Poland that one cannot get a hangover from drinking kosher vodka, and that kosher beer and water are uniquely clean and
healthy (Jutkiewicz and Wrzesiński, 1997: 8–9). If these stories were ever
believed, they must have collapsed under their own weight by now, although the appeal of medical lore does tend to linger. The labels of the
thirty or so brands of kosher vodka reveal a wide spectrum of Polish attitudes toward Jews. There are vodka labels that show alluring and attrac-

Cymes vodka.

tive Jewess stereotypes, such as Rachela brand, which shows the dark-eyed Rachela raising her right hand in a beckoning gesture, her shimmering auburn hair backlit in the glow of a Chanukah menorah. Rachela is the name of the most famous Jewish female in Polish letters, the dynamic and poetic innkeeper's daughter in Stalislaw Wyspiański's 1901 drama *Wesele*. There are vodkas that show images of behatted, bearded older Jewish male stereotypes that may be grotesque, as in the case of Cymes brand vodka, or sympathetic, as in the case of Tevye brand vodka or Jankiel brand vodka, whose label shows the figure of Jankiel the Innkeeper standing beside a hammered dulcimer, lifting a glass of vodka. The images of Jewish men and women fit in with the long-standing orientalist conception of the irresistibly tempting but forbidden Jewess paired (usually in a father-daughter team) with the repellent, sexually rapacious Jewish male. Shylock and Jessica, or Isaac and Rebecca are examples from the English tradition. The labels of some kosher vodkas have abstract designs based on a Star of David motif or a menorah motif, and some kosher vodkas, such as Excite vodka, do not have any recognizably Jewish iconography on the label.

The Jews of Poland, and of the entire pale of the former Soviet empire, have long been associated with the distilling and distributing of vodka, this being one of the few professions in which they were permitted to engage unmolested. The Jews have been gone for many years, but their association with alcohol remains. Several temperance posters show small demons urging drunkards to drink. The demons are all similar to recognizably Jewish male stereotypes. Poland's infamous Cardinal Glemp, after retracting some of his more egregious anti-Semitic statements, popped up again to state that it was Jews who were responsible for the scourge of alcoholism in Poland because of their prewar role in the distilling business (Levine 1991). Into this fray stepped the Polish Jewish distiller Zygmunt Nissenbaum with his own line of Nisskosher kosher vodkas. Nisskosher's presence in the kosher vodka market brings the issue full circle. Nissenbaum did not invent the concept of Jewish vodka; he merely co-opted it. Now a Jewish distiller, borrowing the putatively Jewish display tropes of non-Jewish marketers, whose own images are based on the vanished Jews of Poland, is selling vodka in an almost entirely non-Jewish country, and bottles of this vodka are taken home as souvenirs by Jewish tourists, amused as much by the name, which sounds very much like "Nisht kosher" or "not kosher" in Yiddish, as by the funny pictures on the labels.

Many Jewish and non-Jewish cooks see sweetened gefilte fish as being the Jewish food par excellence. In the public imagination of both Americans and Poles, it is frequently gefilte fish—particularly sweetened gefilte fish—that has outdistanced matzoh as the food that first comes to mind when Jewish food is discussed (Cooper 1993; de Pomiane 1985). Gefilte fish is sometimes referred to as *karp po żydowsku* or "Jewish carp," but *karp po żydowsku* can also be the name of another Polish-Jewish dish made with slices of sweetened poached carp. The *Larousse gastronomique* records this recipe and its variations as *carpe à la juive*. *Larousse* also provides a version of sweetened gefilte fish, confusingly identified as *carpe à la polonaise* (Montagné 1961:215). Many restaurants in Cracow and Warsaw that are in no other way marked as Jewish offer *karp po żydowsku* as either an appetizer or a main course. Stranger still, *karp po żydowsku* has become a traditional dish in many Catholic Polish homes for Christmas Eve and Holy Saturday, traditionally meatless feasts. Herring roe with cinnamon, another Jewish recipe, has become associated with Saint Virgil's Day. In the case of *karp po żydowsku*, gefilte fish, and spiced herring roe, it is the fondly remembered flavors of the dishes rather than any religious or cultural currency that keep them in the Polish cuisine.

Jewish cooking has also entered Polish homes through a handful of new and popular cookbooks. The handsomely produced forty-seven-volume series *Encyklopedia sztuki kulinarnej* (Encyclopedia of Culinary Arts) includes a volume on Jewish cooking, *Kuchnia Żydowska* (Rozycka 1995). Each of the forty-two recipes, including *Kneidlech* and *Zloty joich* (chicken soup) accompanies a photograph of the finished dish. Many of the photographs include lighted candles, which evoke Sabbath or Chanukah candles and give a hint of exoticism to the traditional Jewish dishes not particularly exotic in their styling.

Koszerne i trefne kuchnia Izraelska (Dobrowolska n.d.) is part of a series on national cuisines, *Kuchnie Roznych Narodow*. It includes Israeli recipes, tips on shopping for Israeli ingredients, and brief sketches of Israel's major cities and tourist attractions to guide Polish tourists to Israel. For a readership interested in all things kosher, this is the only Jewish cookbook published in Poland that specifically offers *treyf*, or nonkosher recipes as well.

Israeli cuisine constitutes a major part of *Kuchnia Żydowska i Izraelska* (Pospieszyńskiej 1993, Figure 4-2). The introduction discusses food in the Bible and the ritual calendar, and the kosher dietary laws. Two sections of recipes, one "Jewish" and one "Israeli," form the rest of the book. The Jewish section has recipes of Eastern European and particularly Polish provenance, including *Ryba (karp) po żydowsku* and gefilte fish. The Israeli section also offers Eastern European recipes, as well as other Ashkenazic and Sephardic recipes and many dishes from the Yemenite tradition, including *"Hawayij,"* a pepper and spice mixture, and *"Gulasz z Penisa,"* a stew made with ram or bull penis (112). The resourceful cookery of the Jews in Yemen, where kosher meat was scarce and expensive, made use of penis and udder meat (Kirshenblatt-Gimblett 1987:49).

Most remarkable is *Kuchnia Koszerna*, a facsimile of the 1904 Polish translation of Rebekka Wolf's 1875 *Kochbuch für Israelitische Frauen kosher* cookbook published in Warsaw by Jakoba Klepfisza (Wolf 1995). Facsimiles of old cookbooks are a very sophisticated approach to culinary history.

Eugeniusz Wirkowski's book *Cooking the Polish Jewish Way* (1984), available in English, Polish, and German, makes the case that it is Jewish cooking, especially Galician cooking, that has influenced European cuisine and not the other way around. His reason for approaching the subject at all is that it is not enough merely to cook, but that one must develop a grand theory of gastronomy in the manner of his hero, Brillat-Savarin. A recipe for chopped herring calls for lots of onions, breadcrumbs soaked in vinegar, sugar, black pepper, and dry white wine.

Jewish and Israeli cooking. The caption reads: "How just is God? He gives food to the rich and appetite to the poor."

It is the memory and re-creation of such unremarkable things as a herring with onions that put together a history of a people and a place. Pierre Nora writes that our taste for everyday life in the past "[is] a resort to restoring the flavor of things" (1989:17). Because of the Jewish practice of constantly reenacting rituals, Nora calls Jews "the people of memory." Poles are a people of memory as well, and the Polish fascination with the flavors of things Jewish and with their exotic or health-giving properties is part of a complex system of beliefs that do not fit into such simple categories as anti-Semitism or philosemitism (Sandauer 1982). Both visitors who ache to taste the flavors of their past and natives who want to cobble together a possible Jewish future are haunted by the enormity of the loss suffered in Poland. Barbara Kirshenblatt-Gimblett has noted that the production of heritage, including tourism, restores life to those who have suffered a metaphorical death (1995). In the case of culinary tourism in Poland, it is not metaphorical death, but the real thing, from which visitors and natives alike hope to recover traces and tastes of memory.

Works Cited

I did fieldwork for this essay in 1995, 1996, and 1997, and the rapid change I noted in those years has continued. The lawsuit between the two Ariels has been resolved in favor of the restaurant I call Ariel I. The restaurant I call Ariel II is now Hotel Aleph. Restauracja na Kazimierzu has lost its kosher certification.

I am grateful to Jolanta Ambrosewicz-Jacobs, Andrew Ingall, Monika Krajewska, Lucy Long, and Chana Pollack for their thoughtful and helpful comments, and to Barbara Kirshenblatt-Gimblett for her continuing heroic support of my work.

Cooper, John. 1993. *Eat and Be Satisfied: A Social History of Jewish Food*. London: Aronson.

de Pomiane, Edouard. [1929] 1985. *The Jews of Poland: Recollections and Recipes*. Trans. Josephine Bacon. Garden Grove, Calif.: Philiota Press.

Dobrowolska, Irena. n.d. *Koszerne i trefne kuchnia Izraelska*. Warsaw, Poland: Watra.

Fussell, Paul. 1988. "Travel, Tourism and 'International Understanding.'" In *Thank God for the Atom Bomb*. New York: Summit Books.

Jutkiewicz, Katarzyna and Pawel Wrzesiński. 1997. *Przejadło się?* [Clearing things up?] *Madrasz* 6, no. 6 (October): 8–10. Special issue Polska Koszerna [Kosher Poland].

Kaufman, Michael T. 1985. "After 20 Years, Cracow Marks a Bar Mitzvah." *New York Times*, September 8, section A1.

Kirshenblatt-Gimblett, Barbara. 1987. "Udder and Other Extremities: Recipes from the Jews of Yemen." *Petits propos culinaires* 27 (October): 49–50.

———. 1995. "Theorizing Heritage." *Ethnomusicology* 39(3): 367–80.

Levine, Hillel. 1991. "Cardinal Glemp's Slanted History." *New York Times,* October 5.

Montagné, Prosper. [1938] 1961. *Larousse gastronomique: Encyclopedia of Food, Wine and Cookery.* Trans. Nina Froud, Patience Gray, Maud Murdoch, and Barbara Macrae Taylor. New York: Crown.

Nathan, Joan. 1992. "Jewish Food Traditions Linger in a Poland Bereft of Jews." *New York Times,* September 23: C3.

Nissenbaum Foundation. 1988. *Preserving Traces of Jewish Culture in Poland for the Living and the Dead.* Warsaw, Poland: Krakowa agencja Wydawnicza.

Nora, Pierre. 1989. "Between Memory and History: *Les lieux de memoire.*" *Representations* 26 (spring): 7–19.

Pospieszynskiej, Katarzyny. 1993. *Kuchnia Zydowska i Izraelska.* Warsaw, Poland: Gross.

Roth, Cecil. [1958] 1989. *A History of the Jews.* New York: Schocken.

Rozycka, Maria. 1995. *Kuchnia Zydowska. Encyklopedia sztuki kulinarnej,* vol. 11. Warsaw, Poland: Tenten.

Sandauer, Artur. 1982. *O sytuacji pisarza polskiego pochodzenia zydowskiego w XX wieky.* Warsaw: Czytelnik.

Steinlauf, Michael. 1997. *Bondage to the Dead: Poland and the Memory of the Holocaust.* Syracuse: SUNY Press.

Wirkowski, Eugeniusz. 1984. *Cooking the Jewish Way.* Warsaw, Poland: Interpress.

———. 1988. *Cooking the Polish Jewish Way.* Warsaw, Poland: Interpress.

Wolf, Rebekka. [1904] 1995. *Kuchnia Koszerna.* Warsaw, Poland: Tenten.

CHAPTER 5

Incorporating the Local Tourist at the Big Island Poke Festival

Kristin McAndrews

Sunny weather, white sand beaches, warm blue seas, friendly local people, and visions of paradise (Lofgren 1999:216) have typically attracted tourists to Hawai'i—not the local haute cuisine. Restaurant fare has changed for the better in the past fifteen years due to the creativity and marketing efforts of many of Hawai'i's top chefs who have brought ethnic diversity and cultural traditions into their recipes. But even the best chefs have difficulty incorporating some popular local foods into mainstream tourist food culture. For example, consider the luau. While fire twirlers, hula dancers, and Hawaiian musicians entertain, visitors can experience the cultural performance of a luau, which often includes an extensive buffet including teriyaki chicken and/or beef, rice, macaroni salad, Jell-O, and many other typical buffet dishes. But when local delicacies such as *poi* (fermented taro root) or *poke* (PO-kay; a dish of raw fish, seaweed, oil, and salt) are served, these dishes often go untested or are immediately rejected due to the unique textures and flavors. Through the efforts of Hawai'i's chefs and Aloha Festivals (a six-week celebration of folklife in Hawai'i), not only mainland tourists, but also the local residents have begun to discover the culinary delights of various ethnic groups living in Hawai'i.

Hawai'i's Regional Cuisine chefs have creatively utilized Hawai'i's fish, merging local tastes with nouvelle cuisine. Fish is a staple in Hawai'i. In fact, across ethnic groups we "eat twice as much fish [per person] as mainland Americans" (Apple 2001). Hawai'i's chefs have managed to transform a tired upscale restaurant cuisine based on imported products and replaced it with a cuisine centered on goods grown in Hawai'i but combined in unexpected ways, so "now visitors praise the cuisine and locals who flock to the restaurants, proud of what the Islands have produced" (Lauden 1996:8). The chefs have also impacted regional cuisine from fish markets to restaurants, from grocery stores to home.

Aloha Festivals honor Hawaiian and local folk culture by focusing on crafts or foods specific to Hawai'i's diverse ethnic culture. The island-wide, three-hundred-event festival celebrates Hawaiian heritage and local traditions and attracts both mainland tourists and local people throughout the state. It is the only statewide festival in the United States and lasts for six weeks (Choy 1999:viii). The loss of cultural and ethnic traditions is a concern of many people who live in Hawai'i (Masuoka 1999:A-1). Michael Largey points out "tradition is formed in the present from evidence, perceptions, and impressions of the past. Tradition also uses images that imbue history with power, bringing the past into a relationship with the present" (2000:241). Aloha Festivals mediate the traditional cultural practice of the native people, the Hawaiians, with the local others, or other ethnic and cultural groups established in Hawai'i.

The Poke Festival, a part of Aloha Festivals, held on the Big Island of Hawai'i in mid-September, is an annual celebration of *poke*. As part of the festivities, the festival holds a *poke* contest with up to ninety contestants. Presentations include creative visual displays that incorporate simple or complex *poke* recipes. Local and national politics, local traditions, and ethnic pride are reflected in the displays, which are often presented in a humorous manner. Ingredients in the *poke* recipes are also used as humorous devices.

In this essay I will focus on the use of language and art in relationship to shifting positions of the teller (local) and the audience (local other), especially as it relates to humor. This essay will concentrate on the local tourist who travels within Hawai'i to sample the variations of the cultural and ethnic other.

I tasted my first *poke* dish of raw fish, seaweed, *kukui* nut, and salt twenty-five years ago at a Hawaiian first birthday luau in Hana, Maui. I had been a visitor on Maui for one week. The host led me to a huge buffet table spread with many foods I had never seen before. He scooped a rather substantial amount of *poke* on my plate along with a small, raw blue crab and a couple of raw marinated *opihi* (limpets) and handed me some chopsticks. Thankfully, I was adept at chopsticks, but I had never eaten raw fish before. The fishy, seaweedy flavors and the crunchy but soft texture of the *poke* shocked me. Further, I was stunned to find that I was supposed to eat the entire raw crab, shell and all. As the Hawaiian host stood by, I ate politely, trying to minimize my facial expressions at the new tastes. As soon as the host walked away, I flipped my boyfriend the *opihi*.

Poke is a "popular" food tradition rather than a practice based in traditions of old Hawai'i. The Hawaiian dictionary defines *poke*, "to slice, cut crosswise into pieces, as fish or wood; to press out as the meat of an *opihi* shell; section, slice, piece" (Pukui 1965:311). In other words, *poke* does not refer to the fish dish itself. In her extensive study of Hawaiian cuisine, Rachel Lauden notes that in accounts of Hawaiian uses of fish and the first ethnic cookbooks, there is no mention of *poke* as a fish dish (1996:147). Nor does the Hawaiian dictionary or the major glossary of pidgin have references to *poke* as a fish dish. The Hawaiian liking for raw food is also absent from many anthropological accounts of the Hawaiian people. One account claims that ancient Hawaiian people rarely ate raw fish or meat, and when they did it was only out of necessity. John Wise says, "They [the native Hawaiians] always dried it or preserved it in some way before eating it" (1965:98). Yet, at traditional native Hawaiian luaus numerous raw foods are presented, from limpets, fish, and crab to marinated pig's liver. Sometime during the early 1970s, *poke* became an appetizer to have with beer after work or to bring to a party. It has only been since the mid-1970s that recipes have been recorded. When I interviewed Hari Kojima, a cooking show host (*Hari's Kitchen*), he claimed responsibility for *poke*'s increasing cross-cultural popularity during the past twenty-five years (phone interview, 1998). In 1999, Sam Choy (Hawaiian Regional Cuisine chef) published *Sam Choy's Poke: Hawaiian Soul Food*. The collection represents winning *poke* recipes from the *poke* contest at the Poke Festival. In today's culinary market, *poke* is loosely translated to mean a Hawaiian marinated dish of raw, seared, or cooked seafood (and sometimes tofu). In other words, *poke* is a relative newcomer to the local culinary market.

As reflected in Sam Choy's cookbook title, *poke* is sometimes referred to as Hawai'i's "soul food." One can make it at home, buy it in a fish market or grocery store, and order it in local eateries from Hawaiian Regional Cuisine restaurants to the local fast-food place. Actually, while it is a local acquired taste, *poke*'s popularity is spreading slowly to the mainland. Recently, I found mahi-mahi *poke* on the menu of a popular seafood restaurant in Seattle, Washington. Sam Choy travels around the United States to many food festivals sharing *poke* recipes (Choy 2001). He might argue that the mahi-mahi, a soft white fish, should be used for ceviche-like recipes rather than for *poke*. A firm "red" fish like raw tuna (*ahi* or *aku*) makes a delicious *poke*.

While there are hundreds of variations of the dish, traditional *poke* and *shoyu poke* are the most popular. Traditional poke is typically made of raw *ahi* (tuna), *limu ali'i* or *limu kohu* (seaweed), *'alaea* (large grained salt) and roasted *inamona* (ground *kukui* nut). Traditional *poke* is often available in fish markets rather than in grocery stores, in part because the indigenous seaweeds and *kukui* nuts are considered specialty items—difficult to get, thus expensive. The most popular style of *poke* is *shoyu poke*, which is often made with raw *ahi*, Hawaiian salt, sesame oil, *ogo* (aqua-cultured seaweed), chili pepper, *shoyu* (soy sauce), and chopped white and green onions. At fish markets and grocery stores, *poke* is usually served in a plastic container or a paper bowl and eaten with chopsticks. Alan Young, a second-generation owner of Young's Fish Market, told me that many people buy a bowl of rice or *poi* (fermented taro root) with a dish of *poke*, which makes a complete meal (1999). At upscale restaurants, the *poke* presentation is more complex, such as Alan Wong's (Hawaiian Regional Cuisine chef) "*poke* pines." Chopped *poke* is covered with thin noodle dough shaped to look like a pineapple. They are quickly deep-fried and served on a plate decorated with a wasabi-soy melange, some chopped pink ginger, and thinly grated white horseradish (Ariel 1999). Chopsticks or forks are offered as implements for this dish. *Poke* can be eaten any time, but typically it is served as a snack, lunch, or an appetizer. With *poke*'s rising popularity, it is no wonder that the Poke Festival was created to celebrate this "traditional" dish.

The Poke Festival represents a complex tourist dynamic. While *poke* is becoming increasingly popular in the continental United States, the Poke Festival draws primarily upon local tourists (Zanini 1999). The local tourist has an appreciation for the diverse recipes, which reflect Hawai'i's ethnic mix. Local tourists share aims and fantasies similar to those of mainland tourists, such as to "escape from a perceived mundane environment, exploration and evaluation of self, relaxation, prestige, regression, enhancement of kinship relationships and facilitation of social interaction" (Lofgren 1999:267). The Poke Festival tourist experience is not as simple as the relationship between the mainland tourist and the other, who live in a tropical domain. Like mainland tourists, the local tourist has to travel to the Big Island by plane or boat in order to participate in the Poke Festival. And because of the remote location of the Hapuna Beach Hotel, where the festival is now held (north of Kona, Hawai'i), many people who live on the Big Island have to travel long distances by car in order to attend. Because of the nature of *poke* as a fish dish in progress, the local tourist and the local ethnic or cultural other are the primary audiences for the festival.

In some ways, the Poke Festival reflects MacCannell's vision of the "authentic" or what the mainland tourist cannot hope to find on the "back stage" (1976:106). The local tourist tries to find the "authentic" poke, which is on the "back stage" of each ethnic group consciously and unconsciously represented in the contest.

In Hawai'i, the diverse ethnic mix constitutes a community of others whose number one economic industry is to cater to the visiting other or the tourist. In Hawai'i, otherness is an everyday fact of life. Even the native people, the Hawaiians, have been perceived as the other through colonization, the confiscation of indigenous lands, and the fragmentation of native culture. For two hundred years, a parade of cultures has merged in this community. Sometimes ethnic difference and cultural distinctions have created conflict, but one site where the local others meet is through the appreciation for a rich culinary diversity.

The culinary blending of the other and the local reflects Hawai'i's unique culture. What defines a "local" in Hawai'i is an interesting question. And who is the other? After having lived here for twenty-five years, I still do not consider myself local. I am a Caucasian (*haole*) woman, married to a Caucasian man, who has kept herself immersed in a university environment. But we live in a community of local others or colonizers—Caucasian, Japanese, Chinese, Filipino, Vietnamese, Thai, and Pacific Islanders—either coming to Hawai'i by choice or by historical exploitation. To some factions of the Hawaiian sovereignty movement, the local others are the colonizers who should leave the islands. Obviously, there are cultural strains in our community—subtle and not so subtle. One of the ways in which these struggles are mediated is through food. And until recently, this mingling of culinary diversity, especially with raw fish dishes, did not necessarily extend to the mainland other.

In 1991, the first Poke Contest was held in Waimea on the Big Island of Hawai'i in an old army tent on the fairgrounds. The contest moved to the Waimea Community Center for the second and third year. In 1994, Sam Choy "sold" the *poke* contest to the Hapuna Beach Hotel, a luxury resort, which took over sponsorship and expanded the contest to a festival. In 1999, the festival was so popular that on the day of the contest, there was standing room only in the ballroom at the hotel. Mrs. Glorianna Akau, a coordinator of Aloha Festivals, believes that the Poke Festival shares culture in a positive manner, particularly because it is a cross-cultural, cross-class event. She stated, "Not only does the Poke Festival celebrate Hawaiian culture, fish, and essential foods, but it acknowledges the substantial contributions made from other cultures living in Hawaii" (1999).

Like many public events in Hawai'i, the Poke Festival opens with a ceremonial Hawaiian chant and blessing. The blessing takes place on the golf course preceding a charity golf tournament where local people pay to play with local celebrities. This event has grown in popularity from 60 golfers last year to more than 120 in 1999. The proceeds of this tournament go to a shelter for homeless teens on the Big Island and to a Catholic charity. In the evening there is a celebrity auction and a concert of Hawaiian music. Along with traditional Hawaiian dancing and music, the feast or *poke* contest takes place on Sunday afternoon. In 1999, approximately 1,100 people attended the *poke* tasting, jamming the auditorium.

The Poke Festival commemorates this unique dish not only with various recipes whose ingredients often reflect ethnicity, but also with visual displays that mirror Hawai'i's unique multicultural community. The displays often use visual humor and word play, which speak of our local community, national politics, economics, cultural identity, and tourism. The cultural symbols articulated in the *poke* displays are visualized, and then ritually consumed, thus assimilating the local and the local other.

In 1999, sixty contestants competed in three categories: nonprofessional, professional, and celebrity divisions. Contestants are allowed three square feet of table space to display their *poke* dish. While displays may be as elaborate as the contestant desires, except for the celebrity division, the *poke* judging is based on taste. Twenty-seven judges (including Sam Choy) are selected from the community, representing a variety of community and business concerns—from the mayor of Kona to a dive shop owner. Awards include cash up to $2,500 for the top winner, gift certificates, merchandise, golf packages, and weekends at the Hapuna Beach Hotel. For the contest, there are nine categories for both professional and nonprofessional divisions: best cooked *poke*, hot sauce *poke*, *ogo poke*, *surimi poke*, *hokkigai poke*, macadamia nut *poke*, soy sauce *poke*, tofu *poke*, and lastly, traditional *poke*. Contestants competed for "best tasting *poke*" as well as "best visual display."

As I walked through the *poke* contest exhibits during the judging phase, I was struck by the creativity of the displays and the ingredients. Sometimes the *poke* dishes were so decorative they resembled dessert. Because *poke* is such a flexible dish, it can incorporate many textures and flavors. For the first time in 1999, a dish was entered that did not contain fish or tofu. Interestingly, the dish seemed to have fish in it, because something the color and texture of *ahi* was present. The chef (in the professional division) made reddish-brown gelatin cut to resemble bite-sized chunks of fish. The dish was full of local fruit and nuts such as pineapple, coconut, bananas, and macadamia nuts. I heard several judges commenting on the tastiness of this dish, surprised that raw fish went so well with such an abundance of fruit. It wasn't until later that someone told me that the "fish" was actually gelatin. As it happened, this *poke* dish was one of Sam Choy's favorites. But was it *poke*? Choy commented, "What's important is that it is a labor of love. People tell me how they got their ingredients and what they do. For me, personally that's the bang of the event" (Clark 1999:D4). Not all judges were impressed with the artistry or the combination of ingredients. Noana Kaiwi said, "[I]f you go back to the old days, poke had to do with the sea: raw fish with ocean water was poke. All this new stuff takes away from the Hawaiianness" (Clark 1999:D1). Even Choy expressed a fondness for a simple *poke* dish. He said, "the good ones are the simple ones" (Clark 1999:D4).

Kaiwi questions the authenticity of variations of the *poke* dish. And usually, a simple, "authentic" *poke* of raw fish, ogo, soy sauce, and salt wins. "Hawaiianness," or the cultural and biological connection to the state of being a native Hawaiian, has become a controversial issue in Hawai'i. As indicated, one is not necessarily "Hawaiian" because he lives in Hawai'i. To be Hawaiian, one usually has to have a certain blood quantum or to have been adopted (*hanai*) into a Hawaiian family. While politically marginalized, until recently native Hawaiians had the right to vote for their own representatives in the Office of Hawaiian Affairs (OHA), which was created to maintain checks and balances between the state of Hawai'i, the federal government, and native Hawaiians. But this exclusive right was dissolved by the U.S. Supreme Court last year as discriminatory toward other ethnic groups living in Hawai'i. A new board of trustees was elected that represented a more diverse ethnic mix. OHA's dissembling was very controversial and to some native Hawaiian activists represented just another blow in their fight for cultural recognition and the return of native lands. In some ways the variations of *poke* "mask" the original, or rather they assume a type of "tourist mask" that can often become a grotesque version of authenticity, a prop for a role "designed to accommodate" a tourist audience (Nunez 1989:207–16). Paradoxically, while individuals have strong opinions about what constitutes authentic, traditional Hawaiian culture, *poke* refers only to the type of cut that is made on the fish or tofu—not to the dish itself. *Poke* is actually very representative of our multicultural community.

As we know, food is a system of communication and signifies the culture of those who consume it. In Hawai'i and Asia, raw fish is popular, but as Judith Goode points out: "Many societies do use such aspects of their culinary systems to distinguish between insiders and outsiders and between the good and pure versus the defiling, polluting and dangerous. Thus relationships between social actors and groups as well as those between groups and the forces that govern existence are controlled by rules for food use that define inclusion and encourage discipline, solidarity, and the maintenance of social boundaries" (1992:234). This aspect of insider and outsider, or *poke* artist (local) and audience (local other), is apparent at the Poke Festival.

Hawai'i's tourism industry is a primary economic resource. But like most communities that depend on tourism, the local population is often resentful of the outsiders who consume the natural resources. Local tourists or those who live in Hawai'i were the primary audience at the Poke Festival, while mainland or foreign visitors were not. With an insider's view, the visual displays and recipes become richer; but while outsiders could probably appreciate the complexity and beauty of some of the displays, they are often exempt from a deeper conceptualization of the displays' meaning. Outsiders or mainland tourists wouldn't be able to recognize the multicultural code. Joan Radner calls coding "the expression or transmission of messages potentially accessible to a community under the very eyes of a dominant community for whom these same messages are either inaccessible or inadmissible" (1993:3). While I am excluded from many aspects of the multicultural dimensions of Hawai'i's local culture, I do claim some knowledge of the cultural symbols and stereotypes that predominate in my community. I have some frame of reference for Hawai'i's local multicultural code.

Symbols of Hawaiian culture and elements of exploitation of the environment were very popular at the 1999 Poke Festival. I heard one chef observe that the *poke* presentations seemed to be Hawaiian-themed with earth tones; they were not glitzy like in previous years. For example, in one exhibit, the chef utilized elements of nature in Hawai'i creating a black lava tower approximately twenty inches high, covered with indigenous plants. On the top of the two foot tall tower was a large nest constructed of shredded deep-fried taro noodles. In the nest was a recipe for traditional *poke*. Perched on the edge of the lava tower near the nest was a stuffed *a'ala*, or indigenous Hawaiian crow (an endangered species). Smaller bite-sized taro nests filled with *poke* surrounded the base of the display. Utilizing the *a'ala* and native plants (which are disappearing at an alarming rate in Hawai'i) symbolized the disappearance of Hawai'i's natural environment. Another *poke* display reflected Hawai'i's whaling past. Large pink prawns dangled, tails down, from the side of a foot-long model of a dark brown whaling ship. In the cavity of the ship was a shrimp *poke*. Hawai'i has indigenous freshwater prawns, but these particular shrimp were imports. Whaling, an economic force in Hawai'i in the nineteenth century, led to a declining whale population in this region of the Pacific. Hawai'i now has strict laws protecting whales. A couple of the exhibits focused on Hawaiian popular culture with *shoyu poke* set in *Koa* (an indigenous hardwood) bowls on beds of white or black sand, decorated with white or pink coral and chunks of lava. One of these exhibits had a ukulele standing in one corner.

So what's so funny about the Poke Festival? The interplay between the local and the local other are particularly apparent in the humor expressed in the visual displays at the Poke Contest. But to be able to understand the humorous vision requires a familiarity with a cultural code. Nancy Walker states "humor is a shared activity, a means of communication" (1988:23). But that humor is not always available to an outsider audience. Humor provides "an index to the values and the taboos of the group, and the humor can be so intimately tied to group identity as to be almost unintelligible to anyone outside the group" (Walker 1988:105–06). Henri Bergson calls humor "topsyturvydom" so characteristic of comedy and whose definition might be extended to other forms of humorous discourse as well (1956:118). Mary Douglas argues that joking "consists of a victorious tilting of uncontrol against control, it is an image of leveling of hierarchy, the triumph of intimacy over formality, of unofficial values over official ones" (1975:98).

In the celebrity division, two displays entitled "Taco Poke" and "Poke Pig" dealt humorously with controversies surrounding a couple of Hawai'i's environmental issues. The "Taco Poke" is a play on words and represents environmental concerns and economic necessity. The celebrity *poke* artist combined *ahi* (tuna), tomatoes, onions, Chinese parsley, and jalapeno, stuffing the *poke* into taco shells. Hot sauce and other condiments were present to the side of the dish. *Tako* is the Japanese word for octopus or squid. *Tako poke* happens to be very popular in Hawai'i. According to one fish wholesaler, because of demand most *tako* is imported from Southeast Asia, particularly Thailand. In Hawai'i, *he'e*, the Hawaiian word for octopus is another food source that has become more difficult to find with increasing development, pollution, and the destruction of the reefs. The celebrity artist of "Taco Poke" advised the audience not to try his *poke*, as the raw *tako* and the taco shell did not taste good together.

The "Poke Pig" presentation obviously plays off the image of Porky Pig, that sweet, roundish, pink, stuttering cartoon character. In this display, the *poke* artist pasted a picture of herself carrying a huge, hairy (obviously dead) boar on her back. Inspired by the contest, she hunted and killed a boar and made sausage out of some of it. In the center of her display was homemade Portuguese sausage (another popular local food) surrounded by *shoyu poke*. In Hawai'i, pig hunting is a dangerous quest predominately pursued by men. Each year hunters and hikers are seriously hurt when gored by wild pigs. While traditional local culture values pig hunting, environmentalists blame the wild pigs for the destruction of indigenous plants and want the pigs eradicated from especially vulnerable areas. "Poke Pig" represents mediation between the land and sea.

Local Asian culture was represented with "Thai Poke," "Korean Poke," "Japanese Shrimp Poke," and a "Pake (PA-kay) Poke." The "Pake Poke" display incorporated stereotypical images of local Chinese culture such as a rice steamer, a fan, and Chinese coins. *Pake* (Hawaiian Pidgin) not only refers to Chinese ethnicity, but also connotes the quality of being cheap. In the local community, "You so, *pake*" is usually said in a joking manner when someone doesn't want to pay for something. In this display, the *poke* artist not only takes the symbols of his culture seriously, but makes fun of the *Pake* stereotype as well. This particular display would not necessarily be humorous to an outsider—the mainland tourist. The display was created for the local insiders, who are the audience. Judges chuckled at the connotation of the visual display, as they tasted the "Pake Poke."

Two "Poke-Mon Poke" exhibits specifically used images of popular culture and utilized word play. Pokemon cards surrounded both dishes of *poke* as well as other types of Pokemon paraphernalia. In Hawai'i as well as in other parts of the United States, Pokemon is a popular card game fad among elementary school children. The game was originally marketed in Japan and focuses around a boy, Ash, who tries to catch creatures called Pokemon, who constantly transform. His fantasy is to become the Pokemon master. Matthew Katase, the only child allowed in for the judges' tasting, was impressed with the great collector cards on the display, asking me if he were allowed to take some. He was not impressed with the recipe for the "Poke-mon Poke," screwing up his face as he ate it (1999).

Alan Dundes claims, "[N]o piece of folklore continues to be transmitted unless it means something—even if neither the speaker nor the audience can articulate what that meaning might be. In fact, it usually is essential that the joke's meaning not be crystal clear" (1987:vii). While I do not claim to have a thorough understanding of all the joking relationships going on at the *poke* contest, as a twenty-five-year resident, I can claim some sense of the stereotypes that are played with and the local and national issues that are mocked.

For example, in the 1998 *poke* contest, Kim Gennaula, a local television newscaster, won the celebrity division utilizing word play and themes from national politics. Her display used performance as well as a stationary visual. In the center of her display site sat a large cake adorned with President Bill Clinton's face and a huge cigar. Ms. Gennaula stood next to the display dressed as and impersonating Monica Lewinsky as she held a bowl of *shoyu poke*. She wore a nametag bearing the words "Presidential Poke."

At the 1999 Poke Contest, Ms. Gennaula made fun of a local political event that had torn our community apart. Again she utilized both the visual display and performance as part of the presentation. Her display was named "Loke Poke Left Us Broke" (LO-kay PO-kay left us BRO-kay). She was making fun of Lokelani Lindsey, a former trustee of Bishop Estate and Kamehameha Schools. Kamehameha School is a wealthy private school for children of Hawaiian ancestry. Former trustees of the estate managed substantial assets from the Bernice Pau`ahi Bishop Trust. In 1997, critics claimed that Bishop Estate trustees were mismanaging substantial funds and imposing themselves on curricular matters at the school. Upon investigation by the state and the Internal Revenue Service (IRS), widespread corruption was discovered. Eventually, the IRS threatened the school with the loss of their tax-exempt status if the trustees didn't step down. All the trustees were forced out of their jobs, and new trustees were appointed. The scandal was so vicious, the attorney general, Margery Bronster, who pushed the investigation of the trustees, failed to receive renewal support from the state legislature and was ousted.

In our community, this scandal was emotionally charged. Where many indigenous people live in poverty and have not received the benefit from the educational mandate of the Bishop estate, the idea that trustees were mismanaging funds and paying themselves exorbitant amounts of money was perceived as disgraceful. In addition, in a state stuck in a kind of economic despair for the past ten years, the millions of dollars spent to prosecute these trustees was an additional outrage. Mrs. Lindsey seemed particularly intent on keeping her job despite severe criticism in the media. In press appearances and in court, she was displayed as defensive and unreasonable, justifying her methods of intimidation and calling people testifying against her liars.

At the *poke* contest, on the back of Ms. Gennaula's visual display was a photo of the five trustees along with a headline of the scandal. In addition, a cutout photo of Mrs. Lindsey was pasted with her figure upside down, as if she were going to take a backward dive into a large bowl full of *poke*. Fake paper money surrounded the bowl. Ms. Gennaula played Lokelani Lindsey on stage, complete with a thick graying wig and a large dowdy dress. In her performance she explained why her *shoyu poke* recipe had peanuts as part of the recipe—because that is all that Lokelani Lindsey left the estate and the community with, peanuts. Her impersonation was well received as the crowd howled with delight over her interpretation and *"poke"* at the Bishop Estate scandal. Jokes of this kind function as a socially sanctioned outlet for controversial and emotionally charged subjects.

At the time of the 1999 Poke Festival, the Bishop Estate matter had still not been settled. In fact, after her forced resignation Lokelani Lindsey was brought back to court for money laundering. Gennaula's performance and display reflected many elements of the local other as far as issues of wealth and poverty. As Alan Dundes points out, where there is anxiety, there will be jokes about that anxiety. He argues, "A society with political repression will generate an abundance of political jokes. Indeed, the more repressive the regime, the more numerous the political jokes" (1987:vii). While slightly unappetizing in appearance and texture, the Loke Poke was eaten by participants in the festival. In this way, humor and food function as emotional and physical releases. It is the literal incorporation of food and laughter of the local and the local other that mediates community tension.

Local sports and University of Hawai'i-Manoa politics were reflected in "June Jones Poke." The *poke* artist was commenting on the University of Hawai'i—Manoa football team, the Rainbow Warriors. The *poke* was set in a football-shaped container. In the upper corner of the artist's poster was a very small picture of Fred Von Appen, a Warrior's head coach who was fired after losing fourteen straight games. A significant percentage of Hawai'i's population takes local high school and college football very seriously. There was a general dislike for Von Appen's coaching style and losing streak. The dismissal was messy. Von Appen was first demoted and reassigned to another University of Hawai'i campus. Unhappy with his choices, Von Appen sued and received a settlement. During this process, the university hired June Jones, whose picture was displayed quite prominently on the poster. Jones managed to turn the Warriors around in 1999 and became a local celebrity. The *poke* artist made two kinds of *poke*—one for Von Appen and the other for Jones. Von Appen's *poke* was a combination of all the rotting items that the *poke* artist found in her refrigerator, including an old can of tuna and sardines. She used a food processor to whip the smelly mess together. Fortunately, this *poke* was pushed toward the back of the display so that the judges, and later the general audience, wouldn't taste it. The *poke* for June Jones was a traditional *shoyu poke* with *ahi, shoyu,* and onions, but the artist confessed she had chopped five bulbs of garlic into the dish. She thought the garlic on the breath of the University of Hawai'i—Manoa football players would distract the opponents, resulting in more winning games. Before the artist had a chance to explain her recipe, a couple of the judges who tasted the "June Jones Poke" commented that the dish was hot and hurried over to the bar for a drink. This *poke* and the display won the celebrity division.

The Poke Festival is an eating event that self-consciously makes fun of the local other as well as images of popular culture through punning or outright outrageousness. When I asked Mrs. Akau from Aloha Festivals about the humor of some of the displays, she said, "If you can't laugh with one another then it's a hard job" (1999). In Hawai'i we need to laugh, as our economy has suffered for the past ten years. Our state government has been riddled with scandal, budgets have been cut to the barest of bones, and local institutions once held in high esteem have been reduced to joking matters. After two hours of entertainment, eleven hundred people from a variety of cultural backgrounds grabbed paper bowls and chopsticks and rushed the displays, eager to share the *poke* of the local others. As humor and notions of the other are implicit, the Poke Festival is a site for understanding how a community creates itself and performs its goals and fantasies as well as a place to look at consumption and the local tourist.

Works Cited

Akau, Glorianna. 1999. Personal Interview. Kona, Hawaii.

Apple, R.W. 2001. "Hawaiians and Fish: True Treasures of the Pacific." *New York Times*, January 21.

Ariel, Steven. 1999. Personal Interview.

Bergson, Henri. 1956. "Laughter." In *Comedy*. New York: Doubleday.

Choy, Sam, and Randall Francisco. 1999. *Sam Choy's Poke: Hawai'i's Soul Food*. Honolulu: Mutual.

———. 2001. "Wild About Poke." Lecture. Honolulu, Hawaii.

Clark, Joan. 1999. "New Wave Poke." *Honolulu Advertiser*, September 22. A1.

Douglas, Mary. 1975. *Implicit Meanings: Essays in Anthropology*. London: Routledge & Kegan Paul.

Dundes, Alan. 1987. *Cracking Jokes: Studies of Sick Humor Cycles and Stereotypes*. Berkeley, Calif.: Ten Speed.

Goode, Judith. 1992. Food. *Folklore, Cultural Performance, and Popular Entertainments*. New York: Oxford University Press.

Katase, Matthew. 1999. Personal Interview. Kona, Hawaii.

Kojima, Hari. 1999. Personal Interview. Honolulu, Hawaii.

Largey, Michael. 2000. "Politics on the Pavement: Haitian Rara as a Traditionalizing Process." *Journal of American Folklore* 112 (449): 239–54.

Lauden, Rachel. 1996. *The Food of Paradise: Exploring Hawaii's Culinary Heritage*. Honolulu: University of Hawai'i Press.

Lofgren, Orvar. 1999. *On Holiday: A History of Vacationing*. Berkeley: University of California Press.

MacCannell, Dean. 1976. *The Tourist: A New Theory of the Leisure Class*. New York: Shocken.

Masuoka, Brandon. 1999. "Some Fear Erosion of Local Traditions." *Honolulu Advertiser*, April 26. A1.

Nunez, Theron. 1989. "Touristic Studies in Anthropological Perspective." In *Hosts and Guests: The Anthropology of Tourism, 2nd ed*. Ed. Valene L. Smith. Philadelphia: University of Pennsylvania Press.

Pukui, Mary Kawena, and Samuel H. Elbert. 1965. *Hawaiian Dictionary: Hawaiian-English*. Honolulu: University of Hawaii Press.

Radner, Joan Newlon, and Susan S. Lanser. 1993. "Strategies of Coding in Women's Cultures." *Feminist Messages: Coding in Women's Folk Culture*. Ed. Joan Newlon Radner. Chicago: University of Illinois Press.

Walker, Nancy. 1988. *A Very Serious Thing: Women's Humor and American Culture*. Minneapolis: University of Minnesota Press.

Wise, John H. 1965. "Food and Its Preparation." *Ancient Hawaiian Civilization: A Series of Lectures Delivered at the Kamehameha Schools*. Rutland, Vt.: Charles E. Tuttle.

Young, Alan. 1999. Personal Interview. Honolulu, Hawaii.

Zanini, Marilyn. 1999. Personal Interview. Kona, Hawaii

Culinary Tourism in Private and Domestic Contexts

The essays in part 2 address culinary tourism in private and domestic contexts—in the home, with friends and family, in familiar informal settings. In these contexts, the implications of tourism for personal relationships and for personal identity become paramount. Commensal politics—the politics of eating together—may be especially nuanced and potent since relationships can carry long emotional histories, and the focus tends to be on the individual rather than the group. Individuals may also feel that they can let their guard down in such settings and express their honest responses to new foods. Private rituals develop in these contexts as a way to personalize and localize larger traditions, imbuing them with associations meaningful to particular individuals.

Research on tourism tends to shy away from private contexts, possibly because access to these settings is limited. Food studies, however, particularly by folklorists, have found private contexts to be natural and rich settings for observing foodways. Jill Rudy's essay on the shifting relationship to food she experienced while living in Guatemala demonstrates how food can be used to articulate identity as a dynamic concept of self. She also examines the dilemma posed by the need to balance her own culinary preferences with those of her hosts. Miryam Rotkovitz then explores the ways tourism is shaped within the religious and ethical structures of Judaism. Individuals who want to be adventurous with food while remaining kosher or who want to satisfy curiosity about forbidden foods, manipulate the definitions and boundaries set by Jewish dietary laws. Jacqueline Thursby addresses the use of food to maintain and invent identity among Basques in Spain and Basques living in the United States by exploring her own responses to the cuisines and foodways she has experienced. As do the other authors in this section, Thursby emphasizes tourism as personal experience that differs according to the individual's background, tastes, values, personality, and the circumstances surrounding that experience.

CHAPTER 6

"Of Course, in Guatemala, Bananas are Better"

Exotic and Familiar Eating Experiences of Mormon Missionaries

Jill Terry Rudy

Studying culinary tourism invites a corollary exploration into the realms of experience that emerge during an extended stay in an unfamiliar country or region. Like incidents of culinary tourism, extended-stay eating experiences require the "intentional, exploratory participation in the foodways of an Other" (Long 1998:181). Unlike the touristic desire for "new [culinary] experiences for the sake of the experience itself" (Long 1998:182), however, the extended stay most likely creates compelling twin desires for new *and* familiar eating experiences. For, unlike the tourist, participants in a lengthy stay become more exposed to the "culinary system not one's own" (Long 1998:181). Without significant effort to avoid unfamiliar culinary systems, the long-term visitor or resident will experience more frequent encounters with new aspects of foodways than the culinary tourist: more new food items, new meal systems and cuisines, and new methods of food procurement, preparation, and presentation. This practically unavoidable immersion in an unfamiliar or other culinary system invites an eater to both highlight and shade exotic aspects of eating.

Lucy Long presents three realms of experience to enrich discussions of foodways and the "crux of otherness" (1998:185). By portraying the realms of the exotic, edible, and palatable as axes that form four quadrants, Long invites analysis of how perceptions of particular food items change. Certain foods can be transformed from inedible and unpalatable to palatable and edible (or vice versa) because "individuals' and society's perceptions of edibility and exoticness can shift" (Long 1998:187). In terms of extended-stay eating, the experience of finding edible and palatable food items plays an important role in the perception of foodways of the host culture; however, the continuum of familiar and exotic food items takes on special significance. In contrast to the short encounters with the food items of the touristic other, where novelty and the exotic are highly valued, the extended stay usually requires an ongoing negotiation between the exotic and the familiar. People who live on a military base or another type of compound in a foreign country may be able to avoid unfamiliar foodways during an extended stay. However, the long-term visitor or resident is confronted with more experiences of inedible and unpalatable foodways than the culinary tourist. The long-term visitor also has more incentive to find familiar foods or make exotic foods acceptable, because learning to eat in the new culture is a prime and recurring human necessity and maintaining cultural isolation is often difficult, costly, and undesirable.

Most extended-stay eaters anticipate, either with positive or negative expectations, a longer exposure to the unfamiliar foodways and the other culture; usually these eaters enter relationships and encounter institutions that the tourist may never discover. Only the most adventurous or well-connected culinary tourist starts out procuring unprepared food in local markets or eating in homes of native residents. Because the extended-stay eater often faces frequent and sustained contacts with a new culinary system, familiar food items and well-known ways of procuring and preparing food usually become highly valued and comforting. The extended stay demonstrates dual aspects of eating habits described by foodways historian Donna Gabaccia: "Human eating habits originate in a paradoxical, and perhaps universal, tension between a preference for the culinarily familiar and the equally human pursuit of pleasure in the forms of culinary novelty, creativity, and variety" (1998:6). Such negotiations of exotic and familiar foodways over an extended stay, although not experienced for the sake of experience as with the touristic encounters, invariably become significant personal experiences that reveal as well "the historical, the situated, the contingent, and the diversity within cultures" (Long 1998:186). The length of the stay itself frequently reinforces the eater's need to experience exotic foodways in a manner that does not erase all familiar assumptions about edibility and palatability and that does not preclude experiences with food items and culinary systems from his or her own culture. However, the familiar food items must be experienced within the frame of the new host culture; often the more exotic food experiences in the new culture become some of the most significant, memorable, and recountable aspects of the extended stay. These moments of negotiating the familiar and exotic initiate and inform an eater's quest to align with, respect, and know the cultural other.

One Extended-Stay Group: Mormon Missionaries

Reasons for the extended stay will contour the experiences in unique ways and will allow eaters different latitude in negotiating edible, palatable, and exotic foodways. Some extended-stay situations isolate visitors from new relationships and institutions in the host culture, while other situations require almost constant interaction. The exploratory eating of military personnel in a foreign country will differ for individuals and families living on or off the military base, and military experiences will differ from the experiences of study-abroad students, expatriates, business transfers, diplomats, ethnographers, missionaries, humanitarian workers, or refugees who also spend extended time in an unfamiliar or alien culture. The possibilities for study of extended-stay eating experiences of these groups are fascinating and numerous. While comparative study of various groups in extended-stay situations would be particularly intriguing, a focused study can explore how members of one extended-stay group negotiate the realms of edible, palatable, and exotic eating experiences. To initiate such study and to expand and contribute to the discussion of culinary tourism, this essay offers examples and analysis of the intentional, exploratory eating experiences of Mormon missionaries.[1]

As a former Mormon missionary, I immediately recognized that my eating experiences in the mission corresponded with the culinary tourism model of using food to help negotiate otherness and boundaries of the familiar and strange. I also realized that extended-stay eating would be a useful contrast and comparison with arenas of culinary tourism, such as restaurants, grocery stores, festivals, magazines, and advertising. I drew data from my personal journals written during my time in the highlands of north central Guatemala from 1984 to 1986, as well as from other Mormon mission experiences shared in letters and documented in projects collected by students in folklore courses at Brigham Young University (BYU). William A. Wilson, the doyen of Mormon folklorists, explains why the study of Mormon missionaries requires considering individual and collective identities and experiences: "Mormon missionaries are not uniquely missionaries. Each is a composite of the identities he has brought with him to the field; no two are exactly alike. However, unlike the rest of us, who are constantly changing roles (and therefore identities), missionaries play the same role for the duration of their missions" (1982:7). The Mormon missionary role almost always involves active proselyting, since most missionaries spend a minimum of twelve hours a day contacting and teaching people who may be interested in becoming members of The Church of Jesus Christ of Latter-day Saints (LDS).[2] These contacts require the missionary to interact constantly with people who are other in terms of religion, nationality or region, ethnicity, social class, age, and occupation.

The Mormon missionary learns to negotiate the familiar and the strange in a way that allows prolonged interaction with others during the length of the mission. The standardized mission program of the church exists in historical, contingent, and diverse contexts of situation and is enacted by thousands of individuals attempting to establish relationships with other individuals who all have agency to accept or reject mission contacts. Even when missionaries serve in their home country, they most often are sent by church leaders to live in an unfamiliar region; these missionaries, whether an Idahoan in Alabama or a Quetzalteco in Guatemala City, also experience for a number of months some diversity in language and culture, including foodways. An LDS mission therefore requires the missionary to interact extensively with people in an unfamiliar culture; a missionary who is isolated from others and unable to appreciate and negotiate otherness is an ineffective missionary. Exploratory eating becomes a necessary and significant aspect in this intercultural interaction of the mission. The mission situation requires the missionary to embrace new experiences centering on a religious identity for well over a year in a new and unfamiliar culture, while distancing himself or herself from former experiences with family, home region, peer, and social class groups.[3] The mission tends to form a high-context group sharing esoteric language, pranks, jokes, inspirational or warning legends, and customary events such as dinner appointments; some elements of mission lore are almost universal for all LDS missionaries, while others are unique to a particular geographic location and group of missionaries. Eating familiar food can provide missionaries comfort associated with life experiences before the mission, while the enjoyment of exotic food in the new area integrates the missionary with the mission identity and the host culture.[4]

Thus, the role of a Mormon missionary creates many differentially shared experiences, values, and attitudes toward extended-stay eating experiences. Some of the eating experiences of Mormon missionaries include food initiations, dinner appointments, food disasters, food pranks, celebrations, and food procurement and preparation. Shifts between the exotic and familiar appear in many of these incidents of exploratory eating. Although Long mentions food items as the unit of study for examining shifts along the axes of edible, palatable, and exotic realms of experience (1998:187), the narrated event will be the initial entry into my analysis. First encounters with exotic food invariably become an event that is recounted within the mission, in letters home, and with others after the mission has ended. The strange food event and narrative tend to freeze the perception of the food item in the exotic realm of experience.

After considering exotic food events, I will concentrate on how perceptions of food items shift along the familiar and exotic continuum even if no singular event marks this shift. The search for familiar food items may involve the missionary in exotic contacts with the host culinary system, facing a new market system and unfamiliar cooking utensils. And many food items that initially seem very strange become familiar and very desirable to the missionary. Individual food items evoke desire and stir memories. Finding familiar food items and familiarizing oneself with exotic foods may not be recountable events that easily turn into a humorous or striking story. But these shifting perceptions of specific food items still serve an important, even central, component of extended-stay eating for Mormon missionaries. It is very difficult for a missionary to serve effectively without some familiarization with the host culinary system and without forming relationships of trust with members of the new culture; these relationships often are constructed around food.

While much is shared in an LDS mission, the fact that missionaries retain aspects of their previous identities also significantly affects how any one person will experience, remember, and recount exotic and familiar foodways of the host culture. Analysis of the extended-stay eating of Mormon missionaries must maintain a sense of individual agency and identity. Some missionaries consistently resist the exotic and struggle to maintain the familiar, and most experience a food item that is so inedible and unpalatable that it cannot be made acceptable. Some missionaries experience food-borne illnesses that affect perceptions of new foodways and the host culture. A missionary who served in Thailand lamented that illness from food caused his stomach to reject the spicy food he had come to enjoy (Kruse 2000:71). However, many missionaries use the exploration of foodways during their extended stay to familiarize themselves with the exotic, to change their familiar identities, and to embrace wholeheartedly new foodways as a sign of their missionary identity and as an opportunity to create meaningful relationships with others.

Storytelling to Share Inedible, Unpalatable, and Exotic Eating Experiences

Of all the meals consumed during the months of the extended stay, missionaries most frequently recount incidents of being served inedible, unpalatable, and exotic food items. Unlike the culinary tourist, who intentionally seeks exotic eating opportunities, the missionary often is served unfamiliar foods as a by-product of contacting and teaching people. The missionary intends to live in the area and interact with the people who serve the unfamiliar food, but he or she does not necessarily seek out the unusual eating experience. Narrative becomes a significant instrument for sorting through and sharing the new and strange elements of mission life. Exotic eating incidents therefore demonstrate the necessary interrelationship of narrated event and narrative event, since each experience occurs once but can be recounted often to help explain and answer "What was going on there?" during the mission (Bauman 1986:6). These stories of exotic eating experiences usually are humorous and may be told in a "story war" session of returned missionaries that escalates from accounts of strange to even stranger food items and eating experiences, usually with each person attempting to relate a happening more outlandish than previous narrators.[5] In ways similar to the "kernal stories" identified by Susan Kalčik, these exotic eating experiences of Mormon missionaries easily become a conversational genre by either evoking similar stories or emerging from a conversational context that already involves food, unusual experiences, or missionary work (1975:8). Every time I introduce this research topic, I receive stories about eating unusual food, and Mormons I speak with tend to center these exotic food stories on the mission experience.

My analysis of the narratives identifies certain situational and structural similarities, although the new and strange eating events occur with unique individuals in locations around the world.[6] The narratives usually involve either an initiation into a new area or a dinner appointment. These eating events are performative in the sense that the missionary is accountable to an audience for expressions made during the initial experience and in the oral or written account of what was going on (Bauman 1986:3). Because missionaries are assigned to work and always be with a missionary companion, an individual missionary never negotiates an exotic eating situation alone; there is a built-in audience of companion, other missionaries, or hosts who often gleefully watch the exploratory eating experience. The audience is usually gleeful because the narrated event often is arranged to highlight the most inedible, unpalatable, and exotic food item that could be served. The exploratory eating is an intentional initiation that tests the missionary's ability to confront and consume the exotic aspects of the new culture; displays of disgust or shocked surprise are expected in these events. Other times, however, the exotic food for the missionary is prepared in the familiar manner of the host or hostess and is simply intended to provide a pleasing meal. A positive reaction to the food most often is expected in the dinner appointment scenario, and the missionary has an obligation to confront the exotic in an appropriate manner. The exotic food experience quite easily and necessarily becomes a narrative event revealing how the missionary responds to the new, the strange, and the other.

Examples of food initiation events demonstrate that the missionary often confronts exotic eating experiences in front of a "seasoned" audience already more familiar with the food items. Questions of palatability, defined by Long as the aesthetic and pleasing aspects of a culinary system (1998:186), leap to the forefront of the narratives of food initiations. As Long notes, palatability intertwines with the issue of edibility, because edibility confirms "what we can eat" and palatability affects "what we want to eat" (1998:186). Exotic foods in missionary initiations present the eater with a challenge to confront food that he or she finds neither personally pleasing nor culturally acceptable. For example, Gerald William Galbraith explained how other missionaries initiated him into his Singapore mission with exotic food items: "They take new missionaries, only a couple days out, to what they call Chinatown, and they order some of the most deemed repulsive food, which would include things like chicken claws, turtle soup, pigeon eggs, and just anything that even the appearance freaks you out. They had some sort of dessert that looked like it had worms in it. . . . You're just disgusted as you watch another guy eat the chicken claw. I just lost my appetite and didn't really want to eat any of that" (Kruse 2000:23). Comments like "repulsive" and "even the appearance freaks you out" confirm that the appearance of the food can key the sense of the exotic and inedible. Galbraith's sense of disgust and losing his appetite shows that edibility is seriously affected by food that appears to be too unusual. Further, seeing someone actually partake of an item, such as a chicken claw, which American culture has deemed inedible, minimizes the desire to eat, or palatability of the food.

These narratives of exotic mission eating experiences share a recurring structural pattern of three main sections. The three sections include being served an inedible, unpalatable, and exotic food item; deciding how to respond to the food item; and eating or otherwise disposing of the food item. Several examples from dinner appointment stories demonstrate how the missionary recognizes and negotiates the exotic. The palatability of the food or sense of its edibility keys the strange eating experience. One returned missionary described being served a "Colombian national dish called 'sancocho'. . . I was surprised to look down in my bowl of Sancocho to find both the talon and beak of the chicken!" (Henderson 2000:14). A soup served to a missionary in Brazil also contained an eating experience surprise: "As I dipped my spoon in to take the first bite, I got a spoonful of pigs ear. It was fully formed and you could totally tell what it was. I threw it back into the bowl and I went in to get another bite but this time I pulled out a pigs hoove [sic]" (Henderson 2000:15–16). In another example of the initial appearance of the food item provoking an undesirable response, a returned missionary from a Guatemala mission described being served an unpalatable chicken dish, "When we got our bowls of food, there was a piece of chicken in there and it still had hair all over it" (Henderson 2000:31). In these stories collected by one BYU student, and most others of this type, the missionary is served a food item with an appearance that is very unpleasing. The interconnection of palatability and edibility is confirmed strongly in these stories. The phrase "you could totally tell what it was" clearly states how the sight of the food combines with the identification of the food item as inedible to create a shocking, exotic eating situation.

Because the social situation in these stories often is a dinner appointment with the missionary seeking to establish a relationship for teaching about the LDS faith, the decision of how to respond to the exotic food item becomes very significant. In the case of the talons and beak, the missionary reports seeking help from his companion: "I asked my companion about it and he explained that is was quite an honor—the honored guest usually got the beak or the talon, but never both. What was I supposed to do with them? My companion explained I was to chew on them!!!!" (Henderson 2000:14). The missionary with the clearly identifiable pig parts did not require outside opinions to make a decision: "I said to myself, 'that's it, no more.' I put the spoon back into the bowl and pushed it away" (Henderson 2000:16). The returned missionary who had confronted the hairy chicken also made a quick decision: "I told him [the companion] that there was no way that I was going to eat that stuff and so I had to find another way to get rid of it" (Henderson 2000:31). Because missionaries often are invited to eat with members or church investigators from the host culture, a food item that is inedible and/or unpalatable to the missionary is presented by the host or hostess as a desirable item to eat. The missionary has little control over having been served the item, but he or she can decide how to, or if to, partake of the strange food and how to tell a story about the experience.

Folklorists will not be surprised that unique individuals handle the situation of unavoidably confronting exotic food, and tell stories about this response, in remarkably similar ways; the returned missionaries tell of how they either managed to eat the food or dispose of the food. Responses to narrated and narrative events of eating the food and ways of disposing of the food can become very creative depending on the personality of the missionary. The missionary who received the talon and beak demonstrates a dutiful response to the exotic eating experience: "Not wanting to offend, I nibbled—but with not much enthusiasm—to the delight of our hosts" (Henderson 2000:14). The response of the missionary identifies a key concern in this eating situation—the problem of offending the host. The delighted response of this host acknowledges that the missionary is becoming more familiar with an unusual food item, making a reluctant effort to make the inedible item edible and the unpalatable somehow palatable. In contrast to dutifully attempting to eat the exotic food item, the elder with the pig parts boldly refuses to consume and accepts the consequence of offending the host: "I couldn't eat another bite. The lady ended up getting mad at me and told us that we would not be invited back to here [sic] home to eat. Frankly, I didn't care too much" (Henderson 2000:16). In this situation, the inedible food and the personality of the missionary combine so that the sense of duty to the mission is overcome by the strangeness of the food items in the soup.

While eating or not eating the exotic food seem the most obvious options available to resolve these eating situations and the stories about them, the most popular exotic mission food stories involve creatively disposing of the food. These narratives are popular because creative disposal of the exotic food item appears to be the perfect negotiation of the LDS missionary's exotic eating dilemma; it allows the missionary to avoid ingesting the inedible and unpalatable food while also, hopefully, avoiding the offense of not eating the food. Disposing of the food also involves a slight deception, and the risk of being caught adds intrigue in the narrative and variety to the missionary's image. For these reasons, a stylized aspect of the narrative includes a motif that the person who served the food conveniently leaves the room, allowing the missionary a limited time to hide, fling, share, or otherwise dispose of the food.

The account of the hairy chicken is a good example of this resolution to the exotic eating experience. After deciding to get rid of the food, the missionary explains: "The dog was sitting outside and so i [sic] picked up my bowl, wound up, and chucked it out the front door of the home. While I was in mid swing, the lady walked into the room. I am not sure if the woman saw me or not, but she didn't say anything" (Henderson 2000:31–32). The missionary successfully disposes of the food without eating it and without giving too much offense to his hostess. It is important to note that the personal narratives of these eating encounters describe in some detail the appearance and identification of the unpalatable and inedible food items. The description of exotic food items from a different culture helps someone unfamiliar with the mission area to sympathize with the missionary's response to the food and the unfamiliar culture.

The student who collected these personal narratives of exotic eating experiences also included a story in his project that he remembered hearing in his mission to Venezuela. This narrative is not a personal experience but a more legendlike account of unknown missionaries who are served an inedible soup. Lacking the detail of personal accounts, this legendary version of the missionary's exotic eating experience includes all three sections of the narrative, with highlights on the attempt to creatively dispose of an offending food:

> The lady served them some soup and other things and left the room to do something else in the kitchen. This one elder took one sip of the soup and decided that he could not, in a million years, shovel it down without puking [vomiting], so he looked for an alternative way to get rid of the soup. . . . Well this missionary decided that he would chuck his soup out the window and nobody would ever know, except his companion of course. Well, he did it. The problem was that the window was so clean that it looked like it wasn't even there at all, but in fact it was and it was closed. The soup splatted against the window and dribbled down to the floor. When the sister [female church member] came in and asked what happened, the missionary's lying response was that he had hit his elbow down hard onto the table and caught the edge of the bowl and it flipped up and splashed against the window. The sister replied by saying, "Don't worry Elder, I have plenty more soup in the kitchen. Give me your bowl and I will get you some more." The Elder sheepishly handed over his bowl and learned to gulp down the nasty soup. (Henderson 2000:10)

The conclusion of this story is dually didactic: missionaries who attempt even small deceits will be found out, and dutiful missionaries who encounter exotic or inedible food must learn to "gulp down the nasty soup." The missionary folklore collection of William A. Wilson includes several variants of this story set in countries around the world. This narrative illustrates that LDS missionaries tell each other their own exotic eating stories, or collective versions retold and adapted over the years, to recall the most exotic experiences from the mission and to share the sense of learning to handle extremely sensitive and unfamiliar interpersonal and intercultural situations.

The story sequence of being served unusual food, deciding how to approach it, and disposing of the food is one stylized way of accounting for the numerous and variable events of Mormon missionaries experiencing unfamiliar food during their extended stays in areas around the world. The narrative form of the event highlights the exotic aspects of the eating experience, while also emphasizing the missionary's need and ability to handle the situation appropriately. The food initiation intentionally highlights the strange aspects of the food item, so the missionary is expected to react with shock, disgust, or even a physical response to the food. The dinner appointment highlights the social element of eating, so the missionary is expected not to give offense to the host or hostess and to confront the unexpected and unfamiliar in a mature and sensitive way. The creative disposal-of-food stories represent the gap between the appearance of handling the situation in an appropriate manner and the reality of avoiding a nasty eating experience. The unpalatability of the food, its displeasing appearance and smell, combines with identification of specific items as inedible to create a culinary dilemma that can be resolved in only a few basic ways. These resolutions of the food dilemma seldom shift the food item from the exotic to familiar realm of eating experience; even if the missionary eats the food rather than refusing or disposing of it, partaking of the food becomes a memorable, recountable, and often humorous event, because the item remains unfamiliar and strange.

Creating Familiar, Edible, and Palatable Eating Experiences in an Exotic Culinary System

Extremely exotic eating experiences make a strong impression on missionaries not only because of the strangeness of the food and obligation to respond appropriately in front of others, but also because the length of the mission suggests that each event could be a precursor of other exotic eating situations. The mission situation of living in an unfamiliar culture for an extended period of time strongly encourages some shifting away from exotic foodways to familiar foodways. Missionaries seek out familiar food items and events in various ways, constrained by time, finances, availability of foods, knowledge of preparation techniques, and negotiations with the mission companion and potential food providers. Although some items may be shared with church investigators and members, foods familiar to the missionaries are most often shared with other missionaries, including companions, who frequently are from different regions in the host culture.

Mormon missionaries live in a variety of situations that may or may not allow them to eat familiar foods on a daily basis. Missionaries in a variety of countries stay in rented apartments and shop and cook for themselves. While familiar food and cooking equipment may be readily available in some areas, other places will have limited availability of ingredients and items needed for food preparation. In many areas of the world, the LDS church encourages members to feed dinner to missionaries, saving missionaries the time and expense of preparing the meal and encouraging members to participate in missionary work. Inevitably these dinner appointments will involve a spectrum of familiar and exotic eating experiences depending on differences between the mission area and the missionary's home experience. In her excellent senior seminar project on foodways and missionary identity, Jennifer Kruse conducted extensive interviews with returned missionaries from seventeen different missions. One returned missionary from the Midwest who served in the Ogden, Utah, mission explained that the dinner appointment food was too familiar: "Anyway, everybody was trying to do their best meal for the missionaries. So it was like we had Sunday dinner every night. We had lots and lots of roast beef" (2000:63). This elder sincerely wanted extreme eating experiences and was disappointed to find that his hosts would attempt to provide spicy food by serving "hot sauce packets from Taco Bell" (Kruse 2000:64). Obviously, not every dinner appointment becomes an exotic eating incident, although most student folklore collections tend to center on these narratives. While some missionaries face recurring meals of familiar foods, which they should graciously accept, other missionaries can only obtain familiar food items by negotiating a new, exotic culinary system.

Many missionaries prepare some meals for themselves or eat at dinner appointments, but potential missionaries in the United States often talk favorably about serving a mission in a country with maids or other paid help to provide for meals, laundry, and other housekeeping duties. The age, and possibly gender, of most missionaries factors into the desire for others to handle the procurement and preparation of food, since many missionaries experience their first extended time away from the home of their parents when they serve the mission. Because of their stage of life, even if they live in an area where familiar foods are available, the missionaries may not know how to prepare food that tastes like homemade. On the other hand, missionaries often learn to work within the constraints of the host culinary system to procure and prepare familiar food items. While female missionaries often prepare these familiar foods for themselves and others, male missionaries also may specialize in making particular food items. An elder in Guatemala taught other missionaries to make apple pies before he returned to Utah, and one former missionary turned the breadmaking he did during his mission to Canada into a lifelong career as a baker and bakery owner (Campbell 2000:1).

When I served in areas around Quetzaltenango, Guatemala, the intentional quest for familiar foods involved a few particular items that represented home and American food. In my mission, we lived with families where the *dueña*, or lady of the house, prepared all of the meals. My perception of familiar foods was influenced significantly by mission companions and other missionaries from the United States who taught me where to find the ice cream shops, hamburger and pizza stands, and cooking ingredients to make familiar recipes. My first familiar flavor from home involved learning to drink soda pop—that was poured from a glass bottle into a plastic bag—with a straw. About two weeks after I arrived in my first mission area, the small town of San Juan Ostuncalco, I wrote in my journal, "I drank a Coke. I have wanted one ever since I got here—just to remind me of home I think" (October 2, 1984). Familiarity with the food also is why as missionaries we would meet at Pizza Rica or Don Benito's for pizza, soda pop, and socializing when we were in Quetzaltenango for preparation day or a monthly meeting.[7] This desire and ability to be reminded of home by the consumption of a particular drink or food item demonstrates a significant difference between extended-stay eating and culinary tourism. The constant possibility of encountering exotic food items and events over a lengthy time period more than satisfies the desire for new, exploratory eating experiences, which turns the continuum of valuing the exotic eating experience for its own sake to that of valuing familiar eating experiences for the sake of familiarity.

The drawing power of the familiar during the extended-stay eating of a Mormon missionary overwhelms aspects of edibility and palatability in the case of some food items. For example, my neighbor who serves in a Moscow, Russia, mission did not eat weekly at McDonald's when she lived in our Provo, Utah, neighborhood, but she has written home about eating there frequently on her mission. I seldom ate no-bake cookies, a combination of cocoa, peanut butter, sugar, vanilla, and oatmeal, before or after my mission. But I went through phases in the mission when my companion and I made the cookies often, because they were a food from home that could be made without too much extra effort. My second mission companion also was from my hometown of Draper, Utah; Hermana (Sister) Julie Greenwood taught me to shop for the ingredients for no-bake cookies and chili—teaching me the names of the items in Spanish, how to negotiate prices, where to find certain ingredients, how to use different measurements, and how to cook on the wood-burning adobe stove of our proprietress, Doña Alsi. The desire for the familiar, rather than for the freshness and flavor of the food, also is why elders would purchase McDonald's apple pies and hamburgers on an administrative trip to Guatemala City and several hours later return the order to other missionaries in Quetzaltenango and nearby towns. The extra effort to procure or prepare familiar food defamiliarizes the common food items and allows the missionaries to begin to see their home culture as unfamiliar and different. The food items become familiar and exotic in this new setting, and the missionaries experience their typical foods and methods of preparing and eating them from the perspective of the new mission culture.

Even during the extended stay of the mission, procuring and preparing familiar food items can become a simple aspect of daily life; familiarization with the new culture takes place over time. In her Christmas e-mail, my neighbor Rachel Childs reports: "We had to do our grocery shopping, and run some errands. We dropped some of the fifty trillion candy cane cookies I made to the mission president and his family. We then went to McDonalds for our Christmas treat" (1999:n.d.). Rachel does not describe how she does the grocery shopping or made the candy cane cookies, although accomplishing these tasks in Russia probably is not exactly similar to completing them in the United States. Mentioning the cookies and McDonald's does, however, suggest that these familiar foods were helpful in observing Christmas; because Russians observe the holiday in January, Rachel commented that "Christmas day for us here just felt like any other p-day [preparation day]" (1999:n.d.). The consumption of familiar food items during the LDS mission seldom merits narrative treatment, although efforts to procure and prepare familiar foods may become a noteworthy, memorable, or recountable event when the food is part of another event or celebration or when one is particularly homesick.

The American Thanksgiving is a prime event for highlighting familiar food items in the extended-stay situation of the Mormon mission, while also acknowledging exotic aspects of the mission culinary system. The traditional Thanksgiving dinner can take months of planning and preparation in some parts of the world. Foodways student and returned missionary Miriam Whiting wrote a personal essay describing how she made a Thanksgiving dinner around a pumpkin a family gave her in mid-September in Krasnoyarsk, Russia. She wrote: "A store nearby stocked German evaporated milk for a while, and I bought two cans. I had two carefully hoarded packets of nutmeg I'd found in a market in Novosibirsk. Two members leant me slantsided cake pans that were far larger and deeper than our pie pans, but would do in a pinch" (1999:n.p.). Whiting describes a Thanksgiving meal of chicken, rather than turkey, with mounds of mashed potatoes donated by local residents, and the pumpkin pie: "Maybe it was the fresh pumpkin, maybe it was the fact that we hadn't tasted American food for a while. I don't know. But that pie was as perfect as pies get on this telestial earth" (1999:n.p.).

Hermana Greenwood, for her last Thanksgiving in Guatemala, and my first, also planned for weeks to make our dinner. The quest for familiar food was so strikingly unfamiliar in the mission setting that I described in some detail in my journal how the turkey was prepared. A church member, Hermana Ramirez, bought a live turkey for us, expertly wrung the neck of the bird, and plucked off the feathers: "It was amazing to see the turkey wandering around the yard turned into what looked like a rubber chicken with a wobbly neck and head" (November 21, 1984). We took the turkey and two cakes to a *panederia* (bread shop) to bake because neither the house we lived in nor the church had an oven; the meal of Jell-O salad, turkey, mashed potatoes and gravy, carrots, squash, banana cake, and cheese cake was memorable because of its familiarity in such an unfamiliar setting and cooking situation. Another returned missionary who served in the Philippines in the 1990s described his determination to have an authentic Thanksgiving dinner, which involved him killing the turkey with a machete and taking it to a local bakery to cook (Kruse 2000:133). The involved quest for familiar American food at Thanksgiving obviously can become a notable and important experience for missionaries serving in unfamiliar countries, especially because the extended stay distances the missionary from familiar foodways and identities for a lengthy time period. At some point in the stay, the missionary will seek out some eating experiences because they remind him or her of the familiarity, security, and comfort of home.

Learning to Enjoy Edible, Palatable, and Exotic but Familiar Eating Experiences

Over time in the new mission culture, or with familiar living situations for missionaries in the United States, the comfort of the familiar might evoke desire for more exotic eating experiences or for significant variations on eating traditions. An elder serving in New England described having three dinners for his first Thanksgiving in the mission, but all of them had elements of an unfamiliar cuisine, including seafood and lasagna, because the families he ate with were from the Dominican Republic or Puerto Rico (Kruse 2000:30). By my second Thanksgiving in Guatemala, I was so accustomed to living in the area that my journal does not even record if we had a Thanksgiving meal, and I cannot remember any special preparations or efforts to procure or prepare a turkey dinner. By my second Christmas in the mission, I joyfully wrote about eating six tamales in less than twenty-four hours. The length of the mission and the mandate, and opportunity, to interact with people and institutions such as other churches, businesses, and government offices in the host culture practically require that LDS missionaries minimize the search for the familiar and learn to become comfortable eating, living, and serving in the unfamiliar mission culture.

While some missionaries experience an exotic eating initiation at the beginning of their missions that lingers during the entire length of the mission, most missionaries find at least a few familiar foods and a few new foods that make their mission eating experience both edible and palatable. Some missionaries find many foods that were initially considered entirely unknown, unpalatable, and inedible early in the mission to eventually be edible and even enjoyable later in the mission. Recently returned missionaries in the area encourage the Brigham Young University bookstore and grocery stores in Provo, Utah, to stock quantities of food items from other countries including guarana and Vegemite. One returned missionary describes celebrating Australia Day, January 26, 2000, by preparing Australian hamburgers in his Provo apartment complex. He tells of barbequing with two other returned missionaries from Australia, preparing hamburgers stacked six to eight inches high with fried eggs, pickled beets, and pineapple and then going around the complex handing out extra Australian hamburgers (Kruse 2000:49). Food items that are familiar but prepared or served in different ways in the mission area also can become highly prized eating experiences during and after the mission.

The interviews of Jennifer Kruse with her articulate, returned missionary friends and reflexivity on my own mission experience can demonstrate the powerful transformations in intercultural and interpersonal relationships that occur along with shifts in perception of exotic to familiar foodways. Susan Kalčik explains how this shift in food perception can relate to inclusion in a previously unfamiliar group: "Foodways help mark existing social boundaries and, depending upon one's viewpoint and focus, inclusion within or exclusion from a group" (1984:48). Mormon missionaries recognize that they have eating experiences because they are missionaries that unite them with members of the host culture in a more comprehensive way than short-term visitors. Christian Corbett Wright explicitly contrasted his eating experiences as a missionary in Guatemala City with what he assumed his perception and reaction might be as a tourist:

> If I went to Guatemala as a tourist and someone offered me sompopos [large hairy ants fried in lemon and salt]—never, never . . . but I learned to do away with American ideas about what food should be like—things like you can't eat like cow stomach. My mission broadened my perspective and made me give up paradigms. I changed my eating habits. I actually did eat black beans today, and in the beginning I didn't like black beans at all. Before my mission, I hated bananas. Since I was four, I've hated bananas. Of course, in Guatemala, bananas are better—actually sweet and delicious instead of tasteless like in America. (Kruse 2000:20)

A returned missionary who served in the Dominican Republic also described eating bananas and avocados daily on his mission, although he could not eat them or enjoy them as much when he returned to the United States because they lacked freshness and flavor (Kruse 2000:78). A missionary in Poland reported a similar response to mushrooms: "Those mushrooms [picked from forests in Poland] are much better than the little white ones that we've got" (Kruse 2000:106). The situational contexts, including geographical location, of the mission can alter the familiarity or exoticism of food in ways that transform what was inedible and unpalatable into extremely desirable eating experiences. Wright's sense of broadening perception and the breakdown of paradigms very aptly describes what happens as many LDS missionaries explore foodways and interact with people in their mission areas.

Several of the missionaries interviewed by Jennifer Kruse also associate their openness to exploratory eating experiences in the mission with their increased understanding and appreciation of people in different life situations. Gerald Galbraith explained:

I think after you get over the initial couple of weeks, it's [unfamiliar food is] part of the mission. It's part of the culture. It's part of the experience. You know, they always tell missionaries they need to come to love the people, and you need to come to love the culture too if you're going to love the people. And most, if not all missionaries, save a few—I know a couple missionaries who struggled and held onto their peanut butter and jelly sandwiches three times a day cause they couldn't take anything—but for the most part, people came to embrace it [the food]. And it is delicious. . . . It's part of embracing—the people, the culture, and the mission is just embracing that adventure. (2000:25)

Brian Robert Hanrahan also emphasizes that the food and the people he met introduced him to a new culture and a different way of life that he found enriching and important: "I have a lot more respect for Spanish people. . . . I love their culture. I think it's better than American culture. . . . Loving life. Playing loud meringue music—having huge meals with the best food. So, I really like their culture" (Kruse 2000:30). Another returned missionary describes the impact of his enjoyment of rice and beans in the Dominican Republic: "Rice and beans, let me tell ya, you either like it or you don't, and there were few missionaries who liked it as much as I did. . . . And Dominicans really loved me because they knew that I just had to have rice and beans" (Kruse 2000:80). Susan Kalčik concludes that sharing food implies acceptance of differences: "By ingesting the foods of each new group, we symbolize the acceptance of each group and its culture" (1984:61). The comments of the returned missionaries suggest that the changing perception of familiar and exotic foodways also demonstrates a mutual acceptance between the missionary and the people she or he meets in a previously unfamiliar culture.

A journal description of a farewell dinner prepared by the family I lived with in my third mission area illustrates the complex intertwining of food items, interpersonal and intercultural relationships. I lived with Martita Martinez, her son, live-in maid, and three daughters for only six weeks; the family were not members of the LDS church but enjoyed sharing their home with Mormon missionaries, especially Americans. They were Catholics, and Martita had observed the conclusion of her first year of being a widow while I was living in her household. The night before my transfer to work in a new area, the family prepared the farewell dinner. A recently arrived missionary from the United States, Hermana Wells, had already come to work with my former companion, Hermana Wiseman, so I recognized it was not necessarily a typical Guatemalan meal. I described the meal in my journal:

How could Hermana Wells have culture shock with radio 66 playing English songs, and with a gorgeous table full of food—sandwiches, fresh fruit salad and a banana pie. The table was decorated with flowers and it was so neat—one of the nicest things anyone has ever done for me. The sandwiches were Hermana Wiseman's idea. The fruit salad was wonderful—cantaloupe, watermelon, pineapple, papaya, mango and some plum-like thing. Plus, in the afternoon Martita made garbanzo beans with this yummy sauce and ham. And the banana pie—the crust was $1/2$ inch thick, the filling pure bananas! It was a fun meal. I gave them pictures of me in the corte and huipil [traditional clothing] and bawled. Martita just hugged and kissed me. And I just had to hold Wicha [the live-in maid] because she was crying so hard. (March 16, 1985)

Although the family was middle class and did not wear traditional clothing, it is symbolic of my integration into Guatemalan culture that I gave them a picture of me wearing clothing from the nearby Quetzaltenango area. In turn, the meal was intentionally oriented toward foods familiar to me as an American. Eating sandwiches was an extremely rare experience in Guatemala, and the sandwiches were a menu item suggested by my companion from the United States. Although the sandwiches were nice, I noted in my journal several of the fruits that were not common to me, and the banana pie prepared without a custard or cream filling, because these items were particularly unfamiliar and yet extremely pleasing.[8] The food event celebrated the melding of the exotic and familiar both for me and for the family I had lived with.

The presentation of the food also made the meal extremely palatable and enjoyable. But the situation of leaving a family I had lived with for six weeks, always with the underlying possibility that I might never see them again, keyed the intense emotions described in the journal entry. Such free and intense experience of emotions initially seemed uncomfortable and strange to me when I began living in Guatemala, but after living in the country for six months, I had learned to become very attached and expressive with the people I knew. I am not sure if I loved the food because I loved the people, or if I loved the people I met because I loved the food, especially the fresh fruits, breads, and various ways of eating black beans. The intense reciprocity I felt in the relationships I experienced with people in my areas of service, and with other missionaries, always involved negotiating the strange and unknown with what was familiar and comfortable to create a new level of knowledge and caring.

These examples, and many others, demonstrate the strong feelings of attachment, enjoyment, and love that accompany many of the interpersonal and intercultural experiences of LDS missionaries. The examples also illustrate ways that the shifting perceptions of edible, palatable, and exotic food items actually feed into the relationships of missionaries and the people they work with in the host culture. The comments also suggest that missionaries who cannot participate in the foodways of the other and who do not allow the new ways of the mission culture to become familiar and desirable may miss the adventure of the mission. One returned missionary articulated his awareness that having difficulties in interpersonal relationships and finding the foodways of Chile to be "not very unique" definitely affected his response to his mission: "There were some people that I didn't get along with, like I was pretty much stuck with them and so I never really got that attached to my mission. At the same time I didn't really get attached to the food. . . . I pretty much eat the same as if I hadn't gone on a mission" (Kruse 2000:128). The length of the mission can create a feeling of being "stuck with" people and situations that are difficult and uncomfortable. Because of reluctance, indifference, or physical reaction to trying new and unfamiliar foodways or to making new relationships, some missionaries may not be as warmly embraced by the people they work with as other missionaries who wholeheartedly come to accept the transformation over time from strangeness to familiarity in the host culture and the mission experience. While failure to make the exotic food familiar can maintain social distinctions and the sense of otherness, as Kalčik suggests, eating habits, and changes in eating habits, can become a powerful symbol of "crossing or even breaking down social boundaries" (1984:50). Because of the symbolic as well as the material aspect of foodways, specific food items can represent for LDS missionaries the mission area, culture, and people the missionary has worked with and taught. The transformation of food items from exotic to familiar and desirable illustrates how foodways, especially in an extended stay, can be enmeshed in the accomplishment of human relationships that transcend cultural and religious differences.

Leavetakings: Agency, Relationships, and Extended-Stay Eating

In her article on culinary tourism, Long concludes by discussing the desire to experience the other through exploratory eating. She correctly acknowledges the concern of some scholars who see "the impulse to eat the other as a colonialist, hegemonic act" (1998:195). I fully recognize the concern that proselyting and missionary work also are part of the capitalist, colonialist urge to dominate, exploit, and destroy traditional cultures and the natural environment. In the case of LDS proselyting, I reply to these concerns with the idealistic answer that most Mormon missionaries do what they do with a sincere conviction that the principles they teach will significantly improve the happiness and lives of people who follow the principles. Hopefully, at their most common and their best levels, the mission encounters are not domineering or exploitive. As a consequence of missionary interactions, the lives of the missionaries and those they teach are enriched and expanded by the opportunity to experience significantly new traditions and ways of living in the world. Like the impulse to have a culinary tourism experience, the opportunity to live in another culture for an extended time as an LDS missionary demonstrates "the willingness of humans to experience the cultural worlds of other people" (Long 1998:195). Although missionaries frequently face rejection, this willingness to experience other cultural worlds usually is reciprocal between the missionary and at least some of the people he meets during the months of the mission.

Even with an obligation to eat foods that appear inedible and unpalatable, missionaries decide how to encounter exotic food items, if they should find familiar food items, and when to enjoy newly discovered food items. Some of the most profound realizations during the mission relate to learning to handle transformations of the familiar and the strange. A key to these negotiations of otherness in the LDS mission context is acknowledging the agency of other people to be who they are and live their lives as they choose. At various times I wrote in my mission journal about human agency. After observing situations of drunkenness, domestic abuse, and damaging gossip, I wrote: "I wish I could make everyone be good. . . . It reminds me that I'm wanting something impossible—people have the right to choose" (May 2, 1985). Another returned missionary also commented on the urge to control the behavior of other people: "Instead of helping them grow, I would try to force them to do something. And that's because I just wouldn't look at what they had to offer or how they would discover for themselves. . . . I discovered that to help people grow, you have to see who they are and accept it and love it and see how they can grow through their own efforts" (Kruse 2000:56). The growth that missionaries so desire for people they meet in the mission also comes, reciprocally, to the missionaries themselves.

Foodways inform these transformations in a sensory, personal, interpersonal, intercultural, and spiritual way. Mark William Joseph Nugent grew up in Jamaica and served his mission in Atlanta, Georgia. In his interview with Jennifer Kruse he drew several conclusions about how exploratory foodways in the mission transformed his perception of eating and of his own identity:

> I knew that I wouldn't be the same after my experiences because the food in Atlanta opened up a bunch of new possibilities for my tastes and stuff. And I don't know if it was just the food or what, but I became a lot more adventurous. Now, I'd eat anything. I ate a squirrel. I'd eat anything. And I'm a lot more accepting of things I wasn't accepting of before. Like other food, people I guess. Before there were just certain people I'd hang out with, talk to, but now I can see anybody and know they got a story behind them, that they're very unique. . . . I think food is such a big part of our lives. . . . I wouldn't discover the importance of accepting and integrating new things into my life, or at least as easily as I did. (Kruse 2000:56)

Many of the missionaries in their discussion of new food experiences acknowledge how the exotic foods and the mission relationships taught them tolerance and how to make choices about "integrating new things into my life."

Andrew George Cannon grew up in several university towns around the United States, and he served his mission in Hungary. He also discusses how new foodways and the mission experience profoundly taught him about accepting others: "My food experiences were part of the entire process that I went through of learning to accept people rather than being on a constant crusade to change people. . . . Food was a part of stepping out and saying, 'Okay, I'm going to accept what I run into'" (Kruse 2000:40). In the context of the mission, the connection between relationships with people in a new culture and the new food items can spark insights and awareness of personal growth. Confirming the paradox noted in Matthew 10:39 about losing oneself in the service of others and of God to find oneself, much of the individual improvement and identity change of the LDS missionary comes through intense efforts to reach out to other people while intentionally distancing oneself from familiar aspects of family, region, and peer group.

Understanding the importance of individual agency and relationships with others shows plainly that expanding "horizons of the familiar" is the most significant aspect of the experience of new foodways over the extended stay during the LDS mission (Long 1998:195). The length of the mission is one factor in the transformation of perceiving food items as exotic, inedible, and unpalatable and eventually as familiar and highly desirable. Having time and the responsibility to establish relationships of trust with people in the mission is another significant factor in these transformations. Of course, any missionary's response to the exotic animal parts, insects, and "the nasty soup" served to him or her along with the search for the familiar peanut butter, fast food, or Thanksgiving turkey will be contextually situated with unique historical, contingent, and diverse elements. Some missionaries will eat out of obligation, some will eat out of curiosity or sense of adventure, some will get sick, some won't care if they eat or not, some will absolutely refuse to eat, some will fling food out doors or at windows, and some will crave food items from the area long after the mission concludes.

Food items and events associated with the mission also may index relationships with other people. The presence of a mission companion and other missionaries in the area of service provides for differentially shared experiences and support in the difficult tasks of conducting the mission work. The mandate of the mission to teach people also necessitates interactions that integrate the missionary with the exotic and into familiar realms of experience in the host culture. As Ephesians 2:19 states, the intent of Christian proselyting is to be "no more strangers, but fellow citizens with the saints" in order to negotiate difference to establish common ground and to live by shared principles and values. But the mission also comes to an end, and most relationships are built with an awareness that opportunities for ongoing interactions will change or disappear when the missionary returns home. The impact, however, of having shared profound experiences with others—whether in teaching, eating, or living situations—will remain.

Studying the extended-stay eating experiences of Mormon missionaries demonstrates quite powerfully that the sharing of food often builds human relationships that deftly turn exoticism into familiarity. The ability of missionaries to enjoy previously unfamiliar food or to find freshness and increased palatability in previously familiar food items suggests benefits of an extended stay in a new culture: the opportunity and time to broaden interpersonal experiences and open new avenues of intercultural tastes. Because the food experiences of LDS missionaries are so connected with human relationships, both with other missionaries and with people in the host culture, the response of relishing new food experiences often cannot be separated from the deep bonds of friendship and fellowship that the partaking of food together both informs and celebrates. And as William A. Wilson suggests, "In all this there is nothing unique to Mormon missionaries" (1982:25). As well as encountering food items that remain inedible and unpalatable and desiring some familiar food items that signify the comfort of home, exploratory eaters in other extended-stay situations also will forge friendships and experience new food items in ways that familiarize the exotic. Kalčik refers to a study that showed military personnel wanted to eat food appropriate to the country where they were taking shore leave or coming into port (1984:51). Comparative studies can identify how participation in different groups affects the perception of edibility, palatability, and the exotic. Forming relationships in the host culture will reward the exploratory eater in an extended stay with personal growth, empathy, and long-term, life-changing experience in creating a community and comprehending the unfamiliar.

Experiences of culinary tourism may be sought as a way for individual enhancement (Long 1998:181); likewise, extended-stay eating by Mormon missionaries, whether enjoyed or merely endured, becomes a significant part of a life-changing experience for those missionaries. By accepting the call to serve, LDS missionaries also sign on for intense, difficult, exhilarating, and profound involvement in the lives of other people as they seek to raise awareness of spiritual principles in a temporal existence. The sensory aspects of food, suggested by perceptions of palatability and edibility, draw on the physical properties of food items and the ethereal aspects of taste to deeply embed transformations of the exotic and familiar in the lives of missionaries and all they come to love and those who love them. The extended, but finite, time in the mission creates a permeably bounded experience of losing and finding oneself in otherness; results of such experience are intentionally profound, unforgettable, and infinite. Food items and events experienced during the length of the mission both symbolize and serve as a catalyst for these transformations as the exotic and unfamiliar culture becomes familiar and memorable. The sensory and signifying power of foodways profoundly shapes the ability to experience and accept other cultures and peoples.

Notes

1. Members of The Church of Jesus Christ of Latter-day Saints frequently are called Mormons, referring to their acceptance of the Book of Mormon as scripture along with the Bible. The church and its members also are identified by the acronym LDS, standing for Latter-day Saints, as a parallel reference to the saints in the early Christian church. Founded with six members in New York in 1830 by Joseph Smith, the church expanded throughout the nineteenth and twentieth centuries to over eleven million members through active proselyting in the United States and Canada, Europe, the Pacific Islands, Latin America, Asia, Africa, and the former Soviet Union. Transforming over time from an enclave in the Rocky

Mountains to an internationally recognized religion, the church maintains a highly organized missionary program following the biblical mandate to preach the gospel to people around the world in their own languages.

2. Assigned by church leaders to serve in one of over three hundred mission areas, single young men, known as "elders," ages nineteen to twenty-six and young women, called "sisters," over the age of twenty-one spend twenty-four or eighteen months, respectively, in the mission. LDS missionaries volunteer their time, and they or their families and local congregations pay for their physical needs such as clothing, meals, and lodging. Missionaries are supervised by a mission president—a man and his family called by church leaders to serve in the mission area for three years. Mormon missionaries follow a uniform daily schedule that suggests activities of study, street contacting, and teaching from 6:30 A.M. to 10:30 P.M.; they also observe common dress standards of suits and ties for elders and dresses for sisters.

3. To encourage commitment to the mission, LDS missionaries follow rules of conduct more strict that those followed by other church members, including weekly contact by mail with family members and friends from home, no dating, and limited music, movies, television, or other forms of mass-media entertainment.

4. It is useful to note that gender is an aspect of identity that differentiates male and female mission experiences. Because more males serve missions, many of the examples in this discussion will come from male missionaries; however, I will identify my personal experiences and insights of other female missionaries and collectors to demonstrate, where significant in this discussion related to otherness, how gender and various aspects of personal identity inform exploratory eating in the mission. The experience of married couples that serve missions after their children are grown is not considered in this discussion, although it would offer more insights into exploratory eating and the negotiation of otherness.

5. Although the term "story war" may have appeared in other settings, I first heard it used by Katie Dunn, a student in my American Folklore course during the winter semester of 2000. The phrase aptly described the sense of contest and strategy that these narrative sessions of strange foodways evoke. Interestingly, Katie Dunn is now serving an LDS mission.

6. The narratives in this article have been collected by folklore students at Brigham Young University in Provo, Utah, an excellent setting for the performance and documentation of these stories, with thousands of recently returned missionaries on campus. When these narratives are collected, students usually tape-record and transcribe ten to fifteen stories, providing some contextual and informant information and a cover essay. These focused field projects on missionary food experiences then are catalogued and deposited in the William A. Wilson Folklore Archive. Although the performance of these stories is innumerable at Brigham Young University and anywhere else that returned LDS missionaries congregate, only a handful of projects on this topic have been conducted.

7. One weekday is set aside for a preparation day; known as "P-Day," this is the time missionaries do laundry and other errands, write letters home, and occasionally visit special sites or cultural events in their area. Missionaries attend a

weekly district meeting and a monthly zone conference with other missionaries to plan their work and hear inspirational talks.

8. As Christian Wright exclaimed, the fruit really was better in Guatemala. Although fresh pineapple, papaya, and mango are now available in many American grocery stores, the small and tasteless fruits barely resemble the large and delicious fruits I ate during my mission.

Works Cited

Bauman, Richard. 1986. *Story, Performance, and Event: Contextual Studies of Oral Narrative*. Cambridge, U.K.: Cambridge University Press.

Campbell, Linda. 2000. "This 'Dough Boy' is for Real." *Utah County Journal*, July 6: 1, 6.

Childs, Rachel. 1999. E-mail to Childs family. December.

Gabaccia, Donna R. 1998. *We Are What We Eat: Ethnic Food and the Making of Americans*. Cambridge, Mass.: Harvard University Press.

Henderson, Todd. 2000. "Funny Foreign Food Stories." Unpublished folklore project submitted to Brigham Young University Folklore Archive.

Kalčik, Susan. 1984. "Ethnic Foodways in America: Symbol and the Performance of Identity." In *Ethnic and Regional Foodways of the United States: The Performance of Group Identity*. Eds. Linda Keller Brown and Kay Mussell, pp. 37–65. Knoxville: University of Tennessee Press.

———. 1975. "'. . . like Ann's gynecologist or the time I was almost raped': Personal Narratives in Women's Rap Groups." In *Women and Folklore: Images and Genres*. Ed. Claire R. Farrer, pp. 3–11. Prospect Heights: Waveland Press.

Kruse, Jennifer. 2000. "LDS Missionary Food Experiences: How Tantalizing and Terrifying the Taste Buds Shapes Identity." Unpublished folklore project submitted to Brigham Young University Folklore Archive.

Long, Lucy M. 1998. "Culinary Tourism: A Folkloristic Perspective on Eating and Otherness." *Southern Folklore* 55: 181–204.

Whiting, Miriam. 1999. "A Thanksgiving in Russia." Unpublished essay.

Wilson, William A. 1982–83. "On Being Human: The Folklore of Mormon Missionaries." *New York Folklore* 8–9: 5–27.

CHAPTER 7

Kashering the Melting Pot

Oreos, Sushi Restaurants, "Kosher Treif,"
and the Observant American Jew

Miryam Rotkovitz

> It made us remember our own teenage years, when we had felt the awk-
> wardness of standing out, the shame of being unable to be fully part of
> the crowd. And back then, it had been easier. Many of us had gone to
> public school, and being Jewish, regardless of how observant, was a lot in
> common right there. We had been allowed to join the B'nai Brith youth
> group; our parents were happy that at least our friends would be Jewish.
> The Orthodox world wasn't as strict as it was now. Candy bars that we
> used to think were kosher were no longer considered so, the synagogue
> dances we used to hold were now considered scandalous. It wasn't only
> here that we were becoming more stringent. The whole Orthodox world
> had taken a giant step to the right, and like partners in a dance, we had
> followed.
>
> Tova Mirvis, *The Ladies Auxiliary*, 1999

Historically, there has been enormous fluidity and variety to the way in
which Jews have observed *kashrut* in America. More recently, as reflected
in the above passage from Mirvis's novel, there has also been a growing
move to the "right" and a greater emphasis on technical stringency among
observant Jews in general. Additionally, in recent years, the availability of
foods certified as kosher has grown exponentially. As a result, observant
American Jews have been increasingly able to keep the kosher dietary laws
with more ease on the one hand and greater stringency on the other, while
participating more fully in both American consumer and food cultures.

There are multiple phenomena of culinary tourism in the observant
American Jewish community, several of which are related to the burgeon-

ing *kashrut* certification industry. In fact, a touristic imperative on the part of kosher consumers is arguably responsible—at least in part—for fueling the industry's tremendous growth. Many manufacturers now opt to bring new products to the mainstream market with kosher certification in place and to reformulate formerly nonkosher products to meet the requirements for certification, thereby providing *kashrut*-observant Jews ever-widening access in the marketplace. Of particular interest in the discussion of culinary tourism are products such as the Oreo cookie and M&M candies, which, until their relatively recent certifications, were off-limits and arguably exotic foods, due in part to their iconographic status. Great anticipation preceded their certification, and the swift integration of these foods (versus less special or more common products; for example, a newly certified brand of strawberry jam) into the diet is a point of interest.

Also noteworthy is the proliferation of kosher restaurants serving authentic ethnic (read non-Jewish ethnic) cuisines. There are now kosher Japanese, Thai, Italian, Indian, and French restaurants, to name a few. When, for example, the sushi chef is a non-Jewish native of Japan, so much the better for many kosher diners.

"Legal" experimentation seems key here and is likewise reflected in the consumption of kosher "*treif*" (*treif* is the Yiddish word referring to nonkosher foods). Products including Crisco, beef-frye (a bacon analog), and Bac-O-Bits have enjoyed immense popularity. Kosher versions of "crab" and "shrimp" are available. Even some kosher cookbooks try their hand at "kosher *treif*." The *Kosher Creole Cookbook*, for example, includes a recipe for mock-crawfish salad, suggesting a desire among some kosher cooks to taste the foods other Americans freely enjoy, without transgressing the kosher laws.

Not only may cookbooks offer suggestions for toying with the boundaries of *kashrut* (however artificially), they can also reflect other modes and styles of culinary tourism. As folklorist Barbara Kirshenblatt-Gimblett pointed out in an article entitled "Kitchen Judaism," "cookbooks, though not direct indications of what people ate, nevertheless represent Jewish cuisine and social life." They can serve as excellent barometers of the psychosocial or cultural concerns of the author or of the targeted group, or as reflections of the way those concerns play out through food.

The perceptions that both Jews and non-Jews harbor about the meaning of kosher are vital as well. For while many observant Jews seek out kosher ways to eat like Americans (this includes participating in the non-kosher-observant American's ability to eat through other cultures), many kosher consumers are not Jewish at all. This suggests that many "others" are participating in the foodways of kosher Jews, just as the Jews are trying to emulate the eating patterns of the other.

Perhaps one of the most unique and vital factors to consider is that whatever touristic imperative that the observant Jew feels may be confounded by the very practice of *kashrut* observance. Certainly, *any* individual—observant Jew or not—will likely deal with some sort of barrier when experimenting with unfamiliar foodways. It may be necessary to realign one's mindset in terms of what constitutes an acceptable food, or to acclimate one's palate to an unfamiliar taste or degree of spiciness. But by and large, the choice to pursue knowledge through a particular food or cuisine is one made by the individual, and the degree to which he or she gets involved in that touristic pursuit is self-determined. In the case of the observant Jew, however, there are preset boundaries or external limits set on the ways in which one may indulge the desire to explore the foodways of others. Moreover, those limits ostensibly apply to all *kashrut*-observant Jews as a group, so there is a discipline to follow, permissions to be gained (often represented by kosher certification), and rules to abide by that are unique to kosher tourism. (In the abstract, these very limits may even recast the touristic pursuit as a sort of religious expression.) Though the scope of touristic possibilities may be narrower for the *kashrut*-observant Jew, the significance of that tourism is not lessened.

Along with the questions inherent in any example of culinary tourism—What are the motivating factors? To what extent does novelty play a role?—there are issues unique to kosher tourism to consider. For example, how does culinary tourism impact traditional *kashrut* observance, and vice versa? What impact does the kosher certification industry, with its enormous scope and influence, exert? How does the philosophy of *Torah u'madah* (the integration of Torah and modern science, or secular study, popular among the Modern Orthodox), with its emphasis on living vitally in the modern world while observing the Torah, factor in?

It is tempting to throw one's hands up at the prospect of evaluating the state of America's Jews, not to mention their *kashrut* observance, or varieties and modes of culinary tourism. There is such variety in religious observance and belief or lack thereof. Rather than a cohesive community, there are countless factions, each with their own beliefs and agendas. There are regional variations in practice and philosophy. There are the major splits between Ashkenazic and Sephardic Jews, not to mention Orthodox, Conservative, and Reform. Even within the "major parties," to borrow a political term, there are countless philosophies. Among Orthodox, for example, there are Modern Orthodox, some of whom prefer the term "Centrist," ultra-Orthodox, who affiliate with various subgroups—some of which are Chassidic (i.e. the Lubavitch, Satmar, and Belzer Chassidim)—and others who are anti-Chassidic. It's a bit like looking at an Impressionistic painting up close, with no clear sense of the picture for all of the apparent chaos. But upon stepping back one notices that there are certain commonalties for all of the craziness. It could be said that the freedoms afforded by American culture have encouraged this variety of Jewish identification. In a sense, the preponderance of so many beliefs and practices may be a phenomenon distinct to, if not characteristic of, America.

What then constitutes *kashrut* observance? Which Jews consider themselves mandated to observe the dietary laws, and just how are Jews in America keeping kosher? How in turn do these practices affect, or reflect, acculturation? In the strictest sense, the laws of *kashrut* consist of biblically mandated guidelines and prohibitions regarding permissible food and its preparation. All grains, fruits, and vegetables are kosher, but only certain animals (and their by-products) are permissible and (except for kosher fish) must be ritually slaughtered to retain their kosher status. The laws, however, are far more involved than a review of the written Torah (Pentateuch, or Five Books of Moses) would suggest. Along with the so-called written Torah, an oral tradition, which elaborated on the laws, was passed down. The biblical injunction not to cook a calf in its mother's milk is understood, via the oral tradition, as a prohibition against *any* mixing of milk and meat. During the compilation of the Talmud, scholarly debate served to further elucidate and interpret the laws. In that vein, the continual interpretation and development of *kashrut* has lasted to date. In light of the globalized, highly processed food supply, coupled with the instantaneous information exchange that characterizes the modern era, this sort of debate and the resulting legal rulings necessarily continue—and perhaps have seen an upswing—as demands are made on the *kashrut*-certifying organizations to evaluate new food products and determine their kosher status.

As far as who observes the laws of *kashrut*, that too may be subject to interpretation. Reform Jews are not mandated to keep kosher, as ritual observance is not the focus of Reform theology. At their 1999 Pittsburgh Convention, however, the Reform rabbinate adopted "A Statement of Principals for Reform Judaism," which stated that certain *mitzvot* (sacred obligations) that have not previously been observed by Reform Jews "demand renewed attention as the result of the unique context of our own times." In *Being Jewish*, an exploration of the way Judaism is expressed and observed today by Jews of all affiliations, Ari L. Goldman indicates that *kashrut* observance is one of the *mitzvot* the Reform rabbinate hopes to revisit (2000:228).

The Conservative and Orthodox rabbinates do require the observance of *kashrut*. Only in the case of Orthodoxy, however, is strict observance a given—almost. Goldman points out:

> One of the defining characteristics of Orthodoxy is *kashrut* observance. If someone identifies as Orthodox, most would assume that the home is kosher. Yet, many modern Orthodox Jews are more lax about *kashrut* when eating outside the home. They will not eat non-kosher meat or poultry and will favor the items on the menu that are fish or vegetarian dishes. While Orthodox rabbis frown on this practice, they admit that an earlier generation of Orthodox rabbis accepted such compromises for their congregants if not for themselves. Things have changed, however, the rabbis argue, noting the proliferation of kosher restaurants and kosher supermarket items; there is no longer an excuse for the lax standards of the past. (2000:228)

In short, it is nearly impossible to make valid generalizations about who keeps kosher and how they do it. Some Jews who define themselves as *kashrut*-observant abide by the biblical laws only. Some eat only kosher food on a single set of dishes, while others eat nonkosher food but have separate dishes for milk and dairy foods. Some Jews keep kosher homes but eat food of any variety out of the house. Others are uncompromisingly stringent. Ultra-Orthodox Jews may maintain that it is impossible to keep kosher on a part-time basis. But Jews in America have always personalized their observance and likely will continue to do so.

If the rapid expansion of the *kashrut* industry is any indication, there may be a shift in the nature of this personalization. On the one hand, there is much enthusiasm for the huge availability of kosher-certified foods of all varieties. The ability to purchase so many of the processed foods on the market affords an unprecedented freedom for *kashrut*-observant Jews. Acculturation into American society occurs now on a deeper level, because there is less to delineate the Jew from the non-Jew, at least in the supermarket checkout line. Furthermore, certification puts *kashrut* observance, to a certain degree, into the hands of the consumer. The existence of large *kashrut* supervision bodies, with their known standards, and nationally recognized certification symbols, obviates the need for continual rabbinical consultation on the part of the consumer regarding food purchases.

Paradoxically, the observant Jew today may have less freedom in determining his or her own standards of *kashrut*. While there are seemingly limitless choices on the one hand, there is likewise a great deal of watch-dogging. Those who work in the *kashrut* industry publish newsletters and alerts reminding their fellow Jews that just because a product seems to contain no offensive ingredients, and may perhaps even be inherently kosher, it could have been run on a nonkosher machine, or the wrapper may have been sprayed with a nonkosher lubricant.

Scrupulous *kashrut* observers may find such reminders more a help than a nuisance. But occasionally, unwitting coercion takes place on the part of the *kashrut* industry. Pure, raw vegetables, for example, are un-questionably kosher. They must be washed before preparation because they may harbor bugs, which are not kosher, but there is nothing unto-ward about a *kashrut*-observant Jew walking the produce section of a store and selecting anything sold there. So, too, frozen vegetables, provided the package contains nothing but vegetables and perhaps salt, are kosher re-gardless of whether a certifying mark is present on the package. (Only during Passover might frozen vegetables be of concern, since many manu-facturers now run frozen vegetable and pasta blends on the same machin-ery they use to package pure vegetables.) It is possible, however, to find kosher-certified frozen vegetables. The kosher consumer may feel com-pelled to purchase these over an equally kosher, albeit uncertified, pack-age of frozen broccoli. Widespread certification, then, is not without complicating factors. In a sense, it can be viewed as the impetus for a tug-of-war between acculturation and separation.

The Consumer Imperative, *Kashrut* Certification, and Cookies

A major distinguishing factor of American supermarkets is the sheer vol-ume of products on their shelves. Notable, too, is the proliferation of little symbols on many of those packages, designating their contents as certi-fied kosher. In fact, the kosher food industry has become, by some esti-mates, a multibillion-dollar one, serving countless consumers, both Jewish and non-Jewish (Eidlitz 1999:9). It is not surprising, then, that companies like Nabisco, which have traditionally been nonkosher manufacturers, seek to protect and enhance their market standing by tapping into the kosher market. It is interesting to note, however, that although *kashrut*-observant Jews certainly represent a specialized, stable market niche— after all, they must rely on kosher-certified products—they may not represent the most profitable segment of the kosher market, simply by merit of the fact that Jews are a minority population, and the appeal of kosher also extends to non-Jews.

Hebrew National products, for example, are largely shunned by the Orthodox, secondary to concerns over the validity of a certification that is not overseen by one of the major certifying organizations. But non-Jewish consumers take the company's advertisements—with their tongue-in-cheek assertion that "we answer to a higher authority"—at face value and keep Hebrew National in business.

When Dannon lost certification on its Fruit-on-the-Bottom line of yogurts in 1999, thanks to a reformulation that included gelatin, the company printed a "K" on the label and listed "kosher gelatin" on the ingredient list. Furthermore, the fact that Dannon continued to assert on its website that all of its yogurts were kosher, suggested an equivalency between the Orthodox Union's O-U certification and the "K" (four of Dannon's flavors—lemon, plain, vanilla, and coffee still carry the O-U), and even claimed "the simple K is universally recognized as a symbol of kosher certification. There are currently about 150 different kosher symbols used throughout the world! Many of these are not easily discernible to the eye of the average consumer."

In fact, the eye of the *kashrut*-observant Jew is well trained—and discerning—when it comes to seeking out kosher products. The "K" may be universally recognized, but for reasons that will be discussed later, it is *not* considered a valid mark of kosher certification. Given Dannon's long-standing relationship with the Orthodox Union, the company was surely aware of this. But presumably Dannon was also aware that it has many non-Jewish customers who seek out kosher products but may be ignorant of the intricacies of the laws of *kashrut* and of kosher certification, and apparently had no compunction about capitalizing on that ignorance.

The promise of major profit increase often motivates a manufacturer's decision to "go kosher." From the perspective of observant American Jews, greater availability of kosher-certified products is a welcome convenience, particularly in communities where strictly kosher supermarkets do not exist. Nabisco's recent certification, however, raises issues that tend not to be considered or discussed by American Jews, so thrilled they are by the burgeoning kosher market. Specifically, unlike nearly all products receiving new *kashrut* certification, the Nabisco Oreo cookie bears status as a long-standing American icon. The unveiling of the kosher-certified Oreo cookie, therefore, has significant ramifications for American Jews.

The Oreo Cookie as an American Icon

Since its market launch in 1912, the Oreo cookie has held the imagination and the taste buds of a nation in thrall. Asked simply to name *the* quintessential American cookie, respondents to an informal—and quite unscientific—poll immediately and definitively cited the Oreo. Only one respondent thought for a while, waffled, and then asked, "Um, the Toll House?" When I prompted her by saying "a packaged cookie," her response was instant—the Oreo. (Knowing my general proclivity for freshly baked versus prepackaged cookies, she was perhaps afraid to mention the Oreo off the bat.)

What, though, is the Oreo's appeal? For any product to reign supreme in America for a single year requires formidable marketing and incredible luck. And then whatever is new and most innovative will likely usurp that product's position. Yet even today, despite a ninety-one-year history, the Oreo retains enormous popularity and is a firmly entrenched symbol of popular American culture. Perhaps it is this very history that immunizes the Oreo against an otherwise fickle consumer culture. The cookie was in its infancy in 1914, but nonetheless survived two world wars and the Great Depression—as did the United States. Sentimentality for this classic cookie is even reflected by the trade in both classic and modern Oreo memorabilia.

Moreover, ritual surrounds the eating of Oreos. We recognize the significance of the question "Are you a twister or a dunker?" and associate it with an activity no more illicit than cookie eating. In an article entitled "Creative Eating: The Oreo Syndrome," Elizabeth Mosby Adler frames a thesis regarding our methods of consumption around the recognizable and common phenomenon of Oreo-eating rituals (1983:4–10). A recent national survey conducted by Nabisco regarding Oreo-eating techniques received an overwhelming response. Over 174,000 consumers voluntarily phoned 1-800-EAT-OREO and reported their rituals ("How Do I Love Thee Oreo? America Counts the Ways"). The fact that people were so eager to share their techniques suggests they have quite an attachment to the cookies.

The Oreo seems to have symbolic meaning that extends even beyond more obvious food associations. So familiar are we with its appearance—black on the outside, white on the inside—that "Oreo" has been used as a racial descriptor. In a racial context, the term is not generally applied positively. But the image of the cookie is sufficiently resonant to have served as a useful title for Gerald Thompson's book *Reflections of an Oreo Cookie: Growing Up Black in the 1960s.*

Another example of creative Oreo use is described in the November 1999 issue of *Gourmet* magazine. In "The Last Word" column, Perri Klass wrote about the Oreo's value in the lunchbox trade: "Once, in my older son's day-care class, a little boy traded away his winter coat (in Massachusetts, in midwinter, with snow on the ground), for an Oreo cookie" (1999:244). Thus, it appears that even the toddler set appreciates the value of the Oreo cookie. And the opinions of youngsters matter very much, considering the fervor with which the advertising industry directs its efforts toward them.

Given that, it is important to note that the Oreo cookie contained lard until 1993. So the cookie representative of the United States, land of freedom and equal opportunity, was off-limits to American Jews, or at least to observant ones. It is understood that certain foods are inherently nonkosher—there is a biblical mandate against them; for example, pork and shellfish. But there's no particular reason why a *cookie* ought to be nonkosher. For decades, though, plenty of Jewish kids—and their parents—felt a little "left out" in the cookie aisle.

There could be no speculation about the status of the cookie, no pretending that it might be okay to eat because the ingredient list betrayed no presence of questionable items. If there is one thing that non-Jews know about Jewish dietary restrictions, it is that Jews do not eat pig, or any of its derivatives. What is interesting in the case of the Oreo is that there is no particular reason—at least from the perspective of Jewish consumers—that a cookie ought to contain lard or to be off-limits, but, of course, it did, and it was. The Oreo possessed the aura of a "secret recipe" item—one whose formulation was perfect (aside from that pesky pork fat), yet shrouded in secrecy. It could be savored (by those permitted to enjoy it), but not duplicated.

Jews in America

Why should lack of access to a cookie (even if it is an iconographic cookie) matter? After all, *kashrut*-observant Jews willingly accept a construct that creates a barrier to eating certain foods. The cookie concern may be rooted in the staunch support Jews display for the ideals America represents. In return, there is a desire for inclusion in American society at large.

In the book *Jewish Identity in America*, Henry Feingold addresses this issue in an article entitled "The American Component of Jewish Identity." He points out: "Not only were Jews 'present at the creation' of America, but the creation itself had a Hebraic cast. As late as 1925, Calvin

Coolidge reminded the nation that it was 'Jewish mortar which cemented the foundations of American Democracy.' The Bible was important in eighteenth- and nineteenth-century America, and the Jews were the people of the book. No better legitimation could be asked for" (1991:73).

From the time of America's inception, then, Jews felt a connection to, and had a vested interest in, America's successful future as a nation. The values America was to stand for were familiar ones to Jews. Peace, justice, and liberty were merits to uphold. And Jews have historically been quite active in American cultural and political realms for just that reason. Feingold observes: "American Jews are at once the most separatist and activist constituency in the nation. Adherents of an ancient faith persistently accused of clannishness and separatism, are today ironically, America's fiercest advocates and staunchest citizens. They are exaggerated Americans in acting out the success ethos of American public culture, and yet also retain much of their distinctive communal perspective and style" (1991:72).

In other words, American Jews struggle to remain a distinct people, while embracing American ideals and avidly protecting them, not least in part so other peoples are free to maintain their own distinctions. If freedom for all American citizens is to exist, than sensitivity to and awareness of those distinctions is necessary.

Yet, achieving that balance" "between participation and isolation" has proved difficult for observant Jews, according to Jane Gross. Writing in the *New York Times* about young Modern Orthodox families in New York, Ms. Gross explains that while some Jews have tried to integrate traditional observance with modern life, others view such a move as inappropriate. There is an old joke that concludes that for every two Jews, you have three opinions. In the case of how to best to live as a traditionally committed Jew in the modern world, this seems especially true. But sometimes people want to stop thinking so hard about weighty issues like theology and the optimal expression of religious commitment. Sometimes they just need a cookie.

American Jews B.C. (Before Cookie)

In *The Wonders of America: Reinventing Jewish Culture, 1880–1950*, Jenna Weissman Joselit explains that until the turn of the century, many Jews kept kosher as best they could, particularly in the home. Kosher caterers, however, were as yet unheard of, so large-scale events were handled by caterers who had been prepped as best as possible on the laws of *kashrut*.

This tactic was not always successful, and sometimes dietary laws were ignored outright (1994:174–75). This inconsistent *kashrut* observance can also be linked to the fact that Jews were navigating new terrain. Living in a free country, with potentially unlimited mobility and the opportunity to *choose* one's behavior was a new experience for the immigrant Jew. Outside the confines of an insular Jewish community, experimentation was perhaps to be expected. The period could perhaps be described as an adolescence for American Jewry.

There were likewise many Jews, Weissman Joselit explains, who went to great lengths to convince nonobservers to embrace the laws of *kashrut*: "Borrowing heavily from anthropology and zoology, its defenders alternately sanitized, domesticated, aestheticzed, commodified, and otherwise reinterpreted the practice of keeping kosher" (1994:177). She goes on to say that none of these arguments for keeping kosher proved as powerful as the new availability, at the turn of the century, of mass-produced kosher food products (1994:187). Jews could now participate in the consumerism that defined American culture on a new level.

Manufacturers continued to target Jews with new kosher products, yet into the 1950s and 1960s, there persisted a "make do" mentality, even among strictly observant Jews. There was not a deliberate flouting of the laws of *kashrut* by any means, but there was a smaller availability of products specifically manufactured as kosher. *Kashrut* certification did not have the scope it does today, and there was a greater ignorance regarding mass food production (there was also less technological "tinkering" than there is today, a factor that will be discussed later). What was then considered diligence in the selection of food thought to be kosher would now be considered laxity. For example, in some communities, people might buy packaged products if the ingredients checked out and no offending item was present. If a package had a "K" (which is not today considered a valid certifying mark—just a letter of the alphabet), it would be purchased. Jell-O gelatin is a classic example. Many Jews assumed that the "K" appearing on Jell-O boxes signified an understanding of kosher laws by the manufacturer and the involvement of a supervising rabbi. In the case of gelatin, an animal derivative, there has been much rabbinical debate regarding its *kashrut* status. Some rabbis argue that it is so removed from its original state as to be valid for consumption. Most feel it is problematic, particularly because the bones and hides of nonkosher animals tend to be used in its production. Interestingly, Jell-O is remembered in some Orthodox circles as kosher. In fact, that trick of the collective Jewish unconscious may have much to do with the fact that Jell-O not only once ran advertisements in Yiddish (Wyman 2001:22), but that, as the Jewish Women's Archive Web site notes, the company sponsored a Yiddish-language radio show featuring entertainer Molly Picon.

Though today the "K" is rejected in Orthodox circles, considered unreliable "certification" at best and fraudulent at worst, many people once trusted it. (Letters of the alphabet cannot be trademarked, so a "K" cannot serve as a traceable symbol for any one certifier.) However, before *kashrut* supervision reached the scope and level of organization it boasts today, manufacturers displayed the "K" prominently on foodstuffs marketed as kosher. To the consumer, any mark at all was better than no mark; though the "K" was not the mark of a formal certifying body, such as the Orthodox Union. (Its mark is the "O" encircling a "U".)

Often, consumers would turn to their individual rabbis for guidance, who would extrapolate from *halachic* (legal) texts to determine *kashrut* status of products like jam. My mother remembers that Polaner jam, which was certified as kosher during the year but bore no special mark for Passover, was nonetheless deemed kosher for the holiday by a prominent (and Orthodox) Baltimore rabbi. Velveeta and Sunshine products were also largely "understood" to be kosher.

In the case of Sunshine products, it is likely that once again advertising played a role in the perception that the brand was kosher. Barbara Kirshenblatt-Gimblett's "Kitchen Judaism" includes an advertisement for Sunshine Kosher Crackers that ran on the cover of *The Jewish Examiner Prize Kosher Recipe Book.* Though no supervising rabbi's name or certifying organization's mark appears, "guaranteed kosher and 'parve'" and the word "kosher" in Hebrew print appear in the ad. Sunshine's Hydrox cookies were often regarded as the Jewish person's Oreo, and although they had no official certification, they were associated with kosher eaters. In fact, when I told a friend that I preferred Hydrox cookies to Oreos, he claimed it was because I still associated Oreos with lard.

The history of the Hydrox makes for an interesting side note here, as it has long been considered an inferior knock-off of the Oreo. In fact, Hydrox cookies, introduced in 1908, beat Oreos to the market by five years. Sunshine and Keebler (the one cookie conglomerate that arguably rivals Nabisco in scope and market power) merged in 1996. In a call to investigate whether Hydrox had been manufactured with vegetable (versus animal) shortening since their inception, a Keebler representative informed me that she believed so; she had been told, "the cookies had always been kosher." I wondered both whether she was aware of the significance of formal certification, and if Hydrox's acquisition of the O-U symbol was related to Oreo's certification. Upon further questioning, however, I discovered that she had in fact been referring to O-U certification. Hydrox had it before the merger in 1996. Oreos, conversely, contained lard until 1993 and did not get O-U certification until 1998. The process began earlier and Nabisco's machines were running as kosher in 1997, but certified packages of the cookie were not available until 1998. That year, Hydrox sales flagged sufficiently to inspire a sort of marketing triage. Ninety years after its initial launch, the Hydrox got a makeover: the package and cookie designs were modified, and the name was changed to Droxies. Whether the tactic will work remains to be seen, but whatever edge the Sunshine cookie once had over the Oreo has been leveled.

The Meaning of *Kashrut*

When most people think about Jews and the concept of kosher, they often think first about food. Indeed, this is a logical association and perhaps the most common application of the term. *Kashrut* is a Hebrew word that literally means "fitness." Kosher (*kasher* in Hebrew) is the root of the word *kashrut*. The term extends beyond food, however. Witnesses, properly prepared Torah scrolls, and *mezzuzot*, for example, are referred to as kosher. So too is an ethical, genuinely pious, religiously observant person. Actually, "kosher," as co-opted in American lingo, is very much in line with the true intent of the word. Kosher implies properness and acceptable behavior (Donin 1972:97). Interestingly, the non-Jew's perception of the meaning of *kashrut* is significant too in the mass marketing of kosher products. With this in mind, it is appropriate to consider the *kashrut* industry.

The Rise of "Techno-*Kashrut*"

Food processing is now a huge industry—and a remarkably complex one. This has created an opportunity for the *kashrut* industry's specialization and influence. It has also arguably made a technologically based *kashrut* certification necessary. It could even be said that the *kashrut* industry has raised issues that make such certification necessary; by questioning, for example, whether fourth-generation animal by-products would be considered nonkosher. A *halachic* (legal) debate twice the length of this paper could ensue on this point. In fact, some certifiers hold one opinion, and some hold another. Communities thus determine the validity of various certifications.

Either way, the *kashrut* industry has become as technologically based as the food industry. Huge databases exist to identify the composition and origin of all elements used in food production. Kosher certification and supervision is firmly rooted in the sciences. The Orthodox Union (O-U), one of the world's largest and most influential kashrut certifying bodies, developed "The Kosher Video" for food manufacturers. It explains various intricacies regarding kosher food manufacturing. For example, a butter oil may appear to be kosher. But an emulsifier in that oil may contain an ingredient involving a by-product developed on a growth medium that was of animal origin. The butter oil would have to be replaced by one that had been certified kosher, or the entire product would be *treif* (nonkosher) (Wexler and Luban 1998).

However, the video also stresses the financial rewards of gaining certification. In a press release announcing the launch of kosher Oreos ("Purim Baskets Get an Extra Treat This Year: Certified Kosher Oreos Debut This Month"), Nabisco makes it clear that smart marketing was a major motivator: "With an annual billion-dollar kosher market comprising 6.5 million diverse U.S. consumers O-U certification allows Nabisco deeper market penetration and enables millions more Americans to share in the unmatched taste of Oreo cookies."

The "diverse consumers" Nabisco mentioned are referred to by the O-U when they stress that it's not only the person who keeps a kosher home who qualifies as a kosher consumer. Rather, many people (Jews and non-Jews alike) believe that kosher food is cleaner, free from adulteration and contaminants, and that the extra level of supervision ensures a higher quality product (Wexler and Luban 1998). Wisely, the O-U does not suggest there is validity to the belief that food certified as kosher is more nutritious than nonkosher food, though many consumers believe this is so (*Cooking Light* 2000:28). In fact, it is a bit funny that so many people believe kosher food is cleaner than a comparable version of a nonkosher food. While bug or animal extractives may not be present in kosher products, artificial flavorings and colorings and hydrogenated fats are often present in both kosher and nonkosher products. That may not be much of a consolation for those desiring "clean" food.

So pervasive, though, is the mentality that kosher food is cleaner, more stringently supervised, and more wholesome, that Nabisco addressed these issues in the "Purim Basket" press release designed for the launch of kosher Oreos. They state that the certification "was not primarily based on ingredient changes, but adherence to strict production guidelines stipulated by the premier kosher certification agency." The implication here is that Oreos were essentially kosher anyway (they were not) and that certification was a technicality. Discussing the conversion process, specifically the "high heat and intense cleaning" procedures required to *kasher* equipment on the production lines, Nabisco reassures its public that "long established plant sanitation procedures made this an easier undertaking."

The belief that kosher food is purer, and its production better supervised, than nonkosher food has even been capitalized upon by the kosher food industry. Empire Kosher, the ubiquitous kosher poultry manufacturer, regularly one-ups Frank Perdue's one-line "tough man" patter in its advertising campaigns. In a campaign that ran in magazines such as *Gourmet*, Empire's advertisers assert that "compared to kosher, ordinary chicken doesn't have a prayer." The advertisement clearly targets those ignorant of the laws of *kashrut* and even subtly perpetuates a bit of misinformation. Asking the consumer if he knows what kosher really means, the advertisement states, "It's more than rabbis blessing chickens." In fact, rabbis do not bless kosher food, unless they are about to put it into their mouths. Every observant Jew knows a battery of such blessings, specific to various foods, made before and after eating. But the kosher certification process involves no such "Poof, you are now a kosher chicken" type blessings. Chickens are inherently kosher animals. The only blessings said during their production as a foodstuff are uttered by the *schochet*, or slaughterer, prior to slicing swiftly through the trachea, esophagus, and jugular of the animal. That misnomer aside, the remainder of the advertisement stresses that the stringency of the *kashrut* certification process ensures that Empire's birds are the "cleanest, healthiest, best-tasting" available. The advertisement also mentions "during the kosher process, we routinely reject birds the USDA passes." Having capitalized on fears of preservative-laden, campylobacter-ridden chickens, not to mention worries of governmental incompetence, Empire concludes "the secret's out: kosher is for everyone" (Empire Kosher Poultry, Inc., 1999).

The advertisement is an interesting counterpoint to one targeting observant, or at least *kashrut*-aware, Jews that ran in *Hadassah Magazine*. Less visually slick by far, the second advertisement trades clever Madison Avenue witticisms for a bulleted list of simple assertions. For instance, the advertisement states that Empire Kosher Chickens are antibiotic and hormone free, but refrains from implying that this means a "cleaner" chicken (nowhere, in fact, is the word "clean" mentioned). The chickens are cold-water processed and "grown free roaming in lush Amish country." Heading the advertisement is a little note of thanks to the *New York Times*, *Boston Globe*, and *Cook's Illustrated* magazine, all of which chose Empire Kosher as the best-tasting chicken in taste tests. Written in a style that almost suggests an afterthought, the last statement reads: "And of course [we] adhere to the strictest standards of Kashrus and quality." For this audience, the selling point of "The Chosen Chicken" seems to stem from its acceptance by the nonkosher contingent. The chickens live in Amish Country! People who aren't Jewish think they taste better! So, *nu?* Buy! Eat! This advertisement does not even attempt to sell the merits of *kashrut* to its Jewish audience. This is likely wise, as some Jews take the necessity of *kashrut* observance as a given, or else for granted, while others don't want to hear about it. But most Jews (perhaps especially the observant ones) do not mind hearing that people with a basis for comparison—those who do not have to keep kosher, like the kosher chickens best.

The Conversion

When kosher Oreos made their test-launch debut, they had blue cream centers and were called "Spring Oreos." Perhaps out of awareness that the robin's-egg-blue cream center is more evocative of dyed Easter eggs than it is of springtime, Nabisco pointed out that "Oreo fans nationwide . . . during a contest in 1996" had selected the color. They were so successful, they were being offered again, and this happened to coincide with the February 1998 launch. Skirting the Easter connotation altogether, Nabisco ran a press release with the headline "Purim Baskets Get an Extra Treat This Year: Certified Kosher Oreo Cookies to Debut This Month." Of course, calling them Easter Oreos may have been a poor marketing strategy, to say the least.

Anecdotally, in *The Kosher Video,* the cake from Drake's bakery that is being used as an example for the "conversion" process has red and green sprinkles—a Christmas cake! Is this coincidence? On the one hand, the red sprinkles provide the O-U with an example of the intricacies of certification. Carmine, which provides the red coloring, is a by-product of an insect and therefore not kosher. People unfamiliar with issues of *kashrut* would not have been exposed to such minutiae, so it is a helpful example. It cannot be overlooked, however, that the red and green color combination resonates strongly as symbolic of Christmas. Whether it was a conscious decision or not, the use of this cake as an example for nonkosher food manufacturers represents a suggestion by the O-U that they are capable of more than "converting" nonkosher food products to kosher ones. If manufacturers play their cards right (i.e., choose the most reliable kosher certifier), Jewish consumers may be persuaded to buy even a manufacturer's Christmas or Easter products.

This brings to mind another ticklish proposition—the very "conversion" of foods from nonkosher to kosher. Judaism, after all, is a non-proselytizing religion. Converts are actively discouraged because the obligations incurred are so formidable. And Jews often look askance at religions that seek to bolster their numbers via proselytizing. This may be true in part because on many occasions Jews were subject to forced conversion on penalty of death. So although it may seem merely an argument of semantics, I believe it is significant that the word "conversion" is so often used regarding a company's decision to begin manufacturing kosher products. An animal, for example, that is inherently nonkosher can never become kosher. So, too, no product containing an inherently nonkosher ingredient will ever get certification. But a company can reformulate a recipe to contain only kosher products, and can clean their factories under strict supervision, and thereby convert its products to kosher ones. For a people who have developed "a theology of particularism," as Robert Israel calls it, this strange word choice is notable (*The Kosher Pig* xiv).

Jew Meets Oreo

So anticipated was the debut of the kosher Oreo that the blue cream center appears to have been overlooked. (In fact, because the Spring Oreos were a seasonal line with limited availability, I suspect most observant Jews took their first bite from a classic black-and-white Oreo.) The response, nonetheless, was as varied as it was enthusiastic. One friend reported that the moment she found out that kosher Oreos were on supermarket shelves, she ran out and bought a bag, because she was curious about the cookies.

I also discovered a tongue-in-cheek essay entitled "*Hilkhot* Oreo" (the Laws of Oreo) on the World Wide Web. The anonymous author reported: "Unless we merit the coming of *Mashiach* [the messiah], 5758 [the Hebrew calendar year that corresponds with 1998] will go down in history as The Year That Oreos Became Kosher." The author goes on to address the actual eating of Oreos in the format of a Talmudic debate: "One can postulate that if white represents purity and goodness, and black evil and darkness, then perhaps one should eat the white first, as an example of the *yetzer hatov* [good inclination] triumphing over the *yetzer hora* [evil inclination]?"

Perhaps it was this aspect of ritualistic eating that attracted Jews to the Oreo. After all, Jewish observance is rich with food rituals, even on an everyday basis. Alternately, Lucy Long's paper on culinary tourism provides some insight into the appeal of the Oreo for the *kashrut*-observant

Jew. Most Americans would likely laugh to consider the Oreo an exotic food item. But they were absolutely off-limits (inedible) before their certification. Furthermore, as American icons, Oreos represented a taste of America itself and could therefore be considered exotic. The *kashering* process made the inedible edible. But the Oreo was not familiar until it was finally experienced (1996:4–5).

Eating Out: From *Treif* Chinese to Kosher Sushi

Access to Oreos alone is not sufficient to satisfy the culinary curiosity of the *kashrut*-observant Jew. The presence of kosher-certified Japanese, Indian, Italian, Thai, Chinese, French, and American restaurants is testimony enough that observant Jews want the opportunity to enjoy the foods of other cultures, and to be able to do so with the same freedom as their fellow Americans. "Eating out" no longer requires eating out of the bounds of *kashrut*. It is possible, though, that the enormous interest in the restaurant experience has been fed by the enthusiasm of those who have bent the rules for a taste of the exotic.

In their study entitled "New York Jews and Chinese Food: The Social Construction of an Ethnic Pattern," Gaye Tuchman and Harry Gene Levine theorize about the apparent love affair American Jews (in this case New York Jews of Ashkenazic descent) have with Chinese food. They point out that while Jewish immigrants in the early 1900s had kosher delicatessens or restaurants serving traditional Eastern European fare at their disposal, many eschewed this familiar food. Instead, they sought to shed the image of a ghettoized people and to fully experience the freedoms promised in America. For some, this meant seeking exposure to new cuisines, and Chinese restaurants proved the most useful for fulfilling this desire. The restaurants were easily accessible—as Chinese, Jewish, and Italian immigrants lived in neighboring communities on Manhattan's Lower East Side—and inexpensive, a prerequisite for the generally poor immigrant population. At the same time, Chinese food was perceived as exotic and therefore cosmopolitan, while the Chinese restaurant owners welcomed all diners. The Italian restaurants, by contrast, were intended for an Italian clientele.

Tuchman and Levine quip that Chinese food was "safe *treyf* [nonkosher food]" (1993:166). This is perhaps the most important factor in the immigrant Jew's adoption of the cuisine. While Chinese cooking often relies on the use of pork and shellfish—overtly non-kosher animals—the ingredients are often so well integrated into the dishes as to be almost hidden, or "disguised" (1993:168–69). Chinese cooking technique often involves fine chopping and mincing of the ingredients, so nonkosher elements of the finished foods were hard to detect. Moreover, milk is absent in Chinese cuisine, so Jews were at least able to abide by the biblical prohibition against mixing milk and meat, even if they were eating nonkosher animals (or kosher vegetables prepared in nonkosher pots and thus rendered nonkosher as well). Chinese food may have felt kosher because there were tastes that both Jews and Chinese preferred, such as garlic, onions, and sweet and sour flavors. Both European Jews and the Chinese were tea drinkers (1993:169–70), and just as the Jews hold chicken soup in high esteem for its purported healing powers, so do the Chinese (Simonds 1999: 28).

Immigrant Jews, then, may have found a comfortable medium for acculturation into American society through Chinese food. Tuchman and Levine assert that the habit of eating Chinese food out became so ingrained that by the second generation, a new tradition had emerged. Jews associated–"eating this kind of non-Jewish food—Chinese food—as something modern American Jews, and especially New York Jews, did together" (1993:166). What Tuchman and Levine do not address, however, is that not all Jews were willing to eat nonkosher food—ever. And they do intimate that though Jews may have loved Chinese food, the consumption of it seemed to have its place only in restaurants. Those who did occasionally bring the food home were likely to eat it off of paper plates so kosher dishes would not be rendered nonkosher.

In fact, it may have been the restaurant experience, at least as much as the food, that Jews craved. Perhaps in the exotic setting of a richly decorated Chinese restaurant the otherwise taboo status of nonkosher foods could be overlooked. Perhaps that the food was considered taboo contributed to the exoticism of the experience. Around one's own dining room table, however, some of the intrigue was likely lost. Rationalizing the consumption of a nonkosher meal may have been more difficult for those Jews who still felt a tie to *kashrut* observance.

Granted, some Jews have always observed the laws of *kashrut* uncompromisingly and out of genuine religious conviction. Particularly in America, however, there have been many variations on *kashrut* observance or lack thereof. It would be inaccurate to lament though, as some do, that Jews simply became less religious in the New World than they had been in the Old World. It is true that in *practice* many old-world Jews upheld the laws of *kashrut* and *Shabbat* along with their coreligionists. It should be noted, however, that Jews in Europe were seldom fully or comfortably integrated into the mainstream Christian culture. They often lived together, sometimes by governmental decree, in villages or ghettos, isolated from non-Jews. Living together in this manner made the Jews vulnerable to attack, on the one hand, and allowed them to look out for each other, in whatever capacity they could, on the other. In the face of adversity, religion offered unification of the community, a context for worldly events, and perhaps comfort. But even for those Jews who may have questioned their belief or the way in which Jews observed the Torah would have been hard-pressed *not* to observe the laws in a traditional manner. The food available was kosher, the community structure was built around the synagogue, and the rabbi was the authority, leader, and voice of the community (and often the liaison to the non-Jewish higher-ups). There was little room for variation or personalization of the laws without risk of being ostracized by the community. In fact, Howard M. Sachar points out in *A History of the Jews in America* that most Jewish immigrants had been members of "overwhelmingly secular" political and cultural movements: "Authentically devout Jews (as distinguished from the passively traditional majority) rarely ventured the journey to the United States. They had been forewarned. Letters from family members and reports of Yiddish-press correspondents had emphasized that piety was not survivable in America" (1992:189).

As it turned out, piety could survive not only the secular environment in America, it could also survive a love affair with Chinese food. Recognizing the cuisine's enormous popularity, some Jews responded by offering kosher Chinese options. Bernstein's-on-Essex, a delicatessen on Manhattan's Lower East Side, offered two menus—one deli, one Chinese (Schneider 2000:14:2). Ruth and Bob Grossman published the tongue-in-cheek *Chinese-Kosher Cookbook*, complete with instructions in case "You're using maybe chopsticks?" (1965:5).

Though Chinese food is still popular, it is arguably no longer exotic. Sushi chefs are de rigueur during the cocktail hour at fashionable kosher weddings. There is kosher Persian in Baltimore, kosher barbecue in Chicago, and kosher Thai in New York. Diners may be getting a bit jaded, particularly if they live in cities with very large and active Jewish populations. Today, it may be as much *where* an observant Jew can eat that feels exotic, and therefore touristic, as *what* can be eaten. Several Major League ballparks have kosher concessions. Kosher weddings and events are easily accommodated at mainstream hotels that have facilities for kosher caterers. Cruise ships willingly accommodate kosher guests. A friend selected the hotel for her honeymoon in Hawaii in part because it offered kosher room service. And a special exoticism is afforded to those kosher restaurants deemed "good enough" to share with non-Jewish friends and colleagues. All of this can amount to greater mobility, freedom, and flexibility for the observant Jew, without necessitating the compromise of *kashrut* standards.

Not everyone is pleased with these developments, however. As related by Edward S. Shapiro, in *A Time for Healing: American Jewry Since World War II*:

> The symbiosis between Jewish and non-Jewish cultures manifested by these eateries caused Rabbi Menashe Klein, the leading Hasidic *posek* [authority on and arbiter of Jewish law] in America, to issue a ruling forbidding Jews from eating in such restaurants. . . . In his collection of responses entitled *Mishneh Halakhot* (vol.10), Klein emphasized that these restaurants were defeating one of the major purposes of kashrut—to separate Jews from non-Jews. While Jews might not be walking in the ways of Gentiles, he emphasized, they certainly were eating in their ways, and consequently "it is forbidden to enter restaurants that have non-Jewish names and non-Jewish styles of cooking and food which is given non-Jewish names. It is also forbidden to participate in weddings and affairs where this style of food and drink are served." (1992:183)

What is so astounding about Rabbi Klein's ruling, apart from its extreme nature, is the extent to which it ignores a major Jewish reality—that Jews have, throughout a nearly two-thousand-year exile, lived in virtually every country on the globe. As a natural consequence, they have adopted and adapted local cooking styles, ingredients, and techniques. While the food of India's Jews may differ somewhat from the food of their neighbors, it is distinctly Indian nonetheless. In Rabbi Klein's narrow view of Jewish cuisine, the vast majority of *kashrut*-observant Jews would be deemed nonkosher.

Klein is not alone, however, in his perception of what constitutes Jewish food. American Jews, the majority of whom are Ashkenazic (of Eastern European descent), likewise seem to harbor a very limited view of Jewish food. But to say that Jewish food means chicken soup is about as accurate as saying Mexican food means tacos, or Italian food equals spaghetti. *The Book of Jewish Food: An Odyssey from Samarkand to New York*, by Claudia Roden, is a fantastic testament to just how extensive and varied the Jewish experience with food has been. Interestingly, although Jews are becoming quite familiar with formerly exotic cuisines, eating, for example, kosher Italian food as it is ordinarily prepared and enjoyed by non-Jewish Italians, they are far less familiar with traditionally Jewish versions of foreign cuisines. As the *kashrut*-observant continue to seek out new dining experiences, they may end up returning to the exotic cooking styles of other Jews.

Culinary Tourism by the Book

Cultivating appreciation for the unfamiliar foodways of other Jews seems a priority for Batia Plotch and Patricia Cobe. They make mention throughout *The Kosher Gourmet* of the very rich heritage of international kosher cooking, apparently in hopes of inspiring a sort of Jewish heritage–oriented brand of culinary tourism. But perhaps the deeper purpose of the book is to reinvigorate interest, in whatever way possible, in keeping kosher. Culled from a series of kosher cooking classes offered at Manhattan's Ninety-Second Street YM-YWHA (Young Men's-Young Women's Hebrew Association), many of the recipes were developed by an international core of non-Jewish instructors who adapted those recipes they considered most representative of their native lands according to the laws of *kashrut*. The goal was to provide an "authentic" taste of cuisines that might have been otherwise inaccessible to the kosher cook. There seems to be a dual message at play: to the nonobservant Jew accustomed to eating the foods of all cultures, the authors imply that *kashrut* observance needn't stand in the way of that exploration. At the same time, they communicate to *kashrut*-observers that perhaps they ought to expand their palates and culinary repertoires.

In *Master Chefs Cook Kosher*, Judy Zeidler enlists the aid of culinary heavy hitters such as Roger Vergé, Michel Richard, Joyce Goldstein, and Thomas A. Keller to demonstrate the possibility of imbuing kosher cooking at home with a restaurant-like sophistication, whether with haute cuisine or fashionably rustic inflections. Recipes include former White House chef Stephan Pyles's Pumpkin–White Bean Chowder with Garlic Croutons and Pomegranate Crème Fraîche, Keller's Poached Quail Egg on a Spoon, or Mary Sue Milliken and Susan Feniger's Border Grill Skewered Salmon with Yucatan-Style Marinade and Lime Vinaigrette. There is appeal in the idea that these esteemed culinarians were willing to adapt recipes and cooking techniques—to concede, as it were, to the constructs of *kashrut* (though in many cases, they may have presented recipes that were inherently kosher and needed no adaptation at all). So, too, the notion that one might be able to experience, via a chef's recipe, what it is like to eat at, say, the French Laundry or Border Grill is an exciting one to Jews whose observance prohibits visiting those restaurants (never mind that recipes adapted by chefs for home kitchens are virtually never as labor-intensive or involved as those served in the restaurant).

Interestingly, as *kashrut*-observant Jews have moved away from traditional (or in some cases, stereotypical) Jewish foods, those once familiar foods become exotic. Even at holiday celebrations, when a reversion to traditional foodways might be expected, some strive for "updates," replacing, say, their grandmother's Passover recipes with a seder menu lifted from the pages of *Gourmet*. But sentimentality for the traditional persists, both for nonobservant and *kashrut*-observant Jews. Mitchell Davis's *The Mensch Chef: or Why Delicious Jewish Food Isn't an Oxymoron* wholeheartedly embraces the Ashkenazic foods and culture that some *kashrut*-observant Jews seem to negotiate an uneasy balance with, and defies the idea that Jewish cuisine (whatever that is) is somehow inferior to other cuisines.

Davis, the director of publications for the James Beard Foundation, notes in his "Yiddish for Cooks" glossary entry on *kashrut*, "Me, I eat mostly *traif*." And he does not purport to have written a *kosher* cookbook at all; while all of the recipes can be made kosher, Davis neither requires nor expects *kashrut*-observance of his readers. He does, however, keep the uninitiated informed. He wittily notes the kosher status of each recipe, indicating, for example, that corned beef is *fleishig* (meat), "but, if you put it in a Rueben sandwich with Swiss cheese, it will become *traif*." The book may not be kosher, but it exemplifies—perhaps even more so than many kosher cookbooks—a *Jewish* cookbook. Some authors focus on diminishing the differences between kosher and nonkosher cuisine by stripping away references to Judaism—or, more precisely Jewishness—even while attending to the technical rules of *kashrut* observance. Davis, on the other hand, peppers his book with "Mental Noshes," "A Bissel Advice," and a borscht-belt sense of humor that makes the book read much like a primer on Ashkenazic Jewish culture. As much as *The Mensch Chef* is a cookbook, it is a very entertaining touristic textbook.

Tasting *Treif* (If It's Fake)

For some, the cooking styles of other Jews—no matter how foreign or (formerly) familiar the cuisine—is not exotic enough. Of far more appeal would be finding out what distinctly nonkosher foods taste like, but being able to do it in a kosher fashion. Also of import, is being told that the "safe *treif*" tastes just like the real thing by someone who knows. The desire to explore and to understand what it is other Americans prize in the genuine, nonkosher items may motivate experimentation with the kosher versions. Or it may be that *kashrut*-observant Jews desire the freedom to have unlimited access to all foods and create an artificial construct to fulfill that desire. Jenna Weissman Joselit postulates that the value of foods like beef-frye "was as much symbolic as gustatory: it held out the very real and tantalizing possibility that the observance of *kashrut* posed no barrier to participation in the wider world, at least in a culinary sense. After all, even kosher Jews could now eat bacon!" (1994:193). Convenience too, and the ability to "follow" nonkosher recipes without seemingly significant changes, factors in. "Pepperoni" pizza and "shrimp" salads are no longer off-limits. The line between staunch religious observance and extreme acculturation is blurred.

Just Visiting

Discussions of culinary tourism often center on the experience of, or experimentation with, the exotic. But it is interesting to consider the idea of tourism in the traditional, travel-oriented sense, particularly concerning tourism's temporal or transient nature. In that context, there may be greater psychological openness to experimentation with new foods or foodways; if the tourist is just visiting, the exotic may feel more like a safe adventure and less like a threat to the familiar. Whether the exotic is ultimately abandoned or adopted is another issue entirely. But the initial approach may be eased by the knowledge that back at home the familiar is waiting, in case the new experience turns out to be somehow unsatisfactory.

For the *kashrut*-observant tourist, that notion of a home base is quite important. As a religion that is at once fiercely communal and highly introspective, Judaism lends itself to negotiating between private and public realms, even in terms of culinary tourism. No matter how that tourism finds its expression, it bridges the private, domestic realm with the public, commercial realm. Perhaps more precisely, there's a private ethos or motivation behind this variety of tourism, though it is often acted out in a public or commercial context.

Getting What One Wants, and the Ramifications Thereof (or So What if Oreos Are Kosher?)

Many Jews derive a heightened sense of spirituality from keeping kosher. But it may be a challenge to maintain that spirituality while grabbing

packages by rote from supermarket shelves because they bear an acceptable symbol. Some commentators maintain that the value of *kashrut* is
its elevation of mundane necessities (the preparation of food and the eating of it) to a spiritual level. One such mundane necessity could be the
searching out of kosher symbols. This theory assumes, of course, that one
considers cooking and eating mundane. In fact, though a necessity, it is
arguable that food preparation and eating are rather direct links to spiritual fulfillment. Jewish theology considers each person a partner with
God. It is assumed that God provides the raw materials (water, produce,
animals) necessary to nourish the bodies we occupy. The act of preparing
food provides the opportunity to enhance this partnership by facilitating
the process of nourishing the body. Eating and digestion can be considered
daily miracles. Even without comprehending the Krebs cycle—the complex series of biochemical reactions through which energy is generated
from the metabolites of ingested food—we feel a change in energy level,
mood, and comfort when we eat. The blessings observant Jews say before
and after meals and snacks ideally foster reflection on these matters.

The difficulty, then, is that as opportunities for food preparation (or at
least the likelihood thereof) are diminished, the more tenuous the spiritual connection to food becomes. American Jews are very much a part of
American culture. And American culture is a product culture, with an
emphasis on the well-packaged, the quick and convenient. As *kashrut*
certification proliferates, it is easier than ever to participate in America's
consumer culture, at least with regard to food. As Elizabeth Ehrlich points
out in *Miriam's Kitchen*, even *kashering* meat (the process of salting and
soaking meat to remove any blood), which used to be done in the home, is
now done by the butcher as a convenience to the customer (1997:229). An
individual's active involvement used to be essential to ensuring a food
was kosher; used to even, in the case of *kashering* meat, complete the
process. It is perhaps far more difficult to imbue the quick visual check for
a symbol on a package with meaning.

Haym Soloveitchick, writing about the Modern Orthodox and ultra-
Orthodox Jewish communities, elucidates further:

> Even the accomplishments of Orthodoxy had their untoward conse-
> quences. The smooth incorporation of religious practice into middle-class
> lifestyle meant that observance differentiated less. Apart from their formal
> requirements, religious observances also engender ways of living. Eating
> only kosher food, for example, precludes going out to lunch, vacationing
> where one wishes, and dining out regularly as a form of entertainment. The

proliferation of kosher eateries and the availability of literally thousands of kosher products in the consumer market, opened the way to such pursuits, so the religious way of life became, in one more regard, less distinguishable from that of others. The facilitation of religious practice that occurred in every aspect of daily life was a tribute to the adaptability of the religious and to their new mastery of their environment; it also diminished some of the millennia old impact of observance." (1999:329)

On the other hand, Rabbi Joseph Grunblatt, Rabbinic Vice Chairman of the NCSY (National Conference of Synagogue Youth) National Youth Commission views "high level *kashrut* certification" as a "theological statement." Lucy Long's "other" (non-Jews, nonobservant Jews) may consider the Jewish exegesis a static one—unchanging, perhaps even unyielding—and this may be viewed in a negative sense, as a lack of adaptability. So, too, may the observant Jew appreciate this characteristic from an alternate point of view. The Torah, while a "living" treatise, or blueprint for life, does nonetheless derive its essence from certain inalienable, divinely ordered principals—the truth is unchangeable, but our interpretations or understandings are not. Torah is therefore dynamic and fluid. The emphasis placed on the importance of widespread certification, it is argued, suggests to the world that *kashrut*, indeed Jewish religious observance itself, is vital, adaptable, and relevant to today's world.

The Gastronomic Jew, Redux

Many American Jews, though not religiously observant, nonetheless feel very connected to Judaism in a cultural sense. Often, this connection manifests itself via the consumption of foods perceived to be specifically "Jewish." Bagels and lox, chicken soup, blintzes, *kreplach* (wontonlike dumplings), and brisket are among the foods that resonate as Jewish foods. The term "gastronomic Jew" has long been applied to a person who may not attend synagogue or observe the Sabbath but will eat a corned beef sandwich as if he's fulfilling a sacred commandment.

With the rise in popularity of Orthodoxy, there may be a new kind of gastronomic Jew evolving. In kosher restaurants today, the diner is unlikely to find chopped liver on the menu. It has been replaced by foie gras. This is perhaps a signal of extreme acculturation, on the one hand, or a sign of Jews who are increasingly comfortable with their identities in America, on the other. As Edward S. Shapiro points out, eating out is an indication of the willingness to publicize one's Orthodoxy, and demonstrates "a greater confidence in American Pluralism." Furthermore, he says that kosher restaurants "disclosed an impulse toward cultural amalgamation as the Orthodox strove to combine the best of the Jewish and the outside worlds. The consumption of haute cuisine, even if kosher, was in itself essentially a secular act" (1992:182).

Jews who are not *kashrut*-observant have long been "touring" cuisines of their own accord, and the certification of kosher restaurants may have no significance for them. The Jews who have been keeping kosher all along, both in and out of the house, now have their passports, so to speak. This may be part of the power of the certifying agencies. So, too, the presence of a certifying symbol on a food product communicates social acceptance to the *kashrut*-observant Jew. Major manufacturers not only accommodate the rather intricate and particular requirements of a very small population, but also facilitate comfortable, and public, religious observance. Historically, that level of accommodation was not a privilege afforded most Jews. In some ways, each newly certified food represents an invitation to tourism—the chance to taste, and to get more deeply involved in American culture.

Conclusions

Paradoxically, widespread *kashrut* certification has at once complicated and simplified the experience of keeping kosher. Observant American Jews can now shop with the same convenience, for many of the same foods, as their fellow Americans. They can travel the country or the world, "treasure hunting" for specialties that bear *kashrut* certification. Eating out, discovering the foodways of others, even reconnecting with the exotic foodways of other Jews, is now possible on a scale never before experienced. But there are new considerations to grapple with for every advance of the *kashrut* industry and for each new product launch.

What happens, for example, when Jews are presented as a market niche? Is the marketing of kosher foods and restaurants totally innocuous? As agencies assume the responsibility for ensuring the *kashrut* status of foodstuffs, what happens to the individual's spiritual connection to observance? Is re-creating or remembering meaning for *kashrut* the new discipline for the observant Jew who can now buy a kosher version of nearly every food product?

For much of their history, Jews have been an itinerant people. In the past, though culinary tourism occurred naturally on some level—as Jews adapted available ingredients to suit the dietary laws—it was nonetheless borne of necessity. Perhaps one of the greatest indications that Jews at last feel rooted in America is the desire to—"tour" on a grander, more deliberate scale. Kosher food and branded American products, or international cuisines, or even "safe *treif*" are reconcilable notions. And all can be enjoyed poolside, in a swanky hotel, at a neighborhood bistro, or around the family table. Virtually any version of the American dream that the kosher diner harbors can now be conjured up with relative ease. Or he can stay at home, munching on Oreos.

Works Cited

Adler, Elizabeth Mosby. 1983. "Creative Eating: The Oreo Syndrome." *Foodways and Eating Habits: Directions for Research.* Eds. Michael Owen Jones, Bruce Giuliano, and Roberta Krell. Los Angeles: California Folklore Society.

"A Statement of Principals for Reform Judaism." 2000. Central Conference of American Rabbis Home Page. <http://ccarnet.org/platforms/principles.html>. October 26.

Covert, Mildred L., and Sylvia P. Gerson. 1982. *Kosher Creole Cookbook.* Gretna, La.: Pelican .

Davis, Mitchell. 2002. *The Mensch Chef: or Why Delicious Jewish Food Isn't an Oxymoron.* New York: Clarkson Potter.

Donin, Hayim Halevy. 1972. *To Be a Jew: A Guide to Jewish Observance in Contemporary Life.* New York: Basic Books, .

Ehrlich, Elizabeth. 1997. *Miriam's Kitchen.* New York: Penguin Books.

Eidlitz, Rabbi Eliezer. 1999. *Is It Kosher?: Encyclopedia of Kosher Food Fact and Fallacies.* *Jerusalem*: Feldheim.

Empire Kosher. Advertisement. 1999. *Gourmet,* September: 119.

Empire Kosher. Advertisement. 1998. *Hadassah Magazine,* October: 55.

Feingold, Henry. 1991. "The American Component of Jewish Identity." *Jewish Identity in America.* Eds. David M. Gordis and Yoav Ben-Horin. Los Angeles: Wilstein Institute.

Goldman, Ari L. 2000. *Being Jewish: The Spiritual and Cultural Practice of Judaism Today.* New York: Simon & Schuster.

Gross, Jane. 1999. "Young Orthodox Jews' Quest Is to Blend Word and World." *New York Times. "*September 16(late ed.): A1.

Grossman, Ruth, and Bob Grossman. 1965. *The Kosher Cookbook Trilogy.* New York: Eriksson.

Grunblatt, Rabbi Joseph. 1999. "Thinking Kosher." *Orthodox Union Web Page.* <www.ou.org/kosher/intro.html>. November 3.

"Hilkhot Oreo.""1999. *Lori's Mishmash Humor Page.* <http://www.jewishjokes.tripod.com/index2.html>. December 1.

"How Do I Love Thee, Oreo? America Counts the Ways." 1999. News release. Nabisco. Parsippany, N.J. February 25.

Israel, Richard J. 1993. *The Kosher Pig and Other Curiosities of Modern Jewish Life.* Los Angeles: Alef Design Group.

Keebler Representative. 1999. Telephone Interview. December 2.

Kirshenblatt-Gimblett, Barbara. 1990. "Kitchen Judaism." Exhibition Catalogue: *Getting Comfortable in New York: The American Jewish Home 1880–1950.* Eds. Susan L. Braunstein and Jenna Weissman Joselit. New York: The Jewish Museum, exhibition held September 16–November 15.

Klass, Perri. 1999.–"The Lunch Box as Battlefield." *Gourmet,* November: 244.

"Kosher Catches On." 2000. *Cooking Light.* August: 28.

"Purim Baskets Get an Extra Treat This Year: Certified Kosher Oreo Cookies to Debut this Month.""1999. *Nabisco Home Page.* <www.oreo.com/allabout/ aa-kosher.html>. November 3.

Long, Lucy M. 1996. "Culinary Tourism, Eating an Other; or Adventurous Eating in Small Town Midwest." Joint Nutrition Conference, St. Louis, June.

Mirvis, Tova. 1999. *The Ladies Auxiliary.* New York: Ballantine.

"Molly Picon" 2003. *Jewish Women's Archive Web site.* <www.jwa.org/exhibits/ picon/mp10.htm>. January 9.

Plotch, Batia and Patricia Cobe, eds. 1992. *The Kosher Gourmet.* New York: Fawcett Columbine.

Roden, Claudia. 1997. *The Book of Jewish Food: An Odyssey from Samarkand to New York.* New York: Knopf.

Sachar, Howard M. 1992. *A History of the Jews in America.* New York: Vintage Books.

Schneider, Daniel B. 2000. "F.Y.I.: Egg Rolls Fit for a Rabbi.""*New York Times.* April 16 (late ed.): sec. 14:2.

Shapiro, Edward S. 1992. *A Time for Healing: American Jewry Since World War II.* Baltimore: Johns Hopkins University Press.

Simonds, Nina. 1999. *A Spoonful of Ginger: Irresistible, Health-Giving Recipes from Asian Kitchens.* New York: Knopf.

Soloveitchick, Haym. 1999. "Rupture and Reconstruction: The Transformation of Contemporary Orthodoxy." *Jews in America: A Contemporary Reader.* Eds. Roberta Rosenberg Farber and Chaim I Waxman. Hanover, N.H.: Brandeis University Press.

Spice and Spirit: The Complete Kosher Jewish Cookbook. 1990. Brooklyn, N.Y.: Lubavitch Women's Cookbook Publications.

Tuchman, Gaye, and Harry Gene Levine. 1993. "New York Jews and Chinese Food: The Social Construction of an Ethnic Pattern." *Journal of Contemporary Ethnography* 22, 3 (October): 382–407.

Weissman Joselit, Jenna. 1994. *The Wonders of America: Reinventing Jewish Culture, 1880–1950.* New York: Hill and Wang.

Wexler, Lyle and Rabbi Yaakov Luban. 1998. *The Kosher Video: Kosher Supervision in the Modern Age.* Video. The Orthodox Union.

Wyman, Carolyn. 2001. *Jell-O: A Biography.* San Diego: Harcourt.

Zeidler, Judy. 1998. *Master Chefs Cook Kosher.* San Francisco: Chronicle.

CHAPTER 8

Culinary Tourism among Basques and Basque Americans

Maintenance and Inventions

Jacqueline S. Thursby

Lucy Long has defined culinary tourism as adventurous eating with consideration of contextual significance *and* with consideration of the perspective and motivations of the eater. (1998:181) This definition, and other discussions I have read about tourism and culture since reading Long's work, have named and clarified to me some dimensions of my own decade-long research among the Basque Americans. Cecelia Jouglard, a Basque woman who immigrated to the United States from northern Spain in 1942, served an exquisite cod dinner (*bacalao a la Vizcaina*) in Rupert, Idaho; I was an honored guest at that meal. After dinner she remarked, "To understand the Basques, Jackie, you must eat the food. Then you will understand our people" (interview).

Cecelia's words lingered in my mind as I embarked on a culinary journey that took me through Idaho, Oregon, California, Nevada, Wyoming, Montana, and even across the Atlantic to the Basque Country of northern Spain and southern France in my quest to "understand the Basques." I explored culinary domains of Basque food in the old country and here in the United States to learn for myself what it was about the food that made it so important that simply eating it would yield cultural understanding. Over time, I learned that Basques prepare their food with studied expertise and care in order to serve it in peak form. There was a point at which I realized that Cecelia was right. The finesse practiced in cooking reflects the culture; these are a people who savor not only their food, but also their lives. They live carefully with intelligence, excellence, and self-respect.

My exploration and discovery of their food and their culture is presented in the next few pages.

Long defines culinary tourism as "the intentional, exploratory participation in the foodways of an other, participation including the consumption—or preparation and presentation for consumption—of a food item, cuisine, meal system, or eating style considered as belonging to a culinary system not one's own" (1998:181). Immersion in Basque foodways provided a new aesthetic experience that overlaid my past culinary exploration. I have always had an adventuresome palate, and the Basque foods both meshed and sometimes clashed with what I already knew. "All cultures," Oriol Pi-Sunyer wrote, "engage in taxonomic exercises. The universe of experience is categorized, organized, and then related to in terms of culturally defined measures of equivalence and difference" (1989:193). PI-Sunyer continues to explain that structures like this function like a "template" and allow individuals to relate to others in terms of perceived cultural and social difference. (1989:193).

Cross-cultural culinary seasonings have influenced my personal experience. I grew up in St. Louis, Missouri, where my parents owned a professional dry cleaning business. "Professional" in this sense meant that they handled difficult fabrics and did most of the cleaning and finishing by hand. They had to have highly trained employees, and as it turned out many of their employees were from other countries. The business was small, and it was a place where individual cultures came together on friendly middle ground. Because people shared their cultures, when I was a young child I tasted rabbit prepared in wine by a French war bride. There was also strudel lovingly stretched, folded, and shared frequently by a German seamstress. One woman, a black southerner, took me home with her one day, and I tasted my first sweet potato pie. My grandmother's Jewish neighborhood in the 1940s, and her friendly forays into the delicatessens with me in tow, allowed me to taste bagels, matzo soup, big dill pickles, and delicate pastries long before it was vogue to taste the food of the other. Even so, the variegated template of my experience hardly prepared me for the subtle flavors and varied food phenomena that the Basques offered. I could categorize (vegetables, fruits, meat, dairy, and fats), and I could mentally and physically organize those categories into various recipes and combinations from my past experience, but I was pleasantly unprepared for the Basque "culturally defined measures of equivalence and difference" (Pi-Sunyer 1989:193). I ate carefully prepared foods with the Basques that I didn't even know were edible—from squid ink to elvers (immature eels). Truly, I tasted their culture.

The food exploration I was able to undertake among the Basques, both in the United States and in the old country, revealed nuances of their culinary talent expressed in myriad ways. Throughout the world, the Basque table is defined by an inherited region and culture. There are inventions and syntheses, but the region *of* the Basque Country (situated on the Bay of Biscay at the inner elbow between Spain and France) and the regions *within* the country (coastal, midland plains and hills, and mountains) help define the foods the people prefer and present to onlookers. Food performance arenas among the Basques are many, and food is manipulated as a symbol of identity. Though language is the primary identifying marker of the Basques in the Old World, restaurants, festivals, private celebrations, cookbooks, magazines, and other strategies are used to help define this culture both in the Old and New World. In the New World, it is the food that most clearly defines the Basque American people from other Americans; however, the uniqueness of their food sometimes falls under the shadow of Mexican foods (the beans and *chorizos*), just as the Basque culture in the old country has been greatly diluted by the presence of the Spanish.

In the Old Country

The Basque Country is little more than one hundred miles long and eighty miles wide, and it straddles the Pyrenees Mountains. The traditional view of the country is of one nation encompassing seven provinces: four on the Spanish side and three on the French. The official Basque Country on the Spanish side has an autonomous government linked to Madrid; the three provinces on the French side became unofficial during the French Revolution and are not legally recognized by the French government. There are voices in the Basque Country, in Spain, that call for independence; among them are a few who occasionally resort to terrorism to make their point. However, for the vast majority, life is lived in harmony with their Spanish and French neighbors. The Basque Country is ancient and steeped in traditions that wind back, many Basques claim, to the Neanderthal man and cave paintings found in the rolling foothills of the Pyrenees. Their language is unique and non-Indo-European. Scholars have tried and failed to trace its origins, and that knowledge continues to remain a mystery shrouded with layers of guesses.

Basques continue to enjoy and propagate the essence of mystery they believe surrounds them because of their unidentifiable language and ancient, obscure history. Their tiny homeland looks almost like a fairyland with mountain forests, hidden caves, icy mountain streams, hidden Christian grottos, and ruins of ancient Roman roads. There are many legends and folk stories concerning the origin of the Basque people, and some of the Basques even claim lineage to the Garden of Eden and a pure Adamic language. According to most scholars, however, Iberians first invaded Spain and settled in the north and beyond the Pyrenees into what is now southern France. Other invaders followed (Phoenicians, Greeks, Romans, and Goths), but none succeeded in conquering the *Vascones*, or Basques, who were a clannish mountain people. Further, no invaders succeeded in significantly influencing their language. They governed themselves, declared their entire populace noble and exempt from military conscription by invaders, and to this day continue to nurse their great national pride. The language and the foods of the Basque people still serve as significant historical and cultural markers, and many efforts are still being made to preserve this ancient but dynamic and unique language and way of life.

It was in the old country that I learned the aesthetic of the Basque foods. To eat the carefully prepared dishes and savor the aromas and flavors is to have a deep sensory experience, as Cecelia implied, and Long wrote, the food can take us to "a deeper, more integrated level of experiencing the Other" (1998:182). The basic ingredients, mildly seasoned and for the most part remarkably common, take on a unique and exquisite character when prepared under the hand of an experienced and serious Basque cook. Vegetables are steamed to perfection and seasoned to enhance, not disguise their flavor. Meat is cooked according to its type and cut, not indiscriminately boiled, broiled, or fried. Its quality is considered, and it is prepared to be at its best when it is presented at the table. Seafood, particularly cod, halibut, and squid, are treated with time and care. Custards, cakes, and pastries are flavored delicately, and fruit is served at its peak. The secret of fine Basque cuisine is that the best available ingredients are chosen and prepared with tender care to present them to the eater at their best.

I asked Cecelia how she learned to cook so well. She told me that she had been trained in her sister's four-star restaurant in Guernica, but that her secret was this: "I think it, and I cook it. It is as simple as that" (interview). The traditional recipes that Cecelia still prepares in her daughter's home are common near the seaside in the Basque Country: roast lamb, cod in tomato sauce, squid, halibut, chorizos, garbanzos, potato omelettes, Basque salad, paella, Basque cake, flan, rice pudding, and bread. There is always fresh bread.

On my route to San Sebastian in the Basque Country, I was welcomed into Madrid by a Basque guide. Within a few hours of our small group's arrival, we were settled into an old-world–style hotel owned by a family of Basques and called the Francesco. Soon it was time for dinner, and our small group of travelers was graciously seated at tables spread with pristine white linen tablecloths set with silver, crystal, and one red rose. My dinner was a steaming and generous platter of saffron rice topped with fresh clams, shrimp, chorizos, and vegetables (*Euskalduna Itsasaldeko Paella*). It was served with a crisp green salad, a light dressing, crusty French bread, and wine for those who wanted it. Dessert was a simple flan— custard with caramelized sugar that had lined the cooking dishes before baking. The aroma was a mixture of spices, herbs, mild fish, and candle wax; it was fresh and tantalizing. The bread, particularly the bread, was unforgettable. The texture of the inside of the bread at that first meal was almost like cake; the crust was thin and crisp. How many centuries, I wondered, did it take just to perfect that bread? There is deep symbolism in the fine breads and wine of the Basques, and later interviews revealed meanings and memories that related bread to the fathomless ethos of the people.

Ethnic markers, including language, religion and beliefs, games, folkways, and foods, their authentic expressive culture, traveled with the Basques to South America and the United States during the nineteenth and twentieth centuries. Most of the Basques settled, eventually, in scattered groups throughout the western United States. Basque cultural traits and markers have diluted in the western United States, but it is still safe to say that the majority of Basques in Idaho came from the coastal region of Viscaya. In California, the majority of the Basques come from the French side of the Pyrenees, and in Nevada, the third bastion of the Basques, there is a mixture. Delicate recipes and refined, more expensive cuisines were transmitted to the United States from the coastal regions and tourist cities (Bilbao, Guernica, San Sebastian). In the farmlands and mountains, hearty soups, blood sausage, and eggs, many eggs (often served with mushrooms) are preferred, and menus with those items are still served every evening in some Basque American homes.

Goat and sheep cheese, apples or pears cooked in wine, chestnuts, mushrooms, and other favorites, all receive the same care in selection and table presentation. I took a nine-hour hike in the Pyrenees with fourteen other climbers, and we managed to lose the path. In an opening beside a deep forest, we emerged to find a herder's hutlike cottage. He was there with a few friends and saw us coming. We had our own supplies (bread, salami, fruit, and water), but he insisted that we share his food. He split a small quarter-round of golden-colored sheep cheese that he said he had made himself; I watched him deftly cut thin slices with a razor-sharp pocketknife and hand it to us, one-by-one. There was a coarse white bread, a few crackers, a little red and white wine, two Cokes, and two beers from his hut that he shared with our group. His hands were deep brown and his face was lined with dark mysteries, but his eyes twinkled with delight at this haggard group of mountain-climbing Americans. He spoke Basque and Spanish and offered us ancient hospitality. We received it with delight and relief, and he pointed us in the right direction when we left.

An experience like that echoes with deep memories of ancient host/ guest cordialities, and in such a primeval, pastoral setting it was as though we had stepped into some sort of a time warp. We left him some of our water and meat, and he smiled benignly at us as we made our way back into the forest. Intentional, exploratory participation in the foodways of an other was a reality, not a theory, in that small mountain meadow. There, sheep grazed under the ferns at the edge of the hillside; their copper bells made muffled sounds. Those same sheep provided the cheese we ate. The sweet fragrance of the meadow grass and wildflowers added to the moment. This was authentic, aesthetic, and even spiritual. We hiked on to a monastery knowing that we had each one been involved in Long's "deeper, more integrated level of experiencing the Other" (1998:182). I sometimes wonder if that man is still on the mountain shepherding and comforting misguided hikers.

Each morning in the La Salle monastery where I boarded, breakfast was served very early. It wasn't usually wonderful; there were budget rates for students and scholars during the summer months, and that meant a budget breakfast as well. It was decent enough for the price, but it created in me a further appreciation for the relatively Spartan life of the monks. The "breakfast room," in the basement of an old brick building, was connected to the dorm rooms by a long, outside walkway with arches and benches that opened onto a grassy courtyard. Before breakfast each morning, the walkway was hosed and smelled wet and fresh. The cement floor in the basement had also been hosed; it too was damp and smelled like mildew. Each table was covered with a clean oilcloth, and placed there were prepackaged jellies, butter pats, salt and pepper, an ashtray, and a container of paper napkins.

Rolling carts in the "breakfast room" carried dark, almost thick, coffee and rich cream (*café con leche*), steaming and fragrant in heavy metal coffee pots. Coffee drinkers poured a half-and-half mixture into thick mugs, and there was also steaming water and tea bags for tea drinkers. Cereal, cold milk, bowls, and spoons were set out on a long table. Young men served breakfast most days, and the food varied from cold scrambled eggs with or without olive oil–bathed chorizos, to a container of tepid Yoplait yogurt and cold toast. Cheese omelettes and potatoes were served occasionally. Day-old French bread was piled up on brown trays on a long table.

This was functional food served in a functional way. The food was basically clean and wholesome, and other than the traditional Spanish *café con leche* and the boxed cereals as a nod to American tastes, there was no particular manipulation of food as a symbol. It was plainly served utilitarian sustenance to break the fast of the night. Because of the odor of mildew, no one lingered long inside, and many smoked their after-breakfast cigarette standing outside in the courtyard or sitting on one of the benches.

One of the Basque American women in Idaho gave me a letter of introduction to carry to a woman in San Sebastian who had lived in America for several years and who spoke English fluently. Her "flat" was on the fifth floor of an old, elegant, European-style apartment house. I rang and spoke to her on an intercom before the outer door was unlocked and I could board the elevator to go upstairs. She greeted me when the elevator door opened, and I gave her the letter. Without looking at it, she put it in her apron pocket, put her arm around my shoulder in a welcoming way, and then took me through one of several doors in the hallway. All of the doors from the hall led to their rooms; there were doors to the living/dining room, kitchen, bath, sunroom, and to five bedrooms. Her husband was watching television. She introduced me, and then apologetically excused herself. She returned soon with a pitcher of lemonade, glasses with ice, a plate of plain, lemon cookies, and linen napkins. I was treated with courtesy and consideration, and after a very few minutes, Felicia asked if I would like to stay with them instead of at the monastery. She was sincere, but because I was planning to stay the whole summer, and because her husband seemed frail, I declined. I did stay there the last few days before I left for the United States. I was given a white room with dark woodwork, a feather bed with white sheets, pillows, and a lacy white comforter. The room had white lace curtains over a window that opened onto a balcony rimmed with fine black wrought-iron fencing. Red geraniums were everywhere, and it was very, very beautiful.

I stayed for about an hour that first afternoon and agreed to return the following day for her to take me shopping for some toiletries. The next day, Felicia took me to get those things after she introduced me to San Martin Market, one of the great food markets of San Sebastian. There I saw what I had only seen before in *National Geographic*. The outside of the market is ugly and plain. There would be no reason for a tourist to enter that colorful temple of gastronomic variety unless informed about what was inside. Once through the door it became a visual kaleidoscope of color and contrast. On the first level were individual merchants selling vegetables, fruits, flowers, breads, candies, sausages, cheeses, and all other kinds of beautiful foods. Carts and booths were piled up higher than I would ever think safe for balance, and every one of them was artfully and intricately arranged. The variety of foodstuffs was a sensory delight and nearly a sensory overload. It was hard to know where to look or how to move about in the colorful, crowded space. Especially beautiful were long strings of perfect-looking garlic, shallots, onions, and chili *ristras* hanging from the sides of many booths.

In a huge side room were poultry and meats of every kind imaginable. Some meat was in refrigerated cases, but most was hanging from hooks and looked like paintings from earlier centuries. Colors and smells were varied and vivid: dark reds and purples, bright blue veins on red and fatted white meat, golden chickens, pink hams, and stained white aprons on stout men and women. The smell was a heavy odor of meat and blood, but it was not offensive. Again the floor was cement and had been recently hosed. Many of the men wore dark berets (it was cool in that room), and many of the women wore print headscarves. Almost everyone wore big, black rubber overshoes.

Felicia then took me to the second level of the building. This was the fish market, and it smelled like one would imagine a fish market to smell. Again stout men and women stood behind refrigerated cases wearing stained aprons and rubber gloves. The fish prices were marked, and there wasn't much order to the buying and selling. The men were preparing various seafoods to put into the cases, and the women with aprons were the sellers. They would get the yelled order, throw it in a plastic bag, reach over the case with a long-handled basket for the customer's money, draw in the money, put the change in the basket, and then stretch over the case again to give the change and the purchase to the customer. I am not sure how they kept the customers straight. There was a little bargaining, not much, and Felicia (with a smile) asked me if I would like to buy some cod for our dinner. I was surprised and said I would like cod for dinner, but I would like to watch her buy it. It was graceful. Felicia bought filets at the market price. Salted cod, she said, would be more authentic, but this would do. I told her what Cecelia Jouglard had prepared for me, and she knowingly nodded. We quickly picked up the few things I needed at a nearby store, and then Felicia took me to her home for a cooking lesson.

Interestingly, Felicia prepared almost the identical dinner that I had been served at one of the Basque American homes in Lava Hot Springs, Idaho. It was a very hot July evening, and Felicia served her delicious meal on crystal plates set on a pale pink linen tablecloth. Her menu was breaded and lightly fried cod in olive oil, sliced pork loin (baked), buttery mashed potatoes, chard with onion that had been chopped and steamed, a simple green salad with garlic/oil/white vinegar dressing, white bread slices, butter, and for dessert, *arroz con leche* (rice pudding) and fresh fruit. I had iced water to drink, and Felicia and her husband had a red Navarra wine and water. They had Dry Sack sherry with thin slices of bread and cheese before dinner. Felicia and Leon used their utensils European style, and I switched back and forth between the two styles of eating. We all smiled at that, and I felt like a guest of royalty.

This was a new culture to me, and yet it had been foreshadowed through the transplanted culture in Idaho. The complex template of cultural, social, economic, and aesthetic mores of upper-middle-class Basques was before me, and it quite perfectly fit over the template I had perceived among Basque Americans of the same socioeconomic class in the Intermountain American West. This is a persevering ethnic group, both in the old country and the new, holding tightly to food symbols, even to the exacting requirements of specific menus.

Iruna, the restaurant our group was assigned to for dinner in San Sebastian was interesting, but I found that the food was difficult for me to digest easily. French fries prepared in olive oil accompanied every dinner. Salad was rarely served, and the meal was usually a serving of meat, chicken, or fish prepared in oil, and a warm green vegetable floating in a generous amount of broth and olive oil. There were many bottles of red wine (*tinta*) on each table, and that seemed to please the majority of the clientele. Dessert was usually a small flan or a container of Yoplait yogurt. I stopped eating there and started exploring the restaurants of San Sebastian.

I walked most of the time, though there were taxis and a bus line that I sometimes used. Downtown San Sebastian has a quarter called La Parte Vieja (Old Town) at the tip of the sweep of La Concha (a curved beach named for a conch shell). That is the heart of the city, and there were many fine restaurants and bars in that quarter. Felicia and Leon recommended a place called *Baserri Restaurante* (The Farmstead Restaurant). Though it was clearly a commercialization of the old homesteads in the Basque countryside, it was excellent. There were bright red, checked tablecloths woven with the common Basque symbol (*labouru*: four commas joined at their pointed tips to form a cross), and typical of many Basque restaurants, one had to pass through a bar at the front to be seated in the restaurant in the back. I enjoyed a green salad, fish soup that was something like tomato bisque, *chipirones* (squid in ink sauce), an assortment of bread, and lemon ice for dessert served in a hollow lemon! Patrons in the restaurant were several families, two groups of women, a couple, a table of young men, and a single man. The atmosphere was very relaxed and quiet. I expected that the food would be served family-style, which is the traditional Basque restaurant tradition, but in this case the food was served the same as in any standard restaurant. That is, I am sure, an accommodation for tourists.

Though I did not have the opportunity to visit or eat in one, a tradition that is common throughout the Basque Country is the Basque gastronomic society, clubs for men called *txokos*. They are adult male-only clubs with up to one hundred members, and there the men spend time cooking, eating, drinking, and socializing. "No doubt the clubs originated because men, who were forbidden by custom to cook at home, felt the need of a culinary outlet" (Barrenechea 1998:50). There is no social-economic qualification placed on the membership, so the men's occupations range from laborers to professionals. Sometimes women are invited, but rarely and only as guests. It is said that some of the best food in Spain is prepared and served in these clubs, but when I inquired of a Basque professor who taught in San Sebastian, I was told that I could get food just as fine at the better restaurants in the Old Town and on the coast. He said that the recipes the men used were primarily ones they had stolen from their wives' and mothers' repertoires.

More culinary explorations in the Basque Country worth mentioning were at the festival of Saint Fermin in the city of Pamplona (made internationally famous by Hemingway), the festival of Saint Loyola in San Sebastian (it seemed like there was always a festival going on in San Sebastian), some select bakeries in La Parte Vieja (Old Town), and wayside picnics sponsored by the Basque Studies program. I also found a cookbook of Basque foods, *La Cocina Vasca: sus recetas basicas*, full of wonderful recipes but disappointingly printed in Spanish instead of Basque. I searched several bookshops but was unable to find one written in the Basque language. The foodways of the Basques weave activities, beliefs, and cultural systems in myriad ways, and many of the recipes are passed by word-of-mouth.

Pamplona is in the province of Navarra, and Spanish rather than Basque is the dominant language. I was there during the first week of July for the feast of Saint Fermin, better known as the *Encierro*, or the running of the bulls. It occurred every day at 8:00 A.M., lasted about three minutes, and twelve bulls were run each day. In Pamplona an important part of the ritual is simply talking about the bulls. Part of the tradition is to go to bars after the running and wait for the newspaper to tell how many people got hurt and how serious the injuries were. Being there was an aesthetic and sensory celebration. During the day, the plaza was filled with sleeping youth, and then during the night, the whole city became a riot of noise and light to rival the Mardi Gras at New Orleans. The youth are dressed in sparkling white pants and shirts with a *panuelico* (red neck scarf) and a *gerriko* (red sash) at their waist. (There are coin-operated laundry facilities to help keep the traditional look.)

At Pamplona, the afternoon bullfights are another highlight of the weeklong celebration. In *Death in the Afternoon*, Ernest Hemingway wrote about the bulls surging through the narrow streets of Pamplona behind the running men, and he wrote about the matadors and the exquisite and treacherous traditions of the bullring. He mentioned the fine restaurants of Pamplona in his work and made the city famous. The Basques have such a love for Hemingway that they erected a monument opposite the huge bullring in Pamplona on Paseo de Hemingway. His wife, Mary, an exploratory cook and a culinary tourist, learned to make the cod dish *bacalao a la Pamplona*, and published it in a book called *Great Recipes from the World's Great Cooks* by Peggy Harvey.

Pamplona is known throughout northern Spain as the source of the finest chorizo sausage. The annual tradition of the *mantanza*, or killing of the pig, occurs in November.

> For anyone witnessing pig-killing for the first time the event is undeniably horrific. Two men seize the animal by the legs and cut its throat. As the blood pours out one of the local women shakes it in a bucket kept for this purpose, to prevent it from coagulating. Next the animal is put to hang for several hours. At this stage the woman of the house fries the liver, which traditionally only men eat. Then the women get to work. . . . The onion which was finely chopped and boiled until tender first thing in the morning is now mixed together with small pieces of fat, pounded garlic, sweet and hot *pimenton* [pimento], oregano and the blood of the pig. All the women are sitting next to each other making the *morcillas*, or black puddings, pressing the mixture into the fine tripes [casings]; after this they will be boiled and hung from the ceiling. Next they prepare the *chorizos* mixture of meat, fat, *pimenton*, garlic and salt which has to macerate for twenty-four to forty-eight hours before it is ready to go into the tripes. The men are in charge of the butchering of the animal which is conducted following the rituals es-

tablished since time immemorial; the hams are taken away for curing, some parts of the fats for salting and the meat which is going to be eaten fresh is cut into pieces, while the rest will go directly into the freezer. At the end of the day, presents, known as *txerrimonis*, are given to the neighbors who helped with the pig-killing. They would usually consist of some black pudding, a lump of bacon and some spare ribs, all wrapped in a cabbage-leaf. (1989:34–35)

The running of the bulls, the bullfights, and even the autumn pig-killing represent ancient rites of passage, maintained and practiced in well-defined spaces in the old country. In abstract ways, all of the activity is related to food; even the bulls ultimately killed in the ring are donated to charity for use as food. The self-image of many of these people is one of strength—an independent people of hardy outdoor vigor who eat full meals made of good ingredients well prepared. In the Basque culture, that claimed indefatigable inner strength is called *indarra*. As one of the Basque anthropologists I studied with said, "You have it, or you do not" (del Valle 1990). The foodways are integrated with history and economics, as well as personal taste. The restaurants of Pamplona ranged from simple road-side stands to stylish starred Michelin restaurants. Foods ranged from simple rice dishes to elegantly prepared fish and shellfish, various meats, smoked sheep's milk cheese, and wild mushrooms. For the Basques, inviting tourism of their restaurants and festivals is a continual practice, and outside participation increases revenue; however, the focus of the Basque organizers of restaurants and festivals is a celebration of their own heritage and continued Basqueness, not an effort to trivialize their legacy by commercialization or industrialization of their ethnic heritage.

In the Loyola *barrio* (neighborhood) of San Sebastian, a colorful and lively festival took place in honor of the birth of Saint Ignatius of Loyola, born July 31, 1491, in the castle of Loyola in the Basque province of Guipuscoa. Loyola, a Basque, founded the Roman Catholic Order of the Jesuits, and the people celebrate this with a yearly, several-day fiesta. Like many of the other celebrations in the Basque Country, its origin is based in Catholic beliefs, and it is difficult to discern the beginning and end of the peoples' emotional investment in the event. These types of fiestas seem to group people by neighborhoods, and this was no exception. Each day of the celebration, parades with *gigantes* (giants) and *cabejudos* (bigheads), the *tsistu* (small flute) and *tombril* (playing drum) wound through the streets of the *barrio*. The food and liquor were plentiful and inexpensive, and it seemed to be a time when most restraints on teenagers were dropped. I saw countless inebriated and loud male youth.

The food was not particularly remarkable, but it seemed to be typical of a neighborhood fiesta. There were stands with fried potatoes, chorizos, churros (a deep-fried pastry), cups of beans, fresh fruit, small puddings, small cakes, ices, ice cream bars, and a host of beverages. One of the specialties was fried bread, somewhat like a flour tortilla, wrapped around a chorizo and a strip of white cheese. The celebration was colorful, and there were game booths and dance demonstrations. One of the traditions was a mock bullfight. A young calf was pushed out of the back of a pickup truck into a circular barricade. Young men, from maybe twelve to fifteen or so, then began to run in front and behind of the animal waving red scarves and wooden swords. Added to this were the *gigantes*, costumed male youth, wearing large papier-mâché heads and carrying *pollos* (canvas filled with sawdust and used as soft clubs), who were thumping teenage girls and some women on the back between the shoulders. The fiesta was somewhat chaotic. I did not return the next day, but some of my acquaintances did and reported that it was the same both days. To me, it was almost as if the party were an excuse for youngsters to play out the strong, aggressive reputation that a few Basque nationalists, as mentioned earlier, continue to maintain.

There were fine bakeries in San Sebastian, and each had specialties. Copying the natives and other tourists, for my midday meal I often went to the Saint Martin or La Brecha Market and purchased a little fruit and cheese; I then went to the bakeries to find a bread for the day. One incredible bread, a round about three inches across, was called *pan fruta* (fruit bread). It had a thin, crisp crust and the dough was pink, light, and mildly flavored of yeast and fruit; there were bits of candied fruit sprinkled throughout the bread. I would take my gathered fresh lunch to the beach, find a spot, and enjoy watching the people playing and relaxing there. It was "culinary tourism," I believe, in a personal and intentional way. I was eating *their* food, on *their* beach, watching *their people*, listening to *their* language and snippets of *their* music. I could see, from where I sat, pieces of *their* outdoor art (metal sculptures) and was enhancing my own individual experience.

The Basque Studies group in San Sebastian took the students and scholars on many forays into the countryside to see ancient monasteries, an old iron foundry, wineries, Basque schools and colleges, and other interesting sights. The custom was to stop near a riverside or small park and have a picnic lunch. The meal was good, fresh, and always the same: hard salami, several kinds of cheese, flavorful tomatoes, fruit, olives, many loaves of white French bread, ice cold milk, wine, beer, and soda. It was plain, but typical of Basque food choices, it was plentiful and of the finest quality.

In the United States

Early in this paper I mentioned regional Basque American settlements; that is, a general predominance of Spanish Basques in Idaho (and Oregon), French Basques in California, and a mixture of both in Nevada. These regional designations have diluted over time, and there is presently very little continuing Basque immigration. Many Basques came to the United States initially because of the Gold Rush. Some had previously settled in the pampas region of South America and worked as sheepherders there. Those sheepherding skills turned into a major industry for them in the United States, and for more than one hundred years the Basques were the quintessential sheepherders of North America. Because of the large number of single Basque herders in the United States, a network of Basque hotels was established. There, the herders could store their gear, receive mail, be nursed if they were ill or injured, and enjoy the language, food, music, activities, and games of their homeland.

When ethnic revivals of foods and festivals became popular in the United States in the 1960s and 1970s, the Basque Americans took part and began to hold their own festivals, but for them it was different in many ways; it wasn't really a revival (their culture was alive and well in the United States), but rather, it was an invention to take part in new American festival customs. Because of the Basque hotels, there were herders in the United States who never learned English and ended up aging and dying in hotels that occasionally also served some men as retirement homes. Because of the unique and difficult language, and because of the lonely, isolated lives of the herders, Basque Americans maintained their comfortable ethnic heritage in those scattered hotels in the American West. Many married, of course, but the hotels remained as gathering places, and it was there that the Basque language continued to be spoken, Basque games (*pelota and mus*) continued to be played (*mus* is similar to poker), and the Basque cuisine continued to be maintained and served. At the festivals, the American public was invited to share the unique refinements and tastes of Basque food.

Euzkaldunak, Inc., a Basque American organization, sponsors an international festival in Boise, Idaho, for Basque Americans and guests from the old country every five years. The public is invited, and a tasteful, well-organized fiesta, called *Jaialdi*, takes place. It is a seven-day festival, like Saint Fermin in Pamplona, and begins with a Basque Film Festival and ends with a Basque Mass at St. John's Cathedral in Boise. A French and/or Spanish Basque priest celebrates the Mass, and the Basque dancers from Boise perform a tasteful celebratory dance in the sanctuary. It was at a Basque American *Jaialdi* festival that an elderly gentleman visiting from the old country told me that he liked to attend the *Jaialdi* and didn't mind traveling all the way from the Basque Country, because it reminded him what it really meant to be Basque.

Smaller festivals throughout the summer take place in California, Idaho, and Nevada, and foods served at the various celebrations are similar. There are often food booths where *chorros* and chorizo sandwiches can be purchased. A buffet-style dinner is served for a reasonable cost, and the menu is nearly always the same. There is a green salad with a variety of dressing choices, usually plates of fresh crudites and olives, garbanzos or sometimes a garbanzo/carrot/chorizo mixture, green beans, a warm mixed-bean mixture, roasted lamb, barbequed steak, and flan or *arroza esnearekin* (rice pudding) for dessert. Red wine and loaves of white French bread are always plentiful.

I asked about the white bread, and I was told by one of my elderly Basque friends that during the Spanish Civil War (1936–1939), Franco tried to starve the Basques. It was very difficult to get good grain, and the Basques were reduced to eating bread made of dark grains or corn. For that generation, good white bread represents independence from oppression; many have horrific memories of the deprivations and tortures of the war. The ubiquitous red wine is present at every Basque lunch and dinner; I seldom saw white wine used at their tables. In a sense, the red wine represents a part of their ancient ethos; the bread and wine parallel deep religious beliefs and customs, and its constant presence on most of their dining tables represents a conscious sense of tradition and community. Because of its symbolic and customary meanings, Louise Etcheverry of southeastern Idaho, wife of a now elderly French Basque herder, said, "Jean Pierre would not sit at a lunch or dinner table without his red wine. It is his way; a part of what he has always known" (interview).

These food-related behaviors, as Long said, are complex networks of cultural, social, economic, and aesthetic patterns. (1998:181). For example, one of the women I interviewed representative of this complexity was born in Idaho to a Basque couple who had settled there from the old country a few years before. This woman, in her sixties, told me that she had eaten typical Basque food all of her life at home, in the hotels, and at the festivals; that is, lamb, beef, fried fish, and other favorite and familiar Basque foods. Several months before my interview with her, she had to undergo heart bypass surgery, which she claimed was a direct result of Basque food, but that she still ate small portions of everything at get-togethers. She did not want her name revealed and said, "Who am I to try to change a whole culture and their way of doing?"

Basque American restaurants in the United States serve many of the traditional Basque dishes. *Tortilla de Patata*, a potato omelette, is served at the Bar Gernika in Boise, where the menu is representative of the Basque culture. The Bar Gernika is set up similarly to the bar/restaurants in the old country, and the atmosphere does capture the spirit of the Basque Country bars. Their pork loin sandwich is excellent, and it is a popular place with the locals, both Basque and non-Basque. There is a way of serving common to most Basque American restaurants. The traditional Basque restaurant style is described as follows: "At the appointed hour 7 P.M., a mixed group of strangers files into the spare dining room and systematically fills the seats at the long tables. Tureens of clam chowder, a simple lettuce salad, and bottles of wine are waiting. Just as we finish our salad, a parade of platters begins; pickled tongue, cottage cheese, beef stew, fried fish, spaghetti, roast lamb, French fries and blue cheese, then ice cream. My tablemate sums up the appeal of Basque restaurants: 'This is the real thing—lots of good food, friendly people'" (Anusasananan and Finnegan 2000:180).

In Reno, Nevada, I learned about another side of the Basques, one not unique to ethnic groups serving uninformed outsiders. During my graduate program I researched materials in the Basque Studies Library at the University of Nevada-Reno. My husband was with me, and at that time there was an old Basque restaurant in Reno where we often ate dinner (not Louis' Basque Corner, which is excellent and very popular). The food at this old hotel restaurant was served as described above, and it was always accompanied by red wine. One evening, one of the tourists identified himself as a professor from another state. He was so impressed with the unlabeled wine that he asked to buy a few bottles. The host said that it was a special blend made especially for the house, and that it could not be sold without permission. After some discussion, he sold the professor two labeled bottles. A few nights later, my husband and I dined there again and the bartender recognized us. With a wry smile and twinkle, he explained, "Only the label was unique." He said, "We have them printed up to impress people, but our wine is a cheap, dry red from the grocery store." The Basque Americans, like any other ethnic group under scrutiny, enjoy a good trick now and then. Certainly the professor was none the wiser, appreciative of his culinary tour, and apparently felt that he had integrated his experience of the other by taking some of it away with him.

Another venue for culinary tourism among the Basques is cooking classes. The Basque Cultural Centers in San Francisco, California; Boise, Idaho; and Reno, Nevada, sometimes offer cooking classes for those who would like to learn to experience the Basque cuisine by preparing the foods at home. Basque food is straightforward and simply seasoned. Marcelino Ugalde, sometimes with Basque American Janet Inda, often teaches Basque cooking classes in Reno, Nevada. In Salt Lake City, Larry Osoro and Javier Guerricabelitia, chefs for the Basque Club of Utah's Annual Basque Dinner and Dance, teach cooking techniques from the old country in a bimonthly cooking club held in Basque American homes in the region. Some of their recipes have a French influence and some are more Spanish, according to which side of the Pyrenees the recipe originated. If a person is genuinely interested in learning to cook Basque-style, many Basque American women would be willing to open their own kitchens and demonstrate a recipe or two. They have been generous in teaching me, and my family has been the beneficiary. By participating physically with the selection and preparation of the foods, I have enjoyed a different sensory level of cultural tourism.

Cookbooks are another way of touring Basque foodways, and there are several excellent American-produced recipe collections available. *The Basque Table: Passionate Home Cooking from One of Europe's Great Regional Cuisines* (1998), by Teresa Barrenechea, is accurate and includes contextual background on many of the recipes. The back cover has a blurb that states: "Teresa Barrenechea, the best Basque chef in North America, shows in more than 130 recipes how easy it is to bring classic Basque cooking to the home table. Like other great European cuisines, this is a way to cook that reaches its tastiest and most elegant expression not in fussy techniques but in fresh ingredients simply and lovingly prepared." Cookbooks for the Basque cuisine can be purchased at most of the festivals and at the Basque Cultural Centers in Reno, Boise, and San Francisco. Some of them have long lists of favorite Basque foods, including leeks, coffee royal, anisette, chestnuts, and anchovies. Exemplary ones are *Traditional Basque Cooking: History and Preparation* (1983), by Jose Maria Busca Isusi, and *The Art of Basque Cooking* (1982), by Clara Salaverria Perkins. They have clear instructions, and both include cultural and historical information about the ingredients, traditions associated with the foods, and detailed instructions about the recipe methods.

The language, foods, music, dancing, strength and endurance contests, and even dominant colors (red, green, and white) provide a framework for festivals of the Basques in the old country and in the United States. They have transplanted the essence of the culture, and they have invented new ethnic traditions: music camps for children, Basque American choirs, Basque golf competitions, language and cooking classes, organized tours to the old country, and traditional folkways, particularly the *jota*, a lively dance participated in and performed at many weddings. They invite the public, their guests, to join in their celebrations and tour the networks of activities. The foods served, from procurement and preparation to presentation and consumption, engage a multifaceted universe that involves physical, social, cultural, economic, spiritual, and aesthetic dimensions (Long 1998:183).

> Thinking of tourism as being predominantly a relationship between "real" (i.e., residential) hosts and their guests has become problematic in several respects. Not the least of these is the extent to which most tourism has become a thoroughly mediated activity, dependent on the intervention of others who serve as neither hosts or guests in any conventional manner. . . . It is the increased scale and variety of tourism throughout the world that has added layers of mediation to the fading host/guest relationship. . . . The exploitation of tourism resources, often exemplified in the commoditization and delocalization of place and culture, might be deliberate or might as well be quite unintentional. (Chambers 1997:6)

Having experienced that "fading host/guest relationship" firsthand in the steep Pyrenees Mountains, I believe that congeniality and shared openness are cultural conventions that need to be maintained or revived among those who no longer practice them. The Basque culture, not unlike others around the world, has opened itself up to the public. In doing so, like others, it has lost a part of its perceived mystery and has become a more dynamic, progressive, and open society. It too is more willing to observe and even taste the foods of others. In Boise, Idaho, Basques and Mexicans and other cultural groups present foods and music from their various heritages at a summer festival. In letting outsiders taste the culture and learn the value placed on careful preparation and unhurried and savored enjoyment, the Basques have shared a simple mystery that onlookers can adapt. In tasting the food of others (and dancing to another's music), the Basques have learned to expand their own repertoire and be a part of the larger community.

Being immersed in the culture, as I was that summer in the Basque

Country, I did learn who the Basque people were, what they valued, and some of their dreams. I went as a graduate student to study Basque history and Basque cultural anthropology; I came home with an enriched understanding of what it means to live. There, adapting myself to their pace, I slowed down enough to awaken sensory perceptions that had too often been smothered by my hurried life patterns. My views of culinary tourism changed from simple curiosity to an understanding that foods, and cultural responses to them, sometimes reveal the deepest elements of meaningful human expression.

Most large cities in the United States have multiethnic festivals featuring foods from various homelands, domestic and foreign. The tastes are there to be enjoyed, but the booths are superficial representatives of the deep and complex culinary meanings present in every culture. It is one thing to taste sweet potato pie at a soul-food booth in a local park, but quite another to enjoy the same dish in a savory-smelling kitchen or even café in the Deep South served lovingly, and authentically, by warm, brown hands. As we tour the foodways and folkways of the other by exploring myriad socially constructed identities and behaviors, it might help to note Richard Raspa's words: "One apprehends the world not as a static, sequential, predictable unit of experience, but finally as dynamic, holistic, and mysterious" (1997:192). Culinary tourism, coupled with the attempted apprehension of multiple meanings layered over centuries of tradition, opens us, tentatively, to an almost transcendent understanding of the other. Carefully we savor someone else's heritage, and for a few brief moments we sense who they are.

Works Cited

Anusasananan, Linda Lau, and Lora J. Finnegan. 2000. "A Taste of Basque Country." *Sunset: The Magazine of Western Living.* May: 164–81.

Barrenechea, Teresa. 1998. *The Basque Table: Passionate Home Cooking from One of Europe's Great Regional Cuisines.* Boston, Mass.: Harvard Common Press.

Chambers, Erve, ed. 1997. *Tourism and Culture: An Applied Perspective.* Albany: SUNY Press.

Del Valle, Teresa. 1990. Lecture. Basque Culture Studies. San Sebastian. July 9.

Etcheverry, Louise. 1989. Tape-recorded Interview. Lava Hot Springs, Idaho. October 8.

Isusi, Jose Maria Busca. 1983. *Traditional Basque Cooking: History and Preparation.* Reno: University of Nevada Press.

Jouglard, Cecelia A.A. 1990. Interview by author. Rupert, Idaho. Tape-recorded. March 20.

Long, Lucy M. 1998. "Culinary Tourism: A Folkloristic Perspective on Eating and Otherness." *Southern Folklore* 55.3: 181–204.

Perkins, Clara Salaverria. 1982. *The Art of Basque Cooking.* Woodland, Calif.: Yolo Sheltered Workshop.

Pi-Sunyer, Oriol. 1989. "Changing Perceptions of Tourism and Tourists in a Catalan Resort Town." In *Hosts and Guests: The Anthropology of Tourism, 2nd ed.* Ed. Valene L. Smith. Philadelphia: University of Pennsylvania Press.

Raspa, Richard. 1997. "Exotic Foods among Italian-Americans in Mormon Utah: Food as Nostalgic Enactment of Identity." In *Ethnic and Regional Foodways in the United States: The Performance of Group Identity.* Eds. Linda Keller Brown and Kay Mussell. Knoxville: University of Tennessee Press.

Sevilla, Maria Jose. 1989. *Life and Food in the Basque Country.* New York: New Amsterdam Books.

Smith, Valene L., ed. 1989. *Hosts and Guests: The Anthropology of Tourism, 2nd ed.* Philadelphia: University of Pennsylvania Press.

Culinary Tourism in Constructed and Emerging Contexts

Part 3 addresses culinary tourism as a social phenomena that has supported both the interest in exploring particular others and the development of specific venues for experiencing that tourism. These authors explore otherness—ethnic, nostalgic, religious, ethical, and regional—as well as contexts—restaurants, resorts, grocery stores, and even the home.

These contexts are newer ones with meanings that are neither historically bound nor preset but are actively being invented and negotiated. New social conditions require new relationships between people and food, and these contexts not only respond to those conditions but also emerge from them. In such venues, we can see the appropriation of food traditions and of the meanings historically associated with them, and see new interpretations emerge that do not necessarily represent the intentions of the producer. These new meanings originate in the ways people use that food, and they can take unexpected and unpredictable turns. One basic premise for understanding food, as a cultural production, is that the intended meaning of a tradition does not necessarily correspond with the meaning perceived by the consumer. For example, as Wilson demonstrates in her essay on Asian food among baby boomers, a food that is initially introduced as a marker of ethnic identity may be accepted and used as a viable source of nutritional and spiritual health.

This section explores the varied meanings that culinary tourism can hold for individuals and groups, offering perspectives on tourism particularly in American culture. The United States is rich with constructed contexts for tourism, since immigration into the country as well as migration between regions results in a constant influx of new conditions and new food traditions. Amy Bentley analyzes tourism within the economic structures of American culture, exploring the meanings and uses of the cuisine of the southwestern United States. She examines the appropriation of this cuisine by food industries, and the political implications of the large-scale acceptance of this hybrid cuisine by mainstream America. Rachelle Saltzman's essay describes food in the Catskills resorts, exploring the culinary other not as the unfamiliar but as the ideal. Her work demonstrates the complexity of tourism and the ways it can turn inward as well as lead outward. Liz Wilson writes about the adaptation of Asian foodways by the '60s generation—"aging baby boomers"—tying this movement to specific historical and cultural trends. She explores the changing status of a set of foods from exotic to familiar as well as the incorporation of culinary tourism into an everyday norm for eating. In the final essay, Barbara Shortridge examines a number of public and commercial venues for ethnic food tourism in the Midwestern United States. Restaurants, souvenir shops, and festivals all frame particular foods as representing ethnicity and heritage, and therefore available for tourism. All of these essays demonstrate that culinary tourism manipulates the meaning of food, and that otherness can be a bridge that takes a tourist back home to the familiar as well as to new tastes and experiences.

CHAPTER 9

From Culinary Other to Mainstream America

Meanings and Uses of Southwestern Cuisine

Amy Bentley

The United States is in the midst of a culinary love affair with what is generally known as Southwestern cuisine. From the elite echelons of haute cuisine, to party and recipe ideas in women's magazines, to fast-food conglomerates, Americans can scarcely escape (nor would they want to) ingesting various combinations of tortillas, chiles, beans, cheese, tomatoes, and corn. Witness the following phenomena: for the last several years salsa has outsold ketchup in the United States; Doritos and Tostitos tortilla chips are the second and third most popular-selling snack chips in the country (behind Lay's Potato Chips); nachos are common, popular snacks at football and baseball games; and New Mexico adopted as its state motto "Red or Green?"–in homage to the thousands of times a day restaurant servers ask which kind of chile their customers prefer smothering their burritos and enchiladas (Collins 1997; PepsiCo 1993; *Daily Camera* 1995). Such restaurants as the Coyote Cafe in Santa Fe, Mesa Grill in New York City, and the Frontera Grill in Chicago are the hot dining spots; meanwhile, Taco Bell is rapidly expanding both its number of restaurants worldwide and its volume of business per unit. We have indeed come a long way from the Green Giant canned "Mexicorn" of the 1950s and 1960s, with its indecipherable slivers of red and green intermixed with corn kernels.

When examined through the lens of culinary tourism—understanding "food as other" as a dynamic process running along three axes: from exotic to familiar, inedible to edible, and unpalatable to palatable—most Americans regard mainstream interpretations of Southwestern cuisine as highly familiar and appetizing. Indeed, so familiar has the commercialized "Tex-Mex" version of Southwestern cuisine become that it has been dubbed "Gringo food" by some in the food industry (Collins 1997). Such an assessment is significant given that not too long ago Texas Anglos considered Mexican food unfit for human consumption, even to the point, folklorist Mario Montaño notes, "that Anglos considered Mexican food so bad that they said wild animals did not scavenge on Mexican dead bodies" (1992:108). Similarly, the elite class in Mexico, historian Jeffrey Pilcher explains, considered tamales, enchiladas, and quesadillas "the food of the lower orders" (1998:46).

The entry of Southwestern cuisine into mainstream American foodways is a fascinating and important way to understand how the same cuisine has different meanings to different groups of people depending, among other things, on ethnicity, gender, socioeconomic status, and openness to culinary exploration. On a more concrete level, it is also an important way to examine the place and status of Mexican Americans within the larger cultural milieu. A product of the U.S.–Mexico borderlands region, Southwestern cuisine contains multiple meanings resulting in a "text" replete with cultural contradictions. There are at least three possible ways to think about the nature and function of Southwestern cuisine, and while contradictory in some respects, all three seem valid. First, mainstream Americans' embracing of the cuisine juxtaposed with an intense current national hostility toward Mexico and Mexican Americans indicates a culinary neutralization and cultural domination of borderlands foodways. Second, despite this cultural hegemony, for many Mexican Americans elements of Southwestern cuisine can provide a means of ownership and self-identity. Such events as tamale and tortilla making can be sites of resistance to the dominant culture through which Chicanos and Chicanas can retain and strengthen cultural identity. However, the popularity and even the creation of Southwestern cuisine are not only about appropriation and resistance. Cuisines are never static, but are constantly evolving and are reshaped much like culture in general. Southwestern cuisine, while different from and many would say inferior to its more authentic counterpart, has nonetheless attained legitimacy and positive acceptance, with the potential to function for many Americans as a foray to increased understanding of Latino cultural, economic, and social issues.[1]

Southwestern cuisine is the offspring of Native American and Mexican foodstuffs (chiles, pinto beans, pork, cornmeal, cumin, onions, tomatoes), flavor principles, and cooking techniques, combined with European

American elements (more beef; a variety of cheeses, including cheddar; sour cream; sausage; fewer "variety" meats and dishes) originally imported to the region through the Spanish conquest and later through nineteenth-century German and Anglo settlers, cowboys, and the transcontinental railroad's Harvey Restaurants. Southwestern cuisine extends primarily throughout the states bordering Mexico, California, Arizona, New Mexico, and Texas, with variation among the different regions. Californian Southwestern cuisine, for example, is thought to use more avocado, sprouts, and sour cream; Arizona or Sonoran versions often incorporate Native American influences such as fry bread and mutton stew and employ more often the use of cactus fruits; New Mexican or Santa Fe–style cuisine emphasizes green chiles, blue corn, and *pozole* (hominy or corn kernels soaked in lye); while the Texas "Tex-Mex" version boasts chili con carne, nachos, and barbecue as its most prominent legacies (DeWitt and Gerlach 1995:6). The greatest common denominator for all is the chile. It is important that the basic components of this cuisine—chile, beans, tomatoes, and corn—are native to the Americas, with pork and beef adopted early on from the Spanish colonists (Crosby 1972:114–21; Meier and Ribera 1993:11–15). Chili (spelled with an "I") is perhaps for most Americans the best known and loved Southwestern dish, as indicated by chili enthusiasts' attempt to declare chili con carne "America's Official Food" (DeWitt and Gerlach 1995:122). In fact, so common is its presence in Americans' diets that many may not even regard it as indigenous to the Southwest. There are chili festivals in such non-Southwestern states as Virginia and Vermont. Hot-dog vendors in most urban metropolises offer chili along with relish and sauerkraut as condiments. The cities of Memphis and Cincinnati stage elaborate chili cook offs, where chili aficionados fiercely debate the authenticity of chili with or without beans, the proper assortment of spices, the heat level, and so on. Cincinnati chili is a good example of Southwestern fare gone completely regional, where there one simply orders a "three-way"—mild chili served on a bed of spaghetti and topped with cheddar cheese—or a "four-way," topped with onions as well (Lloyd 1981:28–30).

The relatively recent popularity and general acceptance in the United States of Southwestern cuisine can be explained through several phenomena. First, late-twentieth-century immigration patterns, featuring immigration from Mexico and other Latin American countries, as well as Asia and the Caribbean, are all places where chiles feature prominently in native cuisines. A higher-than-average birthrate also contributes to the growing Latino population, and as a result Latin tastes and preferences are beginning to wield more influence in mainstream American cuisine (Robbins 1992:42). Moreover, changing demographics, combined with the dethroning of French cuisine as the pinnacle of culinary trendsetting, have gradually loosened the rigidity of Americans' diets, allowing greater exploration and acceptance of more complex, spicier foods. The increasing prominence of California as an arbiter of American tastes, for example, accompanied by the rise in so-called celebrity chefs, including many in the West, has allowed Southwestern cuisine and ingredients a prominence and a legitimacy not seen until recently.

Second, Southwestern fare is a relatively inexpensive, palatable, nutritious, and pleasing combination of flavors and ingredients adapted to an "American" palate; that is, an overall acclimation to food often more bland than traditional Latino tastes. In short, it tastes good. Its components are similar to Italian American basics (meat, cheese, tomatoes, and grain products), a cuisine thoroughly accepted by Americans, which provide nutrition, calories, satisfaction, and pleasure. Despite the more mainstream American tendency to turn down the heat, not to be disregarded when considering Southwestern fare's growth in popularity is the allure of the chile pepper. Researchers have hinted at chiles' potentially addictive quality stemming from the heat-generating element capsaicin, which may be a factor in its growing popularity. According to researchers, capsaicin triggers the release of pleasure-producing endorphins in the human brain, thought to be a natural pain reliever and mood elevator, and just like a runner's high, humans can crave and search out this endorphin release (DeWitt and Gerlach 1995:129).

Third, Southwestern cuisine has found such wide acceptance because of its constructed masculine identity allowing for broader general appeal. While the general preparation of this kind of food has been part of the traditional female domain, and specific elements such as tamale and tortilla making are distinctly regarded as "female," the greater emphasis on meat, the outdoors grilling option, the potential high fat and protein content, and especially the chiles give it a masculine edge. Chiles are, as a food writer recently punned, "hot." Self-described "chileheads" get high on the heat; an entire magazine, *Chile Pepper*, with a large readership, is devoted to the topic; and more and more Americans are exploring the merits of the chile pepper. Mark Miller, owner and chef of Santa Fe's Coyote Cafe, observes: "Chiles are a lifestyle. It's an urban cowboy idea of bravado. You have a sense of machismo without running around with a gun rack in the back of your truck. There's got to be a way of proving one's bravado. Chiles are a way of doing that" (DeWitt and Gerlach 1995:41). A recent issue of *Modern Dad* magazine, for example, saw fit to include a feature on the Tex-Mex cookout. Chili and barbecue contests all over the country are comprised of mostly male participants. For example, the father of a former student of mine belongs to not one but two such barbecue teams. Her mother, who never touches the meat or the sauce, is relegated to making the side dishes of coleslaw and cornbread. Finally, what Superbowl gathering of men would be complete without huge plates of nachos? The "maleness" of the cuisine allows a greater variety and number of Americans access to Southwestern fare. People are not afraid of it the way some are of ethnic dishes featuring raw fish or unfamiliar ingredients (Bourdieu 1984:190–94).

This maleness combined with stereotyped notions of Mexican and Latin culture indeed instill a machismo into the cuisine—a sort of dangerousness that the media plays upon, a prime example being the enduring advertising image of the Frito Bandito of a generation ago. The Frito Bandito, as offensive then as today for many, infused an aura of exoticism and dangerousness to Fritos corn chips—inviting consumers to see them as something truly different from other salty snack foods, more daring, more macho. Taco Bell's 1998 advertising campaign featuring a Chihuahua, who stares intently at the viewer and declares, "*Yo quiero Taco Bell,*" plays on some of the same stereotypes, although this time alluding to the cartoon character Speedy Gonzales. Many Mexican Americans, regarding the figure as racist and offensive, staged a national boycott of Taco Bell. Others viewed the advertising character in more complicated terms. Folklorist José Limon, for example, confesses that the "little guy . . .cracks [him] up." At the same time, however, Limon notes: "[T]aking full advantage of the semantic registers of the Spanish word *quiero*, [the dog] wants, desires, loves Taco Bell, arch commodity of American 'Mexicanness,' even as he sits there in all his own evident, though 'small' Mexicanness" (Limon 1998:1).

Finally, Americans embrace Southwestern cuisine in part because of its evocation of a romantic, sanitized version of the American Southwest and understanding of the West in general. This is largely due to the centrality of the chile, resulting in what can be called the icon of the chile pepper. The decorative, bright red strings of dried chiles called *ristras* that are often strung in both private and public spaces symbolize hospitality, evoke a certain ambiance, and are part of the hipness of Southwestern architecture and décor. *Ristras*, for instance, hang in abundance in one upscale restaurant in my former hometown of Boulder, Colorado, whose menu has very little Southwestern influence, simply to appropriate the ambiance of Santa Fe. The chile pepper evokes nostalgic, half-fantasy images of a slower, simpler, less cluttered time, evoking a Western spirit that nicely complements the idealized images Americans hold about the West. In short, the chile pepper, along with its cousins the howling coyote and sprightly mischievous *Kokopelli* (the flute-playing ancient Hopi god of fertility), have replaced the sleepy Mexican under a huge sombrero taking a siesta in the shade of a cactus as icons of the region. The net effect contributes to the exorcising of the actual people and complexities of the region—American Indians, Mexican Americans, and Mexican nationals—and what remains is a warm, romantic feeling connected to the Southwest.

The process by which Southwestern cuisine has evolved from exotic other to familiar favorite is yet another matter. Southwestern cuisine attracts a broad population primarily through a reframing of the food's context and presentation, and through recipe adaptation (Long 1998). First, to ensure the widest and most efficient distribution possible it has been reconfigured to adhere to the priorities of the fast-food industry. When people enter a fast-food eatery such as Taco Bell, they expect efficiency (quick service); calculability (an emphasis on quantity over quality); predictability (a reliable sameness); cleanliness (sanitation over taste); and low cost (Ritzer 1996:1–45). Obviously, these priorities diminish room for creativity, experimentation, substitution, use of seasonal and more expensive ingredients, as well as dishes requiring labor-intensive preparation and extended cooking times. The rapid proliferation of Taco Bells and other Tex-Mex fast-food joints means that for most Americans, Taco Bell equals Southwestern cuisine. Similarly, Southwestern recipes have been "Americanized" to include a greater emphasis on animal protein—more meat (and more expensive cuts of meat), American and cheddar cheese, sour cream—and most prominently, reducing the heat level. Thus, fajitas are made with the tenderloin rather than the traditional skirt steak; one fast-food taco includes bacon ("The Taco Bell BLT"); soft, white-wheat tortillas outsell the more traditional cornmeal version; and the Pace Company has developed a heatless jalapeño for its "cool" salsa (Verhovek 1996).

The results are quite interesting. Old El Paso Products owner, Pillsbury, Inc., located in the decidedly non-Southwestern city of Minneapolis, Minnesota, is now the top producer of Mexican fare in the United States. Moreover, none of Old El Paso's twenty-member development team is of Latino background. Pillsbury executives are eminently aware that its products are not authentic. "We're interested in mainstream America," one is quoted in a newspaper article. "Internally, in our memos, we always put the word Mexican in quotes." Now that Old El Paso's booming sales figures indicate that Pillsbury has captured the attention of mainstream America, the corporation is focusing on narrower segments of the population, specifically Hispanic Americans who see Old El Paso as a "mainstream American food" (Collins 1997).

Multiple Meanings

We know that food conveys meaning as well as calories and nutrients. Thus not only the food, but the preparation, the rituals, the smells, the social conditions and seasons of the year under which the food is sown, gathered, prepared, and eaten are all forms of cultural expression and identity. Anthropologist Arjun Appadurai explains, "In its tangible and material forms, food presupposes and reifies technological arrangements, relations of production and exchange, conditions of field and market, and realities of plenty and want" (1981:494). Because food is an extraordinarily powerful way to transmit ideas, power, and social status, the popularity of Southwestern cuisine can be convincingly interpreted as an act of cultural hegemony, an appropriation of borderlands foods in the hopes of neutralizing the power and voice of people, particularly Latinos, in the region.

The popularity of Southwestern cuisine, in light of the historically negative political climate regarding Mexico and hostility toward Mexican American citizens, indicates a cultural and political blindness. One only needs to think of the overwhelmingly negative construction of Mexico in the U.S. media and thus in the minds of many if not most Americans: the 1990s NAFTA debate and passage and more recent negotiations over fair trade agreements; 1996 Republican presidential candidate Pat Buchanan's defiant and unapologetic use of "José" to refer to all Mexican immigrants, not to mention his pledge to build a "Berlin Wall" on the border; the "us against them" rhetoric contained in nearly all debates over immigration; California's passage of Proposition 187;[2] English-only measures on state ballots; and recent battles over water rights to the Rio Grande River all indicate a national anxiety and prejudice.

In light of this hostility, the mainstreaming and elevation of Southwestern cuisine evinces a cultural amnesia of sorts. Americans embrace, enjoy, and explore literally the fruits of this region, but seem to easily sever the food from the people and region of its origin. While not the only ones in history to do so, in an imperialist fashion enacted repeatedly over the decades, Americans have taken what is compelling (foods, land, other natural resources), altered it to their own tastes, and left the dirty mess behind for someone else to deal with. The Pace Company's heatless jalapeño may be the most interesting, and startling, evidence of this cultural appropriation.

Folklorist Mario Montaño forcefully argues this view in his compelling study of south Texas folk foodways. Food that Anglo Texans used to consider inedible is now all the rage. "How can a food considered repulsive, and unfit for human consumption, and associated with poor working-class people reach the level of acceptance by the dominant culture?" he asks (Montaño 1992:222). In fact, Montaño sees the very name "Tex-Mex" as evidence of this cultural appropriation. "Restaurateurs and food promoters labeled their version of Mexican food as 'Tex-Mex' food, resulting in some of the most alienating and adulterated Mexican food forms ever imagined by a native of the lower Rio Grande Border Region," he exclaims. Montaño observes, "In many of these urban Mexican restaurants the food is classified as ethnic and serves as another form of experiencing the foreign culture without having to deal with the people" (Montaño 1992:224, 237).

Indeed, the process need not be merely part of the political unconscious, but can also exist as an overtly political act. Historian George Sanchez writes that in the early twentieth century there existed a deliberate attempt in the Southwest to rid Mexican Americans of their traditional foods under the guise of making them more American, and perhaps more pliable, easier to control and predict. Sanchez writes: "Reformers encouraged Mexican women to give up their penchant for fried foods, their too frequent consumption of rice and beans, and their custom of serving all members of the family—from infants to grandparents—the same meal. According to proponents of Americanization, the modern Mexican woman should replace tortillas with bread, serve lettuce instead of beans, and broil instead of fry. . . . Within the rubric of Americanization efforts, food and diet management became yet another tool in a system of social control intended to construct a well-behaved, productive citizenry" (1995:102).

An example of this culinary neutralization and cultural domination is Taco Bell's 1997 advertising campaign featuring the slogan "Run to the Border." While no doubt playing on the notion of the borderland as a "dangerous haven" harboring outlaws, Taco Bell advertising executives surely did not intend to evoke any reference to the prevalent "running to the border" debates (of Mexican nationals "running" south to north). Evidently they launched this multimillion-dollar campaign feeling confident that this slogan would not conjure any association with current anti-immigration sentiment and NAFTA debates, an assumption that exposes a remarkable disjuncture between media advertising of Tex-Mex fast food and current political and cultural issues. Moreover, American fast-food restaurants, Taco Bell included, are making their own run across the border. That activists in Mexico City ransacked a McDonald's to protest California Proposition 187 clearly indicates McDonald's function as a symbol of American culture. As the current trend of Tex-Mex fast-food eateries setting up shop in Mexico and other Latin American countries continues—a phenomenon worthy of its own study—it will be interesting to observe any similar markers of resistance to appropriation of Southwestern cuisine ("Protesters in Mexico City" 1994).

Montaño also points out, however, that this cultural appropriation of Mexican cuisine is never airtight, but pockets of resistance always exist, challenges to the dominant cultural forms that provide alternatives for Latinos and others. Intricately tied up with Southwestern cuisine, especially for those of Mexican descent, are meanings of culture and sense of self. Writer Gloria Anzaldua explains: "For me food and certain smells are tied to my identity, to my homeland. . . . Homemade white cheese sizzling in a pan, melting inside a folded *tortilla*. My sister Hilda's hot, spicy *menudo, chile colorado* making it deep red, pieces of panza and hominy floating on top. My brother Carlos barbecuing *fajitas* in the backyard. Even now and 3000 miles away, I can see my mother spicing the ground beef, pork and venison with chile. My mouth salivates at the thought of the hot steaming *tamales* I would be eating if I were home" (1987:61). Sociologist Teresa Martinez similarly writes of her mother's tortilla making: "[M]y most happy images are memories of my mother making tortillas. She was truly a master of this fine art as she worked with a steady, polished rhythm throughout. And I helped her. . . . For me, these were her most delicious creations, and they came to symbolize my culture, my family, and especially my mother" (1996:14).

Tamale making ("tamal" in Spanish) can contain not only powerful, ethnic meaning, but feminist identity as well. Anthropologist Brett Williams argues that for many Chicanas, tamale making is a community ritual, a female-centered, role-affirming process that actually empowers women in their own families and in the public world at large. Educator M.H. de la Peña Brown agrees. The *tamaleada* (tamale making and consuming event) in which Brown participated created shared experience among women, helped develop a sense of unity and community, was important for many of the women who spoke no English or who had only recently arrived in the States, and earned them important recognition for their domestic skills, awarding them dignity and respect (Williams 1984; Brown 1981).

While such identity-affirming food making is traditionally women's work, there are some male-dominated food events that also impart a sense of cultural empowerment and identity. José Limon describes the *carne asada*, the southern Texas all-male ritualistic roasting and consumption of barbecued meat in which bawdy, sexual humor pervades. *Carne*, the word for meat, is closely linked to *carnales*, Limon explains, a kinship term used among brothers or close male friends. Here Mexican-American men can gather, contribute items for the meat and marinade, joke and laugh with friends—in effect, socially bond—in an atmosphere far away from the harsh realities of life as a Chicano in late-capitalist society with seemingly few avenues out of poverty (Limon 1994:137). Limon employs Fredric Jameson's notion of the political unconscious to describe "the socially produced, narratively mediated, and relatively unconscious ideological responses of people . . . to a history of race and class domination" (1994:14). The *carne asada*, with its bawdy humor, is a form of cultural resistance to the (Anglo) capitalist status quo—a flaunting, if you will, of middle-class respectability as a way to protest against it and protest their marginal place in it. I quote Limon at length:

> What kind of meat is this socially, and what, if anything, is its message, its gastropolitics? These men are preparing and consuming those parts of a steer—the internal organs and the faja, or skirt steak—that are clearly undervalued, low-prestige meats in the larger social economy, and, given their economic resources, that is not unexpected. . . . What interests me is the way in which such meat parts—the discards of capitalist cattle ranching— are culturally mediated to convert them from low-prestige, rather rough and stringy protein into tasty, valued, social food. . . . The felt result is another discourse of power, but a power that does not dominate; rather and if only for brief moments, it liberates them from the context of alienation beyond [the scene] where race and class still prevail (1994:136–37).

Similarly, Mario Montaño has explored the cultural meanings of the *barbacoa de cabeza*, the beef-head barbecues popular among borderlands Mexican Americans. While Montaño sees much of popular Southwestern cuisine as an aggressive appropriation of Mexican cuisine by European Americans, it is doubtful that such events as the beef-head barbecues will be subsumed because of the aversion to offal in mainstream American cuisine, largely because the general public can afford to discard the entrails and other less desirable, though no less nutritious and flavorful, parts of an animal. For this reason Taco Bell will never include in its menu *fritada*, a goat stew prepared from the offal meats and blood valued by many borderlands families, and some elements of borderlands cuisine will continue to be solely owned by its originators.

Even given these pockets of resistance and elements of ownership in the mainstreaming of Southwestern cuisine, its evolution is more than just a one-way cultural appropriation of borderlands foodways. As stated earlier, cuisine, like culture, is never static but is in a constant state of change, adding and subtracting elements, creating and being shaped by new boundaries. In this sense, Southwestern fare is not just a crass commercial hijacking, but in a real sense is a legitimate cuisine that is indeed different from Mexican borderlands foodways. In fact, as a product of the place where Mexico and the United States intersect and influence each other, the hyphenated "Tex-Mex" may be the most symbolically accurate that can be found. Moreover, as Sylvia Ferrero points out, the "transnational consumption" of Mexican food through Tex-Mex and other Southwestern cuisines empowers people economically in a very real sense. Ferrero explains, "Mexican food is powerful enough to present Mexicans, Mexican-Americans, and new immigrants with a social opportunity that becomes the bedrock upon which they improve their social position. . . .[I]t lays the ground for new immigrant arrivals and new workforces [and allows them] to gain better positions within the dominant system" (2002:215).

An informal survey of two dozen mostly middle-class Mexican citizens and Mexican immigrants to the United States bears these contradictory meanings and uses out, though gives special credence to the food-as-appropriation premise. When asked about their feelings toward Southwestern, specifically "Tex-Mex" food, many interviewees' comments were emphatically negative: "It seems that it is made out of plastic and very artificial. Everything tastes the same." "It is a very bad adaptation of Mexican food made just for Americans." "It is a reflection of a confused culture." Most resented Tex-Mex's appropriation of Mexican food names. That the word "taco"—in Mexico a meal item consisting of meat and a bit of salsa wrapped in a soft corn tortilla—would be used so ubiquitously for the hard, U-shaped shell filled with not only meat, but also lettuce, cheddar cheese, sour cream, or even other more "exotic" items such as bacon, was an insult. For most the two items had nothing in common. The greatest wrath was reserved for the food served at Taco Bell. "Taco Bell tacos are a corruptive version of the original taco." "Taco Bell is the worst imitation of Mexican food that exists." One person volunteered: "Of Taco Bell: I love it, but I wouldn't consider it Mexican food; it is simply fast food." Yet most respondents' comments were less generous:

"It is not Tex-Mex and it is not Mexican." "It gives a very bad name to our nation." "As a Mexican I think it has no flavor." Some, however, described Tex-Mex in more organic terms: "It is the type of food that was created to satisfy the Chicano needs of Mexican food. Of course it's authentic. It is authentically Tex-Mex food." "The fact that Tex-Mex food is part of two cultures doesn't mean that it is not authentic. . . . [I]t is valid that this type of food exists and that it satisfies a specific group of people." "Tex-Mex is an option but I rarely feel like eating it. I don't find it particularly sophisticated or interesting; it is food by itself with its own traditions, techniques, and very specific flavors. It is the encounter of different cultures and worlds, sometimes with a good result and sometimes not. But after all it has helped to support the creativity of Mexican and American cuisine."[3]

La Frontera

The Mexican-American border, an artificially determined political boundary since the mid-1840s when the United States colonized northern Mexico proper, is the site of the greatest economic disparity between any two nations in the world (Hansen 1981:11). Called by some the Tortilla Curtain, it functions simultaneously to "divide and unite, repel and attract, separate and integrate" (1981:25). While there exists a definite political boundary between Mexico and the United States, upon closer examination it is clear that the borderlands area holds more continuity than distinction between north and south and, in fact, can be divided into four transborder geographical subregions. The Southern California–Baja California region is characterized by the cosmopolitanism of Los Angeles, San Diego, and Tijuana, as well as exoticism of the Baja. The Arizona-Sonora borderlands are shaped by the harshness of the Sonoran Desert, by isolation, and by dominant industries such as copper mining and ranching. The New Mexico/West Texas/Chihuahua region exhibits patterns characteristic of an isolated high-desert zone and a population heavily dependent on the major rivers (Rio Grande, Pecos, Rio Conchos). A major corridor for centuries, migration has been particularly influential. Finally, the southern Texas–northeastern Mexico region has been influenced by the subtropical climate, the large agricultural/ranching societies, and the strong mix of Texas Anglo culture and Mexican Norteño culture (1981:54–55).

The border not only artificially divides, but also actually helps create a country of its own, *la frontera*, as Mexicans call it (Arreola and Curtis 1993:7). The distinctive region is the product of an industrialized country adjacent to a developing country, a so-called Fourth World, producing an economic and cultural in-betweenness, as is evident from the *maquiladoras*, American factories on the Mexican side where mostly Mexican women, desperate for jobs, assemble goods for a pittance of what American workers would be paid. As Anzaldua eloquently observes, "The U.S.–Mexican border *es una herida abieta* [is an open wound] where the Third World grates against the first and bleeds. And before a scab forms it hemorrhages again, the lifeblood of two worlds merging to form a third country—a border culture" (1987:3). Borderlanders are perceived from both sides as the "illegitimate children" of a larger social system. A popular sentiment, for example, holds that the Mexican border communities are more Americanized because of their proximity to the United States; thus, they are not the *real* Mexico (Arreola and Curtis 1993:7–8). "Above all," borderlands scholar Oscar Martinez explains, "the distinctiveness of border Mexicans and Anglos is embedded in the long-term incorporation of many traits from each other's culture, inducing cross-borrowing of such things as language, religion, values, customs, traditions, holidays, foods, clothing, and architecture" (1994:53).

Southwestern food, then, is a product of this borderlands milieu. As the eminent folklorist Américo Paredes observed, Tex-Mex cuisine, with its own versions of tamales, tacos, enchiladas, chalupas, nachos, tostadas, frijoles, and refritos, would be as exotic to many Mexicans as Mexican food is (or was) to many WASP Americans, supporting the assertion that such fare is a hybrid product (1993:20). Thus, in addition to food, the term "Tex-Mex" can apply to many products of the regional culture. Anzaldua describes a hybrid language of Spanish and English as "Tex-Mex," and the term is also used to describe the North-Mexican border music, or *cantina* (bar) music, featuring the button accordion borrowed from the German immigrants settling Central Texas and Mexico in the mid-nineteenth century (1987:56, 60–61).

While there is distinct evidence of culinary neutralization and cultural domination of Mexican borderlands folk foodways, food is a site of enormous capacity for expression and communication, not necessarily negative. In one sense such events as cultural foods nights and ethnic food fairs sponsored by schools, churches, and civic groups can be regarded as contributing to this culinary neutralization and cultural domination; they can also function as just the opposite. Such food events can be and are sites for positive and constructive communication.

A recent personal experience illustrates how food and the sharing of it can provide moments of cultural and political connectedness. At my former place of employment, the University of Colorado, the housekeeping staff invited the faculty in our building to a lunch they would prepare, while we pitched in to provide the basic ingredients. This was an important social event, as there existed many barriers of ethnicity, education, language, and class between the faculty, who were all Caucasian and Asian-American, and housekeeping staff, all Latino and Latina. Rosa, the housekeeping supervisor, served the delicious bean burritos smothered with two kinds of homemade *chile verde* to all, joking that "we'll do it the way they do in Mexico, serve the men first," perhaps to make her male supervisees feel more comfortable. Despite the language and cultural barriers, there ended up a wonderful exchange of goodwill over the food. We learned more about each other's personal lives, enabling each to regard the others as distinct individuals. While the political and economic structures of power did not change, at least from that time on we could call each other by name when exchanging pleasantries—and have more to talk about—because of the shared moment when we broke bread together.

It is perhaps in the realm of language, particularly metaphor, that food has the greatest power to unite and transform. For as the proportion of the U.S. Latina/o population grows greater and greater, North Americans will be forced to sit up and take notice not only culturally but economically as well. The following story from a *National Geographic* article on the borderlands illustrates the potential of food to shape United States language and culture. Robert de la Madrid, a Mexican-American resident of Texas states that inevitably "Mexicans would gradually infuse plainspoken Americans with their humor, their romance, their emotional expressiveness." "For instance?" asked the journalist. "Americans refer to a very handsome man as a hunk," de la Madrid replied. "It could be a hunk of cheese or a hunk of rock. Mexicans call a very handsome man a *mango*, because a mango is a really sensual food. It won't be very long before American women will be referring to Robert Redford as a mango." The author then tries out this theory on a Texas-reared Cajun woman "with a languid way of drawing out a word into all its potential syllables." "'Mango,' she said, lingering over the word—*maa-ynn-go*—and letting a momentarily sublime expression turn up the corners of her mouth. She took a quick pull on her cigarette. 'Not Robert Redford,' she said. 'I don't like my fruit that ripe'" (Sartore and Dale 1996:62).

As this woman's understated but affirmative response indicates, Southwestern cuisine has moved from exotic other to familiar staple, and in so doing has not only altered American food habits, but has also left its imprint on the culture at large.[4] As Southwestern cuisine has become embedded into the lexicon of mainstream American foodways, other Latin American cuisines have followed its lead, emerging as the newest "others." Because of Americans' familiarity with basic ingredients and spices, Brazilian, Caribbean, Cuban, El Salvadorian, and other Latin American cuisines—"Nuevo Latino" or "Floribbean" in their haute cuisine incarnations—are being received positively ("Pan-Latino Cuisine" 1997). Moreover, in an ironic twist, Latin American fast-food chains with stronger, bolder flavors, including Guatemala's Pollo Campero SA, and Mexico's El Tizoncito, Gorditas Doña, and El Fogoncito, are setting up franchises—to great success—north of the border (Bouza and Sama 2002). While these trends are clearly evident, people's different points of view determine the meanings of these transformations. Whether as a form of cultural appropriation, a symbol of resistance, or as a true hybrid providing a medium for mutual regard, Southwestern cuisine is replete with contradictions. This is as it should be, for while food can be an intensely personal experience, it is also a political statement, regardless of the eater's intentions or comprehension. Despite the polite prohibition of political discussions at mealtime, politics is rarely absent at the dinner table—particularly at Taco Bell.

Notes

1. A word on usage: Although there are different nuances to the terms "Chicano/a" and "Mexican American," for the purposes of this essay I will use the terms interchangeably to mean people of Mexican descent inhabiting the United States, whether citizens or not. I use the terms "Latino" and "Latina" to designate members or elements of larger Latin American culture. Similarly, fully aware that people in Canada, Mexico, and Latin America are also "Americans," I use this term and "mainstream Americans" when referring to non-Latino/a U.S. citizens, both because they are less cumbersome, and because they seem most appropriate when naming and discussing mainstream eating habits in the United States.

2. Proposition 187 was an initiative passed in California in November 1994 that eliminated some health and social services, including access to public education, for illegal aliens and their children. The initiative was put on "hold" by a federal court.

3. Special thanks to Natalie Kalb for her research assistance and to Joseph Bentley and Jon Deutsch for their helpful comments.

4. Octavio Paz magnificently explores North American and Latin American cuisine and character in "Eroticism and Gastrosophy" (1972).

Works Cited

Anzaldua, Gloria. 1987. *Borderlands/La Frontera: The New Mestiza*. San Francisco: Aunt Lute Books.

Appadurai, Arjun. 1981. "Gastro-Politics in Hindu South Asia." *American Ethnologist* 18: 494–511.

Arreola, Daniel D., and James R. Curtis. 1993. *The Mexican Border Cities: Landscape Anatomy and Place Personality*. Tucson: University of Arizona Press.

Bourdieu, Pierre. 1984. *Distinction: A Social Critique of the Judgment of Taste*. London: Routledge & Kegan Paul.

Bouza, Teresa, and Gabriel Sama. 2002. "America Adds Salsa to Its Burgers and Fries." *Wall Street Journal*, January 2.

Brown, M. H. de la Peña. 1981. "Una Tamalada: The Special Event." *Western Folklore* 40: 64–71.

Collins, Glen. 1997. "The Americanization of Salsa." *New York Times*, January 9.

Crosby, Alfred, Jr. 1972. *The Columbian Exchange: Biological and Cultural Consequences of 1492*. Westport, Conn.: Greenwood Press.

Daily Camera (Boulder) 1995. October 19.

DeWitt, Dave, and Nancy Gerlach, eds. 1995. *Heat Wave! The Best of Chile Pepper Magazine*. Freedom, Calif.: Crossing Press.

Ferrero, Sylvia. 2002. "*Comida Sin Par*. Consumption of Mexican Food in Los Angeles: 'Foodscapes' in a Transnational Consumer Society." In *Food Nations: Selling Taste in Consumer Societies*. Eds. Warren Belasco and Philip Scranton. New York: Routledge.

Hansen, Niles. 1981. *The Border Economy: Regional Development in the Southwest*. Austin: University of Texas Press.

Limon, José E. 1994. *Dancing with the Devil: Society and Cultural Poetics in Mexican-American South Texas*. Madison: University of Wisconsin Press.

———. 1998. *American Encounters: Greater Mexico, The United States, and the Erotics of Culture*. Boston: Beacon Press.

Lloyd, Timothy Charles. 1981. "The Cincinnati Chili Culinary Complex." *Western Folklore* 40: 28–40.

Long, Lucy M. 1998. "Culinary Tourism: A Folkloristic Perspective on Eating and Otherness." *Journal of Southern Folklore* 55(30): 181–203.

Martinez, Oscar. 1994. *Border People: Life and Society in the U.S.-Mexico Borderlands*. Tucson: University of Arizona Press.

Martinez, Theresa A. 1996. "Tortilla-Making as Feminist Action." *Network*, May 11–14.

Meier, Matt S., and Feliciano Ribera. 1993. *Mexican Americans, American Mexicans: From Conquistadors to Chicanos*. New York: Hill and Wang.

Montaño, Mario. 1992. "The History of Mexican Folk Foodways of South Texas: Street Vendors, Offal Foods, and Barbacoa de Cabeza." Ph.D. dissertation, University of Pennsylvania.

"Pan-Latino Cuisine Stands Poised to Take American Foodservice by Storm." 1997. *Restaurants and Institutions* 107(7): 58–68.

Paredes, Américo. 1993. *Folklore and Culture on the Texas-Mexican Border*. Austin: University of Texas Press.

Paz, Octavio. 1972. "Eroticism and Gastrosophy." *Daedalus* 101(4): 67–85.

PepsiCo, Inc. 1993. Annual Report.

Pilcher, Jeffrey M. 1998. *Que Vivan los Tamales! Food and the Making of Mexican Identity*. Albuquerque: University of New Mexico Press.

"Protesters in Mexico City Ransack a McDonalds." 1994. *New York Times*, November 9.

Ritzer, George. 1996. *The McDonaldization of Society*. Thousand Oaks, Calif.: Pine Forge Press.

Robbins, Jim. 1992. "Care for a Little Hellish Relish?: Or Try a Hotsicle." *Smithsonian Magazine* 22(10): 40–43.

Sanchez, George. 1995. *Becoming Mexican American: Ethnicity, Culture, and Identity in Chicano Los Angeles, 1900–1945*. New York: Oxford University Press.

Sartore, Joel, and Bruce Dale. 1996. "Tex Mex: The Winding Border along the Rio Grande Both Divides and Unites Two Fast-Changing Worlds." *National Geographic* 189(2): 44–62.

Verhovek, Sam Howe. 1996. "Making Jalapeños for Tender Tongues." *New York Times*, May 15.

Williams, Brett. 1984. "Why Migrant Women Feed Their Husbands Tamales: Foodways as a Basis for a Revisionist View of Tejano Family Life." In *Ethnic and Regional Foodways in the United States: The Performance of Group Identity*. Eds. Linda Keller Brown and Kay Mussell, 113–26. Knoxville: University of Tennessee Press.

CHAPTER 10

Rites of Intensification

Eating and Ethnicity in the Catskills

Rachelle H. Saltzman

That's the way it is in the Catskills. You come to eat, eat, eat!
Margaret Hasenkopf Dukarm

Crystal Brook Resort (1991)

The Catskills resort experience was and is about hospitality, comfort, and feeling at home. Unlike modern-day tourist attractions, the family-run resorts in the mountains of upstate New York were and are about re-creating the familiar for their visitors. While second- and third-generation guests looked for innovation and modern improvements such as indoor heated swimming pools, movie theatres, and other entertainment, their parents and grandparents were looking for a place where they could just be in the fresh mountain air with others who spoke the same language, cooked and served familiar foods, and thought the same way. Going to the Catskills was the very antithesis of the touristic experience: it was not about going someplace new—the immigrants who came to the Catskills were already experiencing that on an everyday basis. Seeking out novelty was not the goal; going to the Catskills was about returning year after year to an idealized and re-created version of home and holiday time, complete with all the familiar food you could ever want.

When immigrants came to the United States, they brought with them their religious, regional, and ethnic heritage—including their food traditions. Food, especially homemade food, was and is much more than just nourishment for most ethnic groups. From snacks to everyday meals, from seasonal specialties to holiday dishes, food communicates aesthetic, religious, family, and community values from one person to another. As Mina de Oro restaurant owner Lydia Malave put it, "We keep our sense of being Puerto Rican through our food" (1991).

A stay at the ethnic resorts of the Catskills most closely resembles a homey and festive holiday experience, and, as at holiday time, an abundant supply of carefully prepared food plays a critical part in creating such an atmosphere. Resort menus specifically and consciously offer dishes that evoke family, ethnic, and national traditions; they provide a dining experience that is neither as exclusive as the home kitchen nor as public as a restaurant. Meals are served at designated times and places, but they are not eaten among only family or close friends. Still, "home cooking" has been the model for chefs in Catskills resorts, famous since their beginnings for their elaborate spreads.

In the Catskills, as elsewhere, specific foods—in some cases everyday dishes, and in others holiday specialties—evoke a sense of security and create the feeling of being at home in a new place. Using familiar ingredients and spices, combining certain dishes and ordering the courses, knowing the cook, even being served by someone with a familiar accent—all evoke memories of safe and happy times among family and friends. In many resorts, diners are even assigned tables for their entire stay and get to know their waiters. Although the recollection of such times might sometimes be idealized, resort owners use them to re-create those touches that will make visitors feel comfortable and relaxed—as if their vacation really was an extension of home. For example, Griffin's Irish House in Palenville offered its home cooking as an inducement to visitors in the 1940s. Peni Poulos also described such an atmosphere at Sparta Manor in Windham during the 1950s and '60s, when her parents owned and operated the Greek resort: "This is how [the guests] felt; they went in and out of the kitchen. If they felt like having tea during the late evening, they would go make their own tea, and things like that. It was never, there was no restrictions in those days, you know. It was like having an extension of your home life" (1994).

Joe Sausto, third-generation owner of the Italian resort Pleasant Acres, which started in the town of Lexington in the 1920s, echoed those sentiments. "It's very [much] home cooking; it's really like what you'd make at home. Back then when you came here, whatever my grandmother made that meal, that's what you ate. And there was no choice. We used to ask my grandmother if there was a choice, and she'd say, 'Yeah. You either eat or you don't.' And that was the choice" (1994).

In the 1820s, fresh and abundant country milk, butter, eggs, game, and fish were featured at the Catskill Mountain House. Such cuisine was also a drawing point for wealthy visitors to the Catskills during the Grand Hotel era from the 1870s through the 1880s (Evers 1972:476). And to immigrants and their children, who also began to vacation in the Catskills in the late nineteenth century, the promise of farm-fresh dairy products and produce nourished their bodies as the fresh mountain air did their spirits. As the *American Hebrew* reported in 1928: "The room renters are the families of the men who work at the machines. They rent a room in which live a mother and two or three children. . . . The children are always in the fresh air. They obtain for them milk, in many cases from T.B.–tested cows; eggs, which they themselves can go out and gather in the chicken coops; vegetables which are pulled up right from the ground" (Kanfer 1989:78).

For most immigrant city dwellers, fresh food was often hard to come by. Wilted or rotten fruits and vegetables, milk adulterated with chalk powder and other substances, rancid meat and fish, and aging eggs were all too common in the urban markets that catered to poor immigrants. While these new Americans clearly would have preferred to buy items of better quality, they did not always have the purchasing power to do so, especially during the winter and early spring, when fresh produce was impossible to find unless one paid exorbitant prices. Since many immigrants came originally from rural areas, such deprivation was even harder to bear. One solution to the early-twentieth-century scandals concerning adulterated foods was the passage of the Pure Food and Drug Act in 1906; another was to go directly to the source—to the country—for wholesome produce, dairy products, meat, and fish.

As a small child in the 1920s, my mother, Pearl Sachs Saltzman, stayed with her family at a farm-boardinghouse in Liberty, New York. She recalled: "[We were] served three meals a day, and they had nourishing things in between. . . . I remember my father [who had grown up in the small town of Kaplitza in Lithuania] saying how good everything was and how everything tasted so good. . . . I remember the first time I had that fresh milk from the cow. . . . It was warm, you know—it was warm. And of course the eggs were all from chickens that were on the farm also" (1994).

While food was served at some farm-boardinghouses, at others Jewish women cooked for their families in *kucheleins*. As Saltzman explained, "[I]t means cook alone. You used to cook for yourself. [Each family had its own part of the kitchen.] They probably had their own space, their own shelf in the refrigerator, the icebox, and there must have been more than one. They must have had more than one icebox, but I don't remember that either, but it couldn't have been electric—not up in the country there. It must have been ice. . . . They might have had a wooden cookstove . . . which had the four burners on one side and then the oven on the other. . . . It was an enamel stove and I'm pretty sure it was gas" (1994).

Because most of the resorts started out as farm-boardinghouses, later growing into more elaborate spots, they particularly emphasized the fresh and pure nature of their food, a marketing strategy that awakened nostalgic memories of meals in the old country and played upon the widely publicized importance of consuming fresh and pure food. Sparta Manor featured fresh dandelion greens in late spring and early summer. "That was a big thing!" Peni Poulos recalled. People would ask her mother, "'Sophia, are you going to pick dandelion?' And mom would go out there with the knife and [for] hours pick the dandelion and bring them in. It took very little to please the people in those days. It was mostly wholesome Greek cooking that they wanted" (1994).

Yet it was not only the authenticity and healthful qualities of country food that attracted working-class visitors and later their middle-class children and grandchildren. It was also its abundance. Even if the resorts offered rather sparse amenities in the early days, there was always plenty to eat. Poulos recalled of Sparta Manor, "If you wanted second helpings, it was always, they were very generous with their portions. They were very happy with the, with the meals, but they used to complain about the beds" (1994).

The United States represented a promised land for most immigrants, but the reality of life in densely populated urban neighborhoods was not an idyllic experience. For the hard-working people who had to pinch and save during the year to have a vacation for a week or so in the summer, a plentiful supply of home-cooked food must have seemed the ultimate in luxury; to have as much food as anyone could ever want surely helped create the holiday-like atmosphere of a Catskills vacation.

For those resort-goers who were also wartime or economic refugees, the resorts and their generous menus represented an escape from the deprivations they had earlier experienced. An area that was popular with German-Jewish clientele from the 1940s through the early 1970s was the Delaware County village of Fleischmanns. The Meinstein Lodge, formerly the Villa Meinstein and now the Highland Fling, was one of several German-Jewish hotels that thrived in the village. When German-Jewish émigrés Julius and Frieda Meinstein purchased the hotel in 1944, they left the word "Villa" and added their family name to the original sign. Mrs.

Meinstein, who had trained as a chef in Europe, was famous for her home-cooked and plentiful meals and pastries. Stephen Meinstein, who worked as a waiter when his parents ran the villa, explained what food signified to his family's guests, especially to those who were World War II refugees:

> A lot of these people who frequented the hotels in Fleischmanns were so-called refugees [from Germany and Austria]. . . . Most of these people when they got together still spoke German. . . . There was a small group of Hungarians, too. . . . And food was a very big item to the European people, because having come to this country, and, you know, having eaten over there, I thought American food was pretty darn bland! The bread, you know, the white bread, that was a joke! Because, you know, we had the European-type breads, heavy breads. . . . And the European pastries, which had to be done for the guests, they were rich with nuts and liqueurs. (1994)

Particularly popular among Jewish visitors of Eastern European descent were the hotels in Ulster County around the town of Liberty. Former boardinghouses such as Tamiment were originally opened as vacation places for garment workers from New York City. Months and years of working in overcrowded, poorly ventilated sweatshops in New York City undermined and even destroyed the health of many immigrants. One of the major goals of labor reform in the early twentieth century was to provide vacations to rejuvenate and reinvigorate these workers. Hence labor unions and social service organizations made arrangements to provide paid vacations for workers. And because those workers were so deprived of fresh air and food, as well as of leisure time, the rural Catskills, relatively close by and accessible, provided the perfect vacation spot; for years, Americans with tuberculosis and other lung ailments had come to these mountains, as well as to the Adirondacks and White Mountains, for sanitarium cures. Like the farm-boardinghouses, however, many of those working-class vacation spots had grown larger and fancier by the middle of the century. By the 1940s, these resorts attracted thousands of young people from the Northeast, most of them second-generation Americans. Young women would come up in groups and stay for a week at a time. My mother, who visited Tamiment at that time, recalled: "They had breakfast, lunch, and dinner, and you had—I guess there must have been two sittings, because they had such a large number of people there. It was a very popular place for New York and Philadelphia people. . . . And they had a golf course, tennis courts, and they had two swimming pools. And they had entertainment every night, and tons of food. The food was super.

. . . It was a heavy Jewish style, and of course you had a choice of entrees" (Saltzman 1994).

Stephen Meinstein described the development of the cuisine at his parents' villa in Fleischmanns:

> We started out very small, you know. It was really a private house, you know. And in the dining room there would be four tables, and then after a while you added on another table; after a while on Saturdays and Sundays you had them on the porch. But you were really more of a waiter than you are today, because they could have anything they wanted. . . . For instance, there were two kinds of meat, because if they didn't like one they could have the other. They didn't get anything from a menu, but you were so hard up to keep people satisfied my mother would make anything for them. If they wanted something special, she'd make something special for them. . . . There wasn't a menu. They would ask what you're having, and, like Sunday it was duck. And other days of the week, it would be—because there was a fish store in Fleischmanns, [on a] certain day of the week we always had the carp, which is, the traditional Jewish, you know. And certain days of the week there would be certain food, most of the time.
>
> We never served meat and milk together, and my folks never had pork, you know, because it was not kosher. But it was, you know, it was Jewish, because if you served meat, you didn't serve milk with it, you know. . . . As I remember, there were two big meals [a day]. (1994)

The resorts enabled all visitors, even working-class immigrants, to achieve—if only for a brief time—the promise of the American dream of plenty, for, fundamentally, resort vacations were and are holidays. Such events are by nature brief and characterized by playfulness, excess, and exaggeration of various aspects of everyday life (Smith 1975; Turner 1982; Stern and Cicala 1991; Neustadt 1992). Such festive occasions, like those at resorts, often include singing, playing music, and dancing; playing games and talking into the night; wearing leisure or special clothes; drinking, and, of course, eating generous amounts of specially prepared foods. Religious and secular celebrations such as Christmas, New Year's, the Fourth of July, Thanksgiving, and Passover all include these characteristics, which are also the ones that many of the resorts have made their own. Although they could not re-create totally those traditional holidays, resort owners were able to emphasize the food that was and is such a crucial part of family celebrations and, by extension, the resort experience (Barile 1984; Levenstein 1992).

The significance of food to Catskills resorts is readily apparent in the nicknames by which the mountains have become well known—the Borscht Belt, Yoghurt Belt, Sour Cream Sierras, Derma ("sausage skin") Road, and the Cuchifrito ("fried snacks") Circuit. Entertainers who made the rounds of the different resorts most likely coined these terms, which quickly caught on among the groups who patronized the resorts as well as among local residents. No doubt the popularity of such sobriquets came from their double meaning. They stressed the ethnic dominance of a particular area of the Catskills by invoking a stereotypically alien, foreign, or non-American food associated with particular ethnic groups, a technique that also emphasized the differences among those groups (Leach 1964; Bauman 1972).[1]

The use of food names as labels for ethnic groups is an age-old and widespread practice that occurs among peoples all over the world (Brown and Mussell 1984; Douglas 1966; Humphrey and Humphrey 1988; Leach 1964; Stern and Cicala 1991). One group often uses the stereotypical food preferences of another as an epithet: Germans, whom Americans fought in World War I and II, were known as "krauts" or cabbages; the British have long referred to the French as "frogs"; and the British themselves were once called "limeys" for their sailors' habit of sucking limes to prevent scurvy during long voyages. In certain cultures, the most insulting names one can use are often those of animals one would never eat: *chazer* (pig) for Jews; cur (dog) or ass for European Americans (Leach 1964). The easiest and most accessible part of a culture for those on the outside, food is also so basic to life that when a group's eating practices differ from what another considers to be the norm, members of that latter group tend to react negatively. The timeworn expression "you are what you eat" aptly describes the reaction people have to those who eat strange foods (Humphrey and Humphrey 1988). People fear strangers because they do not understand them, and one of the classic reactions to fear or uncertainty is to mock that which is threatening. Conversely, members of a group also tend to use the fearful stereotypes that others hold about a group to underscore the stupidity of out-group members for believing such nonsense (Paredes 1966:113–28).

In his book about the Jewish Catskills, Stefan Kanfer cited several examples of the way that entertainers used ethnic food stereotypes in their routines to emphasize the fundamentally un-American nature of themselves and their audiences as foreigners—no matter how much they tried to assimilate (Kanfer 1989:68–94):

The anecdotes differ, the morals are identical. Having changed his name and his religion, a former Jew finds himself at dinner with old-line goyim [non-Jews]. All goes well until the hostess serves baked ham.

Horrified, he blurts out the name of forbidden pig meat in Yiddish: *"Hozzer! Oy, vay—"* [Pig! Oh, no!] As the other guests glare at him, he attempts to recoup: *"—whatever that means."* (Kanfer 1989:274)

The humor of this in-group joke comes from the knowledge that no matter how hard the Jewish immigrant tries, he cannot detach himself from his linguistic and cultural roots. For Jews, of course, the food that most signifies gentile culture is pig meat; were Jews truly to assimilate, they would eat ham with no compunction. Only other Yiddish-speaking Jews would even understand such a joke—and understand why food taboos, which seek to separate not only clean from unclean foods, but also Jews from non-Jews, are so basic to Jewish identity (Barth 1969; Douglas 1968:361–76; Howe 1978:92–108; Liebman 1973).

Not everyone was enthralled with ethnic-food jokes, however. By the 1980s, although some Jewish resort owners in Ulster County pressed to retain the food-based tags for the region as a marketing strategy, others felt the terms were outdated and even incomprehensible. The distaste that some express for those terms is directly related to the dismay that ethnic Americans feel at being identified as foreigners. One of the resort owners whom Kanfer quotes explained, "In this day and age the last thing they want are reminders of gluttons and greenhorns." When asked about borscht, the Catskills' most famous dish, another claimed, "Between you and me, I've never tasted it." A third noted, "We don't even use the word "borscht" on our menu. We just call it beet soup, because otherwise people wouldn't know what it was" (Kanfer 1989:275). Although such comments may be a bit disingenuous, they do point out the long-lasting nature of the fear that different habits will enable others to label ethnics as un-American.

Despite the tension over what food-related nicknames for the Catskills mean for in- and out-group members, those terms acquired their popularity because they point to one of the most identifiable features of particular groups—and to the importance that eating came to hold for resorts in the Catskills. While nicknames such as the "Yoghurt Belt" and the "Sour Cream Sierras" certainly seem to signify geographically bounded enclaves, they are in fact more often descriptive of cultural groups. In fact, the Catskills are not cut up into readily identifiable ethnic slices; much like urban neighborhoods, which often have members from several ethnic groups living side by side but not interacting to a very high degree (Barth 1969; Bauman and Abrahams 1981; Stern and Cicala 1991), discrete areas of the mountains often host a wide variety of people of different ethnicities.

Though there are certain towns, including East Durham (Irish), Round Top (German), and Plattekill (Puerto Rican and Latino), that once catered primarily to a particular ethnic group. More often, individual hotels in a region are known to be patronized by a single group. Some resorts, such as the Italian American Villa Vosilla in Tannersville, even serve several different crowds and sponsor "weekends" throughout the summer for such groups as Istrians (from the peninsula south of Trieste that juts into the Adriatic Sea) and Armenians.

Of course there are ethnic group members who visit the resorts or who live part- or full-time in the Catskills, particularly those who have been in this country for several generations and for whom food is not the most important marker of ethnic identity. In such cases, other traditional arts, such as music, dance, or crafts, are culturally more significant than food; hence, the nicknames for the parts of the Catskills where these groups vacation do not focus on food. At those resorts, however, a few well-known dishes tend to assume a greater importance than the overall ethnic character of the cuisine. For instance, very few of the restaurants and resorts in the so-called Irish Alps of East Durham serve food that could be defined as strictly Irish. Yet Fern Cliff House serves corned beef and cabbage once a week, and McGrath's lays on a traditional Irish breakfast of black-and-white puddings (sausages), eggs, and soda bread every day. Sunday breakfast at Erin's Melody also includes the puddings and eggs as well as a grilled tomato half and fried potatoes, typical breakfast garnishes at bed and breakfasts and hotels in Ireland. Food in the Irish resorts probably reflects what vacationers in Ireland would encounter and represents more a tourist experience than a re-creation of home (Bendix 1995; McCannell 1992). A similar situation exists among the German resorts around Round Top, though the cuisine there is more elaborate. The Crystal Brook resort, owned by the Hasenkopf-Dukarm family, serves such specialties as *wursts*, *sauerbraten*, and *wiener schnitzel*, as well as smoked pork chops and potato pancakes. But chicken, pork, and beef dishes, as well as other more "American" mainstays, are also regular menu offerings. One of the owners points out that the kitchen has to be careful not to have only German food, because not all of its guests are of German or Austrian heritage.

On the other hand, because many ethnic resorts market themselves to visitors who may not be members of a particular group, some of the foods served may be more stereotypical—what a wider American public associates with the group—than representative of regular ethnic fare. Certain resorts have become known for specific food traditions: Nellie Gavin's Irish Soda Bread is sold at her resort, Golden Hill in East Durham, while the rye bread for which Jennie Grossinger was known was manufactured and sold nationwide. Such a practice makes resorts as well as local festivals and restaurants more accessible to a broader audience—all an important part of economic survival for today's resort industry. The Jamaican-owned Mountain Valley Resort and Country Club (formerly the Peg Leg Bates Resort and Country Club) in Kerhonkson served the standard Jamaican specialty of curried goat with pigeon peas and rice at its "Blue Drawer" Festival a few years ago (Simmons 1994). Guests at Windham's annual Greek festival, held each August 15 to celebrate Assumption Day (the day on which the Virgin Mary ascended to heaven and the feast day of the Assumption Greek Orthodox Church), are offered *souvlaki*, Greek salad, and *baklava*. The town's Starlight Diner highlights such Greek specialties as *spanikopita, souvlaki,* and rice pudding on its predominantly "American" menu of hamburgers, fries, and the like; many Greek-owned diners located throughout the Northeast offer similar menus combining American foods and Greek dishes that have crossed over, in a sense, into American popular cuisine.

Besides attracting new visitors with popular ethnic foods, resorts also use traditional foods to put an ethnic "frame" around menus, holiday celebrations, and even at the start or finish of a meal or a day (Goffman 1975). Such framing devices point out how ethnic groups identify as both ethnic and American—and use their foods to express this dual identity. For example, the Cold Spring Hotel in Tannersville, now closed but once owned by Syrian American Sabor Khouri, listed Middle Eastern dishes at the beginning and end of its menu and American dishes in-between. The once-famous Mecca Restaurant, which the Khouri family used to run in Manhattan, offered mostly Middle Eastern foods as well as a few broiled meats like Delmonico steak or lamb chops, served with French fries. At the Christmas/New Year's end-of-season celebration on Labor Day weekend at Pleasant Acres, Joe Sausto explained, a traditional Sicilian Christmas Eve dinner introduces the festivities on Friday evening, but as in many Sicilian American family holiday dinners, the foods become more American over the course of the "holiday":

> On Labor Day weekend, the Friday night we serve a traditional Christmas Eve dinner, with all the fish, about ten different types of fish . . . eel and *baccala* and *calamaris, congelie* and . . . all the different Italian types of dishes, shellfishes, clams, and mussels, and things of that nature. . . . And Saturday night is the traditional Christmas dinner, and Sunday is New Year's Eve, and we have a big party afterwards, with champagne and hats and noise-

makers, and entertainment which goes till, you know, two or three o'clock in the morning. . . . The Christmas dinner would be like more of an American-style dinner, with different roasts, a soup-to-nuts type of dinner. . . . And New Year's Eve—more American. You know, like a filet mignon, champagne . . . what you would expect if you went out to a New Year's Eve ball. (1994)

Sausto also pointed out that Columbus Day marks the resort's final holiday before closing for the winter. In celebrating the event, Pleasant Acres makes a day most Americans take for granted into a pan–Italian-American feast day (not just Sicilian), and so closes out the Catskills resort season Italian-style: "Columbus Day's a big deal, and we make a big deal—especially with Columbus being Italian. And we usually, we even have a special song that we sing on that day. . . . And we have a big Italian festival dinner, which is something we do fairly regularly, and we decorate our dining room. We have different linen, we have all the Italian flags hanging in here, we have music; all our servers have uniforms with . . . the Italian flag made into an apron" (1994).

At the Greek-run resorts that once operated in Windham and its vicinity, the day would start off with an American breakfast, but lunch and dinner would feature traditional homemade Greek dishes such as chicken with *pastitsia* or lamb with string beans. Even an American meal ended with Greek pastry as well as Jell-O or rice pudding. Noting the quantities served, Poulos described her mother's plentiful Greek meals at Sparta Manor:

> Three healthy meals! It was a big breakfast in the morning—eggs, pancakes, juice, coffee, whatever it was; for lunch it was soup with a three-course meal, dessert and coffee; six o'clock the cow bell was used to summon all the guests to the dining room. They would sit down and have a three-course dinner—everything. It was three healthy meals, and if I'm not mistaken, I think they used to charge twenty-seven dollars a person. . . . Naturally in the city they wouldn't eat like this, but coming up to the Catskills—the fresh air and walking and hiking—they did, they enjoyed the three meals. . . . All Greek food—wholesome Greek food. . . . [A typical week's menus would include] for lunch Sunday . . . a Greek *avgolemono* soup first, the chicken with the *pastitsia*, then we would have *halatiporico*, which is a Greek pastry made out of farina and milk, eggs, and coffee. For supper, it was a little bit more American-style. . . . It was the same menu week in and week out; it never changed. Monday's menu stayed the same, Tuesday's the same, so Sunday's dinner was veal chop with a slice of liver and pilaf, and watermelon and coffee. . . . They used to break it up a little [with American food], but . . . they all eat the same. (1994)

Different groups or families will often use a particular food or dish to indicate that an event has an ethnic as well as a religious or secular meaning for their members. Conversely, there are also those foods that in and of themselves point to and symbolize the very identity of a particular group. These are not necessarily the same foods with which outsiders are familiar or, if they are, they are often made in more traditional ways and with special ingredients. Examples include Hungarian goulash, Czech pork loin with dumplings, German roast pork, or Ukrainian breads. So important are these special breads that the *Grazhda* of St. John the Baptist Ukrainian Catholic Church in East Jewett sponsors special classes in breadmaking during the summer months. According to Maria Wyznyckyj, a former resident of Brooklyn who now lives in East Jewett, bread and grain symbolize for Ukrainians the connection between earth and heaven, between survival and eternal life.

Like many groups, ethnic and religious, Ukrainians use bread to celebrate every holiday and life-cycle event. What differentiates Ukrainian breads from others, however, are their elaborately sculpted forms, the large number of bread types, and the special names and recipes for each. Wyznyckyj, who came to the United States in 1951, learned to bake from her mother and from watching other Ukrainian women in this country. During World War II and the years afterward, making elaborate breads was not possible. But Wyznyckyj's mother, like other Ukrainian women, remembered the tradition and began to practice it again once conditions improved. Her daughter and the children of friends have been asking their mothers to bake traditional wedding breads for them. Larysa Zeilyk, for instance, whose family has homes in both Greene County and New York City, prepared a traditional wedding bread called *korovoi* for the marriage of her daughter. Decorated with doves, pine cones, and other symbols sculpted out of dough, such elaborate breads call attention to the connection between the fertility of nature and the purpose of marriage. By taking the time to make such ritual foods, Ukrainian mothers pass traditions on to the next generation. Breads are also particularly important for Easter (*paska*), Christmas (*kolache*), Saint Andrew's Day (when young girls predict their fortune), family gatherings, and weddings. A newborn child is greeted with bread, and for Christmas there are three breads, symbolizing the Trinity (Wyznyckyj 1992).

In other communities, style of preparation as well as type of food signified identity. In Fleischmanns, the Oppenheimer-Regis has served strictly kosher foods to its orthodox Jewish clientele since the 1940s. During the 1950s and 1960s, Fleischmanns resident Dottie Cohen recalls, Jewish delicatessens carried corned beef, homemade pickles, and sour green-to-mato pickles (1990). Joyce Wadler remembers that in the 1950s and 1960s, her grandmother would cook Russian Jewish foods for 120 guests at a time at the Maplewood House, "a dairy farm, expanded to a boarding house with pool" in Fleischmanns (1992:6).

In Kerhonkson today, Doreen Richardson and Lloyd Simmons, Jamaican-American owners of the Mountain Valley Resort and Country Club, serve a typically Southern breakfast of bacon, ham and biscuits, grits, home fries, eggs, and toast and dinners of roast beef, pork chops, spare ribs, and chicken to their African-American visitors, many of whose families—and cooking traditions—have roots in the southern United States.[2] On special weekends or for groups of Caribbean origin, however, the menu features such traditional Jamaican or West Indian dishes as *ackee*, a stew of greens and salted codfish, for breakfast and, for dinner, jerked (marinated and grilled) chicken or pork, curried goat and plantains, curried chicken, oxtail stew, *callaloo* (another dish of greens with codfish), and side dishes of pigeon peas and rice (Richardson 1992).

Plattekill's Garden Cathay, formerly the Puerto Rican-owned Villa Nueva, serves its visitors regional dishes from Taiwan, Mainland China, the Philippines, and Hong Kong. Once Latino, the resort's clientele is now predominantly Chinese who come from New York City, New Jersey, Massachusetts, and Connecticut. Although the business changed hands in 1986, it is unusual among resorts that cater to new ethnic groups in that it continues to attract non-Chinese visitors as well—a point that its American-Chinese menu makes clear (there is also another menu printed in Chinese only).

Also located in Plattekill are the Puerto Rican and Latino resorts for which the area is better known. Places such as the Villa Casablanca, which Clemente Rodriguez owns, is open year-round and caters to Dominicans, Cubans, Hondurans, and Colombians as well as to Puerto Ricans. Rodriguez explained that the menu features "octopus, shrimp, lobster, beefsteak, *arroz con gandules* [rice with pigeon peas], chicken, [and] pork chops, but we don't have *cuchifritos*. In winter we make *pastelillos* [meat pies]" (1991, 1994). Mina de Oro, known as "Luis and Lydia's" in New York and Brooklyn, is a favorite Catskills haunt of local residents and urban visitors who come to indulge in *lechon con arroz o tostones* (roast pork, rice, and fried plantains) and other traditional Puerto Rican dishes. According to owner Lydia Malave:

> Sometimes we cook for non-Latino villas, like a roast pork for a picnic,

but we generally don't cook for anyone else. . . . On weekends there are mile-long lines of cars waiting to eat here. . . . This is not a place for rich people, not for very poor either.

. . . During Labor Day and Fourth of July we make one thousand pounds [of pork]. [Luis] cooks it all by himself. We specialize in *lechon* and . . . we only use fresh products. . . . Sometimes the people from the city would drive up just to eat. (1991)

Even at those resorts where guests cook for themselves, ethnic foods help to reinforce identity among visitors. Barbara Konopka, owner with her husband, Richard, of Homestead Farms in New Kingston, caters to a Polish and Polish American clientele who came, or whose parents came, to this country in the 1950s, 1970s, and 1980s. Originally a farm-boardinghouse that served a heterogenous clientele before the war, Homestead Farms was purchased by Polish immigrants in the 1950s and, though it has changed hands, has catered to that ethnic group since. At Homestead Farms, people stay in individual apartments equipped with kitchens and prepare their own meals instead of eating together in a central dining room. Although she describes her visitors as "very Americanized, very much assimilated into American culture," Barbara Konopka notes that they still speak Polish among themselves and prepare traditional, homemade Polish foods such as "stuffed cabbage, that's very popular; and *pirogi*, which is meat pockets; and naturally all the sausages, the barbecued sausages and all that stuff." Because they cannot buy such food nearby, guests "bring their own, all the sausages, and *kielbasi* and all that stuff, they bring with them" (1994).

Many resorts rely not only on home-style ethnic cooking to attract visitors, but they also feature special holiday packages that give resorts a chance to generate income in the off-season. In the fall, one of the most beautiful times of the year in the Catskills, many resorts have apple-picking outings and pumpkin-carving contests, events that attract families and emphasize foods of the region. Religious holidays are also special times for ethnic resorts, which put together special menus to attract families who want a traditional celebration but who do not have the time or the inclination to spend hours in the kitchen.

For those resorts for which food is one of the primary factors of ethnic identification for patrons, meals served during religious holidays provide an even more intensely symbolic experience. At such times of the year, resorts attempt to re-create an authentic festive home atmosphere for in-group members (Handler and Linnekin 1984:273–90; Bendix 1995). Jewish resorts feature Rosh Hashanah/Yom Kippur and Passover packages that include rabbinically supervised meals of gefilte fish (cooked and chopped whitefish or carp formed into balls and served cold with horse-radish), chicken soup with matzoh balls, roast chicken, brisket, potato *kugel* (pudding), *tzmimmes* (carrot and/or sweet potato pudding), stewed dried fruits, and sponge cake.

For Ukrainians as well, many of whom vacationed at resorts in Greene County and who now own second homes around East Jewett, Hunter, and Lexington, religious holidays and cultural events—and the food that ac-companies them—are a critical part of maintaining their identity. St. John the Baptist Ukrainian Catholic Church in East Jewett in Greene County, built thirty years ago, follows the Eastern rite. Patronized by a small com-munity of summer and year-round residents, the church and its women members cook and serve a traditional Ukrainian meal every Sunday after mass. This meal is sold in the *Grazhda,* or community center, where musical performances as well as classes in baking traditional Ukrainian breads, decorating Easter eggs, and creating embroidery and beadwork are often held throughout the summer.

Ukrainian resorts, including the Soyuzivka in Ellenville, also adver-tise holiday specials. People tend to go to the resorts for Christmas, an important family holiday for Ukrainians, to be with other Ukrainians and to ease the women's burden of cooking elaborate holiday meals. Christ-mas Eve dinner includes at least twelve dishes—all made without meat or dairy products. *Cutcha,* made with wheat kernels, poppy seeds, and honey, was traditionally served first. For Ukrainians in New York, however, the sweetened grain and seed dish is often served at the end of the meal, tak-ing the place of dessert for Americanized palates and serving an almost communion-like function in its position at the end of the meal. Accord-ing to Maria Wyznyckyj, without *cutcha* there is no Christmas Eve din-ner. Fish, *borscht* (beet soup) with *vushka* (which translates as "ears" and are small dumplings with wild mushrooms) *cholupche* (stuffed cabbage), beans, cabbage or sauerkraut, and *vereneke* (a sauerkraut and potato dish) with sour cream are among the featured dishes that remind guests of their mother's and grandmother's home cooking (1992). At Easter—a time of community celebration among Ukrainians—a typical meal consists of sausage, ham, cheese, and *bopka* (a sweet egg bread), as well as carefully decorated *pysanki* (eggs). These holiday menus at the Soyuzivka are highly traditional, but at other times of the year, general manager John Fliss says, the food is "half Ukrainian and half American" (1991).

Although most ethnic resort ads are aimed at in-group members, the effort to provide an authentic holiday experience attracts non-group members as well, inadvertently turning a summer rite of intensification into a touristic expedition. Irish resorts open in March for Saint Patrick's Day weekends and serve such well-known dishes as corned beef and cabbage. El Caribe, a Puerto Rican-owned bar and restaurant in Plattekill, featured *pasteles* (pies filled with root vegetables and meat, wrapped in plantain leaves, and boiled), *arroz con gandules* (pigeon peas and rice), *mofongo* (plantains), and roast pig at its Feast of the Holy Cross celebration on the seventh of May.

The *Schlachtfest* put on by Crystal Brook in Round Top every October features a roast pig as its centerpiece, as well as soup made from five different meats (pigs' knuckles and four types of sausage), sauerkraut, potato dumplings, and apple strudel. This festival, which recalls a traditional Germanic harvest meal, begins with costumed pallbearers who lead the pig parade. A mock funeral complete with oratory lamenting the pig's death follows the procession. The mock ritual sacrifice concludes with the ceremonial carving of the animal and redistribution of the meat to all in attendance (Dukarm 1993). Like those actual festivals after which the *Schlachtfest* is modeled, such events invoke symbols of life and death: the autumn harvest celebrates the fullness of life and marks the decline of the natural year. And in the Catskills, October marks the end of the resort season. By feasting, people defy death physically and ensure their survival—as individuals and as a community. By joining together in a community celebration, especially a comedic one like the *Schlachtfest,* they literally laugh in death's face and emphasize the importance of renewing social ties and ensuring the community's survival (Turner et al. 1975; Bakhtin 1968).

At Catskills resorts, food permits visitors from all ethnic backgrounds to revel both in ethnicity and in the comfort and abundance of American life. But, as Joe Sausto notes, a balance between ethnic and "American" elements must be maintained in order for the resorts to survive:

> For us, [Italian identity is preserved] . . . in the food only, I'd say. We've had decisions where we'd say, people really aren't eating this dish anymore, but just for traditional reasons, and especially for the older clients, we won't take it off. . . . Now we have the same basic menu and a lot of the items we serve on the same day that we used to serve—the only thing is now, instead of ordering that, you can order something, you can order a steak or a prime rib or something. . . . We have a lot of choices for the kids: chicken nuggets, and individual pizzas, and hot dogs, hamburgers, peanut butter and jelly sandwiches. There's always something for the kids.
>
> . . . You have to be competitive in today's market, and if you're going to

restrict your market, you're going to hurt yourself. You try to give the customers what they want and what they expect . . . regardless of whether it's Italian or not. . . . It started as, just that my grandparents were Italian, and all their cooking was Italian because that's what they knew, and it's really grown to try to meet the needs of today's travelers, no matter what ethnic background they are. (1994)

Notes

Special thanks to Lucy Long for her patience and forbearance as well as her persistence in encouraging me to complete this work for this volume, and to Kathryn Grover, who provided critical reading, suggestions for revision, and editorial assistance. I am particularly grateful to the other folklorists who were a part of the Catskills Ethnic Resorts project and to the many resort owners, cooks, and residents in the Catskills who shared their thoughts on food, hospitality, ethnicity, and their relationship to the Catskills resorts experience. A grant from the National Endowment for the Humanities funded the research for this essay (part of a larger project on the ethnic resorts of the Catskills), which was originally written for the Delaware County Historical Society, Delhi, New York.

1. Anthropologist Edmund R. Leach has written extensively on the ways in which people all over the world refer to out-group members by their stereotypical food preferences. Dietary taboos in Leviticus are extended to cultural groups and result in name-calling and exclusionary practices.

2. During the 1930s, the Notch Mountain House in Hunter advertised Southern fried chicken and waffles to its clientele, many of them African Americans with Southern roots whose families had migrated North after 1900 (Postcard, c. 1930, Courtesy Mountain Top Historical Society.)

Works Cited

Bakhtin, Mikhail. 1968. *Rabelais and His World.* Cambridge, Mass.: MIT Press.

Barile, Mary. 1984. *Catskill Cookery.* Margaretville, N.Y.: Heritage Publications.

Barth, Fredrik, ed. 1969. *Ethnic Groups and Boundaries.* Boston: Little, Brown.

Bauman, Richard. 1972. "Differential Identity and the Social Base of Folklore." In *Toward New Perspectives in Folklore.* Eds. Américo Parédes and Richard Bauman, 31–41. Austin: University of Texas Press.

Bauman, Richard, and Roger Abrahams, eds. 1981. *And Other Neighborly Names: Social Process and Cultural Image in Texas Folklore.* Austin: University of Texas Press.

Bendix, Regina. 1995. "Vacationing in Ethnic Immersion: Tourism, Cultural Encounter, and the Emergence of Leisure Resorts." Unpublished manuscript.

Brown, Linda Keller, and Kay Mussell. 1984. *Ethnic and Regional Foodways in the United States: The Performance of Group Identity.* Knoxville: University of Tennessee Press.

Cohen, Dottie. 1990. Interview with Mary Zwolinski, Fleischmanns, N.Y., September 13. Delaware County Historical Association (hereafter cited as DCHA) collections.

Douglas, Mary. 1966. *Purity and Danger.* New York: Praeger.

———. 1968. "The Social Control of Cognition: Some Factors in Joke Perception." *Man* 3: 361–76.

Dukarm, Margaret Hasenkopf. 1991. Interview with Janis Benincasa, Round Top, N.Y. DCHA collections.

———. 1993. Interview with author, Round Top, N.Y., December 6. DCHA collections.

Evers, Alf. 1972. *The Catskills: From Wilderness to Woodstock.* New York: Doubleday.

Fliss, John. 1991. Interview with Mary Zwolinski and Rebecca Miller, Kerhonkson, N.Y., August 31. DCHA collections.

Goffman, Erving. 1975. *Frame Analysis.* New York: Harper and Row.

Handler, Richard, and Jocelyn Linnekin. 1984. "Tradition, Genuine or Spurious." *Journal of American Folklore* 97(385): 273–90.

Howe, Irving. 1978. "The Eastern European Jews and American Culture." In *Jewish Life in America.* Ed. Gladys Rosen, 92–108. Hoboken, N.J.: KTAV Publishing House.

Humphrey, Theodore C., and Lin T. Humphrey, eds. 1988. *We Gather Together: Food and Festival in American Life.* Ann Arbor: UMI Research Press.

Kanfer, Stefan. 1989. *A Summer World: The Attempt to Build a Jewish Eden in the Catskills, From the Days of the Ghetto to the Rise and Decline of the Borscht Belt.* New York: Farrar Straus Giroux.

Konopka, Barbara. 1994. Telephone interview with author, January 19. DCHA collections.

Leach, Edmund R. 1964. "Anthropological Aspects of Language: Animal Categories and Verbal Abuse." In *New Directions in the Study of Language.* Ed. Eric H. Lenneberg, 23–63. Cambridge, Mass.: MIT Press.

Levenstein, Harvey. 1992. *Paradox of Plenty: A Social History of Eating in Modern America.* London: Oxford University Press.

Liebman, Charles. 1973. *The Ambivalent American Jew: Politics, Religion, and Family in American Jewish Life.* Philadelphia: Jewish Publication Society of America.

Malave, Lydia. 1991. Interview with Juana Camacho, Plattekill, N.Y., September 27. DCHA collections.

McCannell, Dean. 1992. *Empty Meeting Grounds: The Tourist Papers.* London: Routledge.

Meinstein, Stephen. 1994. Interview with author, Fleischmanns, N.Y., May 18. DCHA collections.

Neustadt, Kathy. 1992. *Clambake: A History and Celebration of an American Tradition.* Boston: University of Massachusetts Press.

Paredes, Américo. 1966. "The Anglo-American in Mexican Folklore." In *New Voices in American Studies.* Ed. Ray Browne, 113–28. West Lafayette, Ind.: Purdue University Press.

———. 1978. "The Problem of Identity in a Changing Culture: Popular Expressions of Culture Conflict along the Lower Rio Grande Border." In *Views Across the Border: The United States and Mexico*. Ed. Stanley Ross, 68–94. Albuquerque: University of New Mexico Press.

Poulos, Peni. 1994. Interview with author, Windham, N.Y. April 19. DCHA collections.

Richardson, Doreen. 1992. Interview with author, Kerhonkson, N.Y., September 2. DCHA collections.

Rodriguez, Clemente. 1991. Interview with Juana Camacho, Plattekill, N.Y., September 27. DCHA collections.

———. 1994. Interview with author, Plattekill, N.Y., January 31. DCHA collections.

Saltzman, Pearl. Telephone interview with author, Bradenton, Fla., January 19, 1994. DCHA collections.

Sausto, Joe. 1994. Interview with author, Leeds, N.Y., April 19. DCHA collections.

Simmons, Lloyd. 1994. Interview with author, Kerhonkson, N.Y., January 31. DCHA collections.

Smith, Robert. 1975. *The Art of the Festival* (Lawrence: University of Kansas Library Publications in Anthropology, no. 6., 1975).

Stern, Stephen, and John Allan Cicala, eds. 1991. *Creative Ethnicity: Symbols and Strategies of Contemporary Ethnic Life*. Logan: Utah State University Press.

Turner, Victor, ed. 1982. *Celebration: Studies in Festivity and Ritual*. Washington, D.C.: Smithsonian Institution Press 1982.

Wadler, Joyce. 1992. *My Breast: One Woman's Cancer Story*. Reading, Mass.: Addison-Wesley.

Wyznyckyj, Maria. 1992. Interview with author, East Jewett, N.Y., August 30. DCHA collections.

CHAPTER 11

Pass the Tofu, Please

Asian Food for Aging Baby Boomers

Liz Wilson

We all know that you are what you eat. Grandmother said so. And now experts like Deepak Chopra, Andrew Weil, and others appear regularly on various media outlets offering evidence to support nutrition-based approaches to health. Weil even confirms the wisdom of our grandmothers' cod-liver-oil fixation in discussing the nutritional benefits of the ingestion of certain fishes high in fatty acids.[1] Clearly nutrition-based approaches to health have well-established roots in the West. This essay suggests that more affluent segments of America's postwar baby-boom generation have contributed to a revival of interest in diet as a means of self-care.[2] But baby boomers' concerns about the quality and purity of food ingested do not simply amplify traditional beliefs about diet as the key to health. Wedded to health issues are status issues. Affluent boomers take the dictum, "you are what you eat" in its declaratory sense, declaring their social identity through the choice of diet and by favoring foods that connote cosmopolitanism and educational attainment. Enjoying a level of income that allows them to spend a little more on the everyday necessities of life such as food and toiletries, affluent baby boomers are adventurous eaters, conducting culinary tourism in their homes and in the restaurants they patronize. Where the consumption of meat served as a marker of status for many prewar Americans, the cosmopolitan baby-boom ethos favors plant-based foods as a substitute for or supplement to meats. Thanks to the mainstreaming and mass marketing of Asian vegetarian foods that were first popularized by members of the counterculture in the 1960s and

'70s, many baby boomers have developed a taste for bean curd, fermented beans and vegetables, seaweed, and other foodstuffs that their parents and grandparents would likely have considered exotic or even inedible. Certain Asian foods, especially those based on traditional Japanese cuisine, are especially in vogue among the baby-boom generation as a healthy alternative to the mainstream, meat-heavy American diet.

In this essay, I briefly sketch some of the historical precedents in American culture for the current vogue that Asian vegetarian foods now enjoy, and attempt to identify what is distinctive in current ethnomimetic food-consumption trends among baby boomers. With the tremendous recent growth in the availability of Asian convenience foods—beverages, food supplements, and soy products—designed to substitute for meat and dairy foods, culinary explorations of Asia have never been easier for American consumers. But just as international tourism can often take the form of journeys to faraway places and encounters with exotic others that shed light on the tourist's own constructions of self and formulations of self-identity, so too culinary tourism can shed light on the self-images of those consumers who are inclined toward adventuresome eating. I analyze material from contemporary women's magazines as well as information gleaned from the marketing and packaging of ethnic and New Age food products, suggesting some ways in which the more romanticized images of Asia these materials reveal serve to confirm consumers' cherished constructions of self. And, finally, I suggest some of the paradoxes that come with the gentrification of the Woodstock generation. While many baby boomers seek to affiliate with non-Western values and express emancipatory social agendas through their choices about what foods and beverages to consume, these declaratory functions of diet operate within a consumer culture that has, since the 1960s, increasingly appropriated the anticapitalistic rhetoric of the '60s to serve corporate interests.

Countercultural America and the Development of Countercuisines

The late 1960s spawned several countercultural movements that contributed to the rise of alternative diets or "countercuisines" as statements of opposition to dominant cultural values.[3] Probably the most significant was the ecological movement, which focused on food as a powerful outlet for activism. *Time* magazine declared the environment "Issue of the Year" for 1970, and Gallup polls showed that pollution surpassed race, crime, and other issues of concern to Americans in late 1969 and early 1970.

Food selection and preparation came to bear a new political significance in light of the warnings of ecological activists about the environmental cost of pesticides, monocropping, resource-wasteful food packaging, and energy-wasteful global food distribution channels. Concerns about over-population and the sustainability of the world's environmental resources also focused attention on meat production. As statistics were gathered about what extent of the world's population went hungry or had nutri-tionally deficient diets, feeding vegetable proteins in the form of corn, grain, and soy to livestock rather than feeding those sources of vegetable protein directly to human beings came to be seen as a squandering of scarce food resources (a grain-fed North American steer, for example, eats twenty-one pounds of vegetable protein for every pound of animal protein it delivers to the human diet).[4]

Meat products and processed American convenience foods brought environmental quandaries into every household. As a concrete and daily fact of life, food provided an outlet for political expression more immedi-ate than other kinds of activism in an era in which leftist politics came to be perceived as beset by endless theorizing and internecine warfare among various activist groups.[5] With food, one could enact one's principles at least three times a day and could teach others through acts of hospitality. How better to realize the emancipatory adage that the personal is the political than to take personal responsibility for the environment and ex-press one's opposition to the dominant culture through one's choice of diet and through a regimen of recycling? Frances Moore Lappé's *Diet for a Small Planet* epitomized this culinary approach to ecological activism.[6] Published in 1971, *Diet for a Small Planet* sold two million copies in the first decade of its publication.[7] The early '70s saw a number of other works dedicated to analyzing the food system and articulating alternative means of providing sustenance, such as Judith Van Allen and Gene Marine's *Food Pollution: The Violation of Our Inner Ecology* (1972), E.F. Schumacher's *Small Is Beautiful* (1973), Jaqueline Verrett and Jean Carpenter's *Eating May Be Hazardous to Your Health* (1974), and Jim Hightower's *Eat Your Heart Out* (1975).[8]

Postwar developments in mass-market food production brought about some rather strange new food fabrications compared to the typical prod-ucts of simpler mechanical food production techniques.[9] By the end of the '60s and the early '70s, mass-market food production techniques were the subject of intense scrutiny.[10] Highly processed, packaged convenience foods were not only recognized as threats to the environment, but also became a powerful symbol of the dominant culture's homogeneity and artificiality. By the end of the '60s, the fascination with modernity and technology that had ushered in the mid-sixties penchant for Day-Glo colors, plastic and foil clothing, and other products of industrialized manufacturing had waned. Handwoven fabrics in natural tones were favored in clothing, and artists and craftspersons tended toward wood, leather, and clay pieces made from natural materials. If extensively packaged processed foods underscored one's membership in a conformist "straight" industrial society, simple grains, nuts, and beans brought home in paper bags, cleaned, husked, and cooked at home, instantiated opposition to mass production and the conformist culture associated with it.

Also fueling this resistance to culinary conformity was the interest in exploring and valorizing ethnic differences that began with the civil rights and negritude movements and blossomed under such mottoes as "Black is Beautiful." White ethnics followed suit by rediscovering and perpetuating the foodways that their parents and grandparents were often all too ready to jettison in the process of assimilation.[11] For countercultural youth eager to shed their WASP cultural identity, ethnic grocery stores and restaurants provided sources of relatively cheap, simply prepared foods. If one could not or would not bake bread at home, purchasing heavy, dark, filling whole grain breads available at ethnic grocery stores was the ideal alternative. As Warren Belasco has noted, the purchase of spongelike white Wonder Bread and other mass-produced breads came to signify not only poor health, but also the artificiality and homogeneity of the dominant white culture.[12] Ethnic foods like dark breads and brown rice allowed countercultural youth to achieve some sense of distance from mainstream culture, while encouraging the eater to identify with the peasant cultures of the past and of the developing world.

Although the countercuisines of the late '60s and '70s tended toward hybrid blends of all manner of ethnic foods, Asian cuisines were given pride of place in many kitchens as interest in vegetarianism increased. In 1977 *Time* magazine noted that the trend in cookbook publishing was "toward more esoteric books on specialized foreign cuisines. . . . The best cooks are learning Indian, Indonesian, Indo-Chinese, and Chinese (especially Szechuan and Hunan) and Japanese recipes."[13] The macrobiotic movement, which gained widespread attention in the late '60s and early '70s, brought Asian foods to many American dinner tables and was the first step in a trend of interest in the traditional Japanese diet as a source of wellness—a trend that has continued unabated into the twenty-first century.

The concept of macrobiotic eating, it should be said, is much older than the contemporary macrobiotic movement. The ancient Greek physician Hippocrates joined the term "macro" (meaning "great" or "large") with "bio" (meaning "life") as a way to denote those whose lifestyles contributed to health and longevity, and Herodotus and Aristotle also similarly used the term. The eighteenth-century German physician and philosopher Christophe W. Hufeland also popularized macrobiotic eating. Hufeland's *Macrobiotics, and the Art of Prolonging Life* revived concepts about diet and longevity first articulated by thinkers of antiquity. In the late nineteenth century, a strong Taoist element was added to existing macrobiotic philosophies by Sagen Ishitska and Yukikazu Sakurazawa (who later took the name George Ohsawa), two Japanese educators who claimed to have recovered from devastating illnesses through eating a diet of such traditional Japanese staples as miso soup, sea vegetables, and rice. Ohsawa went on to establish the modern macrobiotic movement based on such principles as the holistic unity of spiritual and physical wellness and the importance of food as the "key to health and the key to peace."[14]

Although small amounts of chicken and fish are permitted, the macrobiotic regimen is mainly vegetarian. The essentials of a macrobiotic diet include whole cereal grains, beans, fresh local vegetables, and other whole natural foods chosen with attention to the yin (earthly, cold, soft, and contractive) or yang (heavenly, hot, dry, and expansive) values of particular foods. Yin foods are those grown in summer, like vegetables and fruit; yang foods are winter foods, like meat, eggs, and fish. The ideal is to achieve a balance of yin and yang, not by combining extremely yin with extremely yang foods, but by eating those foods that are neither predominantly yin nor yang. In order to calculate yin and yang values, however, one must also pay attention to the way in which season, climate, and geographical place effect these properties. Those living in a tropical environment will need to maintain a different diet from those living in a colder environment. In colder climates, for example, eating meat is advisable for its warming yang properties, whereas elsewhere meat is to be eaten only very sparingly, if at all. Geography is also important in that one should eat only locally grown and seasonally available foods.

While underscoring the need to eat foods that grow naturally in one's own locale, the macrobiotic movement of the 1960s and '70s also stressed the health-enhancing features of Japanese cuisine and encouraged Americans to practice ethnomimesis, imitating the Japanese in their diet and methods of food preparation. The movement's literature, although recognizing the Western roots of macrobiotics, downplayed those roots in contrasting the natural, health-enhancing traditional Eastern ways with the health-destroying ways of the mechanized West: "The natural way of life is the joyous way of life. The alternative to industrialized, chemicalized food, stagnating inactivity and pills for everything are pure and simple food, yoga, and exercise, and healing the natural way with herbs. We Westerners would do well to take a few lessons from our Eastern contemporaries, who, although influenced by Western modes of eating, drinking, and living, have still managed to preserve a certain amount of traditional knowledge concerning the art of eating healthfully."[15] The literature of the contemporary movement distances macrobiotics even more radically from Western traditions. In a recent publication, George Ohsawa asserts that "[Macrobiotics] is a different kind of medicine, totally unknown in the West until recently. . . . This medicine has a history of more than five thousand years. It is a physiological application of the dialectic principle of life that has been totally ignored even in Japan since the importation of Western civilization about a century ago."[16]

If it were not coupled with antimodernist sentiments and did not stress ethnomimesis, the macrobiotic system of food selection could be one that personalizes culinary decisions to a large degree. In its emphasis on determining all the seasonal, climatalogical, and geographical variables that need to be factored into dietary decisions, macrobiotic eating has the potential to position food as an index of geographical and cultural particularity. What one eats would depend on where one lives and what one's environment dictates. What one eats would then truly be tantamount to who one is, as Jean-Anthelme Brillat-Savarin's adage suggests.[17] As we shall see in the next section, interest in food's declarative function, its ability to say something about the identity of the eater, is an important theme in today's culinary tourism. Food has become a preeminent means of self-expression as the countercuisines of the 1960s have influenced mainstream food trends of the '90s.

Multicultural Consumerism and Self-Expression in Contemporary America

As the countercultural youth of the '60s aged, joined the labor force, and acquired more disposable income, countercuisines moved into more public spaces. Plant-based, Asia-inspired cuisines moved from communes to communal restaurants like New York's Moosewood Restaurant (established in 1972 by Mollie Katzen and twenty friends), and ingredients and implements for preparing such foods moved from low-overhead food cooperatives to national supermarket chains.

The mainstreaming of the countercuisine had begun. Concerns about health played a major role in the elaboration and increased commodification of '60s-style countercuisines through the 1970s, '80s, and '90s. As Harvey Levenstein notes, by 1972 even the "straight," conservative *National Review* was extolling natural foods.[18] Concerns about food purity and safety were paramount, especially with regard to suspect additives that food manufacturers incorporated into processed foods to replace taste lost in the food manufacturing process or to enhance the ease of food production. A 1977 Harris poll showed that food manufacturers were chief among the industries the public wished to see investigated by the government.[19] This poll notwithstanding, a majority of Americans also doubted the government's ability to ensure the populace of a safe and nutritious food supply. Only 40 percent of consumers surveyed by the FDA in 1974 thought the government was doing a good job in regulating food safety.[20] Studies published in the 1970s also shifted American attention from the health problems of the world's underfed to the health problems of an overfed but poorly nourished American populace. "Dietary Goals for the United States," published by the U.S. Senate Select Committee on Nutrition and Human Needs in 1977, linked some of the leading causes of death in America, such as stroke, cancer, and cardiovascular disease, with overconsumption of fat and refined sugar and underconsumption of fresh fruits, vegetables, and whole grain products. The report noted that while in 1909, Americans received 40 percent of their daily caloric intake from fruits, vegetables, and grains; in 1976 they were getting only 20 percent from these plant-based sources.[21]

That changes in American food preferences should be increasingly driven by health concerns should come as no surprise. Typically, concerns about nutrition and health issues increase with age. As the vast baby-boom generation of some seventy-six million people approaches middle age, it is reversing the traditional proportions of younger and older generations. In the early '80s, America had some seventy million people under age eighteen and fifty million over age fifty. The U.S. Census Bureau expects that by 2010, the proportion will be reversed, with ninety-six million people over age fifty and only seventy-four million under age eighteen. With the graying of America, health issues have become more visible to the population as a whole.

But if health plays a major role in the late-twentieth-century mainstreaming of cuisines once deemed alternative, other concerns are at work too. A number of food historians and theorists of late-twentieth-century American consumption patterns link culinary tourism with the need for status display and status differentiation. Harvey Levenstein associates the culturally adventurous food preferences of the most affluent sectors of America at the end of the twentieth century with the widening of the class gap in the wake of the oil crisis of the 1970s.[22] Not since Depression-era times, Levenstein argues, when the working classes subsisted on monotonous diets of the cheapest foods, while the affluent worried about weight control, have class differences been so starkly reflected in diet: "Brillat-Savarin's aphorism 'Tell me what you eat: I will tell you what you are' seemed more apt than it had in fifty years, as the social classes again diverged in their food tastes and expectations. . . . The national community of shared values that had persisted for twenty-odd years after World War II—years in which even those in the highest economic and social brackets appeared to share the straightforward national food tastes—seemed to break down, as food again became an important sign of distinction."[23]

Vegetarianism (whether practiced in a meat-free diet or taken as a self-identifying label while eating a meat-restricted diet) has attracted many U.S. adherents and admirers in recent years. If Jon Gregerson is correct, the United States has led the way among Western countries in the practice of vegetarianism in the past thirty years.[24] According to a 1992 survey by *Vegetarian Times* magazine, some 7 percent of Americans (over twelve million people) profess to be vegetarians.[25] While I would not deny that those identifying as vegetarians often do so for a variety of ethical, aesthetic, ecological, and health reasons, I suspect that some contemporary vegetarianism is fueled by the conscious or unconscious desire for status differentiation. The food historian Massimo Mantanari suggests that the widespread vegetarian movements of nineteenth-century Britain may have been, in part, connected to the desire for status differentiation as meat eating became a daily practice for more levels of British society than ever before.[26]

In describing the consumption practices of what he calls the new upper class of the information age, David Brooks suggests that multicultural eating has become a central form of self-identification and status differentiation for bourgeois bohemians, or "Bobos"—those now middle-aged boomers who were youthful bohemians calling for the dismantling of the establishment in the 1960s but who have spent the intervening decades working as professionals, building their investment portfolios, and gradually replacing the old establishment.[27] In an era in which "the rewards for intellectual capital have increased, while the rewards for physical capital have not," many idealistic entrepreneurs combining capitalistic and countercultural values have risen to positions of power through a uniquely postsixties combination of bourgeois industriousness and bohemian individuality, creating in the process a bourgeois establishment that showcases bohemian values such as self-expression, spontaneity, and creativity.[28] According to Brooks, Bobos can be true to their enterprising bohemian ethos only by avoiding conspicuous leisure and ostentatious displays of wealth. For Bobos like us (academics being some of the "founding members" of the new information age elite), work is an expression of creativity—of self-identity—and thus the conspicuous leisure of the old-money classes is déclassé. With "one foot in the bohemian world of creativity" and antiestablishment ideals and "another foot in the bourgeois realm of ambition and worldly success," the new bohemian captains of industry and information management prefer to display wealth in more subtle ways, spending extravagantly only on such necessities as food, exercise, and health.[29] But a great deal of information is communicated by those spending choices. Our kitchens are chrome-plated factories for the production of nutritionally balanced gourmet meals. Our workouts take place in fitness centers that allow us to surf the Internet and read our e-mail while we exercise. Our vacations are Himalayan treks and cultural expeditions, preferably with eco-friendly tour companies. The new elites of the information age simply do not rest: even our leisure time is dedicated to self-expression and self-cultivation; even when idle, we are at work. The only monuments we build are corporal ones, as we shore up the sagging support structures of our aging bodies to maximize future productivity and future self-expression.

What we eat, then, is all-important. Bobos not only seek nutritional antidotes to the stress-related disorders that plague the hyperemployed professional classes, but since the new bohemians must display wealth in unostentatious ways, we spend a good bit of our disposable income on basic necessities like food. Continuing the '60s tradition of identification with distant and downtrodden peoples through culinary tourism, contemporary Bobos now have a much larger range of sources from which to obtain exotic foods, as upscale supermarket chains like Whole Foods (owner of Bread and Circus, Fresh Fields, and Wild Oats) have opened stores throughout suburban America. For the discriminating consumer there are plenty of premium ethnic specialty foods available for purchase.[30] For the producers of these items, the profit margin is excellent. Brooks suggests the cognitive appeal of such foodstuffs in his comments on the Bobo penchant for multicultural shopping. Of the shopping practices of upscale suburbanites in his hometown, who frequent stores with names like

"Anthropologie," Brooks says: "In the information age, shoppers can stroll amidst the radish sprouts, the bins of brown and basmati rice, the jars of powdered fo-ti root, the Mayan Fungus Soap, the Light Mountain All Natural hair coloring, the tree-oil mouthwashes, and the vegetarian dog biscuits, basking in their reflected wholesomeness."[31]

Brooks, however, does little more than document the phenomenon of multicultural shopping, a theme that Kimberly Lau analyzes with great theoretical sophistication in *New Age Capitalism: Making Money East of Eden.*[32] Lau's analysis suggests that every dollar spent on such exotic necessities of life is experienced as a dollar spent in resistance to global capitalism, agribusiness, monocropping, multinational corporate monopolies, environmental degradation, and cultural imperialism. For those who now reap income from companies they once demonized as exploitative and authoritarian, countercultural culinary items and New Age aromatherapy products help to assuage guilt about success and fears of having compromised one's values in order to achieve it. The packaging and marketing of such products often attempts to persuade the consumer that the world can be saved from the ravages of consumer capitalism through high-minded forms of consumption. Money spent on exotic foodstuffs and health and hygiene products is money invested in sustaining cultural diversity in a world becoming all too homogeneous in its commercial landscapes—a "McWorld," as sociologist Benjamin R. Barber puts it.[33]

Updating the bohemian ethos of the 1960s for middle-aged boomers who now value regular bowel movements as much as they once valued "free love," New Age groceries, health food stores, catalogue companies, and Internet "wellness warehouses" can profit by referencing the ideals of the 1960s in order to appeal to those who gained wealth in the '80s and '90s. We Bobos may sport bumper stickers proclaiming that "The Best Things in Life Are Not Things," but such stickers are frequently affixed to sport utility vehicles that display the owner's ability to pay high sticker prices to sustain the illusion of vacation time spent "off road," doing extreme sports in exotic locales. Lau's perspicacious book shows just how convoluted such ostensibly antimaterialistic, anticapitalistic thinking can be and how insidiously companies like Aveda have capitalized on the wishful thinking of former flower children. Aveda products and similarly promoted New Age commodities are often sold in minuscule quantities, but they are ensconced in elaborate, brightly colored, educational packages that explain how this commodity subverts the malignant social effects of global commodity capitalism.

As David Rieff pointed out almost a decade ago, multiculturalism can certainly be a moneymaker in that it helps to legitimate new arenas of consumption.[34] There is money to be made in identifying and promoting Hispanic or African-American writers and developers of cultural products and selling their books and cultural commodities. Multicultural product lines can bring in revenue from previously untapped markets of minority consumers, as Rieff suggests. But ethnicity-based product lines may also have the effect of increasing sales to dominant groups by ensuring that cultural difference can be consumed in nonthreatening, digestible bits.[35]

One can see evidence of the appeal of ethnic commodities almost anywhere one looks today, even in a landscape of Thriftways and Quickstop food markets. Truck stops in Nebraska now sell caffeine-free Chai herbal lattes, "Chinese" herbal tonics, and other packaged foodstuffs and beverages of purported Asian provenance. In Cincinnati, Ohio (a place where one would want to be at the end of the world, Mark Twain once quipped, because it is twenty years behind every other American city), one can now purchase "Chinese" meditation bracelets at a chain of local gas station/ice-cream parlors. These beaded bracelets have now replaced the WWJD ("What Would Jesus Do") bracelets that were top-selling items at this chain of stores last year.

It is obviously not just the most affluent that are seeking health, longevity, and enhanced productivity through multicultural consumption in America today. Donna R. Gabaccia has recently documented the spread of culinary adventurousness at the close of the twentieth century.[36] Beginning with the upscale dining experiences of the more affluent in the 1970s and '80s, exposed to the ethnically Creole creations of California chefs such as Wolfgang Puck, America's fascination with ethnic cuisines spread to more modest consumers. By the 1980s, Gabaccia notes, one out of every ten American restaurants was an ethnic restaurant.[37] Ethnic franchises such as Benihana of Tokyo have succeeded well in the mainstream market by serving modified Japanese hibachi cooking "with no icky, sticky, slimy stuff" in restaurant settings full of Japanese architectural touches.[38] If Bobo sensibilities are now mainstream, the Bobo penchant for declaring one's values and standing through diet choices may shed light on Americans' current appetite for culinary exotica. For many consumers used to a meat-based diet, the exotic qualities of ethnic foods compensate for the absence of meat, a traditional symbol of prosperity.[39] "It's a real challenge and status symbol to come up with something your company hasn't tasted before, something they don't even know how to pronounce," said the food editor of the *Atlantic Constitution* in 1977.[40] Ethnic foods are also seen as ideal for entertaining in that they are more likely to please vegetarians than many meat-rich American regional specialties, and the time it takes to gain access to novel recipes, foodstuffs, and cooking implements suggests that the host enjoys a certain amount of leisure time gained through affluence. And for those dual-career couples and working families who may have little time to dedicate to food preparation, the food industry is rapidly expanding its product lines of ethnic convenience foods.

Food industry reports indicate a strong awareness of the growth potential of ethnic convenience foods, based on their appeal to a wide range of American consumers of all classes. A sales director for one ethnic specialty foods producer credits "the Food Network and New Orleans chef Emeril Lagasse with popularizing a variety of ethnic foods formerly unfamiliar to a mainstream audience."[41] Ethnic convenience foods based on Asian cuisines are multiplying in variety and brand differentiation. *Supermarket News Specialty Foods Supplement* reports: "The Asian products have changed. It's not Chinese, but Korean, Japanese, Thai and Vietnamese, and sales are strong in both suburban and inner-city stores."[42] The rise of salsa, which displaced ketchup as the best-selling condiment in 1991, epitomizes this trend toward ethic eating, although it also suggests the American tendency to incorporate ethnic foods in their diets by using them as sauces to add flavor to more familiar dishes.[43] Fusion foods— blends that bring together more than one ethnic or regional cuisine—have appealed both to consumers with an appetite for something new mixed with something more familiar and to the food industry as a way to tap several ethnic markets at once.

To some extent, the culinary pluralism one sees at the end of the twentieth century may be fueled by tourism. The number of Americans going abroad as tourists tripled in the 1960s, exceeded the four million mark in 1970, and has grown steadily ever since.[44] However, Harvey Levenstein argues that a number of ethnic cuisines grew to prominence in America without any significant travel to the homelands of these cuisines.[45] Japanese foods enjoy a popularity among American eaters that Japan as a tourist destination has never had among American tourists. Chinese food likewise became popular long before China opened its gates to American tourists.

Gabaccia concludes that at the end of the twentieth century, we are not so much a multiethnic nation as a nation of multiethnics, of people who cross cultural boundaries and mingle culinary traditions with ease. As anyone who has ever watched a cable cooking show on television or accessed the recipe banks and other food resources on the Internet knows, the information age has simplified and democratized the process of learning about new cuisines. The United Soybean Board, for example, distributes a brochure entitled "The Soy Solution" to grocery chains such as Kroger.[46] Prominently featuring the statement that "the FDA has approved the following health claim for soy foods: 25 grams of soy protein daily, as part of a diet low in saturated fat and cholesterol, may reduce the risk of heart disease," the brochure gives consumers an easy, one-week meal plan by which to consume at least twenty-five daily grams of soy protein in food preparations that take less than twenty minutes, using soy burgers, soy hot dogs, soy cheeses, and soy milks and beverages. The brochure also lists websites for the dozen or so sponsoring manufacturers of soy products (such as Lightlife, Yves Veggie Cuisine, Morningstar Farms, and Boca Burger) where consumers can access an array of information on health and nutrition research, peruse extensive recipe banks, as well as visit chat rooms and subscribe to Internet newsletters and LISTSERVs. Some websites of sponsoring manufacturers include historical information on vegetarianism through history. The Lightlife website, for example, features a "list of famous vegetarians" including Pythagoras, Gandhi, the Dalai Lama, and a host of contemporary actors and entertainers (this illustrated list is dominated by an animated graphic of Albert Einstein in which Einstein raises his famously bushy eyebrows while hungrily eyeing a soy burger).[47] Illustrating the Lightlife site's link to health information is a sketch of a woman seated in the lotus position, with her hands held in a yogic *mudra* or hand gesture. Through a combination of graphical and discursive information, such media resources make implicit and explicit health claims about the benefits of soy and Eastern lifestyles. Above all, they highlight the convenience of meal preparation using the array of soy-processed food products available in American supermarkets today and suggest that American consumers will have little difficulty following Asian foodways in a landscape of Krogers and Safeways. Whether the incorporation of soy cheeses and dairy substitutes constitutes anything approximating traditional East Asian foodways or not (and probably not, since dairy products are only beginning to appear with any regularity on East Asian dinner tables), such brochures and websites show the growing convergence of ethnomimetic counterculture and capitalism in the diet choices of late-twentieth-century Americans. These new convenience foods alleviate the difficulties faced by earlier generations of countercuisine consumers in America, who had fewer plant-based convenience food options and faced greater difficulties in finding substitutes for hard-to-find or oddly described foodstuffs.[48]

With advertising support from the fashion and beauty industries as well as from the manufacturers of processed foods, women's magazines put a gendered spin on culinary tourism by stressing the importance of a low-fat, plant-based diet in achieving and maintaining a culturally valued slender body shape. My study of women's magazines published in 1999 and 2000 turned up numerous feature articles promoting the consumption of plant-based food preparations for the purpose of weight loss and weight maintenance. Such articles often address concerns about health issues specific to women, while speaking simultaneously to concerns about control of the body as a means of self-esteem and professional advancement.

The April 2000 issue of *McCall's* magazine (billed as a "giant health issue"), for example, ran a feature entitled "75 Natural Cures of PMS and Hormone Hell." Subtitling her piece "Mood Swings? Cramps? Bloating? Insomnia? Surprising Fixes for Womanly Woes," Julia Califano presents research suggesting that the daily ingestion of soy-rich Asian food preparations (containing high concentrations of plant estrogens called isoflavones) may reduce the frequency and intensity of hot flashes and make perimenopause easier for women who experience discomfort and emotional irregularity during this time of fluctuating hormone production.

McCall's ran Califano's informative and fully referenced piece with an illustration that draws on stereotyped representations of the Asian body as lean and slender and suggests the range of psychic benefits attractive to Bobos and those who share the Bobo ethos. The illustration (see illustration 11-1) depicts a slender, attractive twenty-something female of Asian heritage wearing a culturally hybrid costume of black capri pants and a red silk kimono-style tunic. Sitting cross-legged on the ground (an echo of the article's references to yoga as a way of easing menstrual cramps), the model smiles while using chopsticks to fish a cube of tofu out of a dish of soy, mushrooms, and greens presented in a Chinese rice bowl. Her dress and overall presentation of self index cultural difference while assuring the viewer that this is a kindred spirit adhering to Western ideals of female beauty and fashionable dress. Kimberly Lau cites similar examples of how America's culturally widespread obsession with body image, particularly among women, is a clearly discernible subtext within (counter) cultural American discourse on achieving optimal health through yoga and t'ai chi.[49] Examples include the *Mademoiselle* feature "Less Inner Thigh, More Inner Peace: Our Workout Will Give You Lean, Sexy Legs and a Shot of Serenity, Too. Om Sweet Om" as well as the *Buns of Steel Power Yoga* and *Buns of Steel T'ai Chi* videos.

The *McCall's* illustration's caption reads "The Joy of Soy: It Can Ease Symptoms the Asian Way." The invocation of Asia in the caption can be

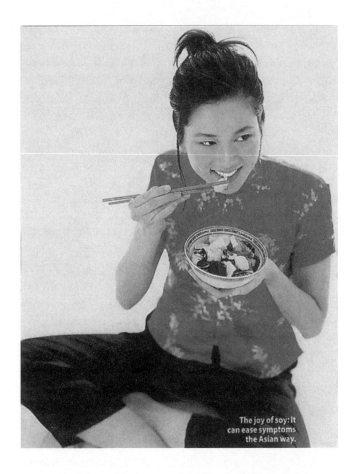

The joy of soy: It
can ease symptoms
the Asian way.

11-1. Asian food has become popular with many baby
boomers who are looking for a healthy alternative to the
mainstream, meat-heavy American diet. *Photo courtesy of
the author.*

read in conjunction with the reference to nature and natural cures in the
title of the essay. It is a common practice in marketing goods of purport-
edly Asian origin to suggest that there is a single, monolithic Asian lifestyle
and that it is a natural one. In his account of Western orientalist thought
from the Enlightenment to the twentieth century, J.J. Clarke suggests that
beliefs about the cultural sickness of the modern West and concomitant
views of Asia as a simpler place where humans live a more peaceful existence in harmony with nature have persisted from the Romantic era to the
present.[50] Although not all modern Western discourse about Asia falls

prey to such simplistic and seductive global polarities, the East has often been idealized by modern Western thinkers of an antimodernist bent who see the West as neurotically hyperactive and out of balance. Asians are said to enjoy longevity and health unheard of in the West by preserving and honoring insights into the healing powers of nature garnered by sages many centuries ago. In contrast to the mechanistic, materialistic West, where advances in technology have caused Westerners to lose touch with the natural world, Asians enjoy simpler, uncomplicated lives in keeping with a less materialistic, more "spiritual" existence. Such antimodernist representations are not entirely benign, for all their outward praise. In associating the East with qualities the West has lost in its frenetic drive for advancement, they position the East as less advanced, if not techno- logically backward. They feed Western nostalgia for a simpler, ideal lifestyle of the past in a way that freezes Asia in a pretechnological, changeless existence in which time does not pass, progress does not occur. In Edward Said's reading of orientalist discourse, conscious or unconscious imperial ambitions are the driving force behind such monolithic constructions of the Oriental other.[51]

Modern thinkers and advertisers did not, of course, invent the romanti- cized image of Asia as a land of natural wellness. This theme has roots in long-circulating legends about exotic peoples living beyond the pale of West- ern cultures. Depictions of Asia as a place where health and longevity pre- vail to an extent unknown in the West date back to early Greek geographers and historians such as Herodotus. Reporting on the peoples living on the borders of the Greek world, writers such as Herodotus marvel at the re- markable physiology of Asian peoples.[52] In addition to such strange traits as being of extraordinary size, having additional or oddly shaped limbs, and sporting feet so large they can be used as parasols to block out the sun simply by lying down and raising the feet over the body, Asians are said also to enjoy less monstrous forms of difference from Westerners as remarkable longevity. Megasthenes, who served as ambassador to the Maurya court and resided in Pataliputra (present-day Patna, India) in the fourth century B.C., described the people of India as free from disease.[53]

Romanticized contemporary images of Asia as a simpler place where people live in harmony with nature preserved from the ills of modernity have their roots in medieval legends in which Asia literally was an Edenic place, home to the terrestrial paradise.[54] Fourteenth-century manuscripts of a letter claimed to have been written by a Christian ruler in Asia by the name of Prester John locate the Garden of Eden in the remote recesses of

Asia. Manuscripts of the letter of this legendary figure tell of how health and vigor could be preserved by drinking from a fountain of eternal youth, located three days' journey from the terrestrial paradise. The fountain of youth changes its taste every hour on the hour, day and night. Anyone who bathes in it three times will remain a thirty-two-year-old as long as he or she lives.[55]

This idealized image of Asians as people who enjoy remarkably long and healthy lives is so pervasive in the West that Asia can be invoked as an icon of wellness by purveyors of multicultural foods, food supplements, hygiene products, and remedies with the most minimal of symbolic cues. An example of this symbolic shorthand can be seen in the packaging of "Indian Arth-right" tea (see illustration 11-2), sold by the Alvita company in its line of "Herbal Remeteas." Describing its contents as "a synergistic blend of Boswellia serrata, turmeric, ginger, devil's claw, licorice, and white willow bark," the package depicts a six-armed figure reminiscent of one of Herodotus's monstrously shaped Asians or perhaps a multilimbed Hindu deity. But where the conventions for representing Hindu deities would dictate that an emblematic object such as a lotus or a sword be held in each hand of the deity, this multiarmed figure is empty-handed. He or she (the figure is androgynously devoid of clear secondary sexual characteristics) stretches forth its arms in an agile and vigorous manner that suggests the practice of yoga and the increased range of flexibility that might be expected from holding yogic postures for extended periods. Thus the packaging of this herbal tea suggests a whole range of associations having to do with the practice of religion in India. From one single graphic image of a multiarmed figure, the buyer may infer an entire symbolic nexus involving extraordinary beings with humanlike bodies that nonetheless transcend the human condition and the practice of bodily disciplines that extend the body's capabilities beyond what is normally seen.

While there is no gainsaying the fact that Asian religio-medical systems and practices of bodily discipline such as yoga and t'ai chi offer many health benefits, Asia is often so romanticized by marketing practices as to bear little resemblance to actual places and persons east of the Khyber Pass. We monied consumers looking toward the Orient while shopping in the multicultural boutiques of the developed world may fancy ourselves to be preserving diverse cultural traditions and patching up the torn social fabric of the global village. But in buying into the idea campaigns of those who promise to deliver us from the hegemony of McWorld, we may be purchasing little more than neatly packaged, rarefied versions of our own self-image.

11-2. An advertisement for an herbal remedy. *Photo courtesy of the author.*

Culinary Tourism: Encounters with Self and Other

In analyzing the appeal of Asian foods and food supplements for American baby boomers, it appears that such forms of culinary tourism reveal a desire to engage and experience a variety of presumed others. The ethnically non–Asian-American consumer can affiliate with spatially and culturally distant peoples of Asia through the consumption of Asian food and beverage products. These products are also a means of traveling back in time, as they are often represented as preserving ancient foodways that allow the modern consumer to experience the temporal otherness of the distant past. In favoring Asian vegetarian foods out of health and ecological concerns, boomers associate themselves with an alternative lifestyle or ethos that is identified simultaneously with the past and the future. This alternative ethos belongs to the past in that it is seen as a perpetuation of premodern foodways and healthways. It is also situated in an ideal, hoped-for future in which rational consumers will act on the findings of the scientific community with regard to the health benefits and ecological wisdom of a plant-based diet. Finally, for those consumers who aspire to membership in a more affluent socioeconomic class, the purchase of Asian foods and food supplements can be a means of experiencing a socioeconomic other within the consumer's home culture. The commercial discourse of alternative foodways and healthways in America (including packaging, advertising, and consumer education resources such as websites) creates communities of consumption that allow the consumer to affiliate with like-minded consumers who are also willing and able to spend a little extra on everyday necessities of life. By paying a little extra for a food or beverage linked with certain goals or values—such as achieving an ideal body size, optimizing health, or preserving cultural diversity in a world grown too homogeneous—consumers can tighten their bonds with other American consumers while expressing solidarity with peoples distant in time and space.

Notes

1. Weil, it should be noted, advocates relying on vegetarian sources for the essential fatty acids that American diets tend to lack. It should also be noted that compared to fishes with higher fat content, such as salmon and sardines, cod is not a good source of fatty acids, particularly the crucial omega-3 fatty acids. See Weil, *Eating Well for Optimal Health,* 115ff.

2. Defined as the generation born between 1946 and 1964, the baby boomers comprise the largest generation in American history.

3. I borrow the phrase "countercuisine" from Warren J. Belasco, *Appetite for Change.*

4. There has been considerable debate since the late '60s as to whether Americans can help alleviate world hunger by shifting to a plant-based diet without a major restructuring of the world's food distribution systems. Lappé came to believe that world hunger cannot be vanquished until food production and distribution problems in the countries where hunger is most acute are addressed. See Belasco, *Appetite for Change,* 56ff.

5. On the ideological battles fragmenting the left in the late '60s, see Todd Gitlin, *The Sixties: Years of Hope, Days of Rage* (New York: Bantam Books, 1986),

pp. 377–419; *The Whole World is Watching: Mass Media in the Making and Un-making of the New Left* (Berkeley: University of California Press, 1980), 180–204.

6. *Diet for a Small Planet,* New York: Ballantine Books, 1971.

7. Sales statistics in the tenth-anniversary edition, *Diet for a Small Planet.*

8. Judith Van Allen and Gene Marine, *Food Pollution, The Violation of Our Inner Ecology* (New York: Holt, Rhinehart, and Winston, 1972); E.F. Schumacher, *Small Is Beautiful* (New York: Harper and Row, 1973); Jaqueline Verrett and Jean Carpenter, *Eating May Be Hazardous to Your Health* (New York: Simon and Schuster, 1974); and Jim Hightower, *Eat Your Heart Out* (New York: Crown Publishers, 1975).

9. On methods the flavor industry uses to make processed foods more palatable, restoring flavor lost in canning, freezing, and dehydrating techniques, see Eric Schlosser, *Fast Food Nation: The Dark Side of the All-American Meal* (Boston: Houghton Mifflin, 2001), chapter 5.

10. Americans expressed fears about food processing techniques as early as the 1930s, according to Harvey Levenstein. Those voices questioning the nutritional price consumers paid for the convenience of processed foods, however, were largely shouted down by professional nutritionists and home economists allied with the food industry. See Harvey Levenstein, *Paradox of Plenty,* 15ff.

11. Michael Novak, *The Rise of the Unmeltable Ethnics*; Sallie Te Selle, ed., *The Rediscovery of Ethnicity.*

12. Warren J. Belasco, *Appetite for Change,* 49ff.

13. Levenstein, *Paradox of Plenty,* 219.

14. George Ohsawa, *Essential Ohsawa* 21.

15. Barbara Rossi and Glory Schloss, *Everyday Macrobiotic Cooking,* 13.

16. George Ohsawa, *Essential Ohsawa,* p. 1.

17. Jean-Anthelme Brillat-Savarin, *Physiology of Taste,* 13.

18. Levenstein, *Paradox of Plenty,* 195.

19. Levenstein, *Paradox of Plenty,* 200.

20. Ibid.

21. On the data used in this pamphlet, see Letitia Brewster and Michael Jacobson, *The Changing American Diet* (Washington: Center for Science and the Public Interest, 1983). For recent dietary guidelines from the U.S. Department of Agriculture, see <http://www.usda.gov/cnpp>, 1999.

22. Levenstein attributes the widening of the class gap after the oil crisis to the crisis' impact on the manufacturing sector and the availability of high-wage manufacturing jobs. See Levenstein, *Paradox of Plenty,* 222ff.

23. Levenstein, *Paradox of Plenty,* 222.

24. Jon Gregerson, *Vegetarianism,* 116.

25. Survey information available at: Nutrition Action Healthletter, <http://www.cspinet.org/nah> 1999.

26. Massimo Mantanari, *Fame e l'abbondanza,* 152ff.

27. David Brooks, *Bobos in Paradise.* Brooks writes in a satirical third-person voice while admitting that he is, in fact, a Bobo. I hope here to emulate the wry satirical style Brooks uses in his discussion of bourgeoisie bohemians while writ-

ing in the first-person plural in acknowledgment of my own affinities to the Bobo ethos.

28. Brooks, 36.

29. Brooks, 11.

30. Ethnic specialty foods, according to Nancy Brumback, are "higher-margin products, typically sold at full price." Nancy Brumback, "Special Treatment," 4.

31. Brooks, 58.

32. Kimberly Lau, *New Age Capitalism: Making Money East of Eden.*

33. Benjamin R. Barber, *Jihad vs. McWorld.*

34. David Rieff, "Multiculturalism's Silent Partner," 62–85.

35. Kimberly Lau, personal communication, July 14, 2000.

36. Donna R. Gabaccia, *We Are What We Eat,* 202ff. While Gabaccia sees the crossing of cultural and regional boundaries as something that has characterized American eating habits from the start, tolerance and appreciation of foreign foodways set the end of the twentieth century apart as a uniquely multicultural era in food consumption. Where xenophobic culinary nativists reacted to earlier waves of immigrants with campaigns to eliminate immigrant foodways, educate enclave eaters, and turn back the tide of crossover foreign foods, immigrants arriving since the reform of U.S. immigration laws in 1965 "now cook and eat in a culture less interested in demonizing them than in enjoying their foods. . . . ordinary Americans today are much more eager than in 1900 to entertain themselves with the culinary gifts of new immigrants." Gabaccia, 202.

37. Gabaccia, 218.

38. Gabaccia, 217.

39. On meat as a status symbol in Europe from the eleventh century onward, see Massimo Mantanari, *Fame e l'abbondanza,* 32–33, 46–77, 73–77; on the ways in which ethnic foods are seen as compensating for the loss of meat and hence ideal for entertaining, see Ahmad Jamal, "Multicultural Eating in the Contemporary U.K.," 12–26.

40. Levenstein, 218.

41. Brumback, p. 4.

42. Ibid.

43. On salsa's place as the new "king of condiments," see Gabaccia, 219; on the assimilation of foreign flavors as condiments, see Levenstein, 220.

44. Levenstein, 215.

45. Ibid.

46. "The Soy Solution: A One-Week Meal Plan to Help You Add Soy to Your Meals," developed by Anne Patterson, R.D., 1999.

47. <http://lightlife.com>, 1999.

48. Regarding the difficulties in identifying ingredients of Chinese recipes, E.N. Anderson suggests that the English names given to Chinese vegetables are often quite whimsical and complicated. E.N. Anderson, "Traditional Medical Values of Food," 80ff. Anderson gives the example of luffa or silk gourd, which has become "Chinese okra" even though it bears no resemblance to okra in taxonomic or morphological features. What might one tell the produce manager at the

local Thriftway when in search of "five-claw Chinese beans" (which resemble pole beans but are shorter) or "four-season beans" (which resemble green beans but are more thick)?

49. Lau, 123ff.

50. J. J. Clarke, *Oriental Enlightenment,*109ff.

51. Edward Said, *Orientalism.*

52. On Herodotus and his sources, see James Oliver Thompson, *History of Ancient Geography;* G. Rawlinson, *History of Herodotus;* J.E. Powell, *History of Herodotus;* and John Watson McCrindle, *Ancient India as Described in Classical Literature.*

53. Donald Lach, *Asia in the Making of Europe,* 1: 10. John Watson McCrindle, *Ancient India as Described by Megasthenes and Arrian;* T.S. Brown, "The Reliability of Megasthenes, *American Journal of Philology* 76 (1955).

54. See Jean Delumeau, *Histoire du paradis,* ch. 4.

55. Ibid., 81.

Works Cited

Anderson, E.N. 1997. "Traditional Medical Values of Food," in *Food and Culture: A Reader.* Eds. C. Counihan and P. Van Esterik. New York: Routledge.

Barber, Benjamin R. 1995. *Jihad vs. McWorld.* New York: Times Books.

Belasco, Warren J. 1989. *Appetite for Change: How the Counterculture Took of the Food Industry, 1966–1988.* New York: Pantheon Books.

Brewster, Letitia and Michael Jacobson. 1983. *The Changing American Diet.* Washington: Center for Science and the Public Interest.

Brillat-Savarin, Jean-Anthelme. 1994 [1825]. *The Physiology of Taste.* Trans. Anne Drayton. New York: Penguin Books.

Brooks, David. 2000. *Bobos in Paradise: The New Upper Class and How They Got There.* New York: Simon and Schuster.

Brown, T.S. "The Reliability of Megasthenes." *American Journal of Philology* 76.

Brumback, Nancy. 1999. "Special Treatment." *Supermarket News Specialty Foods Supplement,* August 30.

Clarke, J.J. 1997. *Oriental Enlightenment: The Encounter Between Asian and Western Thought.* London: Routledge.

Delumeau, Jean. 1995. *Histoire du paradis.* Trans. Matthew O'Connell, *History of Paradise: The Garden of Eden in Myth and Tradition.* New York: Continuum.

Gabaccia, Donna R. 1998. *We Are What We Eat: Ethnic Food and the Making of Americans.* Cambridge, Mass.: Harvard University Press.

Gitlin, Todd. 1986. *The Sixties: Years of Hope, Days of Rage.* New York: Bantam Books.

———. 1980. *The Whole World is Watching: Mass Media in the Making and Unmaking of the New Left.* Berlelely: University of California Press.

Gregerson, Jon. 1994. *Vegetarianism: A History.* Fremont, Calif.: Jain Press.

Hufeland, Christophe W. *Macrobiotics, and the Art of Prolonging Life.*

Jamal, Ahmad. 1996. "Multicultural Eating in the Contemporary U.K." *British Food Journal* 98: 12–26.

Lach, Donald. 1965. *Asia in the Making of Europe*, 4 vols. Chicago: University of Chicago Press.

Lau, Kimberly. 2000. *New Age Capitalism: Making Money East of Eden*. Philadelphia: University of Pennsylvania Press.

Levenstein, Harvey. 1993. *Paradox of Plenty: A Social History of Eating in Modern America*. New York: Oxford.

Mantanari, Massimo. 1994.*Fame e l'abbondanza*. Trans. Carl Ipsen, *The Culture of Food*. Oxford, U.K.: Blackwell.

McCrindle, John Watson. 1960. *Ancient India as Described by Megasthenes and Arrian*. Calcutta: Chatterjee.

———. 1901. *Ancient India as Described in Classical Literature*. Westminister, England: A. Constable and Co.

Novak, Michae. 1971. *The Rise of the Unmeltable Ethnics*. New York: Macmillan.

Ohsawa, Georg. 1994. *Essential Ohsawa: From Food to Health, Happiness to Freedom*. Ed. Carl FerrÈ. Garden City Park, N.Y.: Avery.

Powell, J.E. 1930. *The History of Herodotus*. London: Knox.

Rawlinson, G. 1910. *The History of Herodotus*. New York: E.P. Dutton.

Rieff, David. 1993. "Multiculturalism's Silent Partner." *Harper's Magazine* (August): 62–85.

Rossi, Barbara, and Glory Schloss. 1971. *Everyday Macrobiotic Cooking*. New York: Universal.

Said, Edward. 1979. *Orientalism*. New York: Vintage Books.

Schlosser, Eric. 2001. *Fast Food Nation: The Dark Side of the All-American Meal*. Boston: Houghton Mifflin.

Te Selle, Salli, ed. 1973. *The Rediscovery of Ethnicity*. New York: Harper Collins.

Thompson, James Oliver. 1948. *History of Ancient Geography*. Cambridge, U.K.: Cambridge University Press.

Weil, Andrew. 2000. *Eating Well for Optimal Health: The Essential Guide to Food, Diet, and Nutrition*. New York: Knopf.

CHAPTER 12

Ethnic Heritage Food in Lindsborg, Kansas, and New Glarus, Wisconsin

Barbara G. Shortridge

The Midwest is dotted with small, European ethnic settlements, a legacy from the immigration streams of the nineteenth century. Several of these communities, including New Glarus, Wisconsin (a Swiss settlement established in 1845), and Lindsborg, Kansas (a Swedish settlement of 1869), have purposely reinvented themselves as heritage destinations for tourists. Architecture, signage, music, dance, costumes, and special events are all facets of the fabrication, but food is especially important. To the townspeople, selling ethnic food to tourists is a reliable source of income. To visitors, eating (or taking home a food product) is a major participatory component of their ethnic explorations. Tasting another culture is part of the expected experience for those who want to be Swiss or Swedish for a day.

Culinary tourism has many facets. People who want to experience another culture may eat authentic ethnic foods to gain status among peers and to contribute to their touristic cultural capital. At another level, those who are curious about other places may be dining as part of an imaginary foreign trip. For such people, the goal is a multisensory experience: food plus other visual and auditory markers. Still other visitors, however, may be actively reinforcing their own ethnic identity by returning to nostalgic culinary roots. A dish, for example, that might be difficult or tedious to prepare in a home cooking situation can here be readily provided by professionals. A vague food memory of times past can now be tasted again. The ethnic foods available in these two towns are, in general, familiar to a midwestern palate (without intense spices or unusual cooking methods) and thus provide modest exoticism and not much skepticism. Because of their geographic positions near larger population centers, Lindsborg and New Glarus are well situated for even an abbreviated visit such as an evening meal. Finally, we must not ignore the possibility that many regional patrons return again and again simply because they savor the good-tasting food. In addition to North American tourists wanting to partake of an exotic cuisine, the two towns also attract significant numbers of visitors from Switzerland and Sweden. These people come to participate in food memory tourism, to see what eating and culture was like a hundred years ago in their homelands.

The developers of New Glarus and Lindsborg provide all the classic tourism facilities for shopping, playing, and eating.[1] They do so with a twist, however, by constructing environments that allow the tourist to be readily integrated into an ethnic culture and to have contact with the local populace. This accessibility is facilitated by their rural locations, settings that also enhance the difference factor for a visitor from an urban environment. A person entering these towns is immediately aware that they are constructed and commodified landscapes, but usually pleased that the garishness of many other tourist venues is absent. In Lindsborg and New Glarus, the "foreign" is purposely made familiar to the visitor, and this familiarity is responsible for their success.

In order to see how the process of culinary tourism works from the consumer's point of view, I analyzed promotional material, restaurant menus, food imports from the homeland, food specialty shops, cookbooks, and festival foods; interviewed townspeople; and observed the landscape as a geographer. By examining the carefully constructed presentation of ethnic food from several aspects, I hope to reveal the multiple ways food is important to the tourist experience.

Background

The people of Lindsborg and New Glarus decided to turn themselves into full-scale tourist destinations at almost the same time in the 1960s. These reinventions, led by some strong-willed visionaries but with the agreement of the entire communities, were not abrupt. Both places had hosted well-attended ethnic festivals before and, as a result, were used to accommodating crowds and the associated problems of parking and restrooms. The transition was not a matter of a swelling local pride that had to find an outlet. Instead it was simple economics. Agriculture was in decline and farm towns had to change if they were to survive. Local leaders recognized a growing fascination of Americans with ethnicity and heritage and realized they had something to sell. Tourism became the new focus. The strategy worked better than even the dreamers could have imagined. Today there are no empty storefronts in downtown New Glarus or Lindsborg.

New Glarus and Lindsborg have been studied extensively. Both, in fact, are subjects of recent dissertations in geography. I am indebted to Steve Hoelscher's and Steve Schnell's thoughtful and entertaining analyses for much of the historical background material for this essay.[2] Their works focus on ethnic identity and place, however, and touch only lightly on the important role of food in the overall tourist presentation package. Similarly, other recent academic research about these towns has only minor allusions to food as part of the cultural commodification.[3]

I revisited these communities in the summers of 1999 and 2000 after having kept informal tabs on them for some time. Lindsborg is two hours from my home in Kansas; New Glarus is near where I grew up in Wisconsin. Both are functioning places with churches and schools, doctors and lawyers; with tourism they have just added another layer to their economy. Storekeepers and waitstaff have found a gracious way to combine midwestern friendliness with the practicalities of dealing with busloads of tourists and their demands. Lindsborg and New Glarus are successful not only in generating dollars, but also in presenting their ethnicity to the public in an accessible manner that is seen as authentic. They have been so successful in fact, that they are now among the premier places for this genre of tourism nationally and are imitated by others anxious to tap into the tourist dollar.

I argue that ethnic foods are a large part of the successes of these two towns. The tantalizing smells and gustatory gratification of eating an on-the-spot bakery product or a free sample of locally produced sausage cannot be surpassed in establishing a nonthreatening tie with another culture. Foods provide an immediate opportunity for the visitor to participate without a big investment of time or money. If the dish you order in a restaurant is unsatisfactory to your taste, there is no need to ever eat it again. If it is something that you would like to incorporate into your own cooking repertoire, then local stores are prepared to sell you cookbooks, imported ingredients, and perhaps special cooking utensils so that the experience can be replicated at home. In addition, ethnic foods provide tangible reminders of times past and are a good way to establish a heritage experience or to awaken food memories of past eating occasions. Swiss or Swedish American food is so important to the tourist package in these two towns that it is specially presented in their promotional material. By suggesting possible menu items in advance, food providers encourage the tourist to anticipate the experience they are about to have and to make eating the local part of the visit.

The larger issues of the creation and maintenance of community and ethnic identity underlie my investigation. Religious affiliation, regional loyalty, support of professional sports teams, alumni ties to schools, and participation in the political process are some ways to belong to sometimes overlapping spheres. Ethnic expressions of identity, though, have always been especially important sources of bonding in our society. Ethnic food and culture are linked to the resurgent need for and interest in community-based identity in our postmodern society. Rapid cultural change and personal stress have led many citizens to embrace, reaffirm, and even reinvent their ethnic ties as a way of creating attachment to community.

Scholarly literature on ethnic identity in the United States has dealt first with European immigrant groups and now with other, more recently arrived Americans.[4] Some of this writing notes that many family traditions are maintained through the use of music, dance, language, and especially food at holiday celebrations and at other special occasions such as birthdays.[5] Increasingly, however, these personal celebrations have been extended to the public through once-a-year festivals.[6] The initial motivation may have been to raise money for some worthy cause, but often this event takes on a life of its own and almost literally becomes the community. Working together toward a common goal reinforces the group identity of the planners. The embracing of traditions by visitors of the same ethnicity also raises their consciousnesses, and, finally, the public sharing with outsiders becomes a complex but rewarding two-way exchange. The same ethnic elements that were (and are) important in the seclusion of the family unit are now other-directed: music and dance performances, costumes, pageants, athletic contests, and food—all carefully constructed displays of ethnicity.

New Glarus and Lindsborg have taken the process of community-based ethnicity one step further. Not only do their citizens support several public festivals with large attendance, but they also have opened up their communities to year-round visitors. The display and performance of ethnic identity are constant parts of everyday life in these towns.

New Glarus and Lindsborg make an especially nice pair for study because they are similar yet different. They are both Midwestern and both represent an older, European immigrant group. As far as culinary tourism, however, a fundamental difference exists in presentation. Restaurant food is more prominent in New Glarus, home-cooked food in Lindsborg. These two approaches lead to subtle but important differences in the feel and appearance of the places.

New Glarus

New Glarus today is a town of two thousand people located in the scenic southwestern part of Wisconsin, a land with hilly topography and sharply cut river valleys. This landscape has produced a much-circulated story that Swiss immigrants chose to live there in the mid-nineteenth century because it looked like Switzerland. Maybe it came closest among their choices, but it is a far cry from their former home in the truly mountainous, German-speaking canton of Glarus, near Zurich.

Southwestern Wisconsin is America's dairy land, where Holsteins and Brown Swiss graze contentedly in picturesque settings. Green County, New Glarus's setting, is noted for its cheese making. In addition, many local people worked in the town's Pet Milk condensery until it closed in 1962. The closing date corresponds directly with the advent of tourist boosterism in New Glarus. Currently the two major local employers are New Glarus Foods, which makes semidry sausages, and a retirement community/nursing facility. Both of these enterprises are successful, but they employ only a small proportion of the labor force. Most of the other workers participate in a thriving hotel, restaurant, and gift-shop trade that has been put into place over the past forty years. The people of New Glarus have voluntarily commodified their place and their ethnicity.

The migration from Switzerland to New Glarus was a carefully planned group experience. In 1845, a hundred unemployed textile workers and their families came to land that had been purchased for them by an emigrant association. Hundreds of others from Glarus and other cantons, including Bern, followed in the next several decades in a typical chain migration. These people, from urban backgrounds, knew little about cows and cheese. In fact, their first attempts at farming focused on wheat. They switched to dairy farming in the 1870s at a time when small, European-style cheese factories started to flourish in Wisconsin.

The community was not on major road or railroad lines and so remained a distinctly Swiss enclave for over a century. Of the marriages recorded between 1851 and 1950, 90 percent were Swiss to Swiss.[7] This experience contrasted with that of Swiss Americans in the nearby communities of Monroe and Monticello, who shared their villages with other ethnicities. As a result, New Glarus became the de facto "Little Switzerland" of the state, and the village's isolation helped to preserve the language, religion, costume for festive events, folk music and dance, and food habits of the homeland culture.

New Glarners, like other German-speaking immigrants, found themselves under suspicion by their neighbors during World War I, but this ethnic resentment was short-lived. The 1924 Immigration Restriction Act slowed the infusion of new residents, and a statewide promotional effort heightened awareness of ethnicity. Gradually, "Old World people came to be seen as romantic vestiges from the past."[8] By the 1930s in New Glarus, festival events that used to be attended only by people of Swiss heritage began to attract curious outsiders.

New Glarus Festivals

The first community event to garner statewide interest was an outdoor production of Schiller's *Wilhelm Tell*. This began in September 1938 and has been performed annually on Labor Day weekend ever since. A Heidi Festival, every June, was added in 1964. This includes a play based on the Johanna Spyri classic, entertainment (including polkas and yodeling), a craft fair, a street dance, and a parade. Now the calendar year has been filled nearly completely with a Winterfest in January, Polkafest in May, Volkfest (Swiss Independence Day) in August, and Octoberfest.[9] Food is important in all six of these events, with local restaurant fare being supplemented by concession stands (especially beer and brats[10]) and the occasional chicken barbecue sponsored by a service club. Food figures most prominently in a seventh festival, however, the New Glarus Tastes & Treasures. In recent years, each July local restaurants, food shops, and food manufacturers cooperate to serve samples of Swiss specialties at food stands and outdoor cafes in the downtown area. According to the narrative in the official visitor's guide, "You will find appetizers of locally made cheeses and sausages, and a variety of entrées like Brat and Sauerkraut Kabobs, Chicken Risotto, Sauerbraten, Geschnetzelets, Swiss Pizza, Cheese Spaetzle, Roasted Garlic Mashed Potatoes, Roesti Potatoes, Cheese Fondue, and desserts ranging from Éclairs to Crème Brulée."[11] And fifty-cent beers.

It was the strong interest displayed by outsiders attending these festivals that led townspeople to create an ongoing tourist town. Early visitors had enjoyed the plays and other events but complained about a lack of visual Swissness and the absence of Swiss cheese and Swiss eating places. Business owners at first responded individually, but gradually, unified efforts arose. By the early 1960s new billboards, street signs, geraniums, and

12-1. The New Glarus Hotel serves Swiss food, often accompanied by live polka music. A life-sized Brown Swiss fiberglass cow is a new addition to flowers at the entrance. *Photo courtesy of the author.*

architectural facades were all in place. It was a conscious reinvention of place. A fairly ordinary midwestern town transformed itself, not by city code, as has happened in other ethnic heritage towns such as Pella, Iowa,[12] but in a spontaneous way that is quite charming and gives the illusion of authenticity. A local businessman purchased the dilapidated New Glarus Hotel, for example, and made it "Swiss" by serving specialty foods along with ethnic entertainment. He also decided to accommodate bus tours for lunch, bringing in even more visitors. The year-round tourist business was born and still flourishes alongside the festival crowds.

Today, bus tours also include visitors from Switzerland. These tourists from Europe make nostalgic treks to this community to eat foods of a hundred years ago. They claim New Glarus is more Swiss than Switzerland and say that they travel such distances to participate in food memory tourism.[13] But the connections between homeland and colony are not just one way. A recent survey details the level of interaction between old and New Glarus: 58 percent of the New Glarus Swiss have made pilgrimage visits to the ancestral homeland to visit friends and family.[14]

Traditional Swiss Food

Let me say a few words about traditional Swiss cookery before I discuss how it is interpreted today in New Glarus. Switzerland has an international cuisine that has absorbed many things from its neighbors. In its larger cities, modern fare is as cosmopolitan as anywhere in urban Europe. Folk cooking, which relies upon locally produced foodstuffs, is not as prominent as it once was and survives only in isolated areas. This rustic home cooking of the past was simple and hearty, with large servings and pleasurable flavors. It relied heavily upon dairy products, particularly cheese and butter. Meats were secondary but often included air-dried pork or sausages, specialties of the Glarus canton. Soups of substance were important too; so were fried potatoes and other vegetables, such as beans, cabbage, carrots, and turnips. The Glarus area is known for its intricately constructed pastries. Fruit tarts, puff-pastry creations, and honey cakes are common desserts. Beer, wine, and coffee are the beverages of choice.

Because the first emigrants in New Glarus came in 1845, because there have been further infusions of people from Switzerland in the years since, and because there are continuing contacts between the two Glaruses to this day, it is difficult to date the food now presented to the public in New Glarus. When tourists from Switzerland claim they are eating foods of the past, foods that are relatively unavailable now in their homeland, they are probably speaking a relative truth rather than an absolute one. New Glarus has indeed been isolated from outside influences and has purposefully tried to retain its culture intact. Some culinary evolution was inevitable, of course, including new products and new methods of preparation—a continual reinvention of tradition.

Restaurants

The 1999 visitors guide to New Glarus contains numerous restaurant photographs and advertisements of people eating and enjoying themselves. A montage on the cover includes pictures of such traditional fare as fondue and roesti and the phrases "excellent restaurants" and "brewery tours." Similar information is presented on the town's website, at a toll free number, and in a local visitor's booth. In addition, two of the major restaurants have their own websites. From these sources one learns, for example, that the Glarner Stube provides the finest in Swiss and American cuisine; that the Chateau Landhaus has a Swiss-trained chef; that Flannery's Wilhelm Tell Restaurant serves schnitzels, cheese fondue, and Swiss-style sausages;

12-2. Tourists inspect the menu in front of the Glarner Stube in New Glarus. The restaurant façade features hand painted murals, decorative ironwork, carved woods, and flower boxes. *Photo courtesy of the author.*

and that the New Glarus Hotel has set the standard for Swiss cuisine in the area.

Of the fourteen restaurants in town, only a few serve Swiss food exclusively.[15] A number of taverns exist with limited menus, including a few that have not made it into the official brochure. There are also local restaurants that use the Upper Midwest phenomenon of the Friday Night Fish Fry as their advertising ploy, an event that has nothing to do with Swiss cuisine. Then there is Culver's, the only fast-food restaurant in town. This regional franchise operates out of Sauk City, Wisconsin, and is known for its frozen custard, butterburgers, and blue décor.

The Swiss American restaurants in New Glarus all serve a combination of Swiss, Swiss-American, and American foods, hoping to maximize their appeal to all ages and backgrounds. It is difficult to separate their offerings into categories. Mixed in with American dinners of walleye pike and New York strip steak are Swiss specialties such as *wiener schnitzel* (pan-fried veal), *kalberwurst* (sausage of veal and milk), cheese fondue (flavored with wine and garlic), and *kaesechuechli* (individually baked cheese pie). Swiss onion soup (topped with croutons and Swiss cheese) and *raclette* (aged cheese melted over potatoes and garnished) are common appetizers. They all are folk foods in terms of ingredients, presentation, and perhaps taste, but they assuredly are not exactly the same as they once were. American components of menus include salad bars, baked potatoes, hamburgers, and vegetarian platters. And as for Swiss-American (a combination of the two cuisines), the omnipresence of cheese and sausage plates is the best example. These use a serving presentation common in Switzerland but with cheeses from Green County to construct the dish. Another area where both Wisconsin and Switzerland are represented is beverages. One restaurant features not only a local winery (Botham from Barneveld), but also imported Swiss wines. It restricts beer to products of the New Glarus Brewery (including Edel-Pils and Uff-Da Boch) and a similar establishment in nearby Monroe (Berghoff). Rivella, a soft drink from Switzerland, is also offered, along with Swiss Alp Water, an imported mountain mineral beverage.

Restaurant décor is heavy with Swiss flags, shields of cantons, and murals. They also feature lace curtains, dark, rustic woodwork, and, in some cases, low beams and stone floors. Subdued lighting is the norm. Many have a European-style outdoor garden section. Servers in some are in ethnic costume. The combination is a deliberate presentation to create the right visual ambiance for the first-time visitor. You are being transported to a different place and time.

The bus tour package offered by the New Glarus Hotel perhaps best epitomizes the culinary experience of short-term visitors to the community. It features a cheese fondue demonstration along with samples and a souvenir recipe, a choice of eight entrées (all Swiss specialties such as veal-based dishes *geschnetzelets* and *wiener schnitzel*), and a dessert fruit

tart. The establishment's goal is to make the visitor's trip to Little Switzerland memorable but still manageable—hospitality with structure. It
seems to work well, judging from the smiling faces.

Other Food Retailing

Food shops in New Glarus copy the style of small-shop, European marketing. Although locals utilize them to buy imported and Midwestern-
produced Swiss-American foods (sausage and cheese being the most
common) and also serve as headquarters for mail-order businesses involving these same foods, their primary trade is with tourists. They are there
to provide edible souvenirs of the New Glarus experience. The architectural embellishments make this apparent; so do their highly visible and
carefully constructed food displays.

Landjaeger, kalberwurst, mettwurst, and bratwurst (all locally prepared meats) are featured, with Ruef's Meat Market going so far as to claim
it is "the 'Wurst' store in town."[16] Hoesly's Meats advertises its farm processing and homemade sausage. Swiss cheese along with Gruyère and
butterkäse dominate the extensive cheese displays in Schoco-Laden, "New
Glarus' Finest Cheese and Specialty Shop . . . offering you the best selection of the finest Green County cheese and sausage."[17] The local Alphorn
brand claims that cheese making is "A Swiss Family Tradition," even if it
is produced in South Wayne, Wisconsin. As usual in Wisconsin food souvenir displays, some cheeses are made into the shapes of a Holstein cow
(with an appropriately designed black-and-white wax coating) and capital
letter "W" (waxed in University-of-Wisconsin red). Imported ethnic products from Switzerland range widely but include dried soup and sauce mixes
by Knorr and Maggi and packaged mixes for desserts. Toblerone and other
milk chocolate also are prominently displayed. As with the best of sales-
manship, free samples abound. I declined the horseradish cheddar but accepted a fudge product.

The New Glarus Bakery is an important tourist attraction, perhaps because of its back-in-time atmosphere. Traditional Swiss excellence in baked
goods also plays a role, as does the bakery's decision to share space with a
tearoom, creating a viable tourist combination. "Stop by our bakery to experience scratch baking and ethnic specialties. Try our hearth breads. . . .
Stop by soon. The coffee pot is waiting."[18] Breads are the items most purchased by town residents, while tourists generally prefer the genuine Swiss
items designated by red crosses. *Bratzeli,* anise *springerli,* and *sandbisson*
were among the cookies available on one of the days I was there. All are

12-3. A local brand of Swiss cheese is part of a larger display in Schoco-Laden, "New Glarus' Finest Cheese and Specialty Shop." *Photo courtesy of the author.*

easy to eat on the spot or to carry home. A locally popular *stollen* was the initial offering in the bakery's ten-year-old mail-order business.[19]

A final venue for experiencing Swiss foodways is cookbooks, a way for a visitor to carry memories home for possible re-creation later.[20] A

12-4. The New Glarus Bakery is next to Ruef's Meat Market on First Street. *Photo courtesy of the author.*

representative example was a locally produced thin volume entitled *Swiss Cookery* that starts with potato recipes and ends with *gugelhopf* (coffee cake) recipes. It was authored by two descendents of a Swiss emigrant from 1892. The title page informs us "these recipes have been given to us by Swiss Friends for you to enjoy."[21] A second example was a commemorative volume celebrating 150 years of the local Swiss United Church of Christ.[22] Old photographs, culinary anecdotes, and interviews about church life in the past enhance the spiral-bound collection of recipes, each attributed to a specific cook. These and other cookbooks were displayed in Roberts European Imports and other gift shops along with imported cooking equipment: *raclette* grills (including one imported from Nestal, Glarus Canton), fondue supplies, and *bratzeli* irons. All items can be purchased in the stores, on websites, and through print catalogs. Mail order and gift packages of food are available as well.

Lindsborg

Lindsborg, Kansas, is a town of three thousand that, like New Glarus, sits in a rich agricultural part of its state. The Smoky Hill River Valley of McPherson County is the heart of America's wheat belt. Just south of town is the famous Mennonite farming area of Kansas. Lindsborg also is home to Bethany College, a Lutheran-affiliated school with eight hundred students. When the town was founded in 1869, its early settlers were intent on providing a religious and educational enclave to serve surrounding Swedish-American villages.

The initial emigration from Värmland, Sweden (particularly the villages of Sunnemo and Persberg), was caused by land fragmentation laws that produced many tenant farmers. Between 1851 and 1930, over a million Swedes immigrated to the United States, with many settling in Chicago. From there, groups fanned out across the Midwest, including the Lindsborg colony of 110 people led by Olof Olsson, a Lutheran pastor. The name Lindsborg was selected before settlement and derives from the surnames of four directors of the First Swedish Agricultural Company: Lindh, Lindell, Lindgren, and Lindey. Retaining Swedish culture was important to this group and to those who followed. Swedish language use continued on the streets and in the local newspapers until approximately 1910. It lasted even longer in the churches.

Participation in a national tercentennial celebration in 1938, an event honoring the Swedish pioneers who established New Sweden in the Delaware Valley, was perhaps the awakening of ethnic pride in Lindsborg. The first Lindsborg Svensk Hyllningsfest, a grand celebration of ethnic culture that tied in with "Kansas Homecoming Year," followed three years later. The success of this early celebration of folk Swedishness is indicated by the fact that the volunteer cooks served over fifteen hundred at their smorgasbord.[23]

Lindsborg, also like New Glarus, had been heavily dependent upon traditional agriculture for its economic well-being, and merchants suffered as farms consolidated more and more. A rerouting of an interstate-quality highway to bypass the town added to the woes. The community needed an alternative economic venture and thus had incentive to look to their ethnic culture. They were already well-known for a Messiah Festival held at the college and now for Svensk Hyllningsfest. Thus, a decision was made to bring in visitors on a daily basis. Lindsborg christened itself as "Little Sweden U.S.A." and went about the creation of a Swedescape: new facades on storefronts, heart motifs painted on business windows, flower boxes, metalwork, pastel colors, and sign ordinances.[24]

Traditional Swedish Food

Traditional Swedish cooking, called *husmanskost* (everyday eating), is simple and satisfying. It relies upon locally produced foodstuffs, such as the rye flour used in Swedish *limpa* bread, numerous varieties of berries, potatoes, and an abundant supply of fish. Herring, for example, can be found in any format imaginable. One exemplary frugal dish is *pytt i panna*, a hash made from leftover bits of cooked meat and potatoes, bacon, and onions, with a fried egg over all. Another rustic dish is the nationwide Thursday night supper: a thick yellow pea soup with added salt pork and onions (*ärter med fläsk*). Swedish pancakes (small and thin) served with lingonberry preserves follow the main course. As with Switzerland, modern urban diets in Sweden are international in ingredients and dishes.

Swedish cuisine is probably known best for its use of northern berries in preserves and cakes, its special holiday foods connected with Christmas (*lutfisk* on Christmas Eve, rice pudding on Christmas Day), and its elaborate and delicious baked goods. Cookies and cakes include cinnamon, ginger, and cardamom plus whipped cream, butter, and almonds. Coffee (strong and black) and aquavit, an alcoholic drink made from potatoes, also are important parts of the traditional cuisine.

The smorgasbord is perhaps Sweden's most notable contribution to world cuisine. Served both in the home on special occasions and at restaurants, this lavish buffet presentation of a large variety of foods has been copied in other cultures. Herring, in all its smoked, marinated, and pickled variations, is traditionally the first course. This is followed (each on a clean plate) by seafood; small hot dishes such as Swedish meatballs; cold meats and salads; and a plate of cheeses, fruits, and a light dessert. The number of dishes presented, of course, depends upon how many people are doing the preparation and the number of guests to be served.

The signature hot dish found on a Swedish smorgasbord table is Jansson's Temptation. The story is told that Erik Jansson, the leader of the Swedish colony in Bishop Hill, Illinois, in the mid-nineteenth century, snitched a bite of a parishioner's tasty hot dish. In what was otherwise an ascetic community opposed to pleasures of the flesh, one of his followers saw this culinary indiscretion, became disillusioned, and returned to Sweden with the recipe. It must have been good, for the dish now appears regularly on Swedish tables and is sometimes served as a party-ending climax before sending people on their way. It also is a regular in Swedish-American cookbooks, usually in the appetizer section and sometimes under the alternate name of Jansson's *frestelse*. The ingredients are as follows: strips of potatoes and chopped onions alternated with a crisscross of anchovies (sprat filets used in Sweden), covered with cream, dotted with butter, and baked. It represents a rarity in food history; a dish that was created in a colonial situation that then not only made a return migration to the homeland, but also became immensely popular there.

Lindsborg Festivals

Lindsborg's premier public event was established in 1882. Every Easter week, Bethany College sponsors performances of Handel's *Messiah* on Palm Sunday and Easter Sunday, and Bach's *St. Matthew's Passion* on Good Friday. Although these events are popular and draw large crowds, they have no specific foods associated with them. Visitors must rely upon local restaurants for their sustenance. This music festival, however, is an important demonstration of the high level of town commitment to public events over a long period of time. "Tales still abound about farmers who came through blizzard-like conditions on hay wagons to make it to rehearsal. . . . Nobody much cared whether or not it was 'really' Swedish; the festival was the most important cultural contribution of Lindsborg to their new country."[25]

Two other, somewhat more recent, festivals do have an important food component in the form of an authentic Swedish smorgasbord. The biggest of these, Svensk Hyllningsfest, is a three-day October event celebrated in odd-numbered years. Folk dancers, parade participants, and townspeople in costumes honor the founders of the community by confirming and sharing their Swedishness with thirty thousand visitors.[26]

Established in 1941, the event now is advertised by the heritage slogan "Join us as we remember our past and celebrate our future." A bigger enticement, however, is an alternate motto: "You don't have to be Swedish to enjoy Svensk Hyllningsfest."[27] Since not everyone who attends could possibly be of Swedish ancestry, the opportunity of being Swedish for a day is an important selling point.

On Friday night, in three sittings, a visitor is able to participate in the famous Lindsborg smorgasbord. This is provided he purchases a ticket in advance (it is sold out every year) and is willing to contribute $17.50 (1999 price). To prepare for this event, the home cooks of Lindsborg turn their kitchens into large-scale food preparation centers for weeks.[28] A respondent who grew up in a nearby town told me about the enormity of the task, and then added that she did not quite understand why the women did it. She quickly reversed this last comment, however, by saying she knew how important it was for these women to participate in the community. In addition, it was a matter of pride to display good cooking and baking skills. Home cooking is not only a practical necessity and a tradition, but it also lends an aura of authenticity to the festival.

Measure for Pleasure, a cookbook published by the Bethany College Auxiliary, features the Hyllningsfest menu and some of the recipes.[29] Among the thirty-nine dishes listed are such Swedish specialties as *inlagd sill* (pickled herring), *fläsk-och kalvsylta* (jellied pork and veal), *köttbullar* (meatballs), *potatiskorv* (potato sausage), *lutfisk* (cod), *bruna bönor* (brown beans), *risgrynspudding* (rice pudding), *inglada rödbetor* (pickled beets), *katrinplommonkaka* (prune pudding), and *kaffe* (coffee). Swedish names are given first in the cookbook menu, followed by the English translation. A recipe for coffee, you may ask? Scandinavians claim that they are the greatest coffee drinkers in the world, and Svensk kaffe is steeped and strong. Water is boiled ahead of time. A slightly beaten egg is added to the coffee grounds to coagulate the smaller particles and ensure a clear brew. Next the coffee-egg mixture is poured into the boiling water and stirred. Finally, everything is simmered, strained into a coffee server, and offered with a pastry or other baked good. Food writers have put forth the idea that heavy coffee consumption in the Scandinavian countries is what led to their excellent reputation as bakers. Whenever a home cook would share coffee with a friend or neighbor, she could also showcase her baking expertise.

Another Lindsborg smorgasbord is presented at *Midsommardag* (Midsummer's Day Festival), a family celebration on a Saturday in June.

In Sweden this holiday coincides with the summer solstice, when daylight lasts almost all night long. Kansas, at a lower latitude, does not have a day nearly as long, but solstice is still a good excuse to resurrect a homeland custom. Music, dancing, flower crowns (*blomkraus*), and a maypole (*majstång*) are followed by a midnight swim. Local cooks demonstrate the preparation of rosettes, tea rings, and *kringler* (coffee cake). The highlight, of course, is the smorgasbord, this time prepared by the Lindsborg Swedish Folk Dancers and their parents. Advance tickets are recommended and the cost is twelve dollars, with only one serving.

A final public event involving food, but in a different context, is a holiday bake sale. Swedes celebrate Saint Lucia's Day on December 13, when the eldest daughter in every family dons a white robe and a crown of lighted candles early in the morning to serve a tray of cookies and coffee. Symbolically she heralds the good news of Christmas. In Lindsborg the Lucia Festival is on the Saturday before the thirteenth and involves folk dancing, music, and the crowning of Lucia.[30] But at 9:30 in the morning, before all the entertainment takes place, the famous Holiday Bake Sale takes place, full of homemade goodies of all kinds, including Lucia buns. This event along with the two previously discussed ones provide well-publicized times during which a visitor is able to sample the kind of Swedish American treats usually available only in family homes. This is an unusual opportunity in the world of ethnic culinary tourism.

Restaurants

Lindsborg has only one restaurant that specifically provides an ethnic menu, the Swedish Crown. That their genuine Swedish chef is a point of pride is seen in this advertising copy: "her expertise in Scandinavian cuisine has enhanced the menu."[31] The restaurant is open daily, with a smorgasbord every Saturday. A typical lunch menu features the following offerings: Swedish meatballs (*köttbullar*), a cucumber-and-boiled-egg sandwich, and marinated herring served on Swedish rye with a dill-mustard dressing. In addition to these strictly Swedish specialties, touches of Swedish cuisine are evident in other ways. Sides of caraway cottage cheese, Scandinavian bean salad, dill potatoes, rye crisp crackers (*knäckebröd*), and diced beets are available even with a hamburger order. The restaurant also is well known for its desserts: "When in 'Little Sweden' do as the Swedes do . . . Delight in our desserts, homemade ostkaka is a must."[32] *Ostkaka,* by the way, is a Swedish form of cheesecake now made with

12-5. The Swedish Crown Restaurant in Lindsborg serves Swedish specialties including *ostkaka,* a cheese-based dessert. *Photo courtesy of the author.*

cottage cheese instead of the traditional rennet and whey. In consistency it is a cross between bread pudding and custard. In addition to the usual range of beverages, Swedish mineral water also is offered.

The Swedish Crown opened in the early 1960s once local entrepreneurs decided that ethnic cuisine was necessary for the heritage package.

12-6. Öl Stuga is the setting for the annual *lutfisk*-eating contest in December. Note the Dala horse sign, an icon for Lindsborg that is found on most businesses and many homes. *Photo courtesy of the author.*

Its owners remodeled the building in 1981 to create a place in the heart of Lindsborg that would be reminiscent of many things Scandinavian. The ambiance is achieved with carved woods, costumed waitpeople, and decorative metalwork—elements that provide the pleasurable atmosphere sought after by the restaurant. Blue, the dominant color in the Swedish flag, also is featured. A variety of meeting rooms and facilities for special occasions assure that this is a community center as well as a destination for tourists.

A deli and full bar, called Öl Stuga, is a second source for Swedish food, though only on occasion. It is the location for the annual *lutfisk*-eating contest in December. *Lutfisk*, of course, is the much-demeaned Scandinavian fish dish ritually made from dried cod. What was once a practical way of surviving the winter in Sweden is now symbolically associated with Christmas among Swedes everywhere. The fish is soaked in lye water for days, then drained and cooked. Served with a light cream sauce, even true-blue Swedes say that *lutfisk* stinks as it cooks, has a rubbery consistency, and looks bland. It is simultaneously a source of pride and of jokes.

Other Food Retailing

Lindsborg has a set of shops that provide foods imported from Sweden. Anderson Butik's Scandinavian Shop (where you are encouraged to "Come in for the True Swedish Feeling") and Hemslöjd (best known for personalizing red Dala horse signs) also offer mail-order service. Preserves of lingonberry, black currant, gooseberry, and cloudberry are popular purchases, along with Anna's crisp ginger thins (*pepparkakov*). They are all portable and nonperishable. Marabou milk chocolate bars, Swedish chocolate peppermint creams, and *polkagrisar* (pink dancing pigs) satisfy the sweet tooth. Prepared foods sell well too, including Kungsörnen's Swedish coffee roll mix and Lund's Swedish pancake mix with their simple directions at the level of "add water." Packaged dried beans for Swedish-style brown beans and yellow pea soup line the shelves as well. There is even a Viking pasta made in America by Ole & Lena that has the shapes of ships, helmets, and even the Dala horse symbol. You can make a hot dish with either.

Coffee is the final ubiquitous item. Royal Swedish Classic Coffee and Zoéga's Skåneroast are two popular imported brands. According to my sources, however, belonging to a buying club is the best way to assure a constant supply of Swedish coffee. The club automatically sends you a standing order at specified intervals, typically every month or six weeks. Lingonberries and rye crisp (*knäckebröd*) may be shipped on this basis as well. Lindsborg also has its own brand of coffee that uses the Swedish method of roasting. It sells under the King Oscar label. "No meal is better than its coffee," claims this brand established in 1899 by the Davis Coffee House.

The food displays in each of these shops also feature imported cooking equipment of traditional and modern form. Examples include *plätt*

12-7. Foods imported from Sweden and cooking utensils are displayed in Hemslöjd, a Scandinavian gift store. Note the "We Can Ship" sign. *Photo courtesy of the author.*

pans to make Swedish pancakes (griddle with seven three-inch-round in-dentations), *sandbakkel* tins to make almond tartlets, cookie presses, and almond cake molds. Accessories are there as well: aprons, tea towels, wooden spreaders made out of juniper, and cookie cutters in the shapes of hearts and Dala horses.

12-8. Swedish tea ring is featured in the Courtyard Bakery and Kafe in Lindsborg. *Photo courtesy of the author.*

Lindsborg also has a large Swedish import section within the local Scott's Thriftway grocery store. Most Lindsborgians purchase imports here along with their other groceries. The section is adjacent to the meat department and includes a cooler full of herring and cheeses, with prime shelf space devoted to *bond ost* (cheese), fresh lingonberries, homemade potato sausage (*potatiskorv*), and Swedish meatballs. *Lutfisk* is also available, dry, fresh, or frozen. "At my Dad's store you can find all the things you need to make a Swedish meal (even yukky lutfisk)!!" proclaims the owner's daughter at the top of their 1999 display ad in *Destination Lindsborg*. An in-store poster says they will ship anywhere; so does their ad with fax, Web, and e-mail designations. "You don't have to travel to Sweden to get a taste of Sweden."[33]

One bakery not only serves locals and tourists, but also provides ambient good smells up and down Main Street. The Courtyard Bakery and Kafe counts as its specialties Swedish rusks, homemade cookies, and muffins. Swedish baked goods are indicated on the shelves by a blue symbol. As in New Glarus, these goods are popular with tourists as an immediate and inexpensive ethnic taste treat.

Lindsborg's cookbook selection is large and includes some unusual crossover books. As a sampling, *Superbly Swedish* is a straightforward recipe collection from the traditions of Sweden and Swedish America; *Favorite Swedish Recipes* was originally published in Sweden in 1947 for American tourists; and *Our Beloved Sweden* is based on recipe requests to nearly two thousand churches and organizations with Swedish-American ties.[34] "It's all here—meatballs, ostkaka, pepperkakor, egg coffee, and so much more in easy-to-use, tried and true recipes."[35] My personal favorite is a three-hundred-page spiral-bound volume compiled by the Bethany College Auxiliary, a book that has gone through three editions. All recipes in this *Measure for Pleasure* are attributed to individual cooks, with marginal comments such as "1969 Hyllningsfest Queen."

Finally, although both New Glarus and Lindsborg have bed-and-breakfast lodgings, the only one of these to tout its ethnic food is the Swedish Country Inn. Its full breakfast includes cheeses, Swedish meatballs with lingonberries, hard-boiled eggs, cold meats, pickled herring, fruits, Swedish tea rings and breads, and coffee. The inn also succinctly states the purpose of an ethnic theme town in its advertising copy: "If a trip to Sweden is out of the question this year . . . come and stay with us (passports not necessary) . . . It is all here in Little Sweden, so please, join us. For a step back to a simpler place and time."[36] The words imply that Lindsborg is at least as Swedish as Sweden, with a heritage overlay.

Conclusions

Visitors to New Glarus or Lindsborg have ample opportunity to indulge their appetites for ethnic foods through several venues (restaurants, festival foods, bakeries, and food shops) and also to take home souvenirs of prepared foods, cookbooks, and cooking supplies. Organizers in both towns have worked hard to construct and maintain this aspect of the tourism package. In many other ethnic towns the food presentations are not nearly as enticing, and usually the general level of prosperity is not as high. I submit that these two observations may be related. All ethnic theme towns constantly reassess their viability and make plans for the future. Their people have invested a lot in this economic venture, individually and collectively, and do not want to see it diminish. I suggest that flagging operations and proposed new developments look at the culinary tourism that has evolved in New Glarus and Lindsborg. They provide good models to emulate.

New Glarus and Lindsborg belong to a rare category of ethnic theme town—one that draws tourists year-round and hosts one or more public festival events per year. Other well-known ethnic towns in the Midwest that have opted for this status include Frankenmuth, Michigan (German); Hermann, Missouri (German); New Ulm, Minnesota (German); and Pella, Iowa (Dutch). Western examples include Junction City, Oregon (Scandinavian); Leavenworth, Washington (Bavarian); and Solvang, California (Danish). In all these cases, community-wide, ongoing commitment exists in the public presentation of their ethnicity. Downtowns have been reinvented to combine the everyday activities of town residents and the special needs of tourists. Restaurants, gift shops, lodging, public restrooms, and parking lots occur in greater numbers than in other towns of similar size. Their visual landscapes have been enhanced by deliberate architectural and decorative embellishments, prominent visitor kiosks, large gathering spaces, statues, and decorative motifs such as life-sized fiberglass cows or wooden Dala horses. Shopkeepers sometimes even use sprinklings of the homeland language in conversations with customers, play folk music on their modern sound systems, and appear in costume. And then there is the taste and smell of ethnic foods. The reincarnation of these towns cannot be a halfhearted venture if they are to flourish in this age of great competition for tourist dollars. The landscape and sensory elements must unite to create an integrated effort, one that speaks for community commitment.

The time is right for well-done ethnic presentations to flourish in this country. Cravings for the local and the ethnic distinctiveness have been reawakened, a process interpreted as a countercurrent to the national, even global, commercialism that seeks to homogenize our experiences. Public venues where an outsider can experience the other in a nonthreatening setting have obvious appeal in this situation. They are antidotes to postmodern distress about the lack of attachment to place. Coupling the increasing appeal of small town life to urbanites with exoticism,[37] an ethnic community that presents seemingly authentic experiences, a diversity of entertainment, shopping, and good publicity has a chance to be a successful tourist destination.

A striking commonality of New Glarus, Lindsborg, and other Midwestern ethnic theme towns is their European origins and long-ago ancestral migrations. This prompts the question of whether newer immigrants in big-city neighborhoods can also construct similar tourist oriented presentations as a way to make money and share their culture. Ethnic festivals, often pluralistic, are well established in many large urban areas, but they typically have been confined to neutral, public areas such as churchyards, parks, or malls. In my experience, food stalls are important parts of these presentations. Ethnic restaurants within ethnic neighborhoods are also popular and patronized by locals and outsiders. But that is where the commodification stops, as of now. Perhaps the traditionally rapid turn-over of residents in inner-city neighborhoods and the high costs of acquiring property to provide parking and festival facilities have prohibited restoration of heritage landscapes in these urban areas. Perhaps just not enough time has passed for people yet to perceive a golden age worthy of preservation and visitation.

The type of tourism developed in New Glarus and Lindsborg needs more research to identify common features and reasons for success and failure. When this work is complete, I suspect that the role of food will be more important than many people now think. It is difficult to overstate the importance of smell and taste in our lives. Both of these communities provide multiple venues for eating foods of another culture, and it is this diversity of opportunities that enhances the culinary tourism experience.

Notes

1. For discussions of ethnic marketing see Jacinthe Bessière, "Local Development and Heritage: Traditional Food and Cuisine as Tourist Attractions in Rural Areas," *Sociologia Ruralis* 38 (1998): 21–34; Stephen Frenkel and Judy Walton, "Bavarian Leavenworth and the Symbolic Economy of a Theme Town," *Geographical Review* 90 (2000): 559–84; Marilyn Halter, *Shopping for Identity: The Marketing of Ethnicity* (New York: Schocken Books, 2000); Laurier Turgeon and Madeleine Pastinelli, "'Eat the World': Postcolonial Encounters in Quebec City's Ethnic Restaurants," *Journal of American Folklore* 115 (2002): 247–68.

2. Steven D. Hoelscher, "The Invention of Ethnic Place: Creating and Commemorating Heritage in an Old World Wisconsin Community, 1850–1995" (Ph.D. diss., University of Wisconsin, 1995); Steven M. Schnell, "Little Sweden, U.S.A.: Ethnicity, Tourism, and Identity in Lindsborg, Kansas" (Ph.D. diss., University of Kansas, 1998).

3. For Lindsborg, see Larry W. Danielson, "The Ethnic Festival and Cultural Revivalism in a Small Midwestern Town," (Ph.D. diss., Indiana University, 1972); "Public Swedish-American Ethnicity in Central Kansas: A Festival and Its Functions," *Swedish Pioneer Historical Quarterly* 25 (1974): 13–36; and "St. Lucia in Lindsborg, Kansas," in *Creative Ethnicity: Symbols and Strategies of Contemporary Ethnic Life*, eds. Stephen Stern and John Allan Cicala (Logan: Utah State University Press, 1991), 187–203; and Steven M. Schnell, "The Making of Little Sweden, USA," *Great Plains Quarterly* 22, 1 (2002): 3–21. For New Glarus, see Steven D. Hoelscher, *Heritage on Stage: The Invention of Ethnic Place in America's Little Switzerland* (Madison: University of Wisconsin Press, 1998); "Tourism, Ethnic Memory and the Other-Directed Place," *Ecumene* 5, 4 (1998): 369–98; and Hoelscher and Robert C. Ostergren, "Old European Homelands in the American Middle West," *Journal of Cultural Geography* 13, 2 (1993): 87–106.

4. Richard D. Alba, *Ethnic Identity: The Transformation of White America* (New Haven: Yale University Press, 1990); Fredrik Barth, ed., *Ethnic Groups and Boundaries* (Boston: Little, Brown, 1969); Kathleen Neils Conzen, "Ethnicity as Festive Culture: Nineteenth-Century German Americans on Parade" in *The Invention of Ethnicity*, ed. Werner Sollors (New York: Oxford University Press, 1989), 44–76; Herbert J. Gans, "Symbolic Ethnicity: The Future of Ethnic Groups and Cultures in America," *Ethnic and Racial Studies* 2, 1 (1979): 1–20; Jon Gjerde, *The Minds of the West: Ethnocultural Evolution in the Rural Middle West, 1830–1917* (Chapel Hill: University of North Carolina Press, 1997); Richard Handler and Jocelyn Linnekin, "Tradition, Genuine or Spurious," *Journal of American Folklore* 97 (1984): 273–90; Eric Hobsbawn and Terence Ranger, eds., *The Invention of Tradition* (Cambridge, U.K.: Cambridge University Press, 1983); Stanley Lieberson, "Unhyphenated Whites in the United States, "*Ethnic and Racial Studies* 8, 1 (1985): 159–80; Joane Nagel, "Constructing Identity: Creating and Recreating Ethnic Identity and Culture," *Social Problems* 41, 1 (1994): 152–76; Mary C. Waters, *Ethnic Options: Choosing Identities in America* (Berkeley: University of California Press, 1990).

5. Thelma Barer-Stein, *You Eat What You Are: People, Culture and Food Traditions* (Willowdale, Ont.: Firefly Books, 1999); Linda Keller Brown and Kay Mussell, eds., *Ethnic and Regional Foodways in the United States: The Performance of Group Identity* (Knoxville: University of Tennessee Press, 1984); Donna R. Gabaccia, *We Are What We Eat: Ethnic Food and the Making of Americans* (Cambridge, Mass.: Harvard University Press, 1998); Anne R. Kaplan, Marjorie A. Hoover, and Willard B. Moore, *The Minnesota Ethnic Food Book* (St. Paul: Minnesota Historical Society Press, 1986); Rachel Laudan, *The Food of Paradise: Exploring Hawaii's Culinary Heritage* (Honolulu: University of Hawaii Press, 1996); Deborah Dash Moore and Dan Gebler, "The Ta'am of Tourism," *Pacific Historical Review* 68, 2 (1999): 193–212; Rachelle H. Saltzman, "Rites of Intensification: Eating and Ethnicity in the Catskills," *Southern Folklore* 55, 3 (1998): 205–23; Gaye Tuchman and Harry Gene Levine, "New York Jews and Chinese Food: The Social Construction of an Ethnic Pattern," *Journal of Contemporary Ethnography* 22, 3 (1993): 382–407.

6. Alvar W. Carlson, "America's Growing Observance of *Cinco de Mayo*," *Journal of American Culture* 21, 2 (1998): 7–16; C. Paige Gutierrez, *Cajun Foodways* (Jackson: University of Mississippi Press, 1992); Sabina Magliocco, "Playing with Food: The Negotiation of Identity in the Ethnic Display Event by Italian Americans in Clinton, Indiana," in *Studies in Italian American Folklore*, ed. Luisa Del Giudice (Logan: Utah State University Press, 1993), 107–26; Sheldon Smith, "The Re-Establishment of Community: The Emerging Festival System of the American West," *Journal of American Culture* 8, 3 (1985): 91–100; Penny Van Esterik, "Celebrating Ethnicity: Ethnic Flavor in an Urban Festival," *Ethnic Groups* 4(1982): 207–27; Robert Wood, "Tourist Ethnicity: A Brief Itinerary," *Ethnic and Racial Studies* 21, 2 (1998): 218–41.

7. Hoelscher, *Heritage on Stage*, 1998, 71.

8. Ibid., 84.

9. For context, see Donald G. Tritt, *Swiss Festivals in North America* (Chicago: Swiss-American Historical Society, 1999).

10. Bratwurst is one of several forms of fresh sausage that is not cured and thus must be cooked shortly after purchase. Made of pork, highly seasoned, and individually encased, brats have become regional icons in some parts of the upper Midwest. They are featured, for example, in pregame tailgate parties at Lambeau Field, home of the Green Bay Packers professional football team.

11. New Glarus Chamber of Commerce, "New Glarus 1999 Visitors Guide," 10. *Sauerbraten* is a beef roast marinated in spiced vinegar; *geschnetzelets* is fried veal served with noodles; *spaetzle* is an egg dumpling boiled, topped with cheese, and then broiled; *roesti* is a large potato pancake made with strips of raw potato; and fondue is the communal Swiss dish of bread dipped in melted cheese.

12. Pella, Iowa, a Dutch American town dating from 1843, is thirty miles southeast of Des Moines. Known for its spring tulip festival that attracts one hundred thousand visitors over three days, the town also provides year-round culinary tourism with two bakeries (a pastry specialty is Dutch letters) and two meat shops known for their secret-recipe bologna.

13. They also come to see "Indians" and the Mississippi River, according to the New Glarus Chamber of Commerce director, Susan Foster (July 7, 2000).

14. Hoelscher and Ostergren, 99.

15. Dennis R. Getto, "New Glarus Hotel Delivers Wedge of Switzerland," *Milwaukee Journal Sentinel*, August 27, 2000, sec. 3W.

16. New Glarus Chamber of Commerce, "Your 2000 Visitors Guide to New Glarus, Wisconsin," 20.

17. 1999 Visitors Guide, 18.

18. Ibid., 19.

19. *Bratzeli* is a crisp, thin cookie made from dough that is first formed into a ball and then pressed in a special *bratzeli* iron. A *springerli* is formed by rolling out dough and then stamping it with a wooden board or carved rolling pin. *Sandbisson* cookies are formed by slicing a roll of rich, refrigerated dough. *Stollen* is a powdered-sugar-covered yeast bread associated with Christmas. It contains raisins, spices, rum, and a core of marzipan.

20. Here cookbooks are discussed as mementos of the tourism experience. For the possibilities of content analysis see Anne L. Bower, ed., *Recipes for Reading: Community Cookbooks, Stories, Histories* (Amherst: University of Massachusetts Press, 1997), and Lynne Ireland, "The Compiled Cookbook as Foodways Autobiography," *Western Folklore* 41, 1 (January 1981): 107–14; and Janet Theophano, *Eat My Words: Reading Women's Lives through the Cookbooks They Wrote* (New York: Palgrave, 2002).

21. Marie Matzinger, Elda Schiesser, and Linda Schiesser, *Swiss Cookery* (New Glarus, 1992).

22. Swiss United Church of Christ, *Sesquicentennial Recipes and Recollections, 1850–2000* (New Glarus, 1999).

23. Schnell, 165.

24. Ibid., 263–64.

25. Ibid., 71–72.

26. Jeri Clouston, "*Valkommen* to Svensk Hyllningsfest," *Kansas!* (fall 1997): 26–29.

27. "Join Us at the 1999 Svensk Hyllningsfest" brochure.

28. Marty Hardy, "Legends Among Us," in *Everyday Tales: A Small Book About Lindsborg, a Small Kansas Town* (Lindsborg Arts Council, 1999).

29. Bethany College Auxiliary, *Measure for Pleasure* (Lindsborg, third ed., 1991).

30. Danielson, 1991.

31. *Lindsborg News-Record*, "Destination Lindsborg," spring/summer 1999, 12.

32. *Lindsborg News-Record*, "Destination Lindsborg," spring/summer 2000, 27.

33. Ibid., 26.

34. Martha Wiberg Thompson, ed., *Superbly Swedish: Recipes and Traditions* (Iowa City: Penfield Press, 1983); Selma Wifstrand, ed., *Favorite Swedish Recipes* (New York: Dover Publications, 1975); Janet Letnes Martin and Ilene Letnes Lorenz, *Our Beloved Sweden: Food, Faith, Flowers & Festivals* (Hastings, Minn.: Sentel Publishing, 1996).

35. "Hemslöjd: An Adventure in Scandinavian Tradition, 1999–2000," (catalog), 25.

36. "Destination Lindsborg," 2000, 18.

37. Richard V. Francaviglia, *Main Street Revisited: Time, Space, and Image Building in Small-Town America* (Iowa City: University of Iowa Press, 1996); David M. Hummon, *Commonplaces: Community Ideology and Identity in American Culture* (Albany: SUNY Press, 1990); Thomas W. Paradis, "Conceptualizing Small Towns as Urban Places: The Process of Downtown Redevelopment in Galena, Illinois," *Urban Geography* 21, 1 (2000): 61–82.

Contributors

AMY BENTLEY is an associate professor in the Department of Nutrition, Food Studies, and Public Health at New York University. A cultural historian by training, she is the author of *Eating for Victory: Food Rationing and the Politics of Domesticity* (1998) as well as several articles. She is currently working on two book-length projects, a general history of food in the United States since World War II, and a cultural history of the infant food industry in the United States.

EVE JOCHNOWITZ, Yiddish instructor at Rutgers University and at The Workman's Circle Arbiter Ring, also teaches foodways at Living Traditions Klezkamp. A professional cook and baker, she is conducting a Jewish culinary ethnography for her doctoral dissertation in Performance Studies at New York University. She is the author of "Holy Rolling: Making Sense of Baking Matzo," in *Jews of Brooklyn* (2002), and "Send a Salami to Your Boy in the Army," in *Remembering the Lower East Side* (2000). Ms. Jochnowitz is also known as the Chocolate Lady.

LUCY M. LONG (M.A. Ethnomusicology, University of Maryland; Ph.D. Folklore, University of Pennsylvania) is assistant professor, Department of Popular Culture, Bowling Green State University, where she teaches classes in folklore, traditional music and foodways. She has published on Korean ethnicity and food; Asian ethnic restaurants; Midwestern, Appalachian, Irish, and Spanish food traditions; food as regional symbol; food festivals; family foodways; holiday meals; and culinary tourism. Recent publications include "Holiday Meals: Rituals of Family Tradition" in *Herbert L. Meiselman* (2000); "Nourishing the Academic Imagination: The Use of Food in Teaching Concepts of Culture" in *Food and Foodways; Stirring up the Past: The Grand Rapids Apple Butter Fest* (a documentary video on a Midwestern food festival); "Images of the U.S. in Spanish Food Packaging" (a website for a Spanish university). She is currently working on a reader on folkloristic perspectives on food and on an NEH-funded project on food as a humanities subject. She is also chair of the Foodways Section of the American Folklore Society and editor of *Digest: An Interdisciplinary Study of Food and Foodways.*

KRISTIN MCANDREWS has published articles on gender, humor, and the images of the American West pertaining to the storytelling of women who work with horses. She has done fieldwork in Hawai'i, focusing on issues of land use and heritage tourism. Most recently, she was the project director for a lecture and performance series on five historical figures who influenced the culture of Hawai'i in significant ways. An assistant professor at the University of Hawai'i at Manoa, she teaches composition and literature courses with an emphasis on folklore and food.

JENNIE GERMANN MOLZ is a doctoral candidate in sociology at Lancaster University in northwest England. Her research focuses on the practices and narratives of round-the-world travel and the enactment of belonging in a global context. She has also written on American fast food abroad, including a chapter titled "The Guilty Pleasures of the Golden Arches" that will appear in a forthcoming book entitled *Emotional Geographies.*

JEFFREY M. PILCHER received his Ph.D. in Mexican history from Texas Christian University in 1993. His books include the prize-winning volume *¡Que vivan los tamales! Food and the Making of Mexican Identity* (1998), as well as a forthcoming study of the Mexico City meat supply. His current research examines the globalization of Mexican cuisine. He teaches at The Citadel in Charleston, South Carolina.

MIRYAM ROTKOVITZ, a native of Baltimore, studied theatre at Towson University, and holds an undergraduate degree in theatre and in American studies from Brandeis University. She worked as an actress in Boston and New York, before earning a master's in food studies from New York University, where she also studied clinical nutrition. A former associate editor for the James Beard Foundation, Rotkovitz now works as a clinical nutritionist in Brooklyn. She contributes regularly to the James Beard Foundation's monthly newsletter and to *Beard House* Magazine.

JILL TERRY RUDY, an associate professor of English at Brigham Young University, received a Ph.D. in folklore from Indiana University in 1997. She developed her essay in this volume from teaching a senior seminar titled, "A Feast of Foodways in Life and Literature." She has presented papers on familiar and foreign eating experiences at the Folklore Society of Utah, California Folklore Society, and Passion for Place conferences. Her interest in food studies centers on foodways and intersections of genre, narrativity, and symbolic cultural exchanges. Other research interests involve the historiography of folklore and English studies.

RACHELLE H. SALTZMAN, the folklife coordinator for the Iowa Arts Council, earned a Ph.D. in anthropology/folklore at the University of Texas. She has worked since 1982 in the field of public folklore at private non-profit and state agencies in eight states. Saltzman served as the facilitator for "Global Sounds, Heartland Beats," a regional project with Arts Midwest and six other states as well as activities with the national project, American Traditions. She was the Iowa curator for the Iowa Program for Smithsonian Institution's 1996 Festival of American Folklife and the curator for the Sesquicentennial Commission's 1996 Festival of Iowa Folklife. Saltzman also directed the 2001 Festival of Iowa Folklife, the Iowa Folklife Institute, and "Iowa Traditions in Transition," a program to document and present the traditions of Iowa's refugee and immigrant artists in public libraries. She has conducted scholarly research on a wide range of topics and has published articles in the *Journal of American Folklore, Anthropological Quarterly, Journal of Folklore Research, New York Folklore, Southern Folklore,* and *Southern Exposure* as well as several edited collections.

BARBARA G. SHORTRIDGE is an assistant professor in the department of geography at the University of Kansas. She was born in the bratwurst and dairy land of southern Wisconsin. Her undergraduate degree is from the University of Wisconsin and her advanced degrees from the University of Kansas, all with a cartography concentration. She published a series of articles on map symbolization early in her career. Her *Atlas of American Women* (Macmillan) appeared in 1987. Since then, her research interests have shifted to cultural geography and issues of everyday life in America.

She is the co-editor of *The Taste of American Place: A Reader on Regional and Ethnic Foods* and the author of several articles related to food and culture. Most recently she has written about the Great Plains as a culinary region.

JACQUELINE S. THURSBY, Ph.D., is an associate professor in the English department at Brigham Young University where she teachers undergraduate and graduate classes in folklore, mythology, and secondary English pedagogy. Her first book, *Mother's Table, Father's Chair: Cultural Narratives of Basque American Women* (1999), further discusses the foods and lore of Basque Americans. She is currently writing a multicultural book focused on funerary rituals, mourning, and foods in the contemporary United States.

LIZ WILSON is a professor in the Department of Comparative Religion and Affiliate in Women's Studies at Miami University in Oxford, Ohio. She is author of *Charming Cadavers: Horrific Figurations of the Feminine in Indian Buddhist Hagiographic Literature* (1996) and editor of *The Living and the Dead: The Social Dimensions of Death in South Asian Religions* (forthcoming from SUNY). She is currently working on a book on attitudes toward sexuality and family life among contemporary Western Buddhists.

Index